THE KING AS EXEMPLAR

Society of Biblical Literature

Academia Biblica

Adele Berlin,
Old Testament Editor

Mark Allan Powell,
New Testament Editor

Number 17

THE KING AS EXEMPLAR
The Function of Deuteronomy's Kingship Law
in the Shaping of the Book of Psalms

THE KING AS EXEMPLAR
The Function of Deuteronomy's Kingship Law in the Shaping of the Book of Psalms

Jamie A. Grant

Society of Biblical Literature
Atlanta

THE KING AS EXEMPLAR

Copyright © 2004 by the Society of Biblical Literature

All rights reserved. No part of this work may be reproduced or transmitted in any form or by any means, electronic or mechanical, including photocopying and recording, or by means of any information storage or retrieval system, except as may be expressly permitted by the 1976 Copyright Act or in writing from the publisher. Requests for permission should be addressed in writing to the Rights and Permissions Office, Society of Biblical Literature, 825 Houston Mill Road, Atlanta, GA 30329, USA.

Library of Congress Cataloging-in-Publication Data

Grant, Jamie A.
   The king as exemplar: the function of Deuteronomy's kingship law in the shaping of the book of Psalms / by Jamie A. Grant.
     p. cm. — (Society of Biblical Literature Academia Biblica ; no. 17)
   Includes bibliographical references and index.
   ISBN 1-58983-108-X (paper binding : alk. paper)
   1. Bible. O.T. Psalms—Relation to Deuteronomy XVII, 14-20. 2. Bible. O.T. Deuteronomy XVII, 14-20—Relation to Psalms. 3. Bible. O.T. Psalms—Criticism, Redaction. 4. Kings and rulers—Biblical teaching. 5. God—Kingship—Biblical teaching. 6. Piety—Biblical teaching. 7. Eschatology—Biblical teaching. I. Title. II. Academia Biblica (Series) (Society of Biblical Literature) ; no. 17.
BS1430.52.G73 2004b
223'.2066—dc22
                                2004010177

07 06 05 04   5 4 3 2 1

Printed in the United States of America
on acid-free paper

For Iwona,
with grateful thanks for much love and support
and for Gosia, Debbie and David,
with thanks for all the fun.

TABLE OF CONTENTS

Acknowledgements xiii
Abbreviations xv
INTRODUCTION 1
Chapter 1 METHODOLOGICAL CONSIDERATIONS 7
   1. Introduction 7
          1.1 Outline of the Central Argument 10
   2. Canonical Approach 11
          2.1 Canonical Method in the Study of the Psalms 13
          2.2 Identifying Editorial Agendas 14
          2.3 The Question of Significant Placement 16
          2.4 Cautionary Notes regarding Methodology 17
   3. Choice of Psalms 20
          3.1 Editorial Significance of Torah Psalms 20
          3.2 Editorial Significance of Kingship Psalms 25
   4. Comparative Method 27
          4.1 Biblical Conversation 28
          4.2 Which Deuteronomy? 30
   5. Eschatological Rereading of the Psalms 33

Chapter 2 TORAH-KINGSHIP THEME IN PSALMS 1–2 41
   1. Introduction 41
   2. Analysis of Psalm 1 43
          2.1 Deuteronomic Background to Psalm 1 43
               2.1.1 Psalm 1 and the *Shema* 43
               2.1.2 Centrality of Torah 45
               2.1.3 Dependence on Yahweh 49
               2.1.4 Eschatological Rereading of Psalm 1 50
               2.1.5 Theology of the Two Ways 52

```
            2.2  Assessment of the Theological Significance of Psalm 1 .. 53
      3.  Analysis of Psalm 2 .................................................................. 56
            3.1  Deuteronomic Background to Psalm 2............................. 57
                  3.1.1   The King's Dependence upon Yahweh ............ 58
                  3.1.2   Psalm 2's Association with Psalm 1 ................. 60
      4.  Theological Significance of a Dtr Introduction to the Psalter.......... 65
            4.1  Deuteronomic Worldview................................................ 65
            4.2  Kingship Law and the Psalms ......................................... 66
      5.  Conclusion ................................................................................ 69
Chapter 3  TORAH-KINGSHIP THEME IN PSALMS 18–21 ................ 71
      1.  Introduction .............................................................................. 71
      2.  Choice of Psalms 18–21 ............................................................ 72
      3.  Analysis of Psalm 18 ................................................................ 74
            3.1  Deuteronomic Background to Psalm 18........................... 78
                  3.1.1    Appellatives..................................................... 78
                  3.1.2    Theophany....................................................... 80
                  3.1.3    Torah Centre and Declaration of
                           Blamelessness..................................................81
                  3.1.4    Theology of the Two Ways ............................. 84
                  3.1.5    Appellatives Again .......................................... 85
            3.2  Association of Psalm 18 and Psalms 1 and 2 .................. 86
                  3.2.1    Yahweh as Refuge............................................ 86
                  3.2.2    Torah and Delight ............................................ 87
                  3.2.3    Theology of the Two Ways ............................. 88
                  3.2.4    Universal Dominion ........................................ 88
                  3.2.5    Yahweh's Messiah............................................ 88
            3.3  Conclusion regarding Psalm 18........................................ 89
      4.  Analysis of Psalm 19 ................................................................ 89
            4.1  Structure of Psalm 19 ...................................................... 90
            4.2  Deuteronomic Background to Psalm 19........................... 91
                  4.2.1    Polemic............................................................. 92
                  4.2.2    Torah Theology................................................ 93
                  4.2.3    Prayer of Psalm 19 and Personal Piety............. 95
                  4.2.4    Psalm 19 and Deuteronomy 4........................... 96
            4.3  Link between Psalm 18 and Psalm 19.............................. 97
                  4.3.1    Superscriptions................................................. 97
                  4.3.2    Appellatives..................................................... 97
                  4.3.3    Characteristics of Yahweh and His Torah ........ 98
                  4.3.4    Servant of the Lord.......................................... 98
            4.4  Association of Psalm 19 with Psalms 1 and 2 .................. 99
```

	4.4.1	Expansion of Torah Theme	99
	4.4.2	Psalm 19 as Example of Delight in Yahweh's Torah	100
	4.4.3	Conceptual Associations	100
	4.4.4	Kingship Theme	101

    4.5 Conclusion regarding Psalm 19 101
5. Analysis of Psalms 20 and 21 102
    5.1 Association of Psalms 20 and 21 104
    5.2 Deuteronomic Content of Psalms 20 and 21 105
        5.2.1 Name-Theology 105
        5.2.2 Dependence upon Yahweh 107
        5.2.3 Trust in Yahweh vs. Dependence in Military Power 108
        5.2.4 Salvation/Victory Belonging to Yahweh 109
        5.2.5 Covenant Theme in Psalm 21 110
    5.3 Association with Psalms 18 and 19 112
    5.4 Association with Psalms 1 and 2 112
        5.4.1 Kingship-Torah Theme 113
        5.4.2 Messiah Link 114
        5.4.3 Prayer Theme 114
        5.4.4 Theme of the Two Ways 115
6. Conclusion 116
    6.1 Background in Deuteronomic Theology 116
    6.2 Torah-Kingship Connection 116
    6.3 Democratisation of the King 117
    6.4 Limitation of the Power of the King 118
    6.5 Torah-Prayer Link 118

Chapter 4 TORAH-KINGSHIP THEME IN PSALMS 118–119 121
1. Introduction 121
2. Selection of Psalms 118 and 119 122
3. Analysis of Psalm 118 125
    3.1 Deuteronomic Influences in Psalm 118 127
        3.1.1 Ps 118 as Entrance Liturgy 127
        3.1.2 Eternal *Hesed* of Yahweh 129
        3.1.3 Fearers of Yahweh 130
        3.1.4 Trust in Yahweh 133
        3.1.5 Yahweh as the Psalmist's Help 135
        3.1.6 Trust in Yahweh—Not in Men/Princes 135
        3.1.7 Surrounding Nations, Circumcision, Name Theology 137

		3.1.8	Yahweh as Help and Salvation	139
		3.1.9	This Day, Prosperity, Name Theology	140
		3.1.10	Individual and Community	142
	4.	Psalm 118 in the Light of Psalms 1–2 and 18–21		143
		4.1	Salvation of the Lord's Anointed	143
		4.2	Dependence upon Yahweh	144
		4.3	Yahweh as Refuge	145
		4.4	Theology of the Two Ways	146
		4.5	Prayer Theme	146
		4.6	Torah-Piety	147
		4.7	Conclusion regarding Psalm 118	148
	5.	Analysis of Psalm 119		148
		5.1	Deuteronomic Influences on Psalm 119	157
			5.1.1 Torah Synonyms	157
			5.1.2 Language of Devotion	159
			5.1.3 Dependence upon Yahweh and the Name of Yahweh	161
			5.1.4 Yahweh as Refuge and Torah	163
			5.1.5 Theology of the Two Ways	164
			5.1.6 Meditation and Prosperity	166
			5.1.7 Continuous Torah Meditation	168
			5.1.8 Grace Enabling Obedience	169
			5.1.9 The "I" of Psalm 119 as the Dtr King	171
	6.	Links between Psalms 118 and 119		175
		6.1	Canonical	175
		6.2	Lexical	176
		6.3	Theological	180
	7.	Psalm 119 in the Light of Psalm Groupings 1–2 and 18–21		180
		7.1	Torah-Piety	181
		7.2	Meditation	182
		7.3	Blessedness and Prosperity	183
		7.4	The Two Ways	184
		7.5	Prayer	185
		7.6	Dependence upon Yahweh and the Kingship Law	186
		7.7	Name Theology	186
		7.8	Blamelessness of the King	187
		7.9	Conclusion	187
	8.	Conclusion regarding Torah-Kingship Psalm Groupings		188
Chapter 5	THE KINGSHIP LAW AS A PARADIGM			189
	1.	Introduction		189

| | | Table of Contents | xi |

2. Analysis of the Law of the King (Deut 17:14–20) 191
3. Kingship Law as Inherently Anti-Monarchic? 194
   3.1 Introduction to the Kingship Law 194
   3.2 Kingship and Yahweh's Choice 196
4. Characteristics of the King.. 198
   4.1 Essential Equality: Democratisation 199
   4.2 Restrictions on the Power of the King 201
      4.2.1 Absolute Dependence upon Yahweh.............. 202
      4.2.2 Democratising Effect.. 205
   4.3 Torah-Piety of the King 206
   4.4 Essential Equality 210
   4.5 Conclusion regarding the Characteristics of the King.... 212
5. The Kingship Law as a Paradigm in the Psalter............................ 213
   5.1 King as Chosen by Yahweh 214
      5.1.1 Chosenness in Psalms 1–2............................... 215
      5.1.2 Chosenness in Psalms 18–21............................ 215
      5.1.3 Chosenness in Psalms 118–119....................... 216
   5.2 King's Dependence upon Yahweh 216
      5.2.1 Dependence Theme in Psalms 1–2................. 217
      5.2.2 Dependence Theme in Psalms 18–21............. 217
      5.2.3 Dependence Theme in Psalms 118–119......... 218
   5.3 King as Exemplar of Torah-Piety.................................. 218
      5.3.1 Torah-Piety Theme in Psalms 1–2 219
      5.3.2 Torah-Piety Theme in Psalms 18–21 219
      5.3.3 Torah-Piety Theme in Psalms 118–119 219
   5.4 Humility of the King 220
6. Conclusion 221

Chapter 6 THE EDITORIAL PLACEMENT OF THE
TORAH-KINGSHIP PSALM GROUPINGS................................. 223
1. Introduction 223
2. Assessing Psalm Groupings: Conjunctive and Disjunctive
   Features.. 224
3. Psalms 1–2: Book I, the Davidic Psalter(s) and the Psalter 227
   3.1 Disjunctive: Lack of Superscription.............................. 227
   3.2 Conjunctive: Davidic King in Psalms 1–2 229
   3.3 Conjunctive: Psalms 1–2 cf. Psalm 41 230
   3.4 Conclusion regarding the Placement of Psalms 1–2 230
4. Psalms 18–21 within Book I of Psalter.................................... 234
   4.1 Psalms 18–21: Central to Book I 239
5. Psalms 118–119: Central to Book V 240

xii   *The King as Exemplar*

    6. Bracketing Function of Torah-Kingship Groupings 244
    7. Excursus: A Brief Word about History 246
    8. Conclusion 250

Chapter 7 TORAH, KINGSHIP AND DEMOCRATISATION 253
    1. Introduction 253
    2. Torah 255
        2.1 Torah in the Psalms 256
            2.1.1   Reading Torah in the Torah Psalms 259
            2.1.2   Torah in the Psalms and the Pentateuch 261
        2.2 Torah in Deuteronomy 265
            2.2.1   "This Torah" in the Kingship Law 266
            2.2.2   Sonnet on "This Torah" in Kingship Law 267
        2.3 Torah and Relationship with Yahweh 270
        2.4 Conclusion regarding Torah 271
        2.5 Excursus: Translation of Torah 271
    3. Kingship 273
        3.1 Kingship in Torah-Kingship Psalm Groupings 274
            3.1.1   Conclusion regarding Kingship in the
                     Torah-Kingship Psalm Groupings 277
        3.2 Kingship in the Kingship Law 278
        3.3 Conclusion regarding Kingship 280
    4. Democratisation 280
        4.1 Democratisation of Torah and Kingship Psalms 281
            4.1.1   Reinterpretation of Royal Psalms 282
            4.1.2   Democratisation of the Torah-Kingship
                     Psalm Groupings 284
        4.2 Democratisation in the Kingship Law 286
            4.2.1   The King as One of the Hebrew Brothers 286
            4.2.2   Democratisation in Deuteronomy 287
        4.3 Conclusion regarding Democratisation 288
    5. Conclusion 289

CONCLUSION 291
    Final Words 294

Bibliography 297

Author Index 313

Scripture Index 319

General Index 327

ACKNOWLEDGEMENTS

It is an impossible task to thank everyone who has contributed to this thesis in one way or another. The reality is that "who we are" shapes "what we produce," and those who have influenced my life to bring me to this point are too many to mention—family, friends, ministers, teachers, colleagues and so on. I am grateful to all those who have been of help and encouragement along the way. There are a few who deserve special votes of thanks, however.

Prof. J. Gordon McConville was an excellent doctoral supervisor and I am extremely grateful to him. His wisdom, enthusiasm and encouragement have made the process of doctoral studies as much of a pleasure as it can possibly be! I am grateful also to Prof. Christopher Seitz, of the University of St. Andrews, and Prof. Craig Bartholomew, of Redeemer University College, Canada, for their supervisory contributions at various stages in the development of this thesis. Thanks also go to Prof. Gordon J. Wenham for stimulating Hebrew Reading seminars and for his encouragement.

The members of Psalms Study Group of the Society for Biblical Literature have opened up the study of the Psalter in new and dynamic ways over the last ten years or so and many of us working in the Psalms owe these scholars a great debt of thanks. Thanks also to my post-graduate student colleagues in the Biblical Studies Seminar at the University of Gloucestershire (1999–2002) for being good friends and for many stimulating discussions. The same thanks can be proffered to my colleagues, here, at Highland Theological College in Dingwall, Scotland—they are not a bad bunch, all things considered!

Prof. Adele Berlin, Hebrew Bible editor of the Academia Biblica series, and the editorial team at SBL, especially Leigh Andersen, have been the epitome of courtesy, efficiency and professionalism throughout the process of producing this book. The end product is undoubtedly better as a result of their efforts and I am grateful to them. This work was written using NotaBene Lingua Workstation research software, a great tool for research in Biblical Studies, and my thanks go to Steven Siebert of NotaBene for his technical advice and assistance.

Thanks also to my parents who have provided so much help and support in so many ways—not least of which, first teaching me to read the Scriptures. And most of all I really want to thank my wife, Iwona, and our children, Gosia, Debbie and David for love and support beyond imagination and for much fun always—it is to them that this book is lovingly dedicated.

The introduction to one book (of the many books which I read in my little office with slit windows in Cheltenham) struck me in particular and I would like to echo these words at the beginning of this thesis. 'I pray that the truth will be served and not hindered by this work, which after its fashion is turned towards the greatest mystery of religion, towards the representative figure that carries all the world's agony and hope."[1]

Jamie Grant   Dingwall, April 2004

---

[1] John H. Eaton, *Kingship and the Psalms* (SBT, Vol. 32; London: SCM Press, 1976), Preface.

ABBREVIATIONS

PERIODICALS, SERIES AND REFERENCE WORKS

AB	Anchor Bible Commentary
ACOT	Augsburg Commentaries on the Old Testament
ANET	*Ancient Near Easter Texts*, Pritchard 3rd ed., Princeton, 1969
AOTC	Apollos Old Testament Comentary
AUSS	*Andrews University Seminar Studies*
BDB	Brown, F., S. R. Driver, C. A. Briggs, *Hebrew and English Lexicon of the Old Testament*
Bib	*Biblica*
BibInt	Biblical Interpretation
BJS/UCSD	Biblical and Judaic Studies/University of California San Diego
BT	*The Bible Translator*
BTB	Biblical Theology Bulletin
BZAW	Beihefte zur Zeitschrift für die alttestamentliche Wissenschaft
CBQ	*Catholic Biblical Quarterly*
CBQMS	Catholic Biblical Quarterly Monograph Series
CJT	*Canadian Journal of Theology*
ColT	*Collectanea theologica*
Comm	Communio
ConBOT	Coniectanea biblica: Old Testament Series
CurTM	*Currents in Theology and Mission*
CUP	Cambridge University Press
EBC	Expositor's Bible Commentary
EvQ	*Evangelical Quarterly*
ExAud	*Ex auditu*

FAT	Forschungen Alten Testament
FOTL	Forms of Old Testament Literature
HBT	*Horizons in Biblical Theology*
HSM	Harvard Semitic Monographs
IBC	Interpretation Biblical Commentary
ICC	International Critical Commentary
Int	*Interpretation*
IOTS	*Introduction to the Old Testament as Scripture*. B. S. Childs. London, 1979
JBL	*Journal of Biblical Literature*
JBQ	*Jewish Biblical Quarterly*
JETS	*Journal of the Evangelical Theological Society*
JJS	*Journal of Jewish Studies*
JPSTC	Jewish Publication Society Torah Commentary
JSNTSup	Journal for the Study of the New Testament Supplement Series
JSOT	*Journal for the Study of the Old Testament*
JSOTSup	Journal for the Study of the Old Testament Supplement Series
JSS	*Journal of Semitic Studies*
JTS	*Journal of Theological Studies*
MR	*Modern Reformation*
NCB	New Century Bible
NEchtB	Neue Echter Bibel
NIBCOT	New International Biblical Commentary: Old Testament
NIB	New Interpreter's Biblical
NICOT	New International Commentary on the Old Testament
NIDOTTE	New International Dictionary of Old Testament Theology and Exegesis
NIVAC	New International Version Application Commentary
OBO	Orbis biblicus et orientalis
Or	*Orientalia*
OTG	Old Testament Guides
OTL	Old Testament Library
OTR	Old Testament Readings
OUP	Oxford University Press
Proof	*Prooftexts: A Journal of Jewish Literary History*

PIW	*Psalms in Israel's Worship.* S. Mowinckel. London, 1962.
RestQ	*Restoration Quarterly*
RevExp	*Review and Expositor*
SBET	*Scottish Bulletin of Evangelical Theology*
SBLDS	Society of Biblical Literature Dissertation Series
SBLSP	Society of Biblical Literature Seminar Papers
SBT	Studies in Biblical Theology
SBTS	Sources for Biblical and Theological Study
SHS	Scripture and Hermeneutics Series
SJT	*Scottish Journal of Theology*
SSEJC	Studies in Scripture in Early Judaism and Christianity
ST	*Studia theologica*
SwJT	*Southwestern Journal of Theology*
TLZ	*Theologische Literaturzeitung*
TOTC	Tyndale Old Testament Commentary
TJ	*Trinity Journal*
UF	*Ugarit-Forschungen*
VT	*Vetus Testamentum*
VTSup	Vetus Testamentum Supplements
WBC	Word Biblical Commentary
WTJ	*Westminster Theological Journal*
WW	*Word and World*
ZAW	*Zeitschrift für die alttestamentliche Wissenschaft*

ANCIENT TEXTS, RABBINIC TEXTS AND DEAD SEA SCROLLS

4QPs^a	Qumran Cave 4 portions of the Psalms
11QPs^a	Qumran Cave 11 portions of the Psalms
Ber.	*Berakot*
LXX	Septuagint
MT	Masoretic Text

MODERN BIBLE TRANSLATIONS

ESV	English Standard Version
JPS	Jewish Publication Society *Tanakh*
KJV	King James Version

NASV	New American Standard Version
NEB	New English Bible
NIV	New International Version
NRSV	New Revised Standard Version
RSV	Revised Standard Version

MISCELLANEOUS

ANE	ancient Near East
BCE	before the Common Era
ca.	circa
CE	Common Era
cf.	*confer*, compare
Dtr	Deuteronomic
DtrN	Nomistic Deuteronomic
e.g.	*exampli gratia*, for example
EVV	English versions of the Bible
et al.	*et alii*, and others
etc.	*et cetera*, and the rest
i.e.	*id est*, that is
MS(S)	manuscript(s)
n	note
p(p)	page(s)
Ps(s)	Psalm(s)
RPs(s)	royal psalm(s)
s/s(s)	superscription(s)
vol.	volume
v(v)	verse(s)

INTRODUCTION

In the fourth century C.E., Augustine wrote that "the arrangement of the Psalms, which seems to me to contain a secret of great mystery, has not yet been revealed to me."[1] His observation is one which probably reflects the experience of many readers of the Psalter. On the one hand, the order of the Psalms seems to be entirely random and without recognisable design; yet, on the other, there are occasions when the reader is left with the impression that there is something more to it than that. A psalm answers a question asked in the previous poem, or the themes and language of one composition are echoed in the verses of its neighbour. Then there are the collections of psalms found throughout the Psalter: David, Asaph, Sons of Korah, Songs of Ascents and so on. What is more, there are the five "books" of psalms each ending with a doxology. So the more the reader thinks about it the more he or she empathises with the words of Augustine: there is something "going on" in the ordering of the psalms in the Psalter, but it is hard to define precisely how that ordering may influence our understanding and interpretation of them.

This thesis seeks to plumb some of the depths of Augustine's "great mystery." The task in hand is not to present an over-arching explanation of the ordering of the psalms in the Psalter (as if such a task were possible!). Rather the aim of this study is to discuss one particular paradigm which may have influenced the shape of the Psalms in certain ways. That paradigm is the Deut-

---

[1] "Ordo psalmorum, qui mihi magni sacramenti videtur continere secretum, nondum mihi fuerit revelatus," *Enarrationes in Psalmos* 150.i (translation mine). I am grateful to David Mitchell who included this quote by way of preface to his work *The Message of the Psalter: An Eschatological Programme in the Book of Psalms* (JSOTSup 252; Sheffield: Sheffield Academic Press, 1997), 14.

eronomic Kingship Law (Deut 17:14-20); and the tentative argument of this dissertation is that the Law of the King has been used as an intellectual construct to shape and nuance the psalmic presentation of kingship.

How is the Kingship Law applied as an interpretative paradigm by the editors of the Psalter? The suggestion made herein is that the editors wished to reflect the theology of the Law of the King through the deliberate juxtaposition of kingship psalms alongside torah psalms.[2] Psalms which focus upon the person of the king placed alongside psalms which celebrate the significance of Yahweh's revelation. Psalms in which the king confesses his dependence upon Yahweh (a key idea of the Kingship Law) are set beside psalms which encourage a piety based in the reading and application of the torah (another key concept of the Kingship Law). So the central idea of this thesis is that the placement of kingship psalms alongside torah psalms was a deliberate editorial act through which the Psalter's redactors intended to reflect the theology of the Deuteronomic Law of the King in the Book of Psalms.

Why would they wish to do so? It is always a dangerous task to suggest why an individual (or group of individuals, for that matter) may or may not have prepared a particular text in a certain way. This task is made doubly difficult by distances of time and culture. The only means we have of answering such a question is, as far as is possible, to let the psalms speak for themselves—to let the theological content of these compositions be the basis for our conclusions. It appears, from the detailed exegetical examination of the psalms which feature in this thesis, that the editors had two concerns: proper kingship and proper piety. Proper kingship in that the juxtaposition of royal and torah psalms draws attention to the Dtr *ideal* of kingship rather than the reality of the monarchy as recorded in the history books of Judah and Israel. Proper piety in that Deuteronomy calls upon the king to be an exemplar of right relationship with Yahweh for all the people, and the editors of the Psalms seek to present that exemplary commitment to God as the proper path for their readers to follow.

---

[2] Namely, the placement of the royal Psalm 2 alongside (torah) Psalm 1; Pss 18, 20 and 21 are all kingship psalms which bracket Ps 19, a hymn celebrating Yahweh's torah; and Ps 118 (where the king leads the people into worship in the temple) is juxtaposed alongside the fullest of all the torah psalms, Ps 119.

These concerns (proper kingship and proper piety) should be read in the light of the post-exilic era during which the editors of the Psalter carried out their final work. Therefore, it is highly likely that the editors' presentation of kingship is meant to speak to the people's eschatological image of a restored Davidic king. In the juxtaposition of these psalms, the redactors point out that this expected ruler from a renewed house of David is to reflect the ideal of kingship rather than the reality as experienced in the DtrH. Post-exilic concerns speak to the question of proper piety as well. In the period of the return from exile, Yahweh's torah is seen as key to the renewed community in the land—it is the cornerstone by which they can avoid the fate of exile in the future.[3] So, regardless of the original setting of these royal and torah psalms, they are (as we shall see) to be re-read in the light of the post-exilic final form of the Psalter which focuses attention on these dual themes: definition of the type of kingship which was to characterise the expected king and encouragement of a proper piety based in torah amongst the readers and hearers of the Psalms.

Therefore, the aim of this thesis is to ask a question of the text of the Psalter: is the juxtaposition of kingship and torah psalms designed to reflect the Law of the King? Obviously, there is a certain risk in such method; that is, the answer which one arrives at is inseparably linked to the question which one asks. So, in asking this question, do we risk imposing a paradigm which would not be apparent had we asked a different question? Perhaps. However, the question here asked is not—in its origin—one imposed on the text from without, but one which results from initial (superficial) reading of the final form of the Book of Psalms itself. Psalms 1 and 2 are significant because they head the Psalter; they strike its opening chord, and, therefore, are somehow important to all that follows. It is in the reading of these initial psalms that one is first struck by the overtones of the Kingship Law. These two compostions (as chapter 2 explains) are linked by several significant lexical and thematic repetitions, which associate the figure of the king in Ps 2 with the torah-lover of Ps 1. The king and the איש who delights in Yahweh's torah are read together in creative juxtaposition, and so the voice of the Psalter—at its very outset—speaks in terms of the themes found in the Law of the King. This in turn challenges the reader to look further and more closely at the use of the torah psalms in the Psalter. They are few in number, yet their

---

[3] As reflected, for example, in the prominence of torah in the post-exilic books of Ezra-Nehemiah and the exilic Jeremiah and Ezekiel.

voice is loud in terms of the shape of the book as a whole.[4] A cursory reading of Ps 19 and its surrounds indicates a torah psalm bracketed by kingship psalms and the reader's curiosity is further awakened to a possible link with the Kingship Law. The association of king, leading the people into Temple worship, in Pss 118 and the torah-keeper who orders his life around the divine revelation, in Ps 119, again confirms these observations, and legitimates the question asked. There *appears to be* a link between king and torah in the psalms. There *is* an explicit link between king and torah in Deut 17:14–20. Are these two phenomena connected? Was the Kingship Law used by the editors of the Psalter as a paradigm for the juxtaposition of torah and kingship psalms? Thus, yes, a question is being asked of the text, but it is a question which springs from the text.

How do we proceed from there? How do we go about answering the question asked? The main aim is to let the respective texts speak for themselves as far as possible. Therefore, after dealing with certain questions of methodology in chapter one, chapters two to four will deal with the exegetical consideration of the three torah-kingship psalm groupings respectively. In examining the groups of psalms, the aim is to assess the main theological concerns apparent in each psalm and to highlight any indications of concatenation between the psalms of that group. In chapters three and four, we shall also consider the question of linkage between the three psalm groupings. In particular, as we seek to answer the question of whether or not the Kingship Law has functioned as a paradigm for the placement of torah and kingship psalms alongside one another, we should be aware of any intellectual background in Deuteronomic theology which is to be found in these compositions. It seems reasonable that, if the Law of the King is the paradigm for their juxtaposition, they should reflect something of the Deuteronomic worldview. Or rather, to express the same point negatively, it is unlikely that the Kingship Law has functioned as a paradigm for the placement of these psalms if they bear no other indication of a background in Dtr theology. Therefore, particular (but not exclusive) focus will be placed on the discussion of Deuteronomic themes within the torah-kingship psalm groupings.

Chapter five, in turn, will pay more detailed attention to the Kingship Law itself, concentrating on the exegesis of Deut 17:14–20 in the light of the broader context of the laws concerning the offices in Israel (Deut 16:18–18:22). This

---

[4] As chapter 5 of this thesis seeks to explain. See also James L. Mays, "The Place of the Torah-Psalms in the Psalter," *JBL* 106, no. 1 (1987): 3–12.

Introduction

passage too must be allowed to speak for itself in its own context if we are to properly understand its possible usage in the Psalms. Central to the idea of a canonical reading of the Psalter is the idea of the placement of individual psalms at significant junctures throughout the book. Therefore, following on from the exegetical examination of Pss 1–2, 18–21, 118–119 and Deut 17:14–20 in chapters two to five, attention will turn to consideration of the significance of the placement of the torah-kingship psalm groupings within the Psalter as a whole. Finally, chapter seven compares the main theological themes found in the torah-kingship psalm groupings with those found in the Kingship Law. Both the psalm groupings and the Law of the King speak of matters concerning the torah of Yahweh, kingship in Israel and issues of democratisation; but do the Psalms and Deuteronomy speak with the same voice on these matters? This will be the question considered in chapter seven of this thesis.

In his examination of Pss 18–21 as part of an article dealing with the theology of the psalm grouping Pss 15–24, Patrick Miller points out the echoes of the Law of the King found in these psalms and asks a rhetorical question:

> It almost seems as if we are once more before the Deuteronomistic theology of kingship. It may be that all of this in fact reflects a Deuteronomistic influence on the redaction of the Psalter. I do not know. If it does, then we are made even more aware of the centrality of that particular stream in biblical theology and its influence on the theology of kingship and the royal ideal.[5]

Does the Book of Deuteronomy, and in particular (as Miller suggests) the Kingship Law, influence the redaction of the Psalms? This is the very question that we will address in the coming pages of this thesis.

---

[5] Patrick D. Miller, "Kingship, Torah Obedience and Prayer," in *Neue Wege der Psalmenforschung* (eds. K. Seybold and E. Zenger; Freiburg: Herder, 1995), 141.

CHAPTER 1
METHODOLOGICAL CONSIDERATIONS

1. INTRODUCTION

Since the publication of Gerald Wilson's *Editing of the Hebrew Psalter*[1] in 1985 a quest has been continuing in the field of psalm studies: to define and highlight the theological themes emphasised in the final form of the Book of Psalms. Wilson's ground-breaking work set the tone for the development of psalm studies by arguing that the order of the psalms in the final form of the book was not accidental, but rather "represents the end result of purposeful, editorial organization."[2] Consequently, the suggestion that the ordering of the psalms is the result of deliberate editorial activity has led to the conclusion that the theological concerns of the Psalter's redactors must be apparent in the way in which the Book of Psalms has been put together. This theory has gained wide acceptance within the scholarly community over the last fifteen years, or so, and many scholars have contributed to this work in progress. Most scholars working in this field broadly accept Wilson's main thesis and his methodological approach (discussed in greater detail below), and from that starting point go on to analyse the content of the Psalms, pointing out important themes and indications of editorial activity.

The net effect of this scholarly turn towards a canonical approach to the Psalter has been the publication of various works which emphasising the themes which reflect the prominent theological concerns of those who shaped the final form of the Psalter. Wilson himself highlights the importance of the royal

---

[1] Gerald H. Wilson, *The Editing of the Hebrew Psalter* (SBLDS 76; Chico, CA: Scholars Press, 1985).
[2] Wilson, *Editing*, 4.

psalms which are placed at the "seams" of Books I–III of the Psalter.³ Mays and McCann have emphasised the significant placement of the torah psalms in the overall collection—these compositions are few in number but their influence is substantial.⁴ Closely linked to the torah motif is the "wisdom" theology which many authors see as key to a proper understanding of the Psalms.⁵ Other scholars, like Miller, have emphasised the Deuteronomic overtones found in prominent psalms,⁶ whilst the Exodus pericope, which seems to provide the backdrop to many psalms, has drawn the attention of other scholars.⁷ Finally, the reign of Yahweh (undoubtedly one of the central themes of the Psalter) has been the focus of several works.⁸ This recurrent focus on the reign of Yahweh finds emphasis in psalms celebrating the kingdom of Yahweh (e.g. Pss 93–99⁹) *and* in psalms celebrating the rule of his king (e.g. Pss 2, 72, 110).¹⁰ The continuing prominent placement of the latter (kingship) psalms even in the face of the stark realities of post-exilic Israel when the Psalter was closed, has led many scholars to see marked eschatological overtones in the final form of the Psalms.¹¹

---

³ Wilson, *Editing*, 208. See also Gerald H. Wilson, "The Use of Royal Psalms at the 'Seams' of the Hebrew Psalter," *JSOT* 35 (1986): 85–94.

⁴ See Mays, "Place of the Torah-Psalms." This article was also included in Mays's seminal work *The Lord Reigns* (Louisville: Westminster John Knox Press, 1994). See also J. Clinton McCann, *A Theological Introduction to the Books of Psalms: The Psalms as Torah* (Nashville: Abingdon Press, 1993).

⁵ Gerald T. Sheppard, "Theology and the Book of Psalms," *Int* 46, no. 2 (1992): 143–55. See also the chapter on the Psalms in Brevard S. Childs, *Introduction to the Old Testament as Scripture* (London: SCM Press, 1979) and Anthony R. Ceresko, "The Sage in the Psalms," in *The Sage in Israel and the Ancient Near East* (eds. J. G. Gammie & L. G. Perdue; Winona Lake, IN: Eisenbrauns, 1990), 217–30.

⁶ Patrick D. Miller, "The End of the Psalter: A Response to Erich Zenger," *JSOT* 80 (1998): 103–10. See also Miller's "Kingship" and "Deuteronomy and Psalms: Evoking a Biblical Conversation," *JBL* 118, no. 1 (1999): 3–18.

⁷ Erich Zenger, "The Composition and Theology of the Fifth Book of the Psalter," *JSOT* 80 (1998): 77–102 See also Susan E. Gillingham, "The Exodus Tradition and Israelite Psalmody," *SJT* 52, no. 1 (1999): 19–46, however, it must be said that Gillingham's concern in her thorough examination of the use of the Exodus theme in the Psalms is not to address issues of canonical placement.

⁸ For example, Mays, *The Lord Reigns*.

⁹ See David M. Howard, *The Structure of Psalms 93–100* (BJS/UCSD 5; Winona Lake, IN: Eisenbrauns, 1997).

¹⁰ John I. Durham, "The King as 'Messiah' in the Psalms," *RevExp* 81 (Summer 1984): 426–27.

¹¹ This was one of Childs's main conclusions in the psalms chapter of *IOTS*, and is the central theme of David Mitchell's *Message*. Other authors like Mays, McCann,

The discussion born out of this new approach to the study of the Psalms has been rich and diverse.[12] This thesis seeks to draw upon some of the suggestions already made and to add some further considerations to the on-going discussion—the hope being that through the continuation of this conversation our understanding of the Psalter will be further enriched. The main suggestion of this study is that one of the redactional emphases of the Book of Psalms is the juxtaposition of kingship and torah psalms alongside one another, in an attempt to reflect the theology of the Kingship Law in the Psalter's final form. The purpose of this redaction was two-fold: (1) to shape the reader's understanding of the eschatological king, expected in the period of the closure of the Psalter; and (2) to encourage the type of devotion to Yahweh amongst the readers and hearers of the psalms, which the Kingship Law expected of the king. Eschatological hope in a monarch who will be the true "keeper" of the torah of Yahweh in accordance with the Deuteronomic Law of the King, and a piety based in the keeping of that torah are the joint foci of this redaction.

Taking Deut 17:14-20 at face value, the pattern for kingship in Israel entailed keeping the law of the Lord (תורת יהוה) and each king in the history of Judah and Israel failed in this task to a greater or lesser degree.[13] It appears that the redactors of the Psalter, in line with much of the post-exilic literature, are advocating a return to life in accordance with the terms of the Deuteronomic law, as can also be witnessed in other post-exilic books of the Hebrew Bible, e.g. Ezra-Nehemiah.[14] In this particular case it appears that "the righteous" are pointed to an eschatological messiah (משיח) who will finally keep the Kingship

---

Miller, Murphy, Howard, Vincent and Brueggemann have also picked up on the eschatological thrust of the final form of the Psalter to varying degrees and with varying emphases. This issue merits further consideration, so it shall be discussed below, as one of the methodological considerations of this chapter.

[12] Such breadth and diversity of opinion is not a weakness in the method, as Whybray has suggested (*Reading the Psalms as a Book* [JSOTSup 222; Sheffield: JSOT Press, 1996], 78–81). It is rather the inevitable consequence of any new approach to the study of the psalms. The canonical method has opened several new avenues of discussion in psalms studies and each of these should be researched to their fullest extent.

[13] Obviously, this in itself is a complex historical question, which merits further discussion. Some of the issues connected with the role of the Kingship Law will be addressed below in the detailed examination of that passage in Chapter 5 of this thesis.

[14] See, for example, Freedman's association of Ps 119 with Ezra and his programme of reconstruction based in the Torah (David Noel Freedman, *Psalm 119: The Exaltation of Torah* [BJS/UCSD; Winona Lake, IN: Eisenbrauns, 1999], 29, 91–92).

Law of Deuteronomy 17 by living in accord with the law of the Lord. At the same time, the final form of the Book of Psalms calls upon the reader to live by the torah as their rule for life and godliness in the post-exilic period. Indeed, this eschatological figure is to be the torah-keeping exemplar for the righteous, just as the Israelite king was meant to be.[15] His is the example to be followed.

It is argued that this editorial concern is voiced in the juxtaposition of torah psalms and royal psalms at prominent junctures throughout the Book of Psalms. We see this juxtaposition in the very introduction to the Psalter—Psalms 1 and 2—the hermeneutical prism through which the reader is to understand the book as a whole.[16] It is repeated in the centre of a previous collection which lies at the very heart of Book I.[17] It is also found at the very heart of Book V,[18] thus fulfilling a bracketing function, and influencing the whole Book of Psalms.[19] The combined effect of these juxtapositions, as mentioned above and discussed below, shapes the reader's worldview and her picture of the eschatological king.

Obviously, any thesis which would purport to see editorial activity in the juxtaposition and placement of psalms must be carefully argued both exegetically and theologically. Such examination shall be carried out below.[20] However, prior to the discussion of necessary issues regarding method in the remainder of this chapter, it would be helpful to outline the central idea of this thesis in order to signpost the direction which this study will follow.

1.1 OUTLINE OF THE CENTRAL ARGUMENT

As mentioned above, the first juxtaposition of kingship and torah psalms is seen in the introduction to the Psalter itself. Psalm 1 celebrates the role of the torah in the life of the believer. It contains imagery of stability and fruitfulness and the blessing of God upon all those who would reject evil and live by the torah. Psalm 2 celebrates the rule and reign of Yahweh and his anointed over all the kings and rulers of the nations of the earth. It is a kingship psalm which

---

[15] How to define the word torah is a complex issue, and at this point I merely wish to outline some of the issues involved and to refer to the fuller discussion of this question in chapter 7 below.

[16] See chapter 2 below.

[17] See chapter 3 below.

[18] See chapter 4 below.

[19] See chapter 6, *The Editorial Placement of the Torah-Kingship Psalm Groupings*.

[20] Chapters 2–4 deal with the exegetical examination of the three psalm groupings.

paints a picture of the universal rule of Yahweh via his king from Zion. There are several thematic and lexical links between these two psalms which highlight their connection. In the juxtaposition of these psalms, it appears that the editors of the final form are deliberately trying to link the concepts of torah and kingship. Secondly, Pierre Auffret and Patrick Miller have argued that Psalms 15–24 make up a prior collection of psalms which was incorporated into the broader collections of Book I, the Davidic psalter and, ultimately, the Psalter. They point to a possible chiastic or envelope structure, bounded by two entry psalms (Pss 15 and 24). The focal point of this grouping is the torah psalm, Psalm 19. This psalm—as it is central to the collection's chiastic structure—is bounded by psalms of similar theme, namely Psalms 18 and 20/21.[21] All three of these psalms are kingship psalms, celebrating the Lord's steadfast love towards his "anointed one," his protection of the king and the latter's victory over his enemies. Again we shall see thematic, linguistic and theological connections between these psalms, which indicate that their juxtaposition is not accidental, rather that there has been a deliberate attempt to link these psalms and to hold these concepts of torah and kingship together in creative tension. Thirdly, it shall be argued that the representative leading the people into Temple worship in Ps 118 is, in fact, the Davidic king. What is more, there are good grounds to suggest that the pray-er of Ps 119—who so delights in Yahweh's torah—is also the king, providing an example of proper devotion to God through delight in his revealed instruction. If this was the understanding of the editors of the Psalter then, once more, we see a strong kingship-torah connection at the very heart of Book V of the Psalms. It is the tentative proposal of this thesis that these psalms were deliberately placed alongside one another in order to reflect the theology of the Kingship Law in the final form of the Book of Psalms.

2. CANONICAL APPROACH

Certain preliminary issues must be dealt with before we can address this thesis in detail. Firstly, the texts examined shall be the final form (canonical) Books of Psalms and Deuteronomy.[22] No longer is OT study limited to

---

[21] There is good reason to believe that these two psalms (20 and 21) are deliberately linked and should be treated together. See the discussion in chapter 3.

[22] In other words, whilst reference shall be made to the LXX and to certain Qumran mss, the MT provides the starting point for discussion in this thesis.

discussion of historical-critical questions regarding sources, authorship, redaction layers and the composition history; rather the text of a given OT book in its received form is considered a worthy subject of discussion in itself. Of course, this does not mean that the discussion of diachronic questions has somehow become inappropriate, merely that a synchronic approach has come to be seen as equally valued and significant.[23] So, normally, the adoption of a canonical approach as one's methodology would be non-controversial.

However, the Psalter is hardly a typical case in point. First, it is a "hymnic" collection rather than a book with a narrative plot and structure.[24] Secondly, we know almost nothing about the process by which the psalms were included into the present canonical form, other than the fact that individual compositions or groups of psalms were, probably, gradually added to the growing "Book of Psalms."[25] Thirdly, the form-critical approach (*Gattungsforschung*) was so dominant for so long that the question of an over-arching ordering of the psalms has been subordinated to the discussion of genre.[26] Thus to talk of a canonical approach to the Psalms is a relatively new phenomenon, but is it a "legitimate" approach to the study of the Psalms?

---

[23] This process of change has, largely been due to the significant works of Brevard Childs, and his ground-breaking "canonical approach" to Scripture (*IOTS*; *Old Testament Theology in a Canonical Context* [Philadelphia: Fortress Press, 1986] etc.).

[24] See Wilson, *Editing*, 6–11. It should be remembered that hymnic does not necessarily equate to "cultic." Whilst, most likely, the majority of the psalms did function originally in a cultic setting, this is not true of all psalms. Indeed, the canonical approach suggests that—regardless of the original setting and function of the psalms—ultimately, they came to be read together as a book (Mays, *The Lord Reigns*, 121–23).

[25] James D. Nogalski, "From Psalm to Psalms to Psalter," in *An Introduction to Wisdom Literature and the Psalms: Festschrift Marvin E. Tate* (ed. H. W. Ballard and W. D. Tucker; Macon, GA: Mercer University Press, 2000), 51; Christoph F. Barth, *Introduction to the Psalms* (trans. R. A. Wilson; New York: Charles Scribner's Sons, 1966), 2–3.

[26] Until relatively recently, non-commentary works on the psalms seldom began with Ps 1 and worked systematically through the book. Rather, the hymns or laments or some other form was chosen as a starting-point which led on to the discussion of the remaining genres. Westermann suggests that the reason for this lack of consideration of the shape of the Psalter "lies simply in the fact that in laying the foundation for his interpretation of the Psalms, Gunkel above all had no interest in how the collection was handed down to us," (*Praise and Lament in the Psalms* [trans. Keith R. Crim and Richard N. Soulen; Atlanta: John Knox Press, 1981], 251).

2.1 CANONICAL METHOD IN THE STUDY OF THE PSALMS

The basic thesis of a canonical approach to the Psalter, as mentioned above, is that the ordering and placement of the psalms is not entirely random, but that the Book of Psalms has been shaped by the work of editors in order to emphasise the importance of certain theological themes. Mitchell, summarising Wilson's approach, points out that his "twofold purpose is to demonstrate that purposeful editorial activity lies behind the Psalter, and to identify the agenda that guided the redaction."[27] Indicators of the first of these tasks are to be seen in the tacit[28] signs of editing found in the Psalter. Wilson comments:

> I have been able to show (1) that the "book" divisions of the Psalter are real, editorially-induced divisions and not accidentally introduced; (2) the "separating" and "binding" functions of author and genre groupings; (3) the lack of a s/s [superscription] as an indication of a tradition of combination; (4) the use of *hllwyh* pss to indicate the conclusion of segments; (5) the use of *hwdw* pss to introduce segments; (6) the existence of thematic correspondences between the beginning and ending pss in some books. All of these findings demonstrate the presence of editorial activity at work in the arrangement of the pss.[29]

Wilson goes on to add such features as "the use of author and genre categories in the s/ss to group pss... the function of Ps 1 as an introduction to the whole Psalter[30]... the place of early collections in the final form... the thematic grouping of psalms" as further indicators of editorial activity.[31] As can be seen from the secondary literature cited throughout this thesis, Wilson's suggestion of "purposeful editorial activity" in the Psalter has received very broad support amongst psalms scholars. "Identifying the agenda that guided the redaction" has (perhaps, not surprisingly) led to a much more wide-ranging expression of opinion. How does one go about this task?

---

[27] Mitchell, *Message*, 61.
[28] Wilson, *Editing*, 9–10, 182–85.
[29] Wilson, *Editing*, 199.
[30] It is, however, the suggestion of this thesis that Pss 1 and 2 together form an introduction to the Psalter. Wilson's seeks to exclude Ps 2 from the introduction as he sees it as one of the royal "seam" psalms, the first of Book I. However, it seems likely that the editors of the Psalter sought to associate Ps 2 with Ps 1, rather than associating it with the laments of Ps 3 and the ensuing psalms. (See chapter 2, below.)
[31] Wilson, *Editing*, 11, 199–200.

2.2 IDENTIFYING EDITORIAL AGENDAS

How does one discern editorial activity in the Psalter? Obviously, with regard to the canonical study of the Psalms (as with any methodological approach to the study of the OT), some fairly rigorous ground rules are necessary in order to prevent its misuse and its decline into rampant subjectivity. Gerald Wilson, as well as being one of the originators of this method, has also been a champion of correct and clearly-defined method. Having highlighted the pitfalls of approaching the Psalter with a pre-conceived notion of the editorial themes to be found in the book and then "finding" psalms which fit this theory, Wilson goes on to state:

> My own preference is to work without a hypothesis (other than the cautious one mentioned above) [i.e. that the present arrangement is the result of purposeful editorial activity, and that its purpose can be discerned by careful and exhaustive analysis of the linguistic and thematic relationships between individual psalms and groups of psalms] and to allow any sense of the structure that develops to derive from an intensive and thorough analysis of the psalms in question in terms of their linguistic, thematic, literary and theological links and relationships.[32]

Wilson suggests that editorial themes can be discerned from "linguistic, thematic, literary and theological links and relationships" between psalms. Psalms are linked in order to paint a fuller picture than is seen in their individual parts. Content in context takes on a slightly different meaning.[33] The idea is that the theological concerns of the editors of the Psalter's final form are seen in the way in which they link psalms together and also in their placement of these linked psalms at key junctures throughout the Psalter (see 2.3 *The Question of Significant Placement*, below).

---

[32] Gerald H. Wilson, "Understanding the Purposeful Arrangement of the Psalms: Pitfalls and Promise," in *The Shape and Shaping of the Psalter* (ed. J. Clinton McCann; JSOTSup 159; Sheffield: JSOT Press, 1993), 48.

[33] See the discussion of this idea in James L. Mays, "The Question of Context in Psalm Interpretation," in *The Shape and Shaping of the Psalter* (ed. J. Clinton McCann; JSOTSup 159; Sheffield: JSOT Press, 1993), 21–28 and the response articles Roland E. Murphy, "Reflections on Contextual Interpretations of the Psalms," in *The Shape and Shaping of the Psalter* (ed. J. Clinton McCann; JSOTSup 159; Sheffield: JSOT Press, 1993) and Walter Brueggemann, "Response to Mays, 'The Question of Context,'" in *The Shape and Shaping of the Psalter* (ed. J. Clinton McCann; JSOTSup 159; Sheffield: JSOT Press, 1993).

Methodological Considerations

David Howard also provides helpful comment on canonical methodology with regard to the Book of Psalms. His approach focuses on four areas of linking which show concatenation between individual psalms or groups of psalms—lexical, thematic, structural and genre connections.[34] These categories are further broken down by Howard. Lexical links may include three types of linguistic overlap, i.e. "key-word" (*Leitwörter*) links where the same word or phrase is repeated; "thematic word links" where the same concept is expressed using different words; and "incidental links" where there may be no real significance in the repetition of a word, which could be described as non-essential to both psalms.[35] Thematic links include lexical repetition/similarities and more general linkage of concepts and ideas between psalms.[36] For example, a question asked in one psalm may be answered in the following psalm (e.g. could "The Lord is my Shepherd, I shall not want," in Ps 23:1 be a response to "My God, My God, why have you forsaken me?" from Ps 22:1?) or a theme may be expanded upon throughout a chain of psalms (e.g. the *YHWH mālāk* psalms 93, 95–99). Howard sees structural links as being particularly helpful when dealing with a group of psalms within the larger structure of the Psalter (e.g. see the discussion of the psalm grouping Pss 15–24 in Chapter 3 below). Both Wilson and Howard see genre as being of only limited importance as a tool for deriving thematic association between psalms, it can highlight certain interesting indicators (e.g. the possible transition between groups of psalms[37]) but it seems unlikely that the redactors of the Psalter used genre classification as an organisational tool—content (including superscriptions) rather than type seems to have directed the editorial placement of the psalms.[38]

---

[34] Howard, *Structure*, 99–100.

[35] Howard, *Structure*, 100. Howard's thesis is exhaustive in its analysis of the lexical overlap between the psalms of this group. In terms of lexical analysis, this study will not examine every possible linguistic link, rather it shall focus on the links which seem most relevant to the underlying theological message of the psalms being considered.

[36] Howard, *Structure*, 100–01.

[37] Gerald H. Wilson, "Evidence of Editorial Divisions in the Hebrew Psalter," *VT* XXXIV, no. 3 (1984): 345–47.

[38] Howard, *Structure*, 101–02. See also Wilson, *Editing*, 167. Of course, it should be acknowledged that Gunkel's genre classifications have a strong "content" base therefore some psalm groupings may be informed by this. For example, Pss 3–14 are all laments, with the exception of Ps 8, therefore, in this case genre categories and content coincide (see chapter 6, below, for further discussion).

Obviously, there is a certain degree of overlap in these three categories. Thematic links most often become apparent through the use of lexical concatenation. The use of the same word in consecutive psalms may also indicate a structural connection as well as simple lexical linkage (e.g. the repetition of the "blessed" [אשרי] clause in Psalms 1 and 2 forming an inclusion or envelope structure).[39] However, these ground-rules provide a reasonable framework within which the canonical approach can function and they result in profitable analysis of the psalms and their themes. Therefore, in examining each of the three torah-kingship psalm groupings mentioned above, this study shall apply the following methodology: Analysis of lexical, thematic and structural/literary connections and, on the basis of these analyses, theological conclusions shall be suggested regarding possible editorial emphases in the Psalter.

2.3 THE QUESTION OF SIGNIFICANT PLACEMENT

Having defined some principles for establishing themes by way of concatenation and association,[40] we must also define principles with regard to significant placement within the Psalter.[41] Just what makes the placement of a psalm/group of psalms telling? At its most basic level the answer to that question appears to be quite simple: in essence a psalm/group of psalms placed at the beginning, middle or end of one of the books of the Psalter could be described as having a significant editorial placement. Obviously, the justification of this theory is somewhat more complex than this statement would suggest.

Wilson has pointed out the importance of the so-called "seam" psalms which come at the beginning and the end of the books of the Psalter.[42] These

---

[39] J. Clinton McCann, *The Book of Psalms* (NIB; Nashville: Abingdon Press, 1996), 664–65; Nancy L. deClaissé-Walford, *Reading from the Beginning: The Shaping of the Hebrew Psalter* (Macon, GA: Mercer University Press, 1997), 48.

[40] For the purposes of this thesis, *concatenation* refers to the lexical and thematic linking of immediately juxtaposed psalms. *Association* involves drawing comparisons between groups or pairs of psalms placed at different positions throughout the Psalter, also by way of lexical and thematic connection, and their impact on the book as a whole (see Hossfeld and Zenger's discussion of the canonical method, *Die Psalmen I* [NEchtB; Würzburg: Echter Verlag, 1993], 24 and the fuller discussion in Chapter 6, below).

[41] For example, it is an essential element of Wilson's overall theory that royal psalms were placed at significant junctures throughout the Psalms in order to narrate the failure of the Davidic monarchy and that the editorial centre of the Psalter is the response to that failure in Book IV—the Lord reigns (*Editing*, 215).

[42] Wilson, *Editing*, 207–08. See also Wilson's "Use of Royal Psalms."

Methodological Considerations

have considerable significance for understanding thematic emphases in the Psalter, it is argued. Therefore, the *beginning* and *end* of books are to be seen as points of significant placement.[43] *Centrality* within a book of Psalms is also considered to be of some significance.[44] Zenger, on Ps 119's function in Book V, states:

> According to the theological perspective of the fifth book of psalms which has the Torah Psalm 119 *intentionally placed in the middle of the composition*, the psalms are a means of opening oneself to the living Torah of Yhwh—in accordance with the programme at the beginning of the Psalter, Psalms 1–2, and in accordance with the closing Hallel, Psalms 146–150, which interprets the recitation/signing of psalms as the actualization of the way of life (Torah) instilled in the cosmos.[45]

This shows again the significance of centrality within the respective books of the Psalter. It may be that there is a single, central psalm which clearly lies at the very heart of one of the books (as Wilson and Zenger suggest with regard to Ps 119 in Book V), or it may be a collection which is central (e.g. the Pss 15–24 collection in Book I).[46] The focal point does not, it appears, depend upon mathematical centrality, but rather is reflective of some sort of dominant or emphatic theme present in a roughly central position within a book.

Arguments could probably be made as to the priority of other placements within a given book depending upon the structural breakdown of that collection, but these three positions seem to be key to the understanding of significant editorial placement: introduction, centrality and conclusion. Therefore, our focus in seeking an understanding of the importance of the placement of the torah-kingship psalm groupings will be grounded in these categories.

2.4 Cautionary Notes regarding Methodology

Every method has its limitations. It is helpful to be aware of these when making use of that particular approach. In what areas should we exercise caution in the practice of a canonical approach to the Psalms? The only book-length

---

[43] This is the central thesis of deClaissé-Walford's *Reading from the Beginning*.

[44] See, for example, Wilson's discussion of the centrality of Ps 119 within a Davidic framework in Book V in "Shaping the Psalter: A Consideration of Editorial Linkage in the Book of Psalms," in *The Shape and Shaping of the Psalms* (ed. J. Clinton McCann; JSOTSup 159; Sheffield: JSOT Press, 1993), 79.

[45] Zenger, "Composition," 102 (emphasis added).

[46] See the discussion of these placements in chapter 6, below.

critique of this approach, is R. N. Whybray's *The Psalms as a Book*,[47] which questions the idea of purposeful editorial activity in the psalms—"there is no evidence that there was a systematic and purposeful redaction of the whole Psalter in any of the ways suggested."[48] Whilst Whybray posited some helpful and important questions, it must be said that his critique did not substantially undermine the canonical approach of Wilson *et al.*[49] The fact remains that there are solid indicators of fairly comprehensive editorial activity within the psalms, which must be ignored or explained away if one is to accept that the ordering of the psalms is random. For example, the function of Psalms 1–2 as an introduction; Psalms 146–150 as a concluding voice of praise; the five-book structure of the Psalter; the incorporation and placement of previous collections in the book in its final-form; the existence of the Elohistic psalter. Whybray's critique was largely based upon the fact that any editorial work which may have been carried out was "sporadic" rather than "systematic and purposeful."[50] However, even sporadic editorial activity can change markedly the way in which the entire Book of Psalms is read and understood. Such subtle activity is probably to be expected and its effects should not be minimised.[51]

The canonical approach towards the study of the Psalter has attained broad acceptance within the scholarly community in recent years as there are sufficient "obvious" indicators of editorial activity to provide solid support for this methodological approach. However, questions still remain.[52] For example, viewing

---

[47] *Reading the Psalms as a Book* (JSOTSup 222; Sheffield: JSOT Press, 1996).

[48] Whybray, *Psalms as a Book*, 118–19.

[49] See D. M. Howard's review of *Reading the Psalms as a Book* at the Review of Biblical Literature web-site: http://www.bookreviews.org/pdf/2475_1563.pdf. Howard provides an accurate assessment of the weaknesses in Whybray's overall argument. The basic thrust of Whybray's argument seems to be that "systematic and purposeful" editorial activity cannot be "proven," and that there are only slight and occasional indications of editorial activity in the Psalms. In reply it may be pointed out that, firstly, there are very few theories in the field of OT studies which can be "proven," and, secondly, that there are signs of editorial activity which appear more comprehensive than Whybray is willing to acknowledge (e.g. the five-book division of the Psalter, the Elohistic Psalter, the general movement from lament to praise within the psalms etc.). It seems that if one is to accept that the Psalter did not undergo systematic and purposeful editing, then there are several fortuitous coincidences which give the impression of editorial activity (e.g. kingship psalms at the seams of the Psalter, Pss 1–2 as an introduction, etc.).

[50] Whybray, *Psalms as a Book*, 118–19.

[51] See Wilson on explicit and tacit signs of editorial activity in *Editing*, 139-145.

[52] Mays, *The Lord Reigns*, 126–27.

the collection of psalms as a whole, whilst it can be said that certain themes and emphases are apparent in the Psalter, an element of "randomness" cannot entirely be removed from the book.[53] Theories which would seek to suggest linkage between all 150 psalms testify more to the ingenuity of the author than to the structure of the Psalter.[54] Also, even the definition of themes is a process to be exercised with some caution. We must be careful not to apply thematic interpretations beyond that which can be legitimately supported by the content of the psalms and the structure of the Psalter.[55]

One final expression of caution concerns the increasing popularity of the canonical approach as compared to other methods of analysis. It seems that the application of the canonical method to the study of the Psalter has given a new lease of life to psalm studies, with the exploration of the rich theological motifs and themes which run throughout this great book. This is all good and helpful to the student who seeks to immerse herself in the study of the Psalms. However, it should not lead to the neglect of form-critical analyses, close readings of individual psalms or discussion of the historical function of these poetic compositions. The consistent application of each of these methods alongside one another will lead to the fullest and best understanding of the Psalms.[56] These cautions having been aired, there does appear to be sufficient justification to proceed with a canonical analysis of the final form of the Book of Psalms.

---

[53] At least from our temporal and cultural perspective. It is possible that a more coherent order was apparent to Hebrew readers of the psalms living closer to the period of the book's closure. I suspect, however, that an element of "randomness" would remain even in their view of the collection as a whole.

[54] Ralph Smith, "The Use and Influence of the Psalms," *SwJT* 27, no. 1 (1984): 12.

[55] Wilson, "Understanding."

[56] Murphy has made this point well: "But [the canonical method] is not the *only*, nor the only *authoritative* way, of interpreting the Psalter. The canonical approach does not escape the same kind of hypothesizing that characterizes historical-critical methodology. But neither should be seen in an adversarial position; they do not necessarily preclude one another. Both are levels of understanding with limited but reasonable credibility. One is not more authoritative than the other; the responsible editor(s) do not replace the author(s). The Bible itself does not lay down rules for authoritative interpretation. This is the work of the readers of the Bible, ecclesial or otherwise. And the success of interpretations will depend on factors other than mere authority, such as the carefulness of the reader, the plausibility of the reading, and the relevance of the interpretation. Indeed, different readings may coexist, such as the original one to which the historical-critical method aspires and the canonical one that existed in the context of the entire Psalter." (*The Gift of the Psalms* [Peabody, MA: Hendrickson Publishers, 2000], 21).

3. CHOICE OF PSALMS

The next introductory question which must be addressed is, "Why select these particular psalms as being editorially significant? What makes them any different from all the other psalms in the final form of the book?"

3.1 EDITORIAL SIGNIFICANCE OF TORAH PSALMS

The torah psalms[57] have been problematic for form-critical scholars from the time of Gunkel onwards. They do not really fit into neat categories. They are similar to wisdom psalms, but even the wisdom psalms were problematic because they are frequently of mixed genre and are themselves difficult to categorize. Therefore, these psalms—both torah and wisdom—were traditionally classified as being late and generally of little significance.[58] This pattern continued in the vast majority of psalm works right up to the 1980s along with the continuing stress on form-critical and cultic *Sitz im Leben* questions. Some scholars gave priority to the role of the laments in the Psalter, others to the hymns, but the net effect was that Psalms 1, 19 and 119 always remained "among the leftovers"[59] when the chief organising principle was genre.

Ignoring the torah psalms is not without its problems, however, particularly when the final form of the book is allowed to act as the main organising principle for the interpretation of the psalms. Perhaps the first and most obvious question to spring from a canonical approach to the Psalter is, "Just why is Psalm 1 the first psalm in the book, if the torah psalms are so insignificant?" As Chapter Six of this thesis shall indicate, Pss 19 and 119 also (in different ways) dominate the

---

[57] Pss 1, 19 (or 19B, as it was understood by form-critical scholars) and 119.

[58] For example, Gunkel wrote, "Those psalms which talk about the law in forms of wisdom thus belong to the latest period of the entire development [of the Psalter]..." and also commented that Psalm 119 must be late because it is "utterly filled with legal piety" and "the original liveliness has disappeared," (*Introduction to Psalms: The Genres of the Religious Lyric of Israel* [trans. James D. Nogalski; Macon: Mercer University Press, 1998], 305, 327). Mowinkel also wrote that "the influence of law religion on psalmography is not very discernible," and that "it is significant that no very deep traces can be found in the Psalter of the religion of the law...." (*The Psalms in Israel's Worship* [Vol. II; trans. D. R. Ap-Thomas; Oxford: Basil Blackwell, 1962], 114). He does however acknowledge the *torah* content in Psalms 1, 19B and 119, and categorises these as part of the "learned psalmography" i.e. non-cultic psalmic material (*PIW*, 106, 113–14). It would be fair to say that traditional form-critical approaches tended to minimise the significance of the torah psalms.

[59] Mays, "Place of the Torah-Psalms," 3.

heart of Books I and V respectively. Why so, if these psalms are to be passed off as late, legalistic and unimportant?[60] Psalm 1 was recognised as an introduction to the Psalter as a whole even in the pre-critical period: both Calvin and Luther saw it as providing the hermeneutical glasses for the reading and interpretation of the whole Book of Psalms.[61] However, form-critical preoccupation with genre—which, without doubt, has greatly enhanced our understanding of the psalms—became so much the focus of scholarly activity that the ordering of the psalms and the final form of the book as a whole, came to be seen as somewhat irrelevant.[62] In accordance with this prevailing emphasis on formal categories, the torah psalms were relegated, in scholarly discussion, from the significance which their positioning in the Psalter seems to deserve.

Westermann was one of the first to examine the shaping of the Psalter and to note the prominent placing of the torah-focussed Pss 1 and 119. Having briefly considered the similarities between the two psalms, he concludes:

> We may assume, then, that Ps 1 and Ps 119 form a framework around the intervening Psalms, one which denotes a definite stage in the process which produced our Psalter. We can say therefore that there was once a psalter which began with Ps 1 and ended with Ps 119. Moreover this framework bears witness to an important stage in the "traditioning" process in which the psalter, as

---

[60] We should remember, also, that the question of dating psalms is extremely problematic in most cases and this is, perhaps, especially true of the torah psalms (John H. Eaton, *Psalms of the Way and the Kingdom: A Conference with the Commentators* [JSOTSup 199; Sheffield: Sheffield Academic Press, 1995], 11). It may be the case that Psalms 1 and 119 are "late" in terms of time of writing and inclusion into the Psalter. However, it is also possible that both of these psalms were actually originally connected with the Davidic monarchy (see William H. Brownlee, "Psalms 1-2 as a Coronation Liturgy," *Bib* 52, no. 3 [1971]: 321-36 and Will Soll, *Psalm 119: Matrix, Form and Setting* [CBQMS 23; Washington D.C.: The Catholic Biblical Association of America, 1991]). These are very difficult issues to judge from the content of the psalms alone. When adopting a canonical approach, regardless of the time of writing, the inference that late means legalistic and less important should be rejected. Inclusion into the Psalter and placement within it are of greater importance than period of composition.

[61] See Walter Brueggemann, *The Message of the Psalms: A Theological Commentary* (ACOT; Minneappolis: Augsburg, 1984), 17 and Hans-Joachim Kraus, *Psalms 1–59: A Commentary* (trans. Hilton C. Oswald; Minneapolis: Augsburg, 1988), 117.

[62] As mentioned above (pp 11-12n26), Westermann saw the reason for this being that "Gunkel above all had no interest in how the collection was handed down to us." It would be unfair to lay all the blame at Gunkel's feet, however. A form-critical approach will automatically (and quite naturally, it seems) tend to favour the largest (and therefore, in its own terms, most significant) genre categories.

a collection, no longer had a cultic function primarily, but rather circulated in a tradition devoted to the law. The Psalms have now become the word of God which is read, studied and meditated upon.[63]

Whilst there is no tradition to support Westermann's theory of a truncated Psalter bracketed by torah and royal psalms,[64] his observations are based on the ideas applied in the canonical approach: he associates these psalms because of their textual and theological similarities and assesses the significance of their placement within the final form of the book. The implications of Westermann's argument are significant: (1) when one reads the psalms in order, the torah psalms are no longer to be seen as the "poorer cousins" of the Psalter, on the contrary, they take on a prominent role within the book as a whole; and (2) there is an apparent link between torah and kingship themes in the Book of Psalms.[65]

Form criticism treated Pss 1, 19 (or at least 19B) and 119 as a small generic sub-grouping due to their similarity of subject matter, and a fairly insignificant one because these psalms were late and few in number.[66] However, the transition towards a canonical approach to the Psalter, increased scholarly appreciation of the *significance* of these psalms. The canonical form of the Book of Psalms seems to stress the importance of the torah psalms, giving them a sig-

---

[63] Westermann, *Praise and Lament*, 253. At least amongst modern writers it would be true to say that Westermann was one of the first to re-examine the question of the shaping of the Psalter, there were authors from the nineteenth century—Delitzsch, for example—who had given consideration to the idea that there was a thematic shaping of the Psalter (see David M. Howard, "Editorial Activity in the Psalter: A State-of-the-Field Survey," in *The Shape and Shaping of the Psalter* [ed. J. Clinton McCann; JSOTSup 159; Sheffield: JSOT Press, 1993], 55).

[64] As well as suggesting that the torah psalms (Pss 1 and 119) defined the limits of a previous version of the Psalter, Westermann also draws attention to the significant placement of the neighbouring kingship psalms (Pss 2 and 118), indicating a chiastic inclusio of torah and royal psalms (see *Praise and Lament*, 253–54 and the helpful discussions of his ideas found in Delmar Jacobson, "The Royal Psalms and Jesus Messiah: Preparing to Preach on a Royal Psalm," *WW* 5, no. 2 [1985]: 192–98 and Jerry E. Shepherd, "The Book of Psalms as the Book of Christ: A Christo-Canonical Approach to the Book of Psalms," Ph.D. Diss. [Philadelphia: Westminster Theological Seminary, 1995], 419–20).

[65] It is impossible to determine conclusively (without additional historical evidence) whether there ever was a version of the Psalms which ended at Ps 119, as Westermann suggests. However, the internal evidence—especially the fact that Pss 118-119 are preceded and succeeded by smaller, prior collections (see Chapter 4, below)—tends to indicate that this idea is at least possible. See Patrick D. Miller, "Current Issues in Psalms Studies," *WW* V, no. 2 (Spring 1985): 141.

[66] See, for example, Mowinckel, *PIW*, vol. 2, 113–14.

nificance beyond that which their number would merit. Mays, on this very point, comments:

> Those who composed them wrote them *as psalms* and they were included *in the Psalter*. This double fact means that the latest and smallest group of Psalms may provide the central clue to the way the Psalms, individually and as a book, were read and understood at the time of their composition and inclusion. The problem children of the Psalter do not have a place in the *Gattungen* and *Sitze* of the Psalm criticism, but they do have a place in the book.[67]

Mays emphasis of the placement and role of the torah compositions draws upon Childs's earlier consideration of Ps 1 as introduction to the Psalter.[68] McCann also stresses the torah psalms, "having made the decision to take seriously the canonical shape of the Psalter, we shall begin at the beginning—Psalm 1. The effect is to elevate the concept of torah to one of central significance in understanding the Psalms."[69] Even scholars whose focus is not particularly directed towards torah in their study of the Psalter, generally acknowledge the significance of this psalm group: David Howard, for example, whose work focuses on the Psalms 93–100 and who has a very astute awareness of the historical development of psalms studies, acknowledges the significance of the wisdom/torah redactions of the Psalter in its final form.[70] Gerald Sheppard in his study of the theology of the Psalms writes, "the Book of Psalms can be seen to be fully a part of scripture, whose central subject matter is the Torah, the teaching and law of God."[71] M. Millard also concludes the most significant theme of the Psalms is torah and Yahweh's kingship is the central motif.[72] Jerome Creach highlights the idea of taking refuge in Yahweh as significant to the final form, and adds that the torah psalms are integral to this concept in the Book of Psalms.[73] Patrick Miller has written various pieces on the centrality of the

---

[67] Mays, "Place of the Torah-Psalms," 3.
[68] Childs, *IOTS*, 513–14.
[69] McCann, *Theological Introduction*, 25.
[70] Howard, *Structure*, 205–07.
[71] Sheppard, "Theology," 154.
[72] M. Millard, *Die Komposition des Psalters: Ein formgeschichtlicher Ansatz* (FAT 9; Tübingen: Mohr, Siebeck, 1994), see David M. Howard, "Recent Trends in Psalm Study," in *The Face of Old Testament Study: A Survey of Contemporary Approaches* (ed. D. W. Baker and B. T. Arnold; Leicester: Apollos, 1999), 338.
[73] Jerome F. D. Creach, *Yahweh as Refuge and the Editing of the Hebrew Psalter* (JSOTSup 217; Sheffield: Sheffield Academic Press, 1996), 71–72, 103.

Deuteronomic concept of torah in the Book of Psalms.[74] Such scholarly consensus proves little in itself, except that, when a canonical approach to the Psalter is applied, the torah psalms are central to its final redaction.

The reasons for choosing the torah psalms are two-fold: (1) the function of Ps 1 as an introduction to the Psalter highlights a torah-wisdom paradigm to be applied to the book as a whole; and, (2) Pss 19 and 119 have been placed in locations which are editorially significant. Ps 19, as Pierre Auffret[75] and Patrick Miller[76] suggest, is central to a chiastically ordered prior collection of psalms (Pss 15–24), which lies at the heart of Book I. Ps 119 (along with Ps 118) is the pivotal composition in Book V.[77] This torah emphasis at beginning and end of the canonical Psalter goes beyond the accidental and merits further consideration. There is good exegetical support for the broad acceptance of the redactional significance of the torah psalms highlighted above, and this will be the focus of consideration in chapters 2–4 and chapter 6 of the present thesis.[78]

---

[74] See, for example, Patrick D. Miller, "The Beginning of the Psalter," in *The Shape and Shaping of the Psalter* (ed. J. Clinton McCann; JSOTSup 159; Sheffield: JSOT Press, 1993), 86–87; "Kingship," 127–28.

[75] Pierre Auffret, *La sagesse a bâti sa maison: Études de structures littéraires dans l'Ancient Testament et spécialement dans les psaumes* (OBO 49; Fribourg: Editions Universitaires, 1982), 407–38.

[76] Miller, "Kingship."

[77] See, for example, Wilson, "Shaping" and Zenger, "Composition." However, my own understanding of the centrality of Ps 119 differs slightly from the ideas presented by Wilson and Zenger, see Chapter 6 below.

[78] There are other psalms which contain a certain torah content (Pss 18, 25, 33, 78, 93, 94, 99, 103, 105, 111, 112, 147, 148 are described by Mays as being "developed by torah interests," ["Place of the Torah-Psalms," 8]) and there are other psalms which could possibly be added to this list due to possible association with the Deuteronomic torah (Pss 15, 34, 78, 106, 114, 115; see Miller, "Deuteronomy and Psalms.") However, these psalms could not really be described as *torah psalms* in their own right. They do contain torah overtones and add to the overall torah-wisdom flavour of the Psalter, but these psalms have different central emphases in their theological content (e.g. Temple worship [Ps 15]; wisdom motifs [Ps 34]; history of Israel [Ps 106] etc.). None of these psalms are dominated by the concept of torah as is the case with Pss 1, 19 and 119. Therefore, it would be speculative to argue for the deliberately placement of these psalms as part of a torah redaction, because they are not really "about" torah, *per se*. However, it is at the very least possible in relation to *some* of the psalms mentioned above that they have been influenced by this final form torah redaction. Examination of these torah interjections in other psalms would be a worthy area of study in itself, but falls beyond the remit of this study, where focus is directed towards the psalms *explicitly about* the torah of Yahweh and their editorial placement, particularly in relation to royal psalms.

3.2 Editorial Significance of Kingship Psalms

It has long been understood that a proper understanding of the royal psalms aids proper understanding of the Psalter.[79] The compositions which deal with the king dominate, or at least strongly flavour, the reader's understanding of the whole book. This is especially true when one realises the association between the psalms of individual lament and the person of the king.[80] However, this is not an argument based on weight of numbers alone, a canonical analysis also points to the significant placement of kingship psalms throughout the Psalter.

Brevard Childs and Gerald Wilson have both pointed out the importance of the kingship psalms which are placed throughout the whole of the Book of Psalms.[81] Wilson has argued that the placement of royal psalms (Pss 2, 41, 72,

---

[79] Understanding of what constitutes a royal psalm is still a somewhat difficult question. Some scholars (e.g. Gunkel, Mettinger, Starbuck) take a reductive approach to this question and view royal psalms as being only those poems which refer directly to the "king," "messiah," "son" or to the trappings of kingship like "sceptre," "throne" etc. When the text of the individual compositions of the Psalter is read closely, however, this sort of approach seems unnecessarily reductive. There are several strong indicators that many of the individual psalms (particularly the individual laments) are related to the king and, therefore, in some sense "royal," (see Eaton, *Kingship*, 20–26 and Steven J. L. Croft, *The Identity of the Individual in the Psalms* [JSOTSup 44; Sheffield: JSOT Press, 1987], 73ff). Eaton argues that many, if not most, of the individual psalms may, in fact, be attributed to the king. Croft takes a slightly different approach suggesting various categories of individual who may be speaking in a given psalm of the individual, such as "Cult Prophet," "Temple Singer" and "Wisdom Teacher." The difficulty with Croft's approach, however, is that we have no real idea if such figures actually existed in any sort of official representative capacity, or how (if at all) they were associated with the psalms. Miller comments, "It would not do to characterise major approaches to the understanding of the laments without recognising the view of Birkeland, then later Mowinckel, and others and that the 'I' of the laments is the king acting in behalf of or as representative of the people in crying out for help against national enemies has been taken up afresh and impressively by J. H. Eaton, who sees around fifty psalms of the individual as being in fact royal psalms. Such a construal of the texts is plausible and undergirded by the centrality of the king in ancient Israel and possibly in the official cult, as well as by the ascription of so many psalms to David. The connection of the psalms to the Messiah and the christological use of them by the early church would be even more direct should such an interpretation be on the right track," ("Current Issues," 135–36). Partly to avoid some of these reductive connotations associated with the term "royal psalm," and, partly, to place the royal psalms more fully into the context of the broader OT discussion concerning king and monarchy, the term "kingship psalm" is used throughout this thesis to refer to psalms which deal with royal motifs.

[80] See Footnote 79, above.

[81] Childs, *IOTS*, 517–18; Wilson, *Editing*, 207–08; "Use of Royal Psalms."

89) at the seams of Books I–III of the Psalter provides the reader with a type of narrative, as part of this final redaction, dealing with the Davidic monarchy—a "narrative" of the failure of the Davidic monarchy.[82] Book IV, therefore, he sees as the narrative centre of the Psalter, responding to the problem of this failure.[83] Book IV focuses the reader's attention, Wilson suggests, on the kingdom reign of Yahweh and not the Davidic king.[84] Whilst Wilson's analysis of editorial activity in the Psalms has been ground-breaking and innovative, his "narrative" of the rejection of the Davidic monarchy is not the only possible interpretation to be derived from the editorial presentation of the king in the royal psalms of Books I–III. In fact, if the intent of the editors is to turn the reader's attention from the Davidic king to Yahweh as king, then the narrative does not "read" particularly well. Why reintroduce the king at all in Books IV and V if one seeks to focus attention on Yahweh as King alone?[85] Yet the Davidic king is reintroduced in Books IV and V and some of the expressions of kingship are as strong as any to be found in the Psalter (e.g. Ps 110).

It is the contention of this thesis that the significance of the kingship psalms continues on into Books IV and V even though the presence of David is not as numerically obvious as in Books I–III. The image of the king does not disappear in the last two sections of the Psalter, rather he takes on more obviously eschatological overtones.[86] However, it must be stressed that, in all likelihood, the royal psalms always had at least an element of eschatological expectation about them even during the period of the historical monarchy.[87] The figure of

---

[82] See also Wilson's *Editing*, 208–14.

[83] Wilson, *Editing*, 215.

[84] Wilson, *Editing*, 215.

[85] Perhaps a better explanation of the "Yahweh mālāk" psalms of Book IV is that the editors seek to assure the reader that Yahweh still reigns in heaven and over the earth even although his earthly co-regent has been removed from the picture. Rather than encouraging a focal change from human to divine kingship, Book IV tells of the continuing reign of Yahweh's kingdom and reintroduces the figure of the king, probably implying an eschatological reinterpretation of the monarchy (see Vincent's helpful analysis "The Shape of the Psalter: An Eschatological Dimension?" in *New Heaven and New Earth: Prophecy and the Millenium, Essays in Honour of Anthony Gelston* [P. J. Harland and C. T. R. Hayward; VTSup 77; Leiden: Brill, 1999], 77).

[86] David M. Howard, "The Case for Kingship in the Old Testament Narrative Books and the Psalms," *TJ* 9 (1988): 34.

[87] Speaking of Ps 2, Eaton comments, "Surely royal psalms originally had reference to the monarchy of Israel and functioned in that setting. But from the outset they had a prophetic character: they included vision and oracle, and the purpose of God which they

the king may take on more subtle, eschatological overtones in Books IV–V, but he is still present at the conclusion of the Psalter.[88] So both torah and kingship psalms play a significant role in the final redaction of the Psalter, and the central argument of this thesis is that these important psalms have, at key points in the Psalter, been juxtaposed alongside one another in order to reflect the theology of the Kingship Law.[89] This idea resonates with two prominent currents apparent in the second-temple biblical literature (i.e., in the general timeframe when the Psalter probably reached its canonical form): (1) a concern for the Deuteronomic law,[90] and, (2) a general sense of eschatological hope.[91] It is as a result of such considerations that Pss 1–2, 18–21 and 118–119 have been chosen for consideration in this study.

4. COMPARATIVE METHOD

One of the difficult questions of Old Testament (and, for that matter Biblical) Theology is the issue of how to make comparison and draw parallels between different texts. Historical-critical preoccupation with questions of source and the dating of texts made this task all the more difficult, as one first had to establish, the chronological priority of any given text before even allowing for comparison with another text. The conclusive establishment of dating with regard to OT books or texts is a notoriously difficult task—except, perhaps, in the broadest of terms (e.g., pre-exilic, post-exilic, monarchic etc.). Therefore, theological comparison between books somewhat fell by the wayside in many

---

revealed far transcended the experience of the time. The destiny which they promised David seemed all the more removed as time went on; like the kingdom of God itself, it was a matter of faith, defying appearances on the strength of the divine promise. With the removal of the Davidic monarchy in 586 B.C. the prophetic aspect of such texts came all the more into prominence. For many centuries, incorporated in Scripture, they served to nourish the messianic hope—the belief that the divine promise to David would be fulfilled," (*Psalms* [TBC; London: SPCK, 1967], 33).

[88] Note the Davidic frame in Book V, leaving the final words, prior to the concluding doxology of Pss 146–150, in the mouth of the Davidic king once again (see Ch. 6).

[89] Obviously, there are many more kingship psalms in the Psalter than are considered in this study. The present thesis represents *one aspect* of the theology of kingship in the psalms—the recollection of the ideal of kingship via reflection upon the Kingship Law.

[90] Jon D. Levenson, "The Sources of Torah: Psalm 119 and the Modes of Revelation in Second Temple Judaism," in *Ancient Israelite Religion: Essays in Honor of Frank Moore Cross* (ed. P. D. Miller et al.; Philadelphia: Fortress, 1987).

[91] Mitchell, *Message*, 15.

academic circles, but has been revived in more recent years by the broad adoption of canonical and literary approaches which seek to draw out theological themes from books of the OT.[92] These canonical-literary approaches allow for various comparative methods in analysing one OT text in the light of another — rhetorical methods, reader-response theories, intertextual analysis, and so on. Each of these methods offers its own benefits and has its own difficulties.[93] So, it is important to define the method adopted in making comparison between the torah-kingship psalm groupings and Deuteronomy's Law of the King.

4.1 BIBLICAL CONVERSATION

Recently, Patrick Miller has suggested that a "biblical conversation" may be evoked between the Book of Deuteronomy and the Psalter.[94] Drawing upon canonical and literary approaches, Miller suggests that "the biblical books of Deuteronomy and Psalms are amenable to an interactive relationship, capable of creating or evoking a conversation between them that enlarges our perception of both and contributes to a sense of the whole that is scripture."[95] This thesis picks up on Miller's suggestion and seeks to contribute to our understanding of the conversation between Deuteronomy and the Psalms.

How is a "biblical conversation" to be conducted? Miller suggests that this is a method which "happens on the intertextual level *in its most basic sense*, that is, in the echoes of one text to be found in another text."[96] That is, the idea of

---

[92] See Ellen Van Wolde, "Trendy Intertextuality?" in *Intertextuality in Biblical Writings: Essays in Honour of Bas Van Iersel* (ed. Sipke Draisma; Kampden: J. H. Kok, 1989), 43–49. It should be stressed that methodological focus on literary issues in no way minimises the importance of the historical. Both approaches add to our understanding of the biblical text and neither should dominate to the detriment of the other.

[93] This is the basis of Berry's discussion of Ps 18 (*The Psalms and Their Readers: Interpretive Strategies for Psalm 18* [JSOTSup 153; Sheffield: Sheffield Academic Press, 1993]) where he compares the results of different analytical approaches to the same text.

[94] Patrick D. Miller, "Deuteronomy and Psalms: Evoking a Biblical Conversation," *JBL* 118, no. 1 (1999): 3–18.

[95] Miller, "Deuteronomy and Psalms," 5.

[96] Miller, "Deuteronomy and Psalms," 5 (emphasis mine). Miller goes on to add that this interaction, "also takes place through the interdependencies that are created in redactional and editing processes," (p 5). This is significant for the current discussion as the ideas lying behind the writing of Pss 1, 2, 18, 19, 20, 21, 118 and 119 may have been very different from the emphasis which was given them in their editorial placement alongside one another. Whilst these psalms do reflect key concepts of Dtr theology (see

biblical conversation is not a strict linguistic intertextuality. The aim is neither to prove literary dependence or direct allusion between texts. Obviously, linguistic similarities are an important part of any comparative analysis between texts,[97] but the aim here is not to prove that the Psalms cite Deuteronomy or *vice versa*. The aim, rather, is to see this conversation conducted "both on the very particular level of the textual interaction of particular passages in Deuteronomy and Psalms and also on a larger plane of theology and hermeneutics."[98] The fact that passages use exactly the same (or very similar) words is only significant when it is clear that their intent is to teach the same message.

So the comparative method adopted throughout this thesis will follow Miller's suggestions with regard to a biblical conversation between Deuteronomy and the Psalms. The approach will be broadly intertextual, in that linguistic similarities (of which there is a significant number) between the torah-kingship psalms and Deuteronomy shall be pointed out. However, the conversation between these two books shall also focus on the "larger plane of theology and hermeneutics." The torah-kingship psalm groupings have a message to convey to their reader, as does the Law of the King. Is this the same message? Are these texts concerned with the same theological issues? If so, then there may well be reason to conclude that the Kingship Law was the intellectual paradigm for the placement of torah and kingship laws alongside one another.

---

chapters 2–4, below), it is in the editing process that they come particularly to reflect the theology of the Kingship Law. Thus, it is important to acknowledge that such biblical conversation occurs between the final forms of OT texts and, therefore, editorial processes may be as significant as the writing of a text in establishing this type of intertextual relationship.

[97] *Contra* James L. Crenshaw, "The Deuteronomist and the Writings," in *Those Elusive Deuteronomists: The Phenomenon of Pan-Deuteronomism* (ed. L. S. Schering and S. L. McKenzie; JSOTSup 268; Sheffield: Sheffield Academic Press, 1999), 155. For an alternative view, see Lohfink's article in the same volume ("Was There a Deuteronomistic Movement?" in *Those Elusive Deuteronomists: The Phenomenon of Pan-Deuteronomism* [ed. L. S. Schering and S. L. McKenzie; JSOTSup 268; Sheffield: Sheffield Academic Press, 1999], 41–42), where he points out that—whilst the use of individual words which are thought to be Deuteronomic may not indicate a great deal—the use of combinations or groups of words found in Deuteronomy in other texts, may well indicate a background in Dtr theology.

[98] Miller, "Deuteronomy and Psalms," 5.

4.2 WHICH DEUTERONOMY?

As part of this comparative process, one of the aims of the exegetical examination of the torah-kingship psalm groupings is to assess whether there is a general Deuteronomic background to these compositions. As anyone who has done any work in Dtr studies will be well aware, this theory itself begs a question: what sort of Deuteronomic background? The various theories surrounding the redactions of Deuteronomy and the Deuteronomic History have highlighted a number of different theological emphases which scholars often equate with particular redactions.[99] So the question in our case would be, *"What type of Dtr redaction* has resulted in this reflection of the Kingship Law in the Psalms?'

First, it should be pointed out that the aim of this thesis is not to speak to the possible redactions of Deuteronomy and the Deuteronomistic History. The aim

---

[99] The origins of this process are to be found, of course, in Noth's *Überlieferungsgeschichtliche Studien: Die sammelnden und bearbeitenden Geschichtswerke im Alten Testament* (2nd Edition; Tübingen: Max Niemeymer, 1957) [ET of pp 1–110 of this work has been published as *The Deuteronomistic History* (JSOTSup 15; Sheffield: JSOT Press, 1991)], where he associated Deuteronomy with the Books of Joshua–2 Kings, as the work of a single author or redactor, the DtrG or DtrH (Deuteronomistic historian). Other scholars, who generally accepted Noth's association of Deuteronomy with the succeeding historical books, seeing the theological diversity found within this broad collection, were not convinced that this was the work of a single redactor, and so over a period of time a number of redactions/redactors were brought into the equation. Smend, for example, sees the influence of a later nomistic redactor in some of the historical books and so suggests the addition of another redactor/redaction—DtrN ("Das Gesetz und der Völker: Ein Beitrag zur deuteronomistischen Redaktionsgeschichte," in *Probleme biblischer Theologie: Festschrift Gerhard von Rad* (ed. H. W. Wolff; Munich: Kaiser, 1971) 494–509, ET "The Law and the Nations: A Contribution to Deuteronomistic Tradition History," in *Reconsidering Israel and Judah: Recent Studies on the Deuteronomistic History* [ed. G. N. Knoppers and J. G. McConville; SBTS 8; Grand Rapids: Eisenbrauns, 2000]). Dietrich later added a prophetic redactor/redaction to these suggestions—DtrP (*Prophetie und Geschichte* [FRLANT 108; Göttingen: Vandenhoeck & Ruprecht, 1972). This nomenclature has continued in Dtr studies, but there are substantial differences of opinion as to the extent of these redactions and their chronology. This, of course, is not the only approach to the redactions of Deut/DtrH. Cross has also suggested a different theory consisting of a two-fold redaction of Deut/DtrH in *Canaanite Myth and Hebrew Epic* (Cambridge: Harvard University Press, 1973), and this theory has enjoyed great popularity in some academic circles. Scholars occasionally combine elements of these two main approaches to the shaping of Deut/DtrH (see Knopper's helpful summary article as the introduction to *Reconsidering Israel and Judah: Recent Studies on the Deuteronomistic History* [ed. G. N. Knoppers and J. G. McConville; SBTS, Vol. 8; Winona Lake, IN: Eisenbrauns, 2000], 1–18).

Methodological Considerations 31

is to assess whether a particular passage of the final form of the Book of Deuteronomy could have functioned as the intellectual paradigm for the placement of certain psalms alongside one another. Therefore, the focus herein is not upon whether there was a two-fold or three-fold redaction of Deuteronomy and its associated historical books.[100] The possible redactions of the DtrH[101] are of limited relevance within the remit of this discussion. The only area in which the formation of Deut/DtrH seems relevant to the current discussion is the question of whether the Kingship Law existed as a recognised text prior to the final redaction of the Book of Psalms. There can be little doubt that this is, in fact, the case. Even the latest scholarly estimates for the formation of Deut/DtrH, early in the post-exilic period, precede the closure (and therefore final redaction) of the Psalter.[102] It seems clear that the Kingship Law would have been part of a "canonical" book—and therefore available to the editors of the Psalms—before the Psalter's final redaction.

Secondly, the fact that the redaction of Deut/DtrH is a moot point within this thesis, therefore, requires some clarification of terms used throughout. In his consideration of Gerbrandt's assessment of kingship in Deut/DtrH, Howard comments that:

> The term "Deuteronomistic History" refers to the books from Deuteronomy to 2 Kings. As used by Gerbrandt and most others, it also assumes some type of unified authorship for all of these books in one or more strata of the texts. I use the term here to refer to the same corpus, but I understand the term

---

[100] Important as this question may be in its own right. The recently published collection of essays, *Reconsidering Israel and Judah* (see previous footnote), provides a useful introduction to and summary of many of the issues involved in this discussion. The collection of important articles in one volume allows for easy comparison and analysis of the various approaches to the redaction of Deut/DtrH.

[101] DtrH refers to the Deuteronomistic History in this thesis (i.e. Joshua–2 Kings), as opposed to the use of DtrH as referring to a specific redactor.

[102] Many scholars, of course, do not accept that there was a post-exilic redaction of Deuteronomy (see, for example, Franz Crüsemann, *The Torah: Theology and Social History of Old Testament Law* [trans. A. W. Mahnke; Edinburgh: T&T Clark, 1992], 211). However, even those who do suggest a final redaction in the post-exilic period (e.g. Smend *Die Enstehung des Alten Testaments* (4th ed.; Stuttgart; Kohlhammer, 1989), see this final (DtrN, in Smend's case) redaction taking place in the early period following the return to Israel. By way of contrast, however, it seems (even ignoring some of the excessively late estimates for the closure of the Psalter) that the Book of Psalms took its final form later in the post-exilic period—but, probably, prior to the translation of the LXX (see Mitchell, *Message*, 82–83).

"Deuteronomistic" in a descriptive away—i.e., to refer to those books or ideas reflective of the distinctive viewpoint found in Deuteronomy—with no conclusions concerning authorship of Deuteronomy or the other books implicit in my use of the term. Similarly, when Gerbrandt speaks of the "Deuteronomist" to refer to the author of this unified corpus I would prefer to use a more neutral term, such as the "author(s)" or "editor(s)" of the final work.[103]

Terms borrowed from Deut/DtrH studies are used in a similar way in this thesis. As explained later in this study, it appears that the use of the Kingship Law in the Psalter bears similarities to the "DtrN redaction" of the Deuteronomistic History. However, in adopting "DtrN" for usage in this study, the intention is not to imply that the placement of kingship psalms alongside the torah psalms was necessarily the work of a post-exilic nomistic redactor. Rather, as with Howard's use of DtrH, this term is used descriptively and without comment as to the historical reality of such a redactor. In other words, there is a legal theme which runs throughout Deut/DtrH, which expresses concern for the role of Yahweh's torah in the life of Israel. Some scholars see this theme as the work of a specific (post-exilic) redactor (and they use "DtrN" to refer to this redactor). This study simply does not speak to that point of debate. Rather, the use of "DtrN" herein is descriptive and thematic: that is, it refers to the *legal-torah theme itself*, as found in Deuteronomy and the Deuteronomistic History, without speaking to the idea any specific redactor.[104]

---

[103] David M. Howard, "The Case for Kingship in Deuteronomy and the Former Prophets," *WTJ* 52 (1990): 101 n. 3.

[104] This focus on theme rather than redactor is further motivated by the "modern trend towards reading the books of DtrH as separate works, each with their own tendency and theology," (J. Gordon McConville, "King and Messiah in Deuteronomy and the Deuteronomistic History," in *King and Messiah in Israel and the Ancient Near East: Proceedings of the Oxford Old Testament Seminar* [ed. J. Day; JSOTSup 270; Sheffield: Sheffield Academic Press, 1998], 294–95). Several recent books and articles question the idea of a holistic authorship/redactional association of the books of the DtrH and rather suggest that each book has its own particular emphasis on any given topic and that "the take" on those issues may vary from book to book (see, for example, Gary N. Knoppers, "The Deuteronomist and the Deuteronomic Law of the King: A Reexamination of a Relationship," *ZAW* 108, no. 3 [1996]: 329–46). The implications of this trend have yet to be fully explored, but it does give reason to question the underlying presupposition that a single author-redactor (or, for that matter, a few authors/redactors) produced a unified work encompassing Deuteronomy–2 Kings.

5. Eschatological Re-Reading of the Psalms

One final area of methodological discussion which should be addressed is the question of how the psalms generally (and the kingship psalms particularly) were read and understood at the time of this final redaction of the Psalter. As has been mentioned above, in the consideration of editorial significance of the kingship psalms, it appears that royal (and other) psalms were being reread in an eschatological light by the time of the closure of the Psalter.[105] Indeed, if there has been an area of neglect in some of the recent works which have reopened the study of the Psalter, it is in terms of the *consistent application* of an eschatological rereading throughout the whole of the Psalter's five books.

There has been a tendency to apply an eschatological understanding of certain texts—in particular, the psalms celebrating the Davidic kingship and the glories of Zion—to psalms found in Books IV and V.[106] However, the royal and Zion psalms found in Books I–III are read and interpreted in their historical context and setting without any suggestion of a post-exilic (eschatological) reinterpretation of these texts.[107] The suggestion that these psalms remain as a kind of narrative reminder of the failure of the Davidic monarchy was perhaps partially true, at one stage in the development of the Psalter, but this is not the final editorial word concerning king and monarchy. There *is* a tone of eschatological hope in the coming kingdom of Yahweh in Books IV and V, and it appears that this hope should be read back into the interpretation of Books I–III also. "Yes, these psalms may ring somewhat hollow for now, but they shall ring truer than ever before when the Kingdom of Yahweh comes," the reader is encouraged to think. This eschatological hope is designed to provide a grid for the reinterpretation of *all* of the royal and Zion psalms, and other psalms as well.[108]

---

[105] For example, Mays discusses the eschatological reinterpretation of kingship and torah psalms 18–19 and 118–119 (*The Lord Reigns*, 133–34). See also Mitchell, *Message*, 198; Dennis H. Ormseth, "The Psalms and the Rule of God," *WW* V, no. 2 (Spring 1985): 119–21; Jacobson, "Royal Psalms"; and, Bruce K. Waltke, "A Canonical Process Approach to the Psalms," in *Tradition and Testament: Essays in Honor of Charles Lee Feinberg* (Chicago: Moody Press, 1981), 3–18.

[106] Susan E. Gillingham, "The Messiah in the Psalms: A Question of Reception History and Psalter," in *King and Messiah in Israel and the Ancient Near East* (ed. J. Day; JSOTSup 270; Sheffield: Sheffield Academic Press, 1998), 228.

[107] See Wilson's, *Editing*, 213–14 and "Shaping," 78, 81–82. See also J. Clinton McCann, "Books I–III and the Editorial Purpose of the Psalter," in *The Shape and Shaping of the Psalter* (JSOTSup 159; Sheffield: JSOT Press, 1993), 98–99.

[108] This eschatological reinterpretation was probably an integral part of the readers'

Another area which needs to be called into question is the strong contrast or opposition between the reign of Yahweh and his kingdom, on the one hand, and the co-regent reign of Yahweh's anointed, on the other. For example:

> These psalms [the YHWH-*mālāk* psalms of the 90s] emphasize a "pre-monarchic" reliance on YHWH *alone* that exalts God's wondrous, eternal works in contrast to the weak and transitory nature of humanity. Rather than encouraging confidence in human rulers, these psalms counsel the hearer to find refuge in YHWH who alone is eternal and able to save. These themes provide an appropriate introduction to the central YHWH-*mālāk* psalms that celebrate the kingship of YHWH.[109]

Also:

> Are the final editors seeking to counter the lamentation associated with the collapse of the Davidic hopes in the first three books with a call to praise the only true and eternal King—Israel's only hope? As a result of its final form, the Psalter *counters continuing concern for the restoration of the Davidic dynasty and kingdom* with the wise counsel to seek refuge in a kingdom "not of this world"—the eternal kingdom in which YHWH *alone* is king.[110]

Further:

> ... I propose that an analysis of the final form of Book III reveals an arrangement that serves to assist the community not only to face squarely the disorienting reality of exile, as Wilson would suggest, but also to reach a reorientation based upon the *rejection* of the Davidic/Zion theology that had formerly been Judah's primary grounds for hope. The canonical juxtaposition of the traditional Davidic/Zion theology with community psalms of lament serves to signal the *rejection* of this basis for hope.[111]

This strong dichotomy is unnecessary and inconsistent with the editorial thrust of the Psalter as a whole. There is no need to posit trust in competing sov-e-reignties of Yahweh and his "anointed," rather, according to the royal psalms, theirs is a joint reign.[112] If there is a "narrative plot" which appears in

---

understanding of these psalms even when there was a king in Zion, as we shall see below.

[109] Wilson, "Shaping," 76 (emphasis mine).
[110] Wilson, "Shaping," 81 (emphasis mine).
[111] McCann, "Books I–III," 98–99 (emphasis mine).
[112] Clearly, Yahweh's reign is ultimate and of greatest importance, but the kingship psalms do not present the reign of the chosen Davidic king as competing with Yahweh's sovereignty—on the contrary, this is presented as a public expression of Yahweh's universal reign (e.g., Ps 2). Reading some of the works which posit the idea of a narrative presenting the failure of the David monarchy, one would be inclined to forget that the kingship psalms are actually written about the *human* king, such is the emphasis on the

Book IV having emerged out of the crisis of Book III, it is rather that *Yahweh still rules* and his kingdom remains unchanged even if the visible evidence of that rule—the Davidic monarchy—is no longer.[113] The image of the Davidic king reappears in Book IV with the return of the Davidic superscription (לדוד) in Psalms 101 and 103, an unlikely event if the desire of the redactors is to encourage the reader towards "rejection of the Davidic/Zion theology."[114] What is more, the portrayal of the rule of the Davidic messiah goes on to find strong and explicit expression in Book V (e.g., Ps 110), and in this final section of the

kingdom of Yahweh (see, for example, Wilson, *Editing*, 228 or deClaissé-Walford, *Reading from the Beginning*, 98–99). Yes, they also teach the reign of Yahweh (there was no Davidic rule without the rule of Yahweh), but that is not the sole message of these psalms. They talk about *the king*, and their continued inclusion and prominence in the Psalter indicates a *continued* role for the king within the community thinking—most likely an expectation of a restored king and kingship (again as co-regent in Yahweh's kingdom, but this in no way contradicts the validity of the continued existence of the Davidic king as a part of Yahweh's rule).

[113] Vincent comments to this effect with regard to Book IV, "The second theme central to book 4 is the יהוה מלך motif itself, the assertion that he is king despite it all (despite the individual doubts and national/historical crisis of book 3). In the face of all appearances to the contrary these psalms press the notion that God is king (even if he doesn't have an earthly ruler on his throne!), and that he is in control. In the light of the crisis of captivity the יהוה מלך phrase can on one level be understood as an assertion that *God* is still king, even if the human Davidic king has long since disappeared. The human king may be taken away because of the repeated sinfulness of both him and his people, but God remains enthroned in heaven. Thus he is still to be praised, as the יהוה מלך psalms encouraged, as the lord of all creation. However, as we noted at the outset, this is not the only way of looking at the יהוה מלך psalms. It is also possible to interpret them in an eschatological sense: since God is king his promises will yet be fulfilled and either he himself, or his representative (the future Messianic king) will come. This very assertion forms the climax of two of the יהוה מלך psalms, 96 and 98. Through the body of these psalms there is not a *pronounced* emphasis on this eschatological solution, but there is no doubt that it is discernible," ("Shape of Psalter," 77).

[114] Rather than Book IV denying the validity of the monarchy, it appears that the royal psalms found in this section of the Psalter respond to the crisis of Ps 89, by continuing to hold to the idea of kingship. See Christopher R. Seitz, *Word Without End: The Old Testament as Abiding Theological Witness* (Grand Rapids: Eerdmans, 1998), 164, "David reemerges in Psalm 101 to sing of what? Of God's loyalty and justice, the two matters called into question on his behalf in Psalm 89.... [T]he presence of these psalms [Davidic psalms in Books IV and V], which mention David fourteen times (and Solomon once), signals that David has not been forgotten as Israel's king and chief psalmist, the one to be remembered above all others as having sung God's praises almost without ceasing, as Book 5 has it at its close."

Psalter we see the return of Zion psalms in the Songs of Ascent (שיר המעלות, i.e., Pss 120–134).[115] Therefore, it would appear that the intent of the editors of the final form of the Psalms was not that readers should reject the Davidic king and the centrality of Zion, in favour of commitment to the rule of Yahweh and hope in his eschatological kingdom. Rather, they were pointing the reader towards the *reinterp-retation* of the concepts of kingship and Zion in the light of a future real-isation of Yahweh's rule and plan in the figure of a restored Davidic leader. If there is any degree of corrective going on, it is for those who despair at the loss of the Davidic monarchy—Book IV assures them that Yahweh's reign continues, and Books IV and V point towards a new Davidic reign and a restored Zion. This reinterpretation of the royal psalms is not limited to Books IV and V, however, but should be read into all of the kingship psalms.

As mentioned above, this reinterpretation of the kingship psalms is not merely a post-exilic phenomenon, but is—to a certain degree—inherent to the expression of the royal psalms (e.g., the idea of the king's universal dominion from Zion). There must have been a substantial degree of cognitive dissonance for the reader of the psalms, between the reality of the reigns of the kings of Israel and their rule expressed in the kingship psalms. This variance was heightened all the more when the Davidic king disappeared from view entirely, yet the royal psalms were not only retained in the Psalter, but they retained prominent editorial positions in the Book of Psalms.[116] Why so? It appears that the redactors of the final form of the Psalter expected the Davidic kingship to be restored as part of an eschatological kingdom of Yahweh yet to be revealed.

Brevard Childs has pointed out the inherent eschatological emphases of the Psalter: "However one explains it, the final form of the Psalter is *highly eschatological* in nature.... The perspective of Israel's worship in the Psalter is eschatologically orientated. As a result, the Psalter in its canonical form, far from being different in kind from the prophetic message, joins with the prophets in announcing God's coming kingship."[117] And David Mitchell elaborates on the eschatological nature of the Psalms based on the post-exilic setting during which the canonical Psalter was closed:

---

[115] Mitchell, *Message*, 85–86, 176–77.

[116] See below for further discussion of the principles of discerning deliberate editorial placement.

[117] Childs, *IOTS*, 518.

Methodological Considerations

Several points suggest that the final form of the Psalter may indeed have been redacted in accord with an eschatological agenda. First, it originated within an eschatologically conscious milieu. The period of its redaction was apparently sometime between the end of the Babylonian exile, as the post-exilic psalms attest, and the translation of the LXX. Biblical literature written during this period, when Israel was in subjection and *bet-David* in decline, tends to look for a sudden dramatic divine intervention in history that will restore the nation's fallen fortunes. Thus Ezekiel and Zechariah, in the early post-exilic period, both anticipate a coming golden age of prosperity and dominion for Israel, under a Davidic king.... It therefore seems fair to regard the second temple period as a time of growing eschatological hope. As this was the context of the Psalter's redaction, it seems not unreasonable to suggest that its redactor shared the eschatological concerns of his contemporaries and that an eschatological agenda underlies his work, as it did theirs.[118]

David Howard summarizes the issue concisely:

Despite impressive evidence brought to bear by Wilson, McCann, and others, I maintain that the Psalter does not, in the end, speak of the "failure" and "rejection" of the Davidic Covenant. Rather, the Davidic kingdom and YHWH's kingdom coexist in complementary roles throughout the Psalter. Of the two, YHWH's kingdom is clearly the more important and the one from which the Davidic kingdom derives its legitimacy and authority. Yet Zion and the Davidic kingdom are the earthly expressions of YHWH's kingdom in important ways. Furthermore, in my view, the placement of the royal psalms, along with other considerations, are evidence in the Psalter of a continuing hope that is focused on both Zion and the Davidic Covenant, despite the many flaws of the kings and people who were heirs of that covenant.[119]

M. A. Vincent applies these eschatological themes more specifically to the question of the retention of the kingship psalms in the post-exilic period and their prominent placement in the Psalter:

It is important to stress that this psalm [Ps 2] was chosen (or at the very least allowed to remain) as an introductory psalm for the Psalter when it was finally compiled after the Exile. Victory for God and his son/king is promised and asserted, *at a time when there was no king*, and when the nation had little political significance. To this king God promises the nations and the uttermost part of the world as his inheritance. He will subdue them and reign over them as king from God's holy hill of Zion. Reading the Psalter from the perspective of its final form and taking into account the editorial decision made in placing this psalm in this position we are forced into understanding it eschatologically, whatever its origins may have been.

---

[118] Mitchell, *Message*, 82–83.
[119] Howard, *Structure*, 201–02.

Let me emphasise this point. It is remarkable that this psalm should front a collection which includes a substantial number of psalms which deal with God's *rejection* of Zion and the *failure* of the kingship and kingdom. That this psalm should assert God's rule (when we know what is coming in the rest of the Psalter) makes it almost certain that this Psalm is to be given an eschatological interpretation. All has not been lost despite the captivity and the loss of the kingdom; God will still be vindicated, and will vindicate his people; Zion will still be the centre of the world! So the Psalm asserts. The Davidic promise of 2 Samuel 7 is reasserted here, even though other parts of the Psalter recognise that it was not historically fulfilled. That fulfilment (following a clash between God and the nations, vv 1-5, 8, 9) is yet to come.[120]

Some have sounded cautionary notes with regard to eschatology in the Psalms. Gillingham, for example, creates a distinction between "messiah (small m) and Messiah (capital M). The former denotes the figure of the king and his dynastic rule, and thus refers to many successive figures; the latter, by contrast presumes a once-for-all figure coming either at the end of time, or heralding it."[121] However, as discussed above, such a distinction is difficult to maintain as there were probably elements of "Messianic" understanding of the royal psalms even in the period when there was physical messiah.

Gillingham's view that there is no real messianic content "within canonical psalmody"[122] also seems a little tenuous, and is dependent upon her understanding of the development of eschatological-messianic tendencies "between the period of the editing and collecting of the psalms... and the Christian period."[123] There is no doubt that it is true that eschatological rereadings of the psalms are found in the LXX, the midrashic literature and the *Psalms of Solomon*, as Gillingham points out, but it can be argued that this rereading began much earlier than that. In fact, it is questionable whether, the royal psalms ever did truly fulfil a function *entirely* within the "confines" of the historical realities of Israel, but perhaps during the early stages of the monarchy they could be called "messianic" psalms. There does, however, seem to be a sense in which they were always—at least in part—Messianic psalms, because "from the outset they had a prophetic character."[124] There is good reason to argue that this type of eschatological

---

[120] Vincent, "Shape of Psalter," 66.
[121] Gillingham, "Messiah," 211.
[122] Gillingham, "Messiah," 237.
[123] Gillingham, "Messiah," 229.
[124] Eaton, *Psalms*, 33. See also Keith R. Crim, *The Royal Psalms* (Richmond: John Knox Press, 1962), 60–61.

rereading was broadly understood and applied in the period of the closure of the final form of the Psalms, because it had been (at least partially) inherent to the kingship and Zion psalms from the time of their origin.

Therefore, an eschatological orientation shall be applied consistently throughout our study of the Psalter. The prominent role of the royal psalms was allowed to remain and the redactors, it appears, intended them to be reread in the light of the eschatological hope which was prevalent in the era in which they lived, and which flavours the book as a whole. The result of this reinterpretation of the psalms is that the Kingship Law is also applied to the figure of the eschatological king in the Psalms. This redaction speaks not only as an indicator of proper piety for the readers and hearers of the psalms, but also influences the psalmic picture of the restored Davidic king.

Introductory questions having been dealt with, it is appropriate at this point to turn to the exegetical analysis of the aforementioned psalms. Each torah-kingship psalm grouping shall be considered in turn (chapters 2–4) and then, finally, comparison with the Deuteronomic Law of the King shall be made (chapter 5).

CHAPTER 2
TORAH-KINGSHIP THEME IN PSALMS 1–2

1. INTRODUCTION

The switch in focus which has taken place within Psalm studies over the last fifteen years or so, from a form-critical and cult-functional approach to a canonical reading, has given rise to many new and interesting perspectives, not least of which is the importance of the ordering of the psalms within the Psalter. In the days when Gunkel and Mowinckel set the tone for the study of the psalms, the significance of Ps 1 was minimal. It was, after all, a psalm celebrating the torah, a wisdom psalm, and therefore neither representative of the truly significant psalm genres,[1] nor could it be described as cultic. Therefore, it was seen as representing a later, poorer brand of psalm writing, the so-called "learned psalmography."[2] However, when one treats the final-form of the Psalms seriously, the significance of Ps 1 is greatly increased. Accepting the canonical form as the starting-point of discussion means that certain important questions must be considered. For example, "Why is Psalm 1 the first psalm in the Psalter?" Order is important in the canonical study of any Old Testament book, but its importance is elevated when the book in question is a collection of individual poems: just why does this poem precede all the others?

In recent scholarship, B. S. Childs mooted a response to this question in his *Introduction to the Old Testament as Scripture*, where—amidst discussion of various indicators of editorial activity in the Psalter—he suggests that, "Psalm 1 serves as an introduction to the whole Psalter."[3] Childs suggests that the priority

---

[1] Gunkel, *Introduction*, 305, 327.
[2] Mowinckel, *PIW*, 113–14, 155.
[3] Childs, *IOTS*, 512.

of the first psalm over the other compositions sets it apart as an introduction to the Book of Psalms as a whole. This possible introductory function of Ps 1 is further complicated by an apparent editorial connection between Pss 1 and 2, by way of lexical connection and a common lack of superscription. Could it be that Pss 1 *and* 2 (a torah psalm and a kingship psalm), actually form a *dual* introduction to the Psalms? If so, even more questions are raised: Why these psalms? Why together? What are they trying to communicate? If they are meant to provide "hermeneutical spectacles" through which the reader is to view the book as a whole, then how is that reader meant to read the Psalter?

The repetition of this torah-kingship connection in two other key places in the final form of the Psalms (Book I: Pss 18–21 and Book V: Pss 118–119) makes the discussion all the more relevant. If these torah and kingship psalms have been deliberately juxtaposed, then why did the editors seek to make this link between the torah of Yahweh and the king of Israel? This is the question to which we now turn, dealing with each of these three psalm groupings in turn (chapters 2–4) and, ultimately, comparing them with the theology of Deut 17 (chapter 5). My tentative suggestion is that we see at work here a Deuteronomic redaction in the final shaping of the Psalter—perhaps, more specifically, a nomistic Deuteronomic redaction (DtrN). The thrust of this redaction is to promote a particular view of piety for the post-exilic community and a particular perspective on the Davidic kingship as an eschatological hope in that period. This redaction is designed to be both an encouragement and a corrective for the readers and hearers of the Psalms. The encouragement being the hope of a future Davidic king. The corrective being the addition of a strong torah-focus instead of any simplistic, nominal hope in "David" and "Zion," so often criticised by the prophets. Granted, this is merely part of a broader picture of kingship portrayed in the Psalter, but these texts play an important role in shaping the overall psalmic presentation of the king. This emphasis on torah speaks to both future hope and present reality. Not only is this renewed Davidic king to be the torah-keeper, but the people are to follow the idea of devotion to Yahweh through devotion to his revealed word in the here and now.

However, for this theory to hold true its basis and starting-point must be in exegesis, so now we turn to the analysis of Pss 1 and 2 as an introduction to the Book of Psalms.

2. ANALYSIS OF PSALM 1

BHS	Translation
אַשְׁרֵי־הָאִישׁ אֲשֶׁר לֹא הָלַךְ בַּעֲצַת רְשָׁעִים וּבְדֶרֶךְ חַטָּאִים לֹא עָמָד וּבְמוֹשַׁב לֵצִים לֹא יָשָׁב:	1 Happy is the man who does not walk in the counsel of the wicked, and in the way of sinners does not stand, and in the seat of mockers does not sit.
כִּי אִם בְּתוֹרַת יְהוָה חֶפְצוֹ וּבְתוֹרָתוֹ יֶהְגֶּה יוֹמָם וָלָיְלָה:	2 Rather in the torah of Yahweh is his delight, and upon his torah he meditates day and night.
וְהָיָה כְּעֵץ שָׁתוּל עַל־פַּלְגֵי מָיִם אֲשֶׁר פִּרְיוֹ יִתֵּן בְּעִתּוֹ וְעָלֵהוּ לֹא־יִבּוֹל וְכֹל אֲשֶׁר־יַעֲשֶׂה יַצְלִיחַ:	3 He is like a tree planted by channels of water, which gives its fruit in its season, and its leaf does not wither, and all that he does prospers.
לֹא־כֵן הָרְשָׁעִים כִּי אִם־כַּמֹּץ אֲשֶׁר־תִּדְּפֶנּוּ רוּחַ:	4 Not so the wicked for they are like chaff which is driven about by the wind!
עַל־כֵּן לֹא־יָקֻמוּ רְשָׁעִים בַּמִּשְׁפָּט וְחַטָּאִים בַּעֲדַת צַדִּיקִים:	5 Therefore the wicked will not stand in the judgement, nor sinners in the congregation of the righteous.
כִּי־יוֹדֵעַ יְהוָה דֶּרֶךְ צַדִּיקִים וְדֶרֶךְ רְשָׁעִים תֹּאבֵד:	6 For Yahweh knows the way of the righteous, but the way of the wicked will perish

2.1 DEUTERONOMIC BACKGROUND TO PSALM 1

There are few doubts about the text of the passage, and its meaning seems to be fairly clear.[4] The Psalter begins with a discussion of the "two ways"—the way of the righteous as opposed to the way of the wicked—a theme well-known to both Deuteronomy and the Wisdom literature. Psalm 1 is interesting, however, in the yard-stick which it sets as the test of devotion to Yahweh: The righteous delight in the law of the Lord and meditate upon that torah day and night, a concept which seems to borrow from the theology of Deuteronomy.

2.1.1 PSALM 1 AND THE SHEMA

Deuteronomic overtones are apparent from the beginning of Psalm 1. The psalm starts with blessing or beatitude formula (אשרי האיש), which is not as

---

[4] In terms of structure, Psalm 1 follows a four-fold $A - B - A^1 - B^1$ structure, where:
    A (1–3) = Description of the צדיקים;
    B (4–5) = Description of the רשעים;
    A^1 (6a) = Way of the צדיקים;
    B^1 (6b) = Way of the רשעים.

common as the ברוך formula throughout the OT literature, but is found quite often in the psalms. It is not entirely clear how the two terms—אשרי and ברוך — differ, but the most likely suggestions come from Mays and Kraus. Mays suggests that ברוך is used in traditional blessing formulas and אשרי is used in beatitudes, commonly found in post-exilic psalms.[5] Kraus, on the other hand, (but in a similar vein) writes: "The 'secular' אשרי is to be distinguished from the solemn liturgical ברוך."[6] Whichever approach is adopted the meaning of this introductory phrase is clear, the "blessed" or "happy" person is about to be described to the reader. This is done first negatively and then positively, and in each case Deuteronomic terms are adopted.

The negative description, i.e. what the faithful follower of Yahweh is not like, comes in a parallel three by three structure:

Blessed is the man who...

does not walk	*in the counsel*	*of the wicked*
does not stand	*in the way*	*of sinners*
does not sit	*in the seat*	*of mockers.*

This structure and the vocabulary used has led to Ps 1:1 being read in the light of the *Shema*. Gunnel André points out that much of the focus in the commentaries has emphasised distinctions between the nouns used (who are "sinners" as opposed to "the wicked"),[7] however, she readdresses this trend by focussing attention on the verbs used in Ps 1:1 and its three-fold structure. This André compares with the text of Deut 6, showing both lexical and structural similarities between the two texts. Lexically, the command to talk about the words of Yahweh when one *sits* (ישב), *walks* (הלך), *lies down* (שכב) and *rises* (קום) in Deut 6:7 echoes the vocabulary found in Ps 1:1 (does not *walk* [הלך], *sit* [ישב], *stand* [עמד]). So we find in Deut 6 the positively phrased alternative to the description of what the righteous are *not* like in Ps 1:1. The idea of speaking about the words of Yahweh on all occasions found in the *Shema* also ties in with the positive description of the OT believer as found in Ps 1:2—the one whose delight is in the torah.

---

[5] James L. Mays, *Psalms* (IBC; Louisville: John Knox Press, 1994), 41.

[6] Kraus, *Psalms*, 115. The two observations seem fairly compatible if one associates the beattitudes primarily with the secular (i.e. non-cultic) Wisdom movement.

[7] Gunnel André, "'Walk,' 'Stand,' and 'Sit' in Psalm I 1–2," *VT* XXXII, no. 3 (1982): 327.

André goes on to consider the three-fold emphases of Deut 6 in parallel with the three-fold negative of Ps 1:1. The *Shema* speaks of loving the Lord our God "with all your *lēbāb*, with all your *næpæš*, and with all your *m$^{e\flat}$od*," (Deut 6:5) and v 13 provides another triad of terms, "you shall *fear* YHWH your God; you shall *serve* (him), and *swear* by his name."[8] These, again, she sees as positive alternatives to the triad of negatives in Ps 1:1, which indicate what the "righteous one" is not like. He does not does not walk in the counsel of the wicked, nor stands in the way of sinners, nor sits in the seat of mockers (Ps 1:1), but he does love his God with all his heart, soul and strength (Deut 6:4) and he will fear, serve and swear by Yahweh (Deut 6:13).

We find this Deuteronomy–Psalms link is not entirely new, but is also found in the rabbinic literature. Stefan Reif, in response to André's article, comments:

> It is clear... that Ibn Ezra relates the language and message of the two passages in precisely the manner suggested by André. He regards the Psalms passage as reminiscent of the Deuteronomic one, draws parallels between the vocabulary and regards the theme of each as one of total religious commitment.[9]

Similarly, Patrick Miller points out that: "The activity enjoined in Deut 6:6–9 expresses a constant and total commitment to the law of the Lord comparable to what is pronounced the blessed way of the righteous in Psalm 1."[10] What is more, v 1 introduces us to the main theme of Ps 1 (the two ways), telling the reader that the happy person does not stand in "the way of sinners" (ובדרך חטאים), and, as we shall see in the analysis of v 6, this too is a common Dtr idea.

So we can see that there are similarities in terms of language, form of expression and theme between Deut 6 (a key passage with regard to Dtr theology) and the first verse of Psalm 1. The opening verse of the Psalter serves as a signpost for the contemplative reader, introducing ideas characteristic of a Deuteronomic worldview from the outset of the book.

2.1.2 CENTRALITY OF TORAH

The strong adversative כי אם at the start of v 2 (which Walte and O'Connor suggest should be translated as "rather"[11]), informs the reader that the following

---

[8] André, "Walk, Stand, Sit," 327.
[9] Stefan C. Reif, "Ibn Ezra on Psalm I 1–2," *VT* XXXIV, no. 2 (1984): 234.
[10] Miller, "Deuteronomy and Psalms," 12.
[11] Bruce K. Waltke and M. O'Connor, *An Introduction to Biblical Hebrew Syntax* (Winona Lake: Eisenbrauns, 1990), 670–71.

is the contrasting, positive description of the "happy person." Significantly, this theme is continued in Deuteronomic terms. The key attribute of the faithful believer is that "his delight is in the torah of Yahweh" (בתורת יהוה חפצו). The connection with Deuteronomy would most likely have been obvious to the readers of this psalm, as the concept of torah is, perhaps, most associated with Deuteronomy.[12] It seems likely that this was the editorial intent in placing Ps 1 at the head of the Psalter: to present a call to faithfulness firmly grounded in a Deuteronomic notion of piety. Kraus puts it thus: "The concept תורה that is to be presupposed in Psalm 1 has its origin in Deuteronomic theology."[13]

The characteristically Deuteronomic emphasis regarding the torah of Yahweh continues in the description of the effects of this "delight" in the remainder of v 2. The faithful Israelite delights in the torah by "meditating upon it day and night" (ובתורתו יהגה יומם ולילה). This concept of meditating constantly upon the torah seems, in itself, to be a reflection of ideas found in Deuteronomy and the Deuteronomistic literature, as evidenced by Jos 1:8 and Deut 17:19.[14] Interestingly, both of these exhortations are addressed to the leaders of God's people (Joshua as Moses' successor and to "the kings" who would be called from the ranks of the Hebrew brothers), presumably as exemplars of devotion to Yahweh, whose example was to be followed by all.[15] Jos 1:8 is remarkably

---

[12] Torah appears most often in the Psalms themselves (thanks to Ps 119), but other than that the term is most commonly found in Deuteronomy, which has a strong sense of self-awareness as "this book of the torah" (Deut 1:5, 30:10 etc.), see Jean-Pierre Sonnet, *The Book Within the Book: Writing in Deuteronomy* (BibInt 14; Leiden: Brill, 1997).

[13] Kraus, *Psalms*, 116. Much scholarly debate has focussed on the proper definition of the word "torah" as used in Ps 1. Most commentators point out that the OT understanding of torah goes far beyond our contemporary understanding of what "law" means, to include all of the teaching of Yahweh in a holistic sense. Discussion of just what is meant by "torah" in the torah psalms is an important question, and one which will be a central consideration of chapter 7, *Torah, Kingship and Democratisation*. Suffice it to say for the moment, that the idea of a piety based in torah appears to draw upon Deuteronomy's presentation of devotion to Yahweh.

[14] The similarities between Ps 1:2 and Deut 17:19 will, of course, be discussed in much greater detail in chapter 5, below.

[15] Miller points out that, "The fundamental task of the leader of the people, therefore, is to exemplify and demonstrate true obedience to the Lord for the sake of the wellbeing of both the dynasty and the kingdom. King and subject share a common goal: to learn to fear the Lord (v 19)," (*Deuteronomy* [IBC; Louisville: John Knox Press, 1990], 149). The similarities between the commissioning of Joshua and the Law of the King have led some to posit that Joshua (and also Moses, for that matter) was, in fact, a

similar in its presentation of the role of the torah of Yahweh in the life of the one who was to lead Israel into Canaan. Joshua is commanded "to be careful to keep all of the torah" (לשמר לעשות ככל־התורה) and to "meditate upon it day and night" (והגית בו יומם ולילה). The similarities between Jos 1 and Ps 1 are difficult to ignore and it appears that, just as there is a deliberate attempt to link Joshua (and the DtrH) with the Book of Deuteronomy,[16] so in Ps 1 we see a similar attempt to link the spiritual theology of the Psalms with Deuteronomic theology. "The Psalter and the Deuteronomistic History both begin with an explicit focus on the desirability of a constant attention to the law, which is to be understood to be the Deuteronomic law."[17]

---

kind of *de facto* "king" in the pre-monarchic period (e.g. R. D. Nelson, "Josiah in the Book of Joshua," *JBL* 100, no. 4 [1981]: 531–40; J. Roy Porter, "The Succession of Joshua," in *Reconsidering Israel and Judah: Recent Studies on the Deuteronomistic History* [ed. G. N. Knoppers and J. G. McConville; SBTS 8; Grand Rapids: Eisenbrauns, 2000], 139–62; *Moses and Monarchy: A Study in the Biblical Tradition of Moses* [Oxford: Basil Blackwell, 1963]). This seems to be an unnecessary and somewhat problematic conclusion, however. The commonality is based in the fact that similar expectations surround the office of king and the commissioning of Joshua as leader of the people (e.g. torah-obedience etc.). This, however, is not sufficient to outweigh the indications that Joshua is not to be thought of as a king in Israel (e.g. he is Moses' successor for the task of conquest alone, his is not monarchic succession based on sonship; also, the fact that he fulfils some of the functions later fulfilled by the kings does not, of itself, mean that Joshua *is* king), see McConville, "King and Messiah," 271–72, 285–86. The description of Joshua as monarch or proto-monarch, seems to cloud the issue somewhat. Emphasis is best placed upon the analysis of the content of Yahweh's expectations described in the Kingship Law and the commissioning of Joshua. As Miller points out above, Yahweh expects the same obedience from the people *and* their leaders, so rather than being characteristics particular to the monarchy (thus implying a kingly function for Joshua), these are characteristics expected of the whole community. It seems that the divine expectation is that appointed leaders *excel* in the task of devotion to Yahweh as an example for all the people; and that this expectation is not limited to kings alone, but to any who would lead the people regardless of function (see, for example, Lohfink's comments on the supremacy of torah in Norbert F. Lohfink, "Distribution of the Functions of Powers," in *The Song of Power and the Power of Song: Essays on the Book of Deuteronomy* [ed. D. L. Christensen; SBTS, Vol. 3; Winona Lake: Eisenbrauns, 1993], 350–51). It may be the case that Joshua, as a leader who sought to abide by the divine expectations, served as a model of proper leadership for the kings, but this is something very different from being king himself (Howard, "The Case for Kingship in Deut," 107; G. Widengren, "King and Covenant," *JSS* 2, no. I [January 1957]: 14–15).

[16] A. D. H. Mayes, *Deuteronomy* (NCB; London: Marshall, Morgan & Scott, 1979), 273.

[17] Miller, "Deuteronomy and Psalms," 11. Sarna points out, interestingly, that each of the major sections of the Hebrew Bible begins with a similar focus on the torah: "If not

The final statement of Ps 1:3c (וכל אשר־יעשה יצליח) also focuses attention on the torah-piety of Joshua 1:8 (כי־אז תצליח את־דרכך ואז תשכיל), as is footnoted in both the MT and the LXX. The explanatory expansion upon the metaphor of the tree (discussed immediately below) refers the reader back to the Jos 1 passage where the importance of living according to the torah is so strongly emphasized. Kraus describes the addition of this final phrase of v. 3 thus: "To [the tree simile] is added an insertion that soberly states a fact and makes a transition from illustration to fact: he who is rooted in God's תורה will prosperously bring to a conclusion all that he undertakes. This added part of the verse is modeled after Josh 1:8—a text parallel to Ps 1:2."[18] The thrust of this Deuteronomic connection with Jos 1:8 is that torah-obedience makes a difference in the life and reality of the blessed person.

So we see quite clearly that the introductory verses of the Psalter have a strongly Deuteronomic flavour to them, with a particular focus on the law. The torah is central and true godliness is based upon its study. The purpose of this study is to be equipped to live by Yahweh's torah—not to stray from it either to the right or to the left (cf. Deut 17:20; Jos 1:8)—and such a lifestyle (דרך) is the essence of true faithfulness, according to the introduction to the Book of Psalms.

---

by design, then by happy coincidence, the choice of Psalm 1 makes each major division of the standard Hebrew Bible open with a reference to Torah. The Former Prophets begin with the Book of Joshua, and chapter one contains the following: "You must be very strong and resolute to observe faithfully all the Teaching (*torah*) that My servant Moses enjoined upon you. Do not deviate from it to the right or to the left, that you may be successful whenever you go. Let not this Book of the Teaching (*torah*) cease from your lips, but recite it day and night, so that you may observe faithfully all that is written in it" (vv 7, 8). The Latter Prophets begin with the Book of Isaiah; its opening chapter calls upon Israel to: "Hear the word of the Lord... Give ear to our God's Teaching (*torah*)" (v 10). The final chapter of the prophetic division, the third in the Book of Malachi, likewise exhorts the people: "Be mindful of the Teaching (*torah*) of My servant Moses, whom I charged at Horeb with laws and rules for all Israel" (v 22). Since the Book of Psalms opens the third section of the Hebrew Bible, the *Ketuvim* (*Hagiographa*, or *Writings*, in English), it is to be expected that it, too, would commence with emphasis on *torah* and so a composition with the theme of Torah was selected for the purpose," (*On the Book of Psalms: Exploring the Prayer of Ancient Israel* [New York: Schocken Books, 1993], 28).

[18] Kraus, *Psalms*, 118–19.

2.1.3 Dependence on Yahweh

The Deuteronomic overtones continue into verse three with a simile which describes the effects of life grounded in the torah of Yahweh. The blessed man is likened to "a tree planted by streams of water" (היה כעץ שתול על־פלגי מים), a phrase which is immediately reminiscent of another well-known Deuteronomistic passage, Jer 17:7–8. In Jeremiah it is the man who trusts in Yahweh (יבטח ביהוה) who is described as being "like a tree planted by water" which is conceptually very similar to the blessing formula found in Ps 2:12 (אשרי כל־חוי בו, "Blessed are all who take refuge in him"), which is closely linked with Ps 1 (by way of the אשרי inclusion). The similarities between these two passages are marked:

Ps 1		Jer 17
אַשְׁרֵי־הָאִישׁ	cf.	בָּרוּךְ הַגֶּבֶר
וְהָיָה כְּעֵץ שָׁתוּל	cf.	וְהָיָה כְּעֵץ שָׁתוּל
עַל־פַּלְגֵי מָיִם	cf.	עַל מָיִם
פִּרְיוֹ יִתֵּן בְּעִתּוֹ	cf.	וְלֹא יָמִישׁ מֵעֲשׂוֹת פֶּרִי

Whilst the lexical links are not always exact, the metaphor is essentially the same: The person who is blessed by God (the torah-keeper of Ps 1 or the one who trusts in Jer 17)[19] is like a tree planted by water, denoting permanence, protection and fruitfulness. Jerome Creach has made a good argument connecting the imagery of Ps 1:3 with Ezek 47:12 and accordingly drawing a connection between torah and temple.[20] However, this argument is dependent upon the correlation between secondary aspects of the metaphor (פלגי מים and the phrase פריו יתן בעתו) rather than the primary image of the blessed person being like a tree planted by water. In dealing with intertextual relationships it is always difficult to argue conclusively as to what the original reader would understand or how he would go about internally cross-referencing one text with others. Equally it is difficult to say which text (if any) the author had in mind when writing what he

---

[19] Interestingly, in his study of the idea of refuge, Creach shows how these two concepts, torah obedience and dependence upon Yahweh, are closely associated in the Psalms. He writes: "the association of *torâ* with Yahweh's refuge provides a clue as to how Yahweh's instruction was understood and how the Psalter was meant to be read: the content of the Psalter seemed to be intended as a guide to a life of dependence; the most concrete way of expressing such allegiance was in the study of *torâ*," (*Yahweh as Refuge*, 73).

[20] Jerome F. D. Creach, "Like a Tree Planted by the Temple Stream: The Portrait of the Righteous in Psalm 1:3," *CBQ* 61 (1999): 34–46.

did.²¹ In this case, however, the Jeremiah connection seems to be the more likely because the main metaphors (rather than the secondary descriptions) correspond and also because both passages are clearly metaphors speaking of the faithful believer, whereas it is not immediately clear that the Ezekiel passage is referring to the people of God.²²

The Psalm 1–Jeremiah 17 association is significant. Whilst the exact nature of the relationship between Jeremiah and Deut/DtrH is undoubtedly complex, this prophetic book appears to borrow Dtr concepts and language in its explanation of the exile and its presentation of the hope of restoration and renewal.²³ Jeremiah's explanation of the exile is based in the *rejection* of the torah of Yahweh (Jer 29:19–23; 32:23 etc.), and, equally, the promise of restoration is connected with the *keeping* of the torah (this time as a result of Yahweh's divine help, Jer 31:33). Just as the exilic/post-exilic Book of Jeremiah draws upon Dtr theological concepts both in explanation of the past and in giving hope for the future, could it be that a similar connection with Deuteronomy is being drawn in the final, post-exilic redaction of the Book of Psalms?

Ps 1:1–3, the first section of Ps 1, provide an introduction to the Psalter which is immersed in Deuteronomic theology. It makes use of Deuteronomic concepts and ideas, makes reference to "well-known" Deuteronomistic texts and is thoroughly ensconced in a theology of torah. If indeed Ps 1 is part of an introduction to the whole of the Psalter, then the significance of these opening verses is marked. The reader will be aware that what follows are gathered texts of varied content, but in these verses he is told to take stock of all that follows and to read it from the viewpoint of a Deuteronomic worldview.

2.1.4 ESCHATOLOGICAL REREADING OF PSALM 1

The presentation of the characteristics of the wicked (Ps 1:4–5) follows on from the description of the blessed person with two strongly adversative conjunctions: לא־כן and כי אם. After the description of the righteous in terms of Deuteronomic torah concepts, the psalmist goes on to emphatically say, "*Not so* the wicked! *Rather*, they are like chaff!" There is no halfway-house between the

---

²¹ See Van Wolde, "Intertextuality," 46–47, for good discussion of the issues involved in suggesting textual interconnection.

²² Mays, "Place of the Torah-Psalms," 4.

²³ J. Gordon McConville, *Judgment and Promise* (Leicester: Apollos, 1993), 180–81.

two ways, one either lives in accordance with the torah and prospers, or one is wicked and chaff-like.[24] However, as well as acting as a foil for the imagery of v 3, these verses do add another element to the "hermeneutical spectacles" which result from Ps 1's function as introduction to the Psalter—they add an eschatological twist. It is difficult to know precisely what was v 5's referent in its original historical context, but it seems clear that by the time of the closure of the Psalter its words of judgment had taken on an eschatological character:

> Of course—and we must now emphasize this strongly—it is probably not at all conceivable that the sacral-legal and the cultic institutions [Kraus' suggestion as to the original context of these ideas] still have a real significance for our psalm. The concepts and formulations are indeed molded from that model, but they have been largely spiritualized... Thus those conceptions would finally be proved to be correct which speak—perhaps too quickly and too rashly—of משפט as the final "judgment" and of the עדה as the "messianic congregation of the new world."[25]

Sharing the same view, Mays comments: "Almost certainly verse 5 came to be understood in the light of apocalyptic eschatology like that of Daniel (see Daniel 7; 12) as a reference to a vindicating judgment beyond this life."[26] Kraus is correct to point out that often interpreters have been too quick tox make this jump to a "spiritualised" view of many of the key concepts of the Psalms, but—as he insists—we cannot underestimate the transformation of understanding which took place as a result of the exile. Many institutions (e.g. king, temple, Zion) which were seen as important in the (spiritual) life of the community were removed or radically altered as a result of the Babylonian captivity, and so their meaning underwent radical re-interpretation in later biblical texts.[27]

> In my opinion, it is difficult to overestimate the importance of the exile for theological and religious development, but it must be expected beforehand that the traces of it to so great an extent as possible were obliterated in the literary tradition... *In that respect we can only manage to establish that changing times read different contents into the stereotyped language of the psalms.*[28]

---

[24] The image of "chaff" (מוֹץ) is only ever used figuratively and is chosen as the diametric opposite of the image of the tree in v 3: an image of permanence, security and fruitfulness contrasted with an image of all that is useless, passing and inconsequential.
[25] Kraus, *Psalms*, 119–20.
[26] Mays, *Psalms*, 44.
[27] Waltke, "Canonical Process."
[28] Svend Holm-Nielsen, "The Importance of Late Jewish Psalmody for the Understanding of Old Testament Psalmodic Tradition," *ST* XIV, no. 1 (1960): 13 (emphasis mine).

So we see in Ps 1:5, the concept of (probably) sacral judgment being transformed into a notion of eternal judgment after death. As mentioned in chapter 1, we see this process of eschatological rereading at work with regard to the institution of kingship, however, such reinterpretation is not limited to the royal.

2.1.5 THEOLOGY OF THE TWO WAYS

Verse 6 concludes Psalm 1, by continuing the Dtr theme in much the same vein as we have seen throughout. The idea of the "two ways," the way of the righteous and the way of the wicked, is a common one in the Psalms and Wisdom literature generally (e.g. Prov 8–9). However, it is also an important idea in the theology of the Book of Deuteronomy. Deut 30:11–20 has Moses presenting a climactic exhortation to the Israelites, that they should choose today between "life and prosperity, death and destruction" (v 15, את־החיים ואת־הטוב ואת־המות ואת־הרע). He goes on that they should love Yahweh their God, "walk in his ways" (ללכת בדרכיו), keep his commands and so on. This is presented as one option (obviously, the "right" one), and vv 17–18 show that there is a second option (i.e., to be drawn away to serve other gods and to worship them). In vv 19–20 we see the similar challenge to make a choice between "life and death, blessings and curses" (החיים והמות נתתי לפניך הברכה והקללה). Thus we see that the idea of the "two ways" is also part of Deuteronomic theology, and given the context of the whole psalm, this is at least as likely a connection as any link with the Wisdom tradition.

Again the notion of following in the way of Yahweh is firmly grounded in torah-obedience (Deut 30). So the summary statement of v. 6 presents a very "simple" worldview for the righteous—walk in God's ways by meditating day and night on the torah and your way will be known (and, by implication, blessed) by the Lord. The second alternative is the equivalent of Moses' "death option" in Deut 30—rejection of the torah leads one on the way of the wicked which is fleeting (chaff-like) and ultimately perishing. Kraus summarises Ps 1 thus:

> But, finally, we must not forget that Psalm 1 is the preamble to the Psalter. That person is pronounced happy who, in reading and reflection upon the Psalms, lets himself be guided by the message that shows the path.[29]

---

[29] Kraus, *Psalms*, 122.

2.2 ASSESSMENT OF THE THEOLOGICAL SIGNIFICANCE OF PSALM 1

In summary, it can be seen that Psalm 1—which functions as half of the dual introduction to the Psalter—presents a thoroughly Dtr perspective on life. It suggests that the blessed are those who delight to meditate upon and live by the torah, and that those who reject the torah follow the way of folly and death. The obvious question in response to this conclusion is, "Why? Why does the Psalter begin with this strong presentation of a Deuteronomic worldview?"

There are various levels at which this question can be answered. Historically, it could be answered on the level of pointing out the dominant school of theology at the time of the closure of the Psalter. History is written by the winners, and, it could be said, so is poetry. Canonically, the same would apply: it was, perhaps, the Deuteronomists who appear to have been most involved in the closure of the Old Testament canon.[30] However, this question becomes most interesting when answered from a theological perspective. What were the *theological* reasons for the placement of this psalm at the head of the Psalter?

There seem to be two main reasons for the placement[31] of Ps 1 as the introduction to the Psalter:

1. This is a clear statement that the ensuing Book of Psalms is to be treated as torah itself. The reader is to meditate on all that follows as instruction from God and to seek to live by *its* teaching as much as by the teaching of the Pentateuch.[32] All of these works—praise, lament, wisdom, thanksgiving, individual, corporate—all of these elements are present to teach something about God, or man, or creation, or righteousness, or worship, or daily life, and so on. This Deuteronomic focus on torah-piety addresses the very nature of what the Psalter is. Ps 1 tells the thoughtful reader that the Psalter *is* torah. Seybold puts it thus:

---

[30] Although many view the Deuteronomists as those most associated with the formation of the canon, this was not *necessarily* the case. Lohfink's discussion of whether or not a Dtr movement existed provides an interesting addition to this discussion (see "Deuteronomistic Movement?").

[31] It is unclear whether Psalm 1 was written specifically as an introduction to the Book of Psalms, or if it was a "previously known" psalm which was placed there because of its theological content. For further discussion on this topic see Mitchell, *Message*, 73–75; Patrick D. Miller, *Interpreting the Psalms* (Philadelphia: Fortress, 1986), 81–86; Pierre Auffret, *The Literary Structure of Psalm 2* (trans. D. J. A. Clines; JSOTSup 3; Sheffield: JSOT Press, 1977), 31–34; Wilson, *Editing*, 204–07.

[32] "First, it identifies the function of the book. The book is torah of the Lord. Torah means instruction, teaching, direction that can be given in various literary forms. The psalms provide torah that can be learned by study and meditation. It is scripture where

With the new preface [Psalm 1] and the weight of the reflective proverbial poem [Psalm 119], which in terms of its range is effectively a small collection in itself, the existing Psalter now takes on the character of a documentation of divine revelation, to be used in a way analogous to the torah, the first part of the canon, and becomes a manual of instruction for the theological study of the divine order of salvation and meditation.[33]

Similarly, many commentators would argue that Ps 1 also addresses the usage of the Psalter: that is, that Ps 1 not only declares the Book of Psalms to be torah in a qualitative sense, but also tells the reader the way in which the psalms are to be appropriated. The addition of Ps 1 takes the Psalter out of the remit of the cult and places it firmly into a didactic context. The psalms are no longer primarily designed to be sung in the cult, rather they are to be meditated upon as texts. As Wilson puts it:

> The obvious encouragement to meditate on the psalms as Torah marks an interesting shift in the interpretation of these compositions. For the most part, these works began life as performance pieces in the worship of the temple.... For this reason, the Psalter is often alluded to as the "hymnbook of the second temple"—a collection of hymns to be sung in public worship. The placement of Psalm 1 as introduction decisively explodes this view of the Psalter. The psalms are no longer to be sung as a human response to God but are to be meditated upon day and night as the source of the divine word of life to us.[34]

Adding an introduction with such clear didactic, Wisdom overtones suggests that the Psalms are to be treated more like a book and less like a hymnbook.[35]

2. A second conclusion can reasonably be drawn from the prominent placement of the first psalm: namely, Psalm 1 instructs the reader that the Psalter's presentation of life and spirituality is to be understood from the per-

---

one learns about God and God's way with the world. This identification concerns the comprehensive use of the psalms gathered into the book. It does not deny that many are written to function as prayers and hymns of praise. In the book, the hymns and prayers are to be read as torah of the LORD," (Mays, *The Lord Reigns*, 121–22).

[33] Klaus Seybold, *Introducing the Psalms* (trans. R. G. Dumphy; Edinburgh: T&T Clark, 1990), 24. See also McCann, *Psalms*, 665–66.

[34] Gerald H. Wilson, "The Shape of the Book of Psalms," *Int* 46, no. 2 (April 1992): 137. See also Childs, *IOTS*, 513–14; Willem A. VanGemeren, *Psalms* (EBC; Grand Rapids: Zondervan, 1991), 8 and McCann, *Theological Introduction*, 20–21.

[35] One of the problems involved in making such statements is that we know very little about the historical usage of the Psalter in the post-exilic period, so some caution must be exercised. However, the content of Ps 1 and its prominent placement in the Psalter tends to suggest that a book for reading had overtaken a Psalter for singing in post-exilic Israel.

spective of a Deuteronomic world-and-life view. The Deuteronomic backdrop to Ps 1 is marked, and the theology of Deuteronomy is about more than just ideas; it is about an integrated philosophy of life that impacts every pattern of behaviour. Over and above the issues already mentioned,[36] we see this Dtr worldview presented in the idea of separation from the wicked in Psalm 1.[37] It appears that whoever placed Pss 1 and 2 as the dual introduction to the Psalms wanted the readers of the book to view its varied content from the perspective of a Deuteronomic worldview. So the ideas of personal and communal piety found in the Psalter, or the ideas of the rule and kingship of Yahweh, or the ideas of suffering and lament, or the praise and worship of God, or the kingship of Yahweh and his "anointed one," are all to be viewed from the type of perspective found in Deuteronomy.[38] The psalms, it has often been said, address the whole gamut of human experience and this Deuteronomic introduction encourages sweeping interaction with the lessons and perspectives taught in the psalms. The instruction of Yahweh applies to all things and in all circumstances; and, it is this holistic perspective that is to be applied to the reader's understanding of each of these individual poems. Murphy has phrased it in this way:

> For as the Psalms became Scripture, they did so with an interpretative strategy attached: they were not to be interpreted as self-standing books of prayers and praises, any more than Proverbs was a self-standing collection of wise sayings. Both were adjuncts to the rest of Scripture to be read in the light of the other books....[39]

Ps 1 seems to indicate that the lessons found in the book as a whole should be read in the light of Deuteronomy.[40] Whilst the Psalms should not, because of

---

[36] The importance of meditating upon the torah of Yahweh; connections with significant Dtr texts; the stress on the individual's dependence upon Yahweh etc.

[37] A. D. H. Mayes, "Deuteronomy 14 and the Deuteronomic Worldview," in *Studies in Deuteronomy in Honour of C J Labuschagne on the Occasion of His 65th Birthday* (ed. F. Garcia Martinez; VTSup 53; Leiden: E. J. Brill, 1994).

[38] I use the words "type of perspective" advisedly here. Deuteronomy does not necessarily speak directly to all of these issues within its pages, but its focus is to inculcate a way of thinking and acting in the hearts of the people of God that can be applied to new and changing circumstances. This idea is inherent to the book itself which seems to be a reinterpretation and reapplication of the presentation of the law at Sinai for the new situation of the people in the land.

[39] Murphy, "Reflections," 25.

[40] Not that the voice of Deuteronomy is the only one to be heard in the Psalms—many other voices can be heard in the Psalter, not least of which, as we have seen already

this "derivative" nature, be understood as a lesser type of torah, it does appear that the Psalter was designed to be understood in the light of the Pentateuch. More specifically, given this introduction to the Psalter, and Deuteronomy's self-understanding as "this book of the torah" it seems that there is a particular hermeneutical link to be drawn between the Psalms and Dtr theology.[41]

> Deuteronomy tells of a fundamental dialogue that moves from divine instruction to human prayer. It gives us the instruction part of the conversation but knows about the prayer; the Psalms give us the prayer part of this dialogue, and the redactional shaping of the book turns it into divine instruction.[42]

Historically speaking should we expect anything less? If, as seems to be the case, the dominant school of theology at the time of the Psalter's closure is Deuteronomic, should we not expect to see this type of "interpretative strategy" in the final form of the book?

3. Analysis of Psalm 2

BHS	Translation
לָמָּה רָגְשׁוּ גוֹיִם וּלְאֻמִּים יֶהְגּוּ־רִיק׃ יִתְיַצְּבוּ מַלְכֵי־אֶרֶץ וְרוֹזְנִים נוֹסְדוּ־יָחַד עַל־יְהוָה וְעַל־מְשִׁיחוֹ׃ נְנַתְּקָה אֶת־מוֹסְרוֹתֵימוֹ וְנַשְׁלִיכָה מִמֶּנּוּ עֲבֹתֵימוֹ׃	1 Why do the nations gather tumultuously and the peoples plot in vain. 2 The kings of the earth take their stand and rulers establish themselves together against Yahweh and against his anointed. 3 "Let us break their bonds and let us throw off from ourselves their cords."
יוֹשֵׁב בַּשָּׁמַיִם יִשְׂחָק אֲדֹנָי יִלְעַג־לָמוֹ׃ אָז יְדַבֵּר אֵלֵימוֹ בְאַפּוֹ וּבַחֲרוֹנוֹ יְבַהֲלֵמוֹ׃ וַאֲנִי נָסַכְתִּי מַלְכִּי עַל־צִיּוֹן הַר־קָדְשִׁי׃	4 He who dwells in the heavens laughs. The Lord mocks them. 5 Then he will speak to them in his anger and in his wrath he will terrify them, 6 "I have installed my king on Zion, my holy mountain."
אֲסַפְּרָה אֶל חֹק יְהוָה אָמַר אֵלַי בְּנִי אַתָּה אֲנִי הַיּוֹם יְלִדְתִּיךָ׃ שְׁאַל מִמֶּנִּי וְאֶתְּנָה גוֹיִם נַחֲלָתֶךָ וַאֲחֻזָּתְךָ אַפְסֵי־אָרֶץ׃	7 "I will recount the decree of Yahweh. He said to me, 'You are my son. Today I have begotten you. 8 Ask of me and I shall give the nations as

---

is the voice of Wisdom. However, the prominence of Ps 1 and its close association with Deuteronomy indicate that this perspective in the psalms is probably of greater importance than has been recognised to date.

[41] Obviously, this link should not be overstated. The Psalms correlate with many different types of OT literature (e.g. wisdom themes are also present in Ps 1). My suggestion is merely that Ps 1 as an introduction places an increased emphasis on Dtr theology as a hermeneutical construct in reading the Psalms.

[42] Miller, "Deuteronomy and Psalms," 8–9.

תְּרֹעֵם בְּשֵׁבֶט בַּרְזֶל כִּכְלִי יוֹצֵר תְּנַפְּצֵם:

your inheritance and the ends of the earth as your possession.
9 You will break them with an iron rod, like a fashioned vessel you will dash them to pieces."'

וְעַתָּה מְלָכִים הַשְׂכִּילוּ הִוָּסְרוּ שֹׁפְטֵי אָרֶץ:
עִבְדוּ אֶת־יְהוָה בְּיִרְאָה וְגִילוּ בִּרְעָדָה:
נַשְּׁקוּ־בַר פֶּן־יֶאֱנַף וְתֹאבְדוּ דֶרֶךְ
כִּי־יִבְעַר כִּמְעַט אַפּוֹ אַשְׁרֵי כָּל־חוֹסֵי בוֹ:

10 So now, you kings, pay attention! Be admonished, you judges of the earth!
11 Worship Yahweh with fear and rejoice with trembling!
12 Kiss the son, lest he should become angry and you should perish in your way! For his anger can be ignited quickly. Blessed are all who take refuge in him.

3.1 DEUTERONOMIC BACKGROUND TO PSALM 2

Clearly, Psalm 2 is best described as a royal psalm.[43] This automatically raises questions as to the Deuteronomic nature of this joint introduction. The Dtr associations with a torah psalm may seem fairly obvious, but with regard to a

---

[43] Eaton, *Kingship*, 111–13. Whilst the royal setting of Ps 2 is clear, the structure and text are more complex than was the case with Psalm 1. Structurally, it is difficult to ascertain whose voice is speaking throughout the psalm. Whilst there are other reasonable possibilities, I have opted for a structure reflecting the division of the text above. Verses 1–5 are the words of the psalmist (including a statement of the kings and rulers in v 3); verse 6 is a direct declaration of Yahweh; verses 7–9 reflect a statement of the king himself (his own direct speech in v 7a, followed by his repetition of the words of Yahweh's decree on his behalf); finally, verses 10–12 represent the concluding words of the psalmist (see Peter C. Craigie, *Psalms 1–50* [WBC; Waco: Word Books, 1983], 64–65). It could, of course, be the case that the king speaks the whole psalm, recounting the speech of the kings/rulers and Yahweh (see Eaton, *Psalms of the Way*, 111 and *Psalms*, 31–33), however, when the various statements of direct speech are taken to indicate changes in voice/person it seems to add dramatic emphasis to the poem. Ultimately, this question does not effect in any significant way the overall interpretation of the text.

There is, however, one verse where the text is somewhat unclear. Verse 12 has occasioned much debate in the analyses of Psalm 2. Traditionally translated "Kiss the son", the phrase נַשְּׁקוּ־בַר is problematic because of the switch from the use of the Hebrew בֵּן ("son") in v 7 to the Aramaic בַר ("son") here in v 12. The MT suggests a textual error based in dittography regarding the final phrase of v 11 and this first phrase of v 12. The suggestion is that "Rejoice with trembling. Kiss the son," (וגילו ברעדה: נשקו־בר), could in fact read "With trembling kiss his feet," (ברעדה נשקו ברגליו) the reference therefore being to kissing the feet of Yahweh (see Auffret, *Literary Structure*, 9). This is possible, but perhaps creates as many problems as it solves. This would be an anthropomorphism of an uncommonly radical nature in the OT, which could be interpreted metaphorically, but even this is somewhat unlikely (see Craigie, *Psalms*, 64; A. A. Macintosh, "A Consideration of the Problems Presented by Psalm II.11 and 12," *JTS* XXVII, no. 1 [1976]: 13; David J. A. Clines, "Psalm 2 and the MLF [Moabite Liberation Front]," in *The Bible in*

royal psalm the association is more difficult? Is the Dtr view of kingship positive or negative? Indeed, is there a single Deuteronomic view of kingship or are the voices of Deuteronomy and its associated historical books to be held in tension, presenting the reader with different assessments of kingship?[44] Obviously, the discussion surrounding Ps 2 could become very involved were one to adopt the establishment of the Deuteronomic view of kingship as our starting point for the discussion. Those who associate the DtrN redaction with the reign of Josiah—as a means of legitimising his reforms—may see the connection between the Deuteronomic themes of Ps 1 and the royal themes of Ps 2 as wholly natural and proper. The Josianic reconstruction, however, for all of its scholarly acceptance, is not without its difficulties.[45] Whilst the royal psalms are not, perhaps, obviously associated with the theology of Deuteronomy, there is one feature of their presentation of kingship which echoes strongly with the presentation of the ideal king in Deut 17: that is, the idea of the king as one entirely dependent upon Yahweh. We see this particular presentation of kingship in each of the royal psalms juxtaposed alongside the torah psalms. Besides this echo of the Kingship Law's presentation of the ideal king, Ps 2 is associated with a Dtr perspective by its close lexical and conceptual connections with Ps 1, a poem firmly grounded in the theology of Deuteronomy.

3.1.1   THE KING'S DEPENDENCE UPON YAHWEH

Much has been made of the fact that the kingship psalms speak of the kingship of Yahweh as much as they do about human kingship.[46] This fact is used to

---

Human Society: Essays in Honour of John Rogerson [JSOTSup 200; Sheffield: Sheffield Academic Press, 1995], 165). There are other possible emendations suggested by various commentators ("kiss sincerely," "kiss the mighty one," "you who forget the grave"), but each is problematic in its own way. As other suggestions are equally problematic, this thesis retains the traditional "kiss the son," whilst acknowledging that the text is unclear.

[44] So Knoppers, "Deuteronomist and Deuteronomic Law of the King."

[45] Not least of which is the fact that—whilst it is argued below (chapter 5) that the Kingship Law is not anti-monarchic—Deut 17:14–20 can hardly be described as a ringing endorsement of the monarchy. It is unlikely that this presentation of kingship was the result of a royalist reform programme (see McConville, "King and Messiah," 280; Bernard M. Levinson, "The Reconceptualization of Kingship in Deuteronomy and the Deuteronomistic History's Transformation of Torah," *VT* LI, no. 4 [2001]: 527n41).

[46] See, for example, Nancy L. deClaissé-Walford, "The Canonical Shape of the Psalms," in *An Introduction to Wisdom Literature and the Psalms: Festschrift Marvin E. Tate* (Macon: Mercer University Press, 2000), 101–02, and McCann, *Psalms*, 668–69.

support the assertion that Book IV is the editorial centre of the Psalter, presenting as pivotal the message of the reign of Yahweh.[47] Without doubt the message of the reign of Yahweh is central to the Psalms, however, the importance of the role of the king as Yahweh's co-regent should not be diminished as a result of this. The kingship psalms do focus on the universal reign of Yahweh as Creator God, and on the king as one dependent upon him. This presentation of the king, however, was intended to enhance, rather than diminish, the reader's appreciation of him, because dependence upon Yahweh is a characteristic to be cultivated rather than a weakness according to the Dtr worldview.

The king's attitude of dependence upon Yahweh is seen throughout Ps 2. Rebellion is against Yahweh first and then his anointed (v 2); it is Yahweh who has the power and right to mock in response (vv 4–5); Yahweh has installed him as king, he does not rule at his own prerogative (v 6); any power the king has is derived from Yahweh's universal authority (vv 8–9). As Eaton points out, the warning to the nations is grounded in the fact that: "the all-powerful God, to whom we all owe allegiance, has appointed him as vice-regent and at any moment may drastically vindicate him."[48] In the words spoken by the king in vv 7–9, he freely admits that his power is entirely derivative and the concluding formula of v 12 indicates that such an attitude of dependence ("taking refuge in him," אשרי כל־חוסי בו) results in divine blessing. Creach comments that, "it seems clear that the Psalter contains a 'refuge piety,' in which dependence upon Yahweh is the supreme virtue"[49] and this piety finds clear expression in Ps 2 and the other royal psalms assessed in the course of this study. As Durham comments: "[The king's] rule is guaranteed by Yahweh, and its extent and success are under Yahweh's control. This is made clear not only by the prayers and promises of the Davidic king in the royal psalms, and by the oracles in which Yahweh's words are addressed to him, but also by the clear implication throughout these poems of the king's complete dependence on Yahweh."[50]

This attitude of dependence upon Yahweh is central to the Dtr worldview and is seen as a commendable attribute.[51] The fact that Ps 2 characterises the

---

[47] Wilson, *Editing*, 214–15.
[48] Eaton, *Psalms*, 31.
[49] Creach, *Yahweh as Refuge*, 48.
[50] Durham, "King as Messiah," 428.
[51] Gerald E. Gerbrandt, *Kingship according to the Deuteronomistic History* (SBLDS 87; Atlanta: Scholars Press, 1986), 89; Mayes, *Deuteronomy*, 272 etc.

king in this way places the theological presentation of the monarch firmly within the terms of the Kingship Law, which limits the power of the king in order to ensure that his trust is placed entirely in Yahweh rather than in the trappings of kingship.[52] There are other indications of Dtr influence in Ps 2 (e.g. the torah motif of v 7 and the idea of the "two ways"), however, these shall be dealt with in the following section on the association of Pss 1 and 2.

3.1.2 PSALM 2'S ASSOCIATION WITH PSALM 1

As has been argued above, Ps 1 rehearses many classically Deuteronomic themes in its presentation of the "blessed person" and the "two ways." Some of these are echoed in the second psalm by way of lexical and thematic connection between these two compositions.[53] These juxtaposed psalms are deliberately linked to form a dual introduction to the Psalter. These links exist on lexical, thematic and perhaps even structural levels[54] (which are examined below), however, there are also good arguments to be drawn from older traditions which associate these psalms.

1. Older Traditions and the Association of Pss 1 and 2

i. Neither of Pss 1 and 2 contains a superscription, which is unusual in the context of Book I of the Psalter where almost all of the psalms are headed by Davidic superscriptions.[55] Indeed, Barth comments that "the ancient Greek translation... provided all the psalms—with the exception of Pss 1 and 2—with headings," which tends to indicate that there was an early tradition treating these psalms as a paired introduction to the Psalter, something slightly separate from the rest of the Psalter.[56]

ii. The Western text of Acts 13:33 in referring to Ps 2:7-8, writes "as it is written in the first psalm" (ἐν τῷ ψαλμῷ...τῷ πρώτῳ). It would be presumptuous

---

[52] See the detailed discussion of the Kingship Law in chapter 5.

[53] This connection between Pss 1 and 2 has been widely discussed by most scholars working on the questions of the canonical shaping of the Psalter. See, for example, Auffret, *Literary Structure*, 31–34; Miller, *Interpreting*, 81–91; Mays, *Psalms*, 44; McCann, *Psalms*, 664–65 and Howard, *Structure*, 202–05, to name but a few.

[54] This argument is made by Auffret in *Literary Structure*, 32. However, I am not convinced that his analysis of the structure of Ps 1 is correct, therefore I do not rely on this as evidence of linkage between Pss 1 and 2.

[55] Wilson argues with regard to the two other psalms in Book I which are without superscription (i.e. Pss 10 and 33) that their designation is to be derived from their association with the preceding psalms which do contain superscriptions (*Editing*, 173–76).

[56] Barth, *Introduction*, 6. See also, Mitchell, *Message*, 73–4. For further discussion of Pss 1–2's function as an introduction to the Psalter and their association with Book I and the whole Book of Psalms, see chapter 6 below.

to draw definitive conclusions from this variant reading, but it could indicate that Pss 1 and 2 were read together at the time of the writing of this text.[57]

iii. The Talmud describes Pss 1 and 2 as forming "one lesson or division."[58]

These traditions appear to point to the association of Pss 1 and 2 from the early days of Jewish and Christian exegesis of the Psalter. However, perhaps even more convincing is the lexical association between Pss 1 and 2.

2. *Lexical Association of Pss 1 and 2*

i. The אשרי Inclusio (Ps 1:1 cf. 2:12). Psalm 1 begins with a description of the "happy person" (אשרי האיש) and Ps 2 ends with a similar benediction upon all those who take refuge in the Lord (אשרי כל־חוסי בו). The occurrence of this word in juxtaposed psalms could conceivably be coincidental,[59] however, the positioning of these words at the very beginning of the first psalm and the very end of the second makes this unlikely. It seems more probable that the repetition of אשרי ("blessed") is a deliberate literary device conjoining the two psalms.[60]

ii. The Contrasting Functions of הגה. The verb הגה figures prominently in both Psalms 1 and 2. In Ps 1:2 the righteous person is exhorted to "meditate" (יהגה) upon the torah day and night, which stands in contrast to the attitude of the nations and their leaders who "plot" (יהגו, Ps 2:1) against Yahweh and his anointed. The repetition of this verb serves to contrast the attitudes of the personae which represent opposing worldviews in these two psalms.[61] According to BDB the word הגה can have both positive and negative overtones based around the idea of making a noise—one is either "murmuring" in recitative meditation

---

[57] James W. Watts, "Psalm 2 in the Context of Biblical Theology," *HBT* 12 (1990): 74. It could, of course, also indicate that Ps 1 had not yet been added to the beginning of the Psalter, but this seems less likely as the evidence from the LXX indicates that the ordering of the Psalms was fairly firmly established by the time of the translation of the Greek OT (see Mitchell, *Message*, 82–83).

[58] *Ber.* 9b–10a. See also the discussion found in Watts, "Psalm 2," 74, and Mitchell, *Message*, 74.

[59] אשרי does appear to function as a type of key-word which appears in juxtaposed psalms or a few times in the same psalm (e.g. 32:1, 2; 33:12; 34:9, or 40:3, 5; 41:2, or 84:5, 6, 13, or 127:5; 128:1), however (as Miller points out) nowhere else does it have this inclusio function marking the beginning of one psalm and the end of the next.

[60] Miller, "Beginning," 84.

[61] A parallel drawn between the "blessed person" in Psalm 1 and the "king/all who take refuge in Yahweh" in Psalm 2, as those who receive God's blessing. Equally, there is a parallel between the רשאים of Psalm 1 and the גוים (and especially their leaders) of Psalm 2, as those whose way is perishing. This parallel in itself must have been a strong challenge to its original hearers, as those among the ranks of God's chosen people who chose not to live by the torah are placed on a par with the pagan nations.

(upon the torah in the case of Ps 1:2)⁶² or one could be "plotting" under one's breath (as is the case in Ps 2:1).⁶³ We see these two possibilities reflected in the contrasting figures in these juxtaposed psalms. When viewed in the light of all the other lexical links between these poems, this connection seems to be the result of design rather than accident.⁶⁴

iii. The דרך Motif. Central to both psalms is the idea of "the way" (דרך) which one takes (Ps 1:1, 6 and 2:12). The idea of the "two ways" is explicit in Ps 1, but it is also, more tacitly, present throughout Ps 2 until its explicit mention in v 12. Rebellion against Yahweh is clearly representative of "the other way", the rebellion of the kings and rulers of the peoples is parallel to the "way of the wicked" in Psalm 1. This point is made clear in v 12 where the option of rebellion is warned against lest "you should perish in the way" (ותאבדו דרך). The combination of דרך and אבד makes this parallel with Ps 1:6 all the more clear—just as the wicked are following a way of destruction, so also are the nations and their leaders who rebel against Yahweh and his "anointed one."⁶⁵

iv. The Dwelling Motif. "Dwelling" or "sitting" (ישב) is another linguistic parallel between the two psalms. Psalm 1:1 tells the reader that the blessed person does not "sit" (ישב) in the "seat" (מושב, probably meaning "place in an assembly"⁶⁶) of mockers. The converse implication is, obviously, that the wicked do sit in this seat. This is contrasted with the image found in Ps 2:4 that "he who dwells in heaven laughs" (יושב בשמים ישחק) at the vanity of the rebellion of the kings and rulers. These contrasting images again seem to reflect deliberate connection between Pss 1 and 2—those who reject Yahweh may sit in their assembly and mock, but really all rebellion is in vain and it is Yahweh who has the last laugh.⁶⁷

v. The Torah Motif. There is also a link between the centrality of torah in Psalm 1 and the centrality of the king's declaration that he will "recount the decree of Yahweh" (אספרה אל חק יהוה) in Psalm 2:7. Commonly, in the Psalms

---

⁶² Sarna, *On the Book of Psalms*, 37–39.

⁶³ F. Brown et al., *A Hebrew and English Lexicon of the Old Testament* (Peabody, MA: Hendrickson Publishers, 1997), 211.

⁶⁴ See Howard, *Structure*, 202–05; Mitchell, *Message*, 74f; McCann, *Theological Introduction*, 48; and Auffret, *Literary Structure*, 33.

⁶⁵ Mays, *The Lord Reigns*, 132–33; Mitchell, *Message*, 73–74; and Auffret, *Literary Structure*, 34.

⁶⁶ A. F. Kirkpatrick, *The Book of Psalms* (Cambridge: CUP, 1910), 2–3.

⁶⁷ Auffret, *Literary Structure*, 34.

and Deuteronomy, these two words (חק and תורה) are used interchangeably as synonyms or are used in conjunction.[68] Torah is clearly central to the meaning of Ps 1, and although חק is only found in this one phrase in Ps 2, the function of v 7a is significant in establishing the attitude of the king in this royal psalm. First, structurally, this phrase is central to the psalm. Thirteen cola precede this phrase and thirteen cola follow it.[69] Secondly, if my description of the voices in Ps 2 is correct, this is the only autonomous statement of the "king-son-anointed one."[70] Verse 7a is the only phrase where the king speaks for himself not repeating the words of Yahweh and his statement declares allegiance to Yahweh in keeping his decree. Thirdly, it is possible that the חק יהוה of Ps 2:7, in fact, refers to Deuteronomy or a pre-canonical version of the book.[71] This idea will receive more detailed attention in the study of the Kingship Law in chapter 5. However, Deut 17:18 tells the king to "write a copy of this law into a book" (וכתב לו את־משנה התורה הזאת על־ספר) in order (by implication) to guide him in the task of kingship. The interesting factor in this instruction to the king is its temporal frame: the king is to write this out this copy of the law for himself "when he sits upon the throne of his kingdom" (והיה כשבתו על כסא ממלכתו). It is possible that Psalm 2 was originally connected with a coronation ceremony[72] and that this declaration that the king will "declare the decree of Yahweh" is a reference to his adoption of "book of the torah" as commanded in the Kingship Law.[73] If this is the case then, once again, we see a strong association with Deuteronomy and especially the Kingship Law.[74]

---

[68] Ps 119 is an example where we see this interplay between תורה and חק apparently as synonyms. Deuteronomy 17:19, part of the kingship law, provides a similar example where the two words appear to function as synonyms.

[69] It is interesting that the central section of Ps 18 also focuses on the role of the torah in the life of the king (see chapter 3, below).

[70] See above, pp 55–56n44.

[71] Sonnet, *The Book Within the Book*, 79–80.

[72] Brownlee, "Psalms 1–2," passim; Crim, *The Royal Psalms*, 62–63.

[73] Brownlee, "Psalms 1–2," 332–33.

[74] It is possible that the content of the decree of Yahweh is merely the declaration of sonship that follows in vv 7–9 of Psalm 2 (see, for example, deClaissé-Walford, *Reading from the Beginning*, 45). There is little OT material dealing with the practice of coronation to guide us regarding this question. However, Gerbrandt suggests that the document received by Joash (2 Kgs 11:12) contains both of the these elements: "At a king's coronation he was formally granted the document which both confirmed that Yahweh had chosen him to continue the Davidic dynasty, and confirmed his responsibility to obey the law, and as the leader of Israel, to lead the people in obedience," (*Kingship*, 185).

3. Thematic Association of Psalms 1 and 2

As well as these lexical connections, Pss 1 and 2 share a central theme: the idea of the two ways. This is seen in the imagery of contrasting worldviews common to both psalms. On the one hand, we find images of stability and fruitfulness typifying the righteous in both psalms, and, on the other hand, there are images of vanity and temporality which typify the wicked in each psalm.

Imagery of the Righteous	*Imagery of the Wicked*
1:3a A tree: stable, permanent (כעץ)	1:4b Chaff: Passing/temporal (כמץ)
1:3b Fruitful (יתן פריו)	1:4b Useless/blown away (תדפנו רוח)
1:3c Successful (יצליח)	2:1 Activity in vain (יהגו־ריק)
2:6 Set, installed (נסך)	1:5 Will not stand/be established (לא־יקמו)
2:7b–9 Ruling (various images)	2:1–3 Ruled over (various images, 2:10–12)
2:12 Having a refuge (חסה, 1:6)	2:12 Way is perishing (תאבדו דרך, 1:6)

This thematic link which makes use of a common imagery—the success and permanence of the righteous contrasted with the fruitless and fleeting activity of the wicked—adds to the impression that these two poems are connected

> The relationship of the two psalms thus appears to be closer than simple recurrences of vocabulary or allusions to themes would permit one to imagine. The righteous and the anointed one experience very similar trials and opposition, but the covenant of God is promised to them, and therewith success and prosperity, as contrasted with their adversaries who, if they persist in their opposition, can only run headlong to destruction.[75]

It seems that the close affinity of these psalms goes beyond the realms of reasonable coincidence, but, rather, reflects a deliberate attempt to link these poetic works. Indeed, such is the degree of overlap between Pss 1 and 2 that there have been suggestions that at some point they were in fact a single composition.[76] However, the style and genre are too diverse for this to be the case.[77] The best conclusion seems to be that these psalms were deliberately placed alongside one another because of their lexical, thematic and theological similarity as the dual introduction to the Psalter.[78] The question remains, why

---

[75] Auffret, *Literary Structure*, 31–34.
[76] Brownlee, "Psalms 1–2," 321–25.
[77] John T. Willis, "Psalm 1—An Entity," *ZAW* 91, no. 3 (1979): 381–401.
[78] It is unclear whether this phenomenon arose from the placement of two similar, pre-existing psalms alongside one another or if, for example, Psalm 1 was specifically written in order to complement Psalm 2 in introduction to the Psalms (see Mitchell, *Message*, 73–74, and Nogalski, "From Psalm to Psalms," 53–54).

so? Why is the reader being encouraged to put on these particular "hermeneutical spectacles?" It is to this question that we now turn our attention.

4. Theological Significance of a Dtr Introduction to the Psalter

One of Whybray's criticisms of the approach of the canonical school to the study of the Psalter is that most of the scholars are agreed that Pss 1 and 2 form a joint introduction to the Psalter but that none of them suggest what this is meant to communicate.[79] Whilst this criticism is not strictly true,[80] there is scope for more discussion of the significance of this introduction to the Psalms and its implications for the reader's understanding of the Psalms as a book.

4.1 Deuteronomic Worldview

The placement of Psalms 1 and 2 at the head of the Psalter points towards a particular agenda, which the reader is to look out for in reading the book: that is, a Deuteronomic worldview. The voice of Deuteronomy speaks clearly in Pss 1 and 2, resulting in the presentation of a holistic worldview which is reflective of certain Deuteronomic concerns:

1. The individual's devotion to Yahweh;
2. The centrality of torah in the life of the OT believer;
3. The rule and reign of Yahweh over the whole of creation;
4. The king, as Yahweh's co-regent, is completely reliant upon him;
5. The idea of choice between "two ways" to follow God or to rebel.

These themes present a Deuteronomic agenda (perhaps more specifically a DtrN agenda), thus providing a context for the reader, as she approaches the variegated content of the Psalms. Not that the voice of Deuteronomy excludes all others: by no means would this be the case.[81] However, the introduction is a constant call to return to the fundamentals of the Hebrew faith, as presented in the Book of Deuteronomy. Therefore, the laments (individual or corporate) are real and reflect the trials of life, yet the introduction puts that cry of pain in

---

[79] Whybray, *Psalms as a Book*, 41.

[80] See Miller, "Beginning," 85 and *Interpreting*, 86. Also Mays, *Psalms*, 40–41 and McCann, *Theological Introduction*, 41.

[81] As is seen in the Wisdom content also apparent in Pss 1 and 2 (see Gerald T. Sheppard, *Wisdom as a Hermeneutical Construct: A Study in Sapientializing of the Old Testament* [BZAW 151; Berlin: Walter de Gruyter, 1980], 139–44).

context—Yahweh, the covenant God, still reigns. Or the confusion of the pious as they witness the prosperity of the wicked (e.g., Ps 73) is read through the paradigm of the two ways (as presented in this Dtr introduction). Thus the reader is reminded of the temporality of the way of the wicked, and the blessing of Yahweh upon those who follow his way. Quite simply, this Deuteronomic introduction to the Psalter provides a consistent backdrop to the many voices found in the Psalms—the voice of the royalist, the scribe, the cultic priest are all allowed to speak freely, yet at the same time kingship and wisdom and the cult are to be understood from a Deuteronomic perspective.[82] As such this type of introduction does not limit the reader's engagement with the text of the Psalms, but rather encourages holistic engagement with every aspect of the piety and theology of the Psalter. Therefore, the reader of the Psalms, like the reader of Deuteronomy is to live out "the fear of the Lord" in every aspect of his life.[83]

4.2 KINGSHIP LAW AND THE PSALMS

The eschatological rereading of the royal psalms (discussed above) plays an important role role in understanding the function of Pss 1 and 2 as an introduction to the Book of Psalms. This is particularly so because of the inclusion of Ps 2 as part of this introduction. If, as is broadly assumed, this introduction was added in the post-exilic period, why should a royal psalm be included? Why include a psalm which celebrates the victories and international rule of the Davidic king at a time when this king is no more? What is more, why is it placed in such a prominent position?

As suggested above, the simplest answer to this question is that Ps 2 was included as part of a *Deuteronomic* agenda of future hope in a restored kingdom where Yahweh's reign is represented once more by the co-regency of his kingly messiah on earth.[84] However, this eschatological rereading should be understood not so much in the terms of the history of Israel, but more in terms of the ideal of the Deuteronomic Kingship Law (Deut 17:14–20). This is not a

---

[82] It must be added that this Deuteronomic voice cannot be equated with simple legalism (as some of the scholars working in the Psalms seem to imply). Rather, this refers to a whole life engagement in the ways of Yahweh. It refers to a holistic application of the torah in a way that effects every area of the believers being.

[83] Miller, "Deuteronomy and Psalms," 15, passim.

[84] Mitchell, *Message*, 85–86; Childs, *IOTS*, 516–17; Howard, *Structure*, 302–05 and Mays, *The Lord Reigns*, 96–98.

Torah-Kingship Theme in Psalms 1–2

longing after Josiah or Hezekiah or even the great king David. Rather, the introduction to the Psalter presents an eschatological hope for a new leader who would be the fulfillment of the Law of the King. The introduction acknowledges the voice of royal hope which seems to play a prominent role in the editorial placement of the psalms,[85] but it puts a particular slant on the understanding of the psalmic presentation of kingship. Pss 1 and 2 do not reflect some form of reconstituted hope based in the historical kings of the past, rather this is a hope based in the Kingship Law as the "ideal" of monarchic rule.

The parallels are easily spotted: Ps 1 celebrates the law of the Lord and Ps 2 the reign of Yahweh and the co-reign of his anointed king. The only task assigned the king in Deut 17 is that he should "write out for himself on a scroll a copy of this law" (v 18). That scroll is "to be with him and he is to read it all the days of his life, so that he may learn to revere Yahweh his God and follow carefully all the words of this law and the decrees... and he is not to turn from it to the left or to the right" (vv 19–20). Deut 17 presents a picture of kingship which cannot be separated from a life of devotion to Yahweh through the study and keeping of his torah: Ps 1 presents a picture of exactly this type of torah-piety.[86] Ps 2 represents an eschatological hope for the restoration of Yahweh's king, but he is a king who is entirely dependent upon God rather than the trappings of kingship, as is the instruction of Deut 17:16–17. Furthermore, he is to be an exemplar of the piety represented by Ps 1, as is indicated by the close lexical links between the two psalms, in much the same way as Deut 17 presents Israel's king as an example of true devotion to Yahweh. This is seen in the thematic links between Ps 1 and Deut 17:

Psalm 1	Deut 17
בתורת יהוה חפצו	וכתב לו את־משנה התורה הזאת
בתורתו יהגה יומם ולילה	וקרא בו כל־ימי חייו

Obviously, these connections are not exact, lexically speaking, but the emphasis is essentially the same; i.e., a torah-based piety in following the ways of Yahweh.[87] The connection of Pss 1 and 2 and the Dtr Law of the King raises

---

[85] Wilson, *Editing*, 208–14; "Use of Royal Psalms."
[86] Mays, "Place of the Torah-Psalms," 4.
[87] Obviously, the association between the torah-kingship psalm groupings and the Kingship Law requires more detailed discussion than is offered at this stage. These connections are merely mentioned here, but will be developed in more detail in chapter 5.

68   *The King as Exemplar*

a number of hermeneutical points worthy of discussion. Miller comments upon some of these hermeneutical issues:

> At this point, therefore, one recognizes a major link between Psalms 1 and 2 and that is provided by Deuteronomy in its latest editorial stages.... In the Deuteronomic ideal of human rule, the *'îš* or "one" whose delight is in the law of the Lord, and who meditates on it continually, is the king. The ideal ruler is thus the model Israelite.[88]

We shall discuss the democratising principles at work in Deuteronomy and the torah-kingship psalms at a later point,[89] however, the important point for now is Miller's suggestion that the Deuteronomic paradigm for kingship is the conceptual paradigm behind this introduction to the Book of Psalms. Furthermore, Howard writes:

> YHWH's anointed king in Psalm 2 functions as the *ideal exemplar* of a divinely appointed king; he exemplifies in his own person the qualities of the righteous one in Psalm 1. The focus on study of the Torah links Psalm 1 back to the Charter for Kingship in Deut 17:14–20, where the ideal king is instructed to make the study of Torah his all-consuming concern, leaving military and other concerns to YHWH.[90]

Mays has made similar observations:

> An important connection between the introductory Psalm 1 and the psalms on the Davidic kingship should be noted. *The anointed king is portrayed as one who conforms to the instruction given at the book's beginning.* The law of the LORD is the norm by which Davidic kings are to be judged (89:30–33). The king loves righteousness and hates wickedness (45:7). He keeps the ways of the LORD whose ordinances are always before him (18:20–22). When other psalms attributed to David are brought into consideration, like Ps 15 and 19, the psalmic David appears as teacher and advocate of torah. In the Psalter as a whole, the messiah is one who keeps and teaches the torah and combines in his identity and role the two emphases of the twofold introduction to the Psalter.[91]

There is, therefore, a two-fold purpose in this dual introduction to the Psalms based in the Deuteronomic law of the king. First, to encourage the readers to adopt a Dtr worldview, especially a piety that is rooted in the torah of the Lord. Just as the king was to be commanded to keep the law, so every individual (איש) is to be commended for doing so, for emulating the example that the king

---

[88] Miller, "Beginning," 91.
[89] See chapter 7, below.
[90] Howard, *Structure*, 201.
[91] Mays, *The Lord Reigns*, 125.

was supposed to set. Secondly, these psalms reflect an eschatological hope in a coming messiah who will be the one who meets the Deuteronomic ideal of kingship. Mitchell has expressed the latter point in this way:

> There is good ground, as was noted above, for regarding Psalm 2, together with Psalm 1, as functioning as an introduction to the Psalter. As such, it sets the tone and determines the interpretation of what is to follow.... The combined effect of Psalms 1 and 2 together may be that Psalm 1 foretells the triumph of the righteous divine king who meditates on YHWH's Torah, and Psalm 2 shows him going forth to battle with its predicted outcome. Or Psalm 1 delineates the person who will share in the king's triumph, possibly as a warrior, and Psalm 2 pronounces that one's blessedness. The two psalms together announce that the ensuing collection is a handbook for the eschatological wars of the Lord, describing the coming events and the YHWH-allegiance required of those who would triumph.[92]

Mitchell goes on to highlight the eschatological elements present in Pss 1 and 2, and that is an important part of the interpretative model being set up by the introduction. However, we must not forget that the practical reality of the Psalms, which were just as much a handbook of individual and corporate piety at the time of their closure into final book form, as they are in Jewish and Christian communities today. The Old Testament community of faith were not simply to wait for the coming of a *truly* ideal king, but they were also to follow that example of piety which was the basis for the ideal of kingship.

5. CONCLUSION

The dual introduction to the Book of Psalms is steeped in concepts borrowed from Deuteronomic theology. More specifically the juxtaposition of a torah psalm with a royal psalm in this introduction seems to direct the reader towards the Deuteronomic Law of the King found in Deut 17:14–20.[93] The reasons for this paradigm being placed at the head of the Psalter reflect two of the primary theological concerns of the period of the Psalter's closure:

1. The torah as the proper rule for the life of Israel, and;
2. Eschatological hope in the "renewal" of the Davidic kingship.

---

[92] Mitchell, *Message*, 87.
[93] This passage also needs to be considered in its own context, which will follow the analysis of the remain torah-kingship psalm groupings.

Returning to Miller's rhetorical question, asked in the introduction to this thesis,[94] it seems that Pss 1 and 2 do, indeed, point the reader towards Deuteronomy's theology of kingship, but are they alone in doing so? Our initial, superficial reading of the Psalms suggested that Pss 18–21 reflect a similar torah-kingship focus: now we must see whether this impression bears up to closer scrutiny, as we turn to the exegetical study of these psalms.

---

[94] See above, p 5.

CHAPTER 3
TORAH-KINGSHIP THEME IN PSALMS 18–21

1. INTRODUCTION

Following on from the examination of the Deuteronomic themes present in Psalms 1 and 2 as an introduction to the Psalter, we now turn to the next group of psalms where the themes of kingship and torah dominate: Psalms 18–21. This psalm grouping forms the central section of a larger pre-existing collection of psalms (Pss 15–24) which has, at some later date, been incorporated into Book I of the Psalter. Psalms 18, 20 and 21 are all royal psalms and Psalm 19 is, of course, one of the Psalter's three torah psalms which celebrate Yahweh's revelation. This juxtaposition of kingship and torah psalms, at least on a superficial level, appears to echo the introductory themes of Pss 1 and 2, which (as was discussed in the previous chapter) reflects a Deuteronomic agenda in the redaction of the final form of the Psalter. This Dtr agenda apparent in Pss 1 and 2 seems, in particular, to resonate with the theology and priorities of the Kingship Law, which gives rise to a question: "Could it be that the next group of psalms which focus on these dual themes of kingship and torah also reflect this same editorial concern?" In seeking to answer this question, the exegetical study of Pss 18–21 will follow the same approach as did the examination of Pss 1–2; namely, 1) to see if a general Deuteronomic milieu is present in the content of these psalms, and 2) if so, to analyse any possible overlap with the Kingship Law of Deut 17:14–20.[1]

---

[1] As was the case in the previous chapter, comparison with the Law of the King will be at the level of observation at this stage. Detailed examination of the actual overlap with Deut 17:14–20 will be made in chapter 5, where this passage is examined in detail in its proper context within the book of Deuteronomy.

2. Choice of Psalms 18–21

The first question to be addressed, however, is the choice of psalms in this psalm grouping. Why should these four psalms be singled out for analysis? Commentators have pointed out a kingship-torah link between Psalms 18 and 19,[2] but why should Psalms 20 and 21 be included in this discussion? It is important that the current study does not import external paradigms and impose these upon the text of the Psalter. If this theory is to be established, the voice of the Psalms must be allowed to speak for itself. Therefore, we must begin our discussion with a reminder of the rationale behind the choice of this psalm grouping.

The selection of texts for examination is entirely dependent upon the goal of our study. In the Kingship Law of Deut 17:14–20 the king is presented as one who is devoted to the study and application of the torah of Yahweh—king and torah bound together. There is, at least, *prima facie* evidence of deliberate juxtaposition of kingship and torah themes within the Psalter, and the goal of this study is the detailed, exegetical examination of these texts in an attempt to ascertain whether or not there is sufficient lexical and thematic evidence to indicate that deliberate concatenation of these psalms—following the Kingship Law as an intellectual construct—was likely. The theme of kingship is a broad one within the Psalter: royal psalms seem to dominate the first three books of the canonical Book of Psalms, and this possible link with the Dtr Law of the King is merely one aspect of a broader theology of kingship apparent in the Psalter. Therefore, it is the smaller category of torah psalms which dictates the choice of material for examination. Whilst there are fourteen psalms within the canonical Psalter which contain some element of torah-theology,[3] there are only three psalms which are centred upon Yahweh's torah—namely, Pss 1, 19 and 119. Thus, if we are to expect deliberate editorial juxtaposition of kingship-torah themes, we should expect it around these three psalms. Hence our discussion is drawn towards Psalm 19.

---

[2] For example, Westermann, *Praise and Lament*, 256–57.
[3] Mays, "Place of the Torah-Psalms," 12. Interestingly, this list includes another of the psalms in the grouping under consideration—Psalm 18—and we shall see that the torah theme is significant if we are to come to a proper understanding of the theology of this psalm also.

However, the question remains why these four psalms as a grouping, rather than simply the analysis of Psalms 18 and 19?[4] To answer this question, we have to look at Psalms 18–21 within their broader context as part of Book I of the Psalter. Pierre Auffret and Patrick Miller have pointed out that Psalms 18–21 form the focal point of a collection of psalms which are arranged in a chiastic or envelope pattern.[5] They suggest that Pss 15–24, in fact, represent an independent collection of psalms which was later included within Book I, and point out an interesting pattern of parallels in content between these psalms. Psalms 15 and 24 are both Entrance Psalms, which discuss issues of righteousness and entrance into God's presence in worship—these two psalms demarcate the beginning and end of this psalm grouping. Psalms 16 and 23 are both psalms of comfort, which celebrate Yahweh's protection in the face of danger. Psalms 17 and 22 are both psalms of lament, which express the depths of despair and anxiety felt by the psalmist. This brings us to the grouping of psalms which is to come under examination: Psalms 18 and 20–21 (many commentators highlight the close association which exists between Psalms 20 and 21[6]) are all royal psalms, what is more they all appear to be kingship psalms connected with Yahweh's deliverance of his "anointed one" in the context of battle.[7] Psalm 19 is the central psalm in this chiastic pattern, a torah psalm, and both Auffret and Miller suggest that this indicates the thematic centrality of the torah of Yahweh within

---

[4] Claus Westermann was considerably ahead of his time in promoting the discussion of the placement of the psalms within the Psalter at a time when this was not a popular endeavour. Westermann rejected the common notion that there was no significance in the placement of the psalms and included a chapter on "The Formation of the Psalter" in his work *Praise and Lament*. In this chapter Westermann suggests the deliberate juxtaposition of Pss 18 and 19 based on form-critical (*Gattungen*) considerations (*Praise and Lament*, 256n18, 257). However, it appears that there may be broader organisational factors at work with regard to these psalms in the context of a pre-existent, chiastically-arranged, collection of psalms which would justify the expansion of our examination beyond that indicated by genre considerations alone (see chapter 6 below, *The Editorial Placement of the Torah-Kingship Psalm Groupings*, for more detailed discussion concerning the formation of the Psalter).

[5] Auffret, *La Sagesse*, 407–38; Miller, "Kingship," 127–42.

[6] See, for example, Mays, *Psalms*, 90; McCann, *Psalms*, 757; Kraus, *Psalms*, 281. Older commentaries have also drawn attention to the links between these two psalms, e.g. Kirkpatrick, *Psalms*, 106.

[7] Exegetical examination will show that there are several lexical and thematic links between these psalms which go some way to support Auffret and Miller's suggestion of deliberate concatenation.

this small collection.[8] Therefore, it seems appropriate that we should examine all four of these psalms (18–21) in order to see how they interact with one another and also to see if they do reflect themes which draw upon Deuteronomy's Kingship Law. As well as consideration of the interaction between these four psalms, comparison will be made with the content and message of Pss 1–2. If the juxtaposition of kingship and torah psalms is the result of editorial activity, then similarities of emphasis should be apparent between these groups of psalms, therefore the content of each group will be compared with the others.

3. Analysis of Psalm 18

BHS	Translation
לַמְנַצֵּחַ לְעֶבֶד יְהוָה לְדָוִד אֲשֶׁר דִּבֶּר לַיהוָה אֶת־דִּבְרֵי הַשִּׁירָה הַזֹּאת בְּיוֹם הִצִּיל־יְהוָה אוֹתוֹ מִכַּף כָּל־אֹיְבָיו וּמִיַּד שָׁאוּל: וַיֹּאמַר אֶרְחָמְךָ יְהוָה חִזְקִי: יְהוָה סַלְעִי וּמְצוּדָתִי וּמְפַלְטִי אֵלִי צוּרִי אֶחֱסֶה־בּוֹ מָגִנִּי וְקֶרֶן־יִשְׁעִי מִשְׂגַּבִּי:	1 To the director of music. Of David, the servant of Yahweh, who spoke the words of this song to Yahweh on the day of Yahweh's deliverence of him from the hand of all his enemies and from the hand of Saul. 2 He said, I love you, O Yahweh, my strength. 3 Yahweh is my rock, my stronghold and my refuge; My God is my rock, I take refuge in him; My shield and the horn of my salvation, my refuge.
מְהֻלָּל אֶקְרָא יְהוָה וּמִן־אֹיְבַי אִוָּשֵׁעַ: אֲפָפוּנִי חֶבְלֵי־מָוֶת וְנַחֲלֵי בְלִיַּעַל יְבַעֲתוּנִי: חֶבְלֵי שְׁאוֹל סְבָבוּנִי קִדְּמוּנִי מוֹקְשֵׁי מָוֶת: בַּצַּר־לִי אֶקְרָא יְהוָה וְאֶל־אֱלֹהַי אֲשַׁוֵּעַ יִשְׁמַע מֵהֵיכָלוֹ קוֹלִי וְשַׁוְעָתִי לְפָנָיו תָּבוֹא בְאָזְנָיו:	4 I called out to Yahweh, being worthy of praise; Then from my enemies, I was saved. 5 The cords of death encompassed me; And the torrents of destruction overwhelmed me. 6 The cords of Sheol surrounded me; The snares of death confronted me. 7 In my straits, I called to Yahweh and to my God I cried out for help; He heard my voice from his temple, my cry for help before him came to his ears
וַתִּגְעַשׁ וַתִּרְעַשׁ הָאָרֶץ וּמוֹסְדֵי הָרִים יִרְגָּזוּ וַיִּתְגָּעֲשׁוּ כִּי־חָרָה לוֹ:	8 The earth shook and quaked and the foundations of the hills trembled; They trembled because he himself was angry.

---
[8] Auffret, *La Sagesse*, 407–38; Miller, "Kingship," 127.

עָלָה עָשָׁן בְּאַפּוֹ וְאֵשׁ־מִפִּיו תֹּאכֵל גֶּחָלִים בָּעֲרוּ מִמֶּנּוּ:
וַיֵּט שָׁמַיִם וַיֵּרַד וַעֲרָפֶל תַּחַת רַגְלָיו:
וַיִּרְכַּב עַל־כְּרוּב וַיָּעֹף וַיֵּדֶא עַל־כַּנְפֵי־רוּחַ:
יָשֶׁת חֹשֶׁךְ סִתְרוֹ סְבִיבוֹתָיו סֻכָּתוֹ חֶשְׁכַת־מַיִם עָבֵי שְׁחָקִים:
מִנֹּגַהּ נֶגְדּוֹ עָבָיו עָבְרוּ בָּרָד וְגַחֲלֵי־אֵשׁ:
וַיַּרְעֵם בַּשָּׁמַיִם יְהוָה וְעֶלְיוֹן יִתֵּן קֹלוֹ בָּרָד וְגַחֲלֵי־אֵשׁ:
וַיִּשְׁלַח חִצָּיו וַיְפִיצֵם וּבְרָקִים רָב וַיְהֻמֵּם:

9 Smoke rose from his nostril and fire from his mouth consumed; Burning coals blazed from him.
10 He parted the skies and came down; And a cloud was under his feet.
11 He mounted the cherubim and flew; He flew swiftly upon the wings of the wind.
12 He set darkness as his covering all around him; dark rain clouds.
13 From the brightness of his presence cloud, hail and burning coals pass through
14 And Yahweh thunders from the heavens and the Most High gives forth his voice; Hail and coals of fire!
15 He sends his arrows and he causes them to scatter; and many lightening bolts confuse them.

וַיֵּרָאוּ אֲפִיקֵי מַיִם וַיִּגָּלוּ מוֹסְדוֹת תֵּבֵל מִגַּעֲרָתְךָ יְהוָה מִנִּשְׁמַת רוּחַ אַפֶּךָ:
יִשְׁלַח מִמָּרוֹם יִקָּחֵנִי יַמְשֵׁנִי מִמַּיִם רַבִּים:
יַצִּילֵנִי מֵאֹיְבִי עָז וּמִשֹּׂנְאַי כִּי־אָמְצוּ מִמֶּנִּי:
יְקַדְּמוּנִי בְיוֹם־אֵידִי וַיְהִי־יְהוָה לְמִשְׁעָן לִי:
וַיּוֹצִיאֵנִי לַמֶּרְחָב יְחַלְּצֵנִי כִּי חָפֵץ בִּי:

16 And channels of water appeared and the foundations of the earth were revealed; At your rebuke, O Yahweh, at the blast of the breath of your nostril.
17 He reached out from on high and he took [hold of] me; He drew me out from the great waters.
18 He delivered me from my mighty enemy; From the ones who hate me, because they are mightier than I.
19 They confronted me on the day of my disaster; but Yahweh was my support.
20 He brought me out to a broad place; He rescued me because he delighted in me.

יִגְמְלֵנִי יְהוָה כְּצִדְקִי כְּבֹר יָדַי יָשִׁיב לִי:
כִּי־שָׁמַרְתִּי דַּרְכֵי יְהוָה וְלֹא־רָשַׁעְתִּי מֵאֱלֹהָי:
כִּי כָל־מִשְׁפָּטָיו לְנֶגְדִּי וְחֻקֹּתָיו לֹא־אָסִיר מֶנִּי:
וָאֱהִי תָמִים עִמּוֹ וָאֶשְׁתַּמֵּר מֵעֲוֹנִי:
וַיָּשֶׁב־יְהוָה לִי כְצִדְקִי כְּבֹר יָדַי לְנֶגֶד עֵינָיו:

21 Yahweh has dealt bountifully with me, according to my righteousness; According to the cleanness of my hands he repaid me.
22 For I have kept the ways of Yahweh; And I have not done evil against my God
23 For all his judgements are before me; I have not turned away from his decrees.
24 I have been blameless with him; And I have kept myself from sin.
25 Yahweh has rewarded me according to my righteousness; According to the cleanness of my hands before his eyes.

The King as Exemplar

עִם־חָסִיד תִּתְחַסָּד עִם־גְּבַר תָּמִים תִּתַּמָּם:
עִם־נָבָר תִּתְבָּרָר וְעִם־עִקֵּשׁ תִּתְפַּתָּל:
כִּי־אַתָּה עַם־עָנִי תוֹשִׁיעַ וְעֵינַיִם רָמוֹת תַּשְׁפִּיל:
כִּי־אַתָּה תָּאִיר נֵרִי יְהוָה אֱלֹהַי יַגִּיהַּ חָשְׁכִּי:
כִּי־בְךָ אָרֻץ גְּדוּד וּבֵאלֹהַי אֲדַלֶּג־שׁוּר:

26 To the faithful, you show yourself faithful; To the blameless, you show yourself blameless.
27 To the pure, you show yourself pure. But to the twisted you show yourself shrewd.
28 For you save a humble people, but proud eyes you bring low.
29 For you make my lamp shine, O Yahweh; My God makes my darkness light.
30 Because with you I can run through a troop; And in my God I can leap over a wall.

הָאֵל תָּמִים דַּרְכּוֹ אִמְרַת־יְהוָה צְרוּפָה מָגֵן הוּא לְכֹל הַחֹסִים בּוֹ:
כִּי מִי אֱלוֹהַּ מִבַּלְעֲדֵי יְהוָה וּמִי צוּר זוּלָתִי אֱלֹהֵינוּ:
הָאֵל הַמְאַזְּרֵנִי חָיִל וַיִּתֵּן תָּמִים דַּרְכִּי:
מְשַׁוֶּה רַגְלַי כָּאַיָּלוֹת וְעַל בָּמֹתַי יַעֲמִידֵנִי:
מְלַמֵּד יָדַי לַמִּלְחָמָה וְנִחֲתָה קֶשֶׁת־נְחוּשָׁה זְרוֹעֹתָי:
וַתִּתֶּן־לִי מָגֵן יִשְׁעֶךָ וִימִינְךָ תִסְעָדֵנִי וְעַנְוַתְךָ תַרְבֵּנִי:
תַּרְחִיב צַעֲדִי תַחְתָּי וְלֹא מָעֲדוּ קַרְסֻלָּי:

31 As for God, his ways are perfect; The words of Yahweh are flawless; He is a shield to all those who take refuge in him.
32 For who is God apart from Yahweh? And who is a rock apart from our God?
33 As for God, he girds me with strength; And he makes my way perfect.
34 He places my feet like deer; And upon high places he makes me stand.
35 He trains my hands for battle; And my arms can bend a bow of bronze.
36 You give me the shield of your salvation, and your right hand supports me; And your answering makes me great.
37 You broaden my stride under me; And my ankles do not turn over.

אֶרְדּוֹף אוֹיְבַי וְאַשִּׂיגֵם וְלֹא־אָשׁוּב עַד־כַּלּוֹתָם:
אֶמְחָצֵם וְלֹא־יֻכְלוּ קוּם יִפְּלוּ תַּחַת רַגְלָי:
וַתְּאַזְּרֵנִי חַיִל לַמִּלְחָמָה תַּכְרִיעַ קָמַי תַּחְתָּי:
וְאֹיְבַי נָתַתָּה לִּי עֹרֶף וּמְשַׂנְאַי אַצְמִיתֵם:
יְשַׁוְּעוּ וְאֵין־מוֹשִׁיעַ עַל־יְהוָה וְלֹא עָנָם:
וְאֶשְׁחָקֵם כְּעָפָר עַל־פְּנֵי־רוּחַ כְּטִיט חוּצוֹת אֲרִיקֵם:
תְּפַלְּטֵנִי מֵרִיבֵי עָם תְּשִׂימֵנִי לְרֹאשׁ גּוֹיִם

38 I pursued my enemies and overtook them; And I did not return until they were finished.
39 I struck them and they could not rise; They fell under my feet.
40 And you girded me with strength for the battle; You made my adversaries bow down before me.
41 My enemies turned and ran; And those who hated me I destroyed.
42 They cried for help, but there was no deliverer—unto Yahweh, but he did not answer them.
43 So I beat till they were like dust carried

עַם לֹא־יָדַעְתִּי יַעַבְדוּנִי:
לְשֵׁמַע אֹזֶן יִשָּׁמְעוּ לִי בְּנֵי־נֵכָר יְכַחֲשׁוּ־לִי:
בְּנֵי־נֵכָר יִבֹּלוּ וְיַחְרְגוּ מִמִּסְגְּרוֹתֵיהֶם:

on the wind—like mud outside I poured them out.
44 You have delivered me from the struggles of people—you placed me at the head of nations; People I do not know serve me.
45 They listen carefully to me—foreigners cringe before me.
46 Foreigners loose heart and come quaking from their stronghold.

חַי־יְהוָה וּבָרוּךְ צוּרִי וְיָרוּם אֱלֹהֵי יִשְׁעִי:
הָאֵל הַנּוֹתֵן נְקָמוֹת לִי וַיַּדְבֵּר עַמִּים תַּחְתָּי:
מְפַלְּטִי מֵאֹיְבָי אַף מִן־קָמַי תְּרוֹמְמֵנִי מֵאִישׁ חָמָס תַּצִּילֵנִי:
עַל־כֵּן אוֹדְךָ בַגּוֹיִם יְהוָה וּלְשִׁמְךָ אֲזַמֵּרָה:
מִגְדֹּל יְשׁוּעוֹת מַלְכּוֹ וְעֹשֶׂה חֶסֶד לִמְשִׁיחוֹ לְדָוִד וּלְזַרְעוֹ עַד־עוֹלָם:

47 Yahweh lives! And blessed be my Rock! And let the God of my salvation be exalted!
48 As for God, who gives me vengeance, Who subdues people under me.
49 Who delivers me from my enemies! Surely, you have exalted me above my enemies; From the man of violence you have delivered me.
50 Therefore, I will give thanks to you among the nations, O Yahweh; And I will sing praises to your name.
51 He gives great victories to his king! He shows steadfast love to his anointed—to David and to his seed forever.

Psalm 18[9] is undoubtedly one of the most discussed psalms in the Psalter. Kenneth Kuntz, for example, describes it as a "Hebrew poem that continues to fascinate biblical scholars."[10] From a variety of perspectives, Psalm 18 provokes debate. First, it is one of very few psalms which is cited almost in its entirety in a narrative passage (2 Samuel 22), therefore it is of great interest from a source-critical perspective and is often discussed in this light. Secondly, it is a lengthy psalm whose themes seem to be picked up on by other Old Testament writers, so there is much scope for assessing the intertextuality of Psalm 18; for example,

---

[9] The text of Ps 18 is fairly straightforward, with most of the textual questions revolving around relatively minor differences when compared with the text of 2 Samuel 22. בן־נכר (vv 45–46) may be better rendered "enemies" rather than "foreigners" (Eaton, *Psalms*, 64) also it is unclear whether v 51 speaks of מִגְדֹּל יְשׁוּעוֹת "a tower of victories" according to the Kethib or מַגְדִּיל יְשׁוּעוֹת "he gives great victories" according to the Qere. In terms of structure, the major stanzas are indicated by the divisions in the translation.

[10] J. Kenneth Kuntz, "Review of 'The Psalms and Their Readers: Interpretive Strategies for Psalm 18,'" *Int* 48 (1994): 426.

the link between the book of Habakkuk and Psalm 18 is much discussed. Thirdly, the mixture of genres has prompted much debate from a form-critical perspective; is this a hymn of praise or a song of thanksgiving? Are these the words of the king, and what is the role of the theophany in this psalm? Many of the classic questions of form-critical studies concerning *Gattungen* and *Sitz im Leben* can be richly applied to Psalm 18. Fourthly, the length of this psalm and its somewhat unusual composition make Psalm 18 a "classic text" for rhetorical-critical assessment; how does this psalm break down into stanzas? Is this, in fact, two psalms which have been joined together by an editor, or a single work with a strong and deliberate breakdown into stanzas which reflect a thematic progression? It was the richness of Psalm 18 from many methodological perspectives which inspired Donald Berry to choose this psalm as his test case for the application and evaluation of various methods for the analysis of psalms.[11]

3.1 DEUTERONOMIC BACKGROUND TO PSALM 18

Our focus, however, is on the theological analysis of this psalm. As with Pss 1–2, if Psalm 18 is to be seen as part of a Dtr redaction of the Psalter, its content should be expected to reflect the concerns associated with that school of thought. So does the content of Ps 18 reflect a Dtr worldview?

3.1.1   APPELLATIVES

Perhaps the most striking feature of Ps 18 is the rich and varied use of appellatives in addressing Yahweh. Seldom, if anywhere, do we find such a wealth of metaphors to describe Yahweh and the psalmist's relationship with him. Throughout the psalm Yahweh is variously described as the psalmist's "rock" (סלעי and צורי), "stronghold" (מצודתי), "refuge" (מפלטי and משׂגבי), "shield" (מגני), "horn of salvation" (קרן־ישעי) and "God of salvation" (אלוהי ישעי). Whilst some of the images used are fairly common, such a preponderance of appellatives is rare within the Psalter.[12] It is in this use of appellatives that many of the commentators find a strong link between Psalm 18 and Deuteronomy (esp. Deut 32).

---

[11] Berry, *Psalms and Readers*.

[12] Each of these terms appears several times within the canonical Psalter, but the only other psalms where there is any degree of repetition of these appellatives are Pss 31 and 71, but even here not to the same extent as is found in Ps 18. Mays, *Psalms*, 91, describes this as "the longest series of predicates for God found in the Psalter."

The idea of viewing Yahweh as one's "rock" and "refuge" reflects an attitude of dependence upon him which is viewed as commendable in the Book of Deuteronomy. Many commentators point out the link that exists between Psalm 18:3 and Deut 32:4, 18, 30–31 and 37. Each passage encourages total dependence upon Yahweh as provider of refuge and strength. Mays puts it thus:

> Verse 2 [MT, v 3] extends "my strength" [18:2] into confessional praise that recites the longest series of predicates for God found in the Psalter. Most are metaphors identifying the LORD as provider of protection. All are qualified by the possessive pronoun "my" so that their repetition emphasizes the dependence of the person of the psalmist on the person of God. The metaphor "my rock" (represented by two Hebrew words) is the most frequent in Psalms and in poetry elsewhere. The metaphorical sense seems to lie in the firm and strong character of rock as support. A god is called "rock" as the deity who provides refuge for those who belong to the deity, as the references in Deuteronomy 32:4, 30–31, and 37 show.[13]

The Song of Moses in Deut 32 presents itself as an exhortation and challenge to the people of Israel, as a covenantal sign or witness calling them to faithfulness and trust in Yahweh. The Song seems to function as a paraenetic, didactic reminder to the people of Israel prior to their entry into the Promised Land, encouraging them to place their trust entirely in Yahweh and not to wander off after other gods.[14] Similarly, the king in Psalm 18 expresses just this type of ideology—in the face of his enemies, in the face of battle, he declares his trust in Yahweh alone (v 4). Whilst there are many appellatives which are used in Psalm 18, it appears that the succeeding descriptives act as extrapolations upon the theme of "my rock." In 18:3 we see that each colon begins with a declaration that God is the psalmist's "rock" (either סלעי or צורי)[15] and these general concepts are expanded upon by the use of the ensuing terms ("stronghold," "refuge" etc.). The governing thought appears to be that of Yahweh as "rock" (צור), and this is the concept which is prominent in Deut 32's call to faithfulness. So it can be seen that the theological backdrop to the use of these appellatives in Ps 18 appears to be drawn from a Deuteronomic idea of trust in Yahweh.[16] Of

---

[13] Mays, *Psalms*, 91.

[14] Christopher J. H. Wright, *Deuteronomy* (NIBCOT; Peabody, MA/Carlisle: Hendrickson/Paternoster Press, 1996), 298, 306.

[15] These two Hebrew words should be understood as poetic synonyms in this context, both reflecting the same idea—Yahweh as the psalmist's "Rock."

[16] Most of the commentators make this connection. See, for example, Charles A. Briggs, and E. G. Briggs, *The Book of Psalms* (ICC; Edinburgh: T&T Clark, 1906), 140–

course, in and of itself, this would not constitute proof of a Dtr background to Ps 18, however, the use of appellatives is merely the first of several indicators which together point to a Dtr worldview underpinning the text of this poem.

3.1.2 THEOPHANY

As one reads Psalm 18, the next striking element of the poem is the account of the theophany in vv 8–16. As is to be expected in such descriptions, this stanza is full of remarkable and supernatural images of the appearance of Yahweh in support of his king. Obviously, there are several theophanic accounts throughout the Old Testament, and there are many similarities between each of them. The theophany which is repeated most often in the pages of the Old Testament is, clearly, the account of Yahweh's appearance before the people at Mt. Horeb following their exodus from Egypt. Whilst it is difficult, if not impossible, to establish conclusively that the psalmist is drawing upon one particular theophanic description as opposed to the others, several of the commentators point out similarities between Psalm 18:9–16 and the Deuteronomic accounts of the Horeb theophany. There are two areas of lexical and thematic overlap between the book of Deuteronomy and Psalm 18 in relation to its account of the appearance of Yahweh. Firstly, Kraus and Craigie both point out that the announcement of Yahweh's intervention by way of an earthquake (18:8) is a sign which Moses draws attention to when reminding the people about the Sinai theophany in Deut 33:2–3.[17] Kraus also points out that the bright and fiery appearance (18:13) of Yahweh is reminiscent of the imagery of "dawning" in Deut 33:2.[18] The second area of theophanic overlap is pointed out by Briggs in his commentary, where he indicates similarities between the cloud imagery of Psalm 18:10 and the Deuteronomic account of the Horeb revelation in Deut 4:11 and 5:22.[19] Whilst it cannot be said that these similarities exist in parallel exclusively between the Dtr accounts and Psalm 18, it does appear that similarities may deliberately have been drawn between Deuteronomy's description of the Sinai theophany and the psalmist's representation of Yahweh's appearance in response to his cry for help in Psalm 18.

41; A. A. Anderson, *The Book of Psalms, vol. I* (NCB; London: Marshall, Morgan & Scott, 1972), 153; Kirkpatrick, *Psalms*, 87 or McCann, *Psalms*, 747.

[17] Kraus, *Psalms*, 260; Craigie, *Psalms*, 174.
[18] Kraus, *Psalms*, 260.
[19] Briggs, *Psalms*, 143.

3.1.3   TORAH CENTRE AND DECLARATION OF BLAMELESSNESS

Whilst this possible Dtr connection with the Psalm 18 theophany cannot be described as conclusive, in the succeeding verses we move into more characteristically Deuteronomic material. Ps 18:17-25 is filled with concepts which are considered to be "classically Deuteronomic." This stanza (vv 21-25) lies at the structural centre of Psalm 18, and is dominated by the type of torah-theology which was apparent in Pss 1 and 2.[20] In fact, these five verses are set out in a chiastic pattern which serves to further emphasise the significance of Yahweh's torah in the life of the king, the speaker of the psalm.

v 21   Declaration of righteousness and Yahweh's reward
   v 22   Declaration of blamelessness
      v 23   Declaration of the centrality of torah in the life of the king
   v 24   Declaration of blamelessness
v 25   Declaration of righteousness and Yahweh's reward

Berry comments upon the *structural* significance of this stanza:

> Verses 21-25 form an envelope structure (or staircase parallelism), and again, the structure occurs on the level of complete verses rather than individual lines. An outline of the strophe shows an *a b c b a* pattern with the most significant statement of righteousness in the central verse (v 23). More general claims (verses 21 and 25) frame this verse, and the closest parallel relationship shows itself in the bracketing lines (verses 22 and 24). The occurrence of this structure at the midpoint of the psalm sets it off as the structural key to the understanding of its combined themes.[21]

Mays and McCann point out the *theological* significance of this "most significant statement of righteousness in the central verse." First, Mays:

> The report of salvation is typically followed by praise of the LORD that draws implications from the experience and bears testimony to what it discloses about the LORD. That happens in this section, but in a strange way. The king begins with a recitation of his own righteousness. The explanation lies in the last line of the preceding section: "He delivered me, because he delighted in me" (see 22:8, 47:11-12). Verses 20-24 [MT 21-25] are an exposition of that sentence, a

---

[20] Berry, *Psalms and Readers*, 95; J. Kenneth Kuntz, "Psalm 18: A Rhetorical-Critical Analysis," in *Beyond Form Criticism: Essays in Old Testament Literary Criticism* (ed. P. R. House; SBTS, vol. 2; Winona Lake, IN: Eisenbrauns, 1992), 79. Kuntz, to be fair, does not explicitly highlight the centrality of this stanza, but his structural breakdown of the stanzas which make up Ps 18 indicates centrality.

[21] Berry, *Psalms and Readers*, 95.

section marked off by the theme, "The LORD dealt with me according to my righteousness" (vv 20, 24). God's deliverance was evidence of his favor, his pleasure in the king. The claim is not a crass assertion of self-righteousness by the king but a confession that he had been true to the righteousness in which the divine choice to be king had set him. He had not created the righteousness but had lived within it and according to it. *He had fulfilled the vocation given the king to embody the law of the divine king. This ideal is particularly important in the Deuteronomic tradition (Jos 1:7; 23:6; Deut 17:19-20).*[22]

McCann concurs and adds:

> Vv 20-24 [MT vv 21-25] sound like the self-righteous boasting of the king, but the chiastic structure of verses 20-24 focuses attention on v. 22 [v 23]. That is, God's "ordinances" (more literally, "justices") and "statutes" are the source of the king's "righteousness" and "cleanness" (verses 20, 24; see Psalms 24:4; 72:1). *In short, the king is simply saying that he has been what God has intended and enabled him to be (see Deut 17:18-20; Psalm 72:1-7). In fact, v 22 is reminiscent of Psalm 1:1-2; the king is constantly open to God's instruction.*[23]

Just as the king's focus on torah is characteristically Deuteronomic, so also are the claims of blamelessness and righteousness which surround the torah-centre of the chiastic structure found in these verses. Anderson, drawing upon von Rad, points out that, "it is not moral or religious perfection which is demanded from Israel, but rather an undivided commitment... to the conditions of fellowship with Yahweh."[24] (This challenge from Deut 18:13 is drawn from the very context of the kingship law [i.e. Deut 16:18–18:22]). Anderson continues that the declaration of reward received from Yahweh is not, "self-righteous boasting, but an indirect affirmation of faith in the covenant loyalty of Yahweh... the obedience to the covenant, and the consequent blessings, do not stress the merits of man, but rather the graciousness of God. Loyalty to him may become a legal righteousness, but its misunderstanding does not discredit its true function."[25] So we see that the claims of the king made in this stanza are not in

---

[22] Mays, *Psalms*, 92–93 (emphasis added).

[23] McCann, *Psalms*, 748 (emphasis mine). Miller further points out the Dtr connection in this central stanza of Ps 18: "At this point, it is important to note the echoes of Deuteronomy in these verses of Ps 18, and particularly the language of the laws of leadership reflected in the psalm. The pairing of *mispatim* and *huqqim* is familiar as the Deuteronomic designation of the statutes of the torah," ("Kingship," 129).

[24] Anderson, *Psalms*, 161.

[25] Anderson, *Psalms*, 160. Unfortunately, this true function of the Dtr constitution is often forgotten by commentators who end up presenting Dtr theology as simplistic and legalistic. As Anderson notes, Deuteronomy's "true function" is much deeper than that.

fact self-centred declarations of his own righteousness—this is not the idle boasting of kings which is so prominent in the ancient Near Eastern literature—but rather this stanza reflects an understanding of life and religion which draws upon a Deuteronomic theology of covenant allegiance.[26]

The background in the Deuteronomic theology does not end at this point in the psalm, but continues through the ensuing stanzas to the very end of the poem. The next stanza (verses 26–30) highlights the role of Yahweh in this declaration of the psalmist's "blamelessness." As Psalm 19 will show, "blamelessness" is not the same as sinlessness, and this stanza highlights the important role of Yahweh's faithfulness as the ultimate source of the king's blamelessness. This stanza is a transitional section of the poem, linking the first part of the psalm to the second, and just as it provides a summary and conclusion to the preceding verses, so it provides an introduction to the concepts to be introduced in the succeeding verses. Kraus comments on these verses:

> Yahweh's "causality in all things" sees to it that in the salvation area of צדקה the effects of God's protection and rescue reach the צדיק. On the basis of these precedents we are to understand also the statements of vv. 25 and 26. There is a single great correspondence: the דסיד [*sic.* surely חסיד] experiences God's חסד. And yet, the עקש experiences Yahweh's destructive activity. Here we are dealing neither with the principles of strict retribution... nor with the tenets of the *ius talionis*.... Rather, he who belongs to Yahweh's congregation and lives within the regulations of God's covenant, he by that very fact lives in an area of salvific power. But he who despises Yahweh excludes himself from the area of salvation. All these are regulations of the community of Yahweh that takes salvation for granted.[27]

These verses introduce us to another key aspect of Deuteronomic theology which echoes the theological introduction of Psalm 1—namely, the concept of the "two ways." Verses 26–30 make it clear that the king is the beneficiary of Yahweh's help only because he has chosen to follow faithfully in the way of the divine command.[28]

---

[26] These ideas also overlap with the hermeneutical paradigm presented in Pss 1 and 2 as an introduction to the Psalms. Further consideration of this connection with Pss 1–2 will follow the discussion of the Dtr background of Ps 18.

[27] Kraus, *Psalms*, 262–63.

[28] The mirroring style which is used to represent the two ways in these verses ("faithful... to the faithful; blameless to the blameless" etc.) is reminiscent of Deut 6:24-25 which balances the prospect of prosperity and longevity with the responsibility to keep the law and live in righteousness.

3.1.4 THEOLOGY OF THE TWO WAYS

The theology of the two ways is explicitly discussed in the following stanza (vv 31–37) which celebrates God's help for the king as a representative of the righteous, those who chose the right way. This stanza draws upon Deuteronomic concepts in its expression of the notion that as God's ways are perfect (תמים) and he makes the ways of the psalmist perfect (תמים). These are ideas which clearly reflect the Dtr presentation of life and religious purity found in Pss 1 and 2.

> The salvation is a vindication of the Messiah, a revelation of God's "delight" in his king (v 19). The subject of the divine delight is a coherence between the way of the Messiah and the way of the Lord. Both are "perfect" in their ways (vv 23–30; the Hebrew word is *tamim*, translated "blameless" in v. 23 and "perfect" in v 30 by NRSV). The Messiah has been perfect in the righteousness of holding to the ways of the Lord known through the Lord's ordinances and statutes. He has been obedient to the will of the divine sovereignty (vv 20–24). The Lord is *perfect* in the consistency of his rule and the correspondence between what he promises and does (vv 25–30). In the salvation of the Messiah, the *"perfection"* of the faithfulness of the Messiah and the faithfulness of God is known.[29]

Briggs and Anderson also call attention to the almost formulaic interaction between the "perfection" of God and of the psalmist and, once again, associate this connection with the theology of Deuteronomy.[30] This declaration of the source of the psalmist's blamelessness appears to be drawn, again, from the Song of Moses (Deut 32:4). In Ps 18:31 the psalmist, having earlier described God as his צוּר, declares הָאֵל תָּמִים דַּרְכּוֹ ("As for God, his ways are perfect") which is strikingly similar to Deut 32:4 where the Song of Moses proclaims הַצּוּר תָּמִים פָּעֳלוֹ ("As for the Rock, his works are perfect"). Further connection with Deuteronomy 32 and its presentation of the two ways is, perhaps, represented in the use of אֱלוֹהַּ in reference to God (vv 29–30)—this uncommon form of "God" is also used in Deut 32:15 as part of Moses' presentation of the one who rejects Yahweh's perfect way. In addition the psalmist describes those who reject God's way as "twisted" or "perverse" (עקשׁ, Ps 18:27)—a rather uncommon term paral-

---

[29] Mays, *The Lord Reigns*, 104. Mays further comments in his commentary, "The concluding exclamation (v 30) states the theme of the whole: 'This God—his way is perfect.' (The same theological sentence is the theme of the great song at the end of Deuteronomy, chap. 32 v 4). The term 'perfect' (*tamim*) means 'whole, of a piece, integral.' *Tamim* marks the character of one whose conduct is coherent, consistent, reliable," (*Psalms*, 93).

[30] Briggs, *Psalms*, 146; Anderson, *Psalms*, 162.

leling the "wicked" (רשעים) of Ps 1—and the same adjective is used in Deut 32:5 to describe the generation of Israelites who reject Yahweh. Therefore, it seems that the psalmist is drawing upon a Deuteronomic theology of the two ways in his declaration of the reasons why Yahweh heard and answered his prayer and came to his aid—Yahweh's anointed was faithful to the call to walk in God's ways and so his prayer for help was heard.[31]

3.1.5   APPELLATIVES AGAIN

The final stanza (vv 47–51) returns to the psalmist's celebration of the fact that Yahweh is his "Rock" forming a bracketing structure around the psalm. As Berry points out, there is a sense in which the whole of Ps 18 can, in fact, be considered, "an expansion of a single, pithy sentence, notably, the one which occurs in v 3."[32] We return, therefore, to the theme with which the psalm started—Yahweh as the sole source of strength, security and ability for the psalmist. As we saw above, this notion of dependence upon Yahweh is actively promoted in Deuteronomy.[33] The idea of total dependence upon God is further developed in this final stanza where the psalmist acknowledges that it is Yahweh who has given him victory over his enemies and who subdues the nations under him. Therefore the king ends as he began—celebrating God's protection in battle and rejoicing in the covenant relationship which has given him victory. The final verse of the psalm (v 51) causes the reader to recollect Psalm 2: the king rejoices in Yahweh's steadfast love (חסד) shown to his messiah, and

---

[31] It should also be pointed out that the idea of the דרכי־יהוה is not only found in the Song of Moses, but is a common concept in Deuteronomy (see 8:6, 10:12, 11:22, 19:9, 26:17 and 30:16). What is more, consideration of the "way of Yahweh" and the two ways is not unique to Deuteronomy, but is an idea which is often found in the Wisdom Literature. אֱלוֹהַּ is also used three times in the Book of Job, furthering a possible Wisdom connection in Ps 18. The issue here is not so much a question of either a Dtr or Wisdom presentation of the "two ways," but rather how the two traditions relate to each other more generally. Weinfeld has pointed out the presence of Wisdom themes in Deuteronomy (*Deuteronomy and the Deuteronomic School* [Oxford: Clarendon Press, 1972], 244–247), and the present study has noted the presence of both schools of thought in the psalms which have come under consideration. There appears to be a link between Wisdom and Dtr traditions, but a simple connection via the royal court of Josiah is problematic from a number of perspectives. This link between Deuteronomy and Wisdom is an area where further study would be of benefit to the academic community.

[32] Berry, *Psalms and Readers*, 67.

[33] Closer attention is given to the idea of the importance of dependence upon Yahweh in the treatment of the Kingship Law in chapter 5, below.

extended to all the descendants of David, the continuation the line of the king installed by God in Zion. This reminds us of the ongoing relationship between Yahweh and his anointed one, and so the idea, or perhaps better the ideal, of kingship continues to play a significant role in the theology of this psalm and, indeed, in the theology of the Book of Psalms. The kings themselves may have disappeared in the post-exilic period when the Psalter reached its final form, but the institution and concept remain important in the theology of the Psalms.

3.2 ASSOCIATION OF PSALM 18 AND PSALMS 1 AND 2

> Psalm 18 is a psalm of praise for the steadfast love of the Lord manifest in saving help given to the Lord's Messiah, to David and his seed. *It is a substantive sequel to the introduction in Psalms 1–2... because it testifies that the Messiah who holds the torah of the Lord and is promised rule over the nations is vindicated in person and vocation when he cries out for the Lord's salvation.*[34]

If the idea of a Dtr redaction emphasising the Kingship Law in the final form of the Psalter is to hold true, then we should expect a degree of overlap and continuance between the psalm groupings which juxtapose kingship and torah psalms. Accordingly, there should be a degree of thematic repetition from Pss 1–2 in Pss 18–21. As Mays points out in the above quote, *there is* a substantial degree of continuance between the themes and theology of Ps 18 and Pss 1–2.

3.2.1 YAHWEH AS REFUGE

The first and most obvious connection between Ps 18 and the introduction to the Psalter is seen in the bracketing device which begins and ends the poem (v 3 and v 47). As discussed above, we see the use of a group of appellatives which emphasise the theme of Yahweh as the king's refuge. This notion echoes one of the key structural devices used in the introduction, that is, the אשרי clauses which form an inclusio bracketing Pss 1 and 2. In the introduction to the Psalter the use of this device emphasises a link between the blessed man who delights in the torah of Yahweh and "all those who take refuge in him" (אשרי כל־חוסי בו). We see that Ps 18 begins with a similar theme, the king declares that Yahweh is his Rock, Stronghold and Refuge; he then reiterates the fact that Yahweh is his Rock before going on to express the same idea again using language of Ps 2:12—"I will take refuge in him" (אחסה־בו). This conceptual and lexical overlap indicates,

---

[34] Mays, *The Lord Reigns*, 102 (emphasis mine).

perhaps, that the psalmist is drawing a deliberate link between the content of this poem and Ps 2.[35] It could be the case that Ps 2:12b and the appellatives which bracket Ps 18 were additions designed to give further theological nuance to psalms which the editors saw as already reflecting their theological concerns. Whatever mechanism was used, Ps 18 is clearly linked to the Psalter's introduction by its use of the "refuge" (חסה) semantic field.

3.2.2 TORAH AND DELIGHT

A second parallel between Pss 1 and 2 as introduction and Ps 18 is found in the central stanza of the latter psalm where the king declares his commitment to the "judgements" and "decrees" of Yahweh. This verse is steeped in the torah theology which is the focal point of Pss 1 and 2. The use of "his judgements" and "his decrees" (משפטיו and חקתיו) instead of torah (תורה) introduces the reader to two of the most common synonyms for torah which are often repeated in the Psalter and in Deuteronomy. Ps 19 makes it clear that these judgements and ordinances refer to exactly the same thing as does Ps 1—the king delights in the torah of Yahweh—and these Hebrew synonyms are probably used in order to link Ps 18 with Ps 19 as a part of this psalm grouping. It is also very interesting that the reason which the psalmist gives as to why Yahweh has helped them in his time of trouble is that "he delighted in me" (כי חפצו בי, v 20). This is the same root word (חפץ) that is used concerning the "blessed person" of Ps 1:3. The king is saved because Yahweh delighted in him and then the king goes on to explain why Yahweh delighted in him and central to that explanation is his own delight in torah. There seems to be a deliberate correlation here: Yahweh delights in those who delight in his Law. Once again, we see an emphasis on the centrality of torah for the faithful. If they are to please Yahweh, if they are to secure his aid, then his torah must be central to their life and practice. As was pointed out in the previous chapter concerning Pss 1 and 2, this type of torah-piety is characteristically Deuteronomic.

---

[35] Whether this linking is the work of the original psalmist or of later editors is difficult to establish. It seems most likely that Ps 2:12b is an editorial addition, placed there in order to link Ps 2 with Ps 1 as an introduction and also to connect the introduction with other psalms which have a "refuge" content (see Creach, *Yahweh as Refuge*, 103), but it is also possible that this is an addition to the beginning and end of Ps 18.

3.2.3 THEOLOGY OF THE TWO WAYS

As mentioned briefly above, Ps 18 highlights another theme first mentioned in the introduction to the Psalter—that of the two ways. This theme is expressed in Ps 1 in the contrast between the "blessed man" and the "wicked," and in Ps 2 in the contrast between the rebellious kings and rulers, one the one hand, and the king and "those who take refuge in Yahweh," on the other. The introduction to the Psalms exhorts the righteous to follow in the way of Yahweh, and in Ps 18 we find the king pleading his case that he has, indeed, walked in the way of Yahweh (v 22) and it is due to this fact that Yahweh has come to his rescue. Again, this seems to be a theme which links Ps 18 with the introductory Pss 1–2.

3.2.4 UNIVERSAL DOMINION

One unmistakable feature of the royal psalms which provokes much discussion is the tone of dominion and rule over other nations. This is a central feature of Ps 2, and we see a similar sort of tone in Ps 18. The rebellion of the nations is mocked as futile and pointless in Ps 2 and Ps 18:38–46 celebrates David's triumph and rule over foreign nations. Whilst one cannot make too much of this point as a sign of deliberate linking between Pss 2 and 18 because this type of language is common in the royal psalms,[36] the continuance of this theme is worthy of note from a canonical perspective as it is the *first* repetition of this type of statement of the king's rule over the nations since Ps 2. The possibility of intentional linkage with this regard is further strengthened by the next point.

3.2.5 YAHWEH'S MESSIAH

The language of universal dominion may not be conclusive in and of itself as an indication of deliberate association, but when this language is combined with the elusive figure of the Yahweh's messiah the likelihood that Ps 18 is repeating important themes from Ps 2 increases. The noun "anointed" (משיח) is only used in eight psalms within the canonical Psalter, and Ps 18:51 is the first time that it is used since its appearance in Ps 2:2. Again, it is quite possible that this verse is an editorial addition to a pre-existing psalm coming as it does at the end of the work, and the first repetition of this word is probably designed to set bells ringing in the mind of the reader of the Psalter, directing his or her thoughts

---

[36] Kraus describes this as "the usual theme of the royal psalms," (*Psalms*, 264).

back to Ps 2 and the introduction to the Book of Psalms. The inclusion of the figure of the messiah in this psalm also adds to the eschatological overtones of this redaction in the post-exilic period. As McCann has put it, "In the post-exilic era—indeed, always—the assertion of God's sovereignty is made amidst circumstances and powers that deny it (see vv 4–5). Psalm 18, therefore, like Psalm 2, is eschatological."[37]

3.3 Conclusion regarding Psalm 18

Exegetical examination of the content and theology of Ps 18 indicates: First, that the psalm draws heavily upon a Deuteronomic worldview in its presentation of the king's total dependence upon Yahweh and total commitment to his torah as his source of acceptance before God in prayer; and, secondly, there are signs that Ps 18 deliberately repeats themes which have been highlighted in Pss 1 and 2 as the introduction to the Psalter. It now remains to consider these same questions in relation to Psalms 19, 20 and 21, to see if there is further support for the suggestion of a Dtr redaction in the remaining texts of this group of psalms. Ps 18 is highly significant from another perspective, that is, the question of democratisation and the king's association with the people and representation of the people as the archetypal "righteous one" and keeper of the torah—this topic is part of the overall argument of this thesis, and so shall be dealt with in chapter 7.

4. Analysis of Psalm 19

BHS	**Translation**
לַמְנַצֵּחַ מִזְמוֹר לְדָוִד: הַשָּׁמַיִם מְסַפְּרִים כְּבוֹד־אֵל וּמַעֲשֵׂה יָדָיו מַגִּיד הָרָקִיעַ: יוֹם לְיוֹם יַבִּיעַ אֹמֶר וְלַיְלָה לְּלַיְלָה יְחַוֶּה־דָּעַת: אֵין־אֹמֶר וְאֵין דְּבָרִים בְּלִי נִשְׁמָע קוֹלָם: בְּכָל־הָאָרֶץ יָצָא קַוָּם וּבִקְצֵה תֵבֵל מִלֵּיהֶם לַשֶּׁמֶשׁ שָׂם־אֹהֶל בָּהֶם: וְהוּא כְּחָתָן יֹצֵא מֵחֻפָּתוֹ יָשִׂישׂ כְּגִבּוֹר לָרוּץ אֹרַח:	1 To the director of music. A psalm of David. 2 The heavens declare the glory of God; and the firmament proclaims the work of his hands. 3 Day to day pours forth its speech; And night by night it declares knowledge. 4 There is no speech and there are no words, their voice is heard. 5 Their voice goes out in all the earth and their speech to the end of the world; He has put a tent in them for the sun. 6 And he, like a bridegroom, goes out

---

[37] McCann, *Psalms*, 749.

מִקְצֵה הַשָּׁמַיִם מוֹצָאוֹ וּתְקוּפָתוֹ עַל־
קְצוֹתָם וְאֵין נִסְתָּר מֵחַמָּתוֹ:

from his chamber; And like a warrior he rejoices to run his path.
7 From the ends of the heavens he goes forth and he completes his circuit; And there is nothing hidden from his heat.

תּוֹרַת יְהוָה תְּמִימָה מְשִׁיבַת נָפֶשׁ עֵדוּת
יְהוָה נֶאֱמָנָה מַחְכִּימַת פֶּתִי:
פִּקּוּדֵי יְהוָה יְשָׁרִים מְשַׂמְּחֵי־לֵב מִצְוַת
יְהוָה בָּרָה מְאִירַת עֵינָיִם:
יִרְאַת יְהוָה טְהוֹרָה עוֹמֶדֶת לָעַד מִשְׁפְּטֵי־
יְהוָה אֱמֶת צָדְקוּ יַחְדָּו:
הַנֶּחֱמָדִים מִזָּהָב וּמִפַּז רָב וּמְתוּקִים
מִדְּבַשׁ וְנֹפֶת צוּפִים:
גַּם־עַבְדְּךָ נִזְהָר בָּהֶם בְּשָׁמְרָם עֵקֶב רָב:

8 The law of Yahweh is perfect, reviving the soul; The statutes of Yahweh are faithful making wise the simple.
9 The precepts of Yahweh are upright, making the heart rejoice; The commandments of Yahweh are pure giving light to the eyes.
10 The fear of Yahweh is pure, standing forever; The judgements of Yahweh are true and altogether righteous.
11 More desirable than gold, than much pure gold; and sweeter than honey, than honey from the comb.
12 Also your servant is taught by them; and in keeping them is great reward.

שְׁגִיאוֹת מִי־יָבִין מִנִּסְתָּרוֹת נַקֵּנִי:
גַּם מִזֵּדִים חֲשֹׂךְ עַבְדֶּךָ אַל־יִמְשְׁלוּ־בִי אָז
אֵיתָם וְנִקֵּיתִי מִפֶּשַׁע רָב:
יִהְיוּ לְרָצוֹן אִמְרֵי־פִי וְהֶגְיוֹן לִבִּי לְפָנֶיךָ
יְהוָה צוּרִי וְגֹאֲלִי:

13 Who can discern his errors? Acquit me of the hidden things!
14 Also keep your servant from deliberate sins, let them not rule over me. Then I will be finished with them and I will be innocent of many transgressions.
15 May the words of my mouth and the meditation of my heart be pleasing before you, O Yahweh, my Rock and my Redeemer.

4.1 STRUCTURE OF PSALM 19

Psalm 18 has drawn much attention from scholars over the years, yet it would be fair to say that Psalm 19[38] has probably attracted even more discussion. C. S. Lewis has famously described Psalm 19 as "the greatest poem in the Psalter

---

[38] The text is fairly straightforward, with one notable exception, i.e. v 4 of the MT. The difficulty with this verse is in knowing how the combination of verb and negation is to be read (בלי נשמע). This is often interpreted to mean either that there is no place on the earth where the voice of the heavens is not heard (i.e. the voice is heard everywhere) or, alternatively, to mean simply that the voice of the heavens is not heard on the earth (see the discussion below, p 93). Ultimately, this message of Ps 19 remains the same: Yahweh's revelation in his torah is superior to the revelation in creation.

and one of the greatest lyrics in the world"[39] and whilst many would agree with this assessment, Psalm 19 has also attracted a good deal of criticism as well. Most of the discussion concerning Psalm 19 has centred around the question of whether it is a single work or whether, in fact, an editor has conjoined two separate pre-existing psalms—one an ancient poem derived from a naturalistic, (probably) Canaanite poem worshipping the sun and the second a wisdom poem which celebrates the torah of Yahweh. Whilst this latter theory is, of course, possible, it does not take proper account of one of the central features of the psalm: namely, Psalm 19 naturally divides into three stanzas and not two stanzas as has been suggested for many years. Discussion has centred, classically, around the relationship between Ps 19A (vv 1–7) and 19B (vv 8–15), however, the psalm really consists of three strophes:[40] (1) vv 1–7: Discussion of revelation in nature, focusing on the Creator God (אל); (2) vv 8–12: Discussion of revelation in torah, focusing on the Covenant God (יהוה); (3) vv 13–15: Prayer addressed directly to God using personal appellatives (צורי וגאלי).

As Wagner, Mays and others point out, there seems to be a progression inherent within Ps 19 from "El" to "Yahweh" to "my Rock and my Redeemer."[41] The psalmist moves from the presentation of the works of the Creator God and the way in which these works speak to mankind in general, to the express revelation of the Covenant God to his people and this leads the poet to directly address the Lord in prayer. Therefore, Ps 19 shall be considered as a united whole, and the text will be addressed as it appears in the final form of the Psalter.[42]

4.2 Deuteronomic Background to Psalm 19

The first task, will be to assess any possible Dtr background to be found within this poem; secondly, we will examine how Ps 19 relates to Ps 18 within this

---

[39] C. S. Lewis, *Reflections on the Psalms* (London: G. Bles, 1958), 63.

[40] Mays, *Psalms*, 98–100; J. Ross Wagner, "From the Heavens to the Heart: The Dynamics of Psalm 19 as Prayer," *CBQ* 61 (1999): 245–61.

[41] Mays, *Psalms*, 98–100; Wagner, "Psalm 19 as Prayer," 246. Wagner states that, "the unity and power of Psalm 19 lies in its progressive narrowing of focus from the heavens' praise of El as Creator to the petition of the human heart addressed to Yahweh as rock and redeemer." See also Michael Landon, "God and the Sciences: A Sermon on Psalm 19," *RestQ* 38, no. 4 (1996): 239; Daniel G. Ashburn, "Creation and Torah in Psalm 19," *JBQ* 22 (1994): 248 and Sarna, *On the Book of Psalms*, 70–71.

[42] As Sarna comments, "a persuasive case can be made for the unity of Psalm 19 in its present form," (*On the Book of Psalms*, 74).

group of psalms; thirdly, we shall discuss any overlap between this psalm and the introductory themes of Pss 1 and 2.

4.2.1 POLEMIC

It must be said that, at first sight, vv 1–7 of Ps 19 do not appear to be in the least Deuteronomic in the content. These verses are concerned with nature, the sun, the heavens and their voice—these are not the concerns of Deuteronomy or the Deuteronomistic literature. In fact, many commentators point out that these are not really the concerns of Israel's religion at all and so this must be an adaptation of an older ANE religious hymn.[43] Yet Nahum Sarna has made a strong argument which stands in contrast to this view of Ps 19. The primary reason for rejecting Deuteronomic content in the first strophe is the positing of a strong separation between the two stanzas—nature poem vs. torah hymn. A more unitary view of the content of Ps 19 sees a merging of these themes, and it is from this basis that Sarna argues that Ps 19—as a whole—serves as a "tacit polemic" against Assyrian-influenced astral worship.[44] Now, if this is the case, the reader is drawn into Deuteronomic themes throughout the whole poem, i.e. the rejection of false religion in favour of the sole worship of Yahweh through the study of his torah. Perhaps this rejection of the religions of Israel's neighbours is seen most clearly in Deut 18:9–13 where such practices are condemned as being "detestable things" (תועבת) in the eyes of Yahweh.[45] It is interesting that this passage also challenges the reader to be blameless (תמים, Deut 18:13), one of the repeated themes throughout Psalms 18–21. Whilst we should not overemphasize the role of polemic in the Hebrew Bible,[46] it is quite possible that Ps 19 is

---

[43] See, for example, W. O. E. Oesterley, *The Psalms: Translated with Text-Critical and Exegetical Notes* (London: SPCK, 1959), 167–68; N. Wyatt, "The Liturgical Context of Psalm 19 and Its Mythical and Ritual Origins," *UF* 27 (1995): 559–96. However, it is not necessarily the case that this part of the poem is born out of the religious practices of Israel's neighbours, D. J. A. Clines points out the Genesis themes which are suggested by Ps 19 in "The Tree of Knowledge and the Law of Yahweh," *VT* 24 (1974): 8–14.

[44] Sarna, *On the Book of Psalms*, 71–74.

[45] It should be noted that this passage is drawn from the broader context of the Kingship Law (Deut 16:18–18:22).

[46] One must be careful not to simply posit "polemic" wherever there is any overlap between the text of the Hebrew Bible and the known religious practices of her near neighbours. We cannot assume that any "borrowing" (if, indeed, this is borrowing) functions as polemic against the prevalent religious practices of the day. Whilst such polemic may well be found frequently in the OT—texts may well be used polemically by simply

intended to act as a critique of false religious practice and as a commendation of the proper worship of Yahweh based in his torah. If this is the case then Ps 19 as a whole can be described as being typical of a Deuteronomic worldview.[47]

4.2.2 TORAH THEOLOGY

Regardless of whether or not we accept that Ps 19 functions as a polemic, the fact that the first strophe may or may not be described as typically Deuteronomic in itself is in no way detrimental to the overall argument that the psalm as a whole has a Deuteronomic flavour to it. The function of the first strophe seems to be setting nature, and the revelation which comes from it, as a foil for the celebration of the superior revelation that comes from Yahweh's torah. Much of the discussion of Ps 19 has centred upon the differences between the general and special revelation, and whether or not revelation from nature fails and is contrasted with the efficacious revelation that is the torah.[48] Many of the commentators who take a unitary approach to Ps 19 point out that the transition from the first strophe to the second strophe, regardless of the distinctions that are clearly being drawn, is not so abrupt. McCann, for example, reflects upon the conceptual link between the sun and its function in providing heat for the whole of the earth and the torah of Yahweh and its function in addressing the whole of life.

> Verse 7a [MT v 8a] would be translated better as: "The instruction of the Lord is all-encompassing, restoring life." As vv 4b–6 describe the all-encompassing circuit of the sun, so v 7a asserts that God's *torah* is all-encompassing.

---

twisting them slightly—it is difficult to assess conclusively when this is happening. On the other hand, nor can we simply assume that any degree of overlap with external practices proves that other ancient Near Eastern religious practices were commonplace within Israel. Just as one cannot automatically assume a function in polemic, nor should we automatically assume influence from other ANE practices into all Hebrew texts which appear to be similar to foreign religious texts of that period and area. Each case of similarity must be treated on its own merits, knee-jerk conclusions in favour of either polemic or borrowing are equally wrongheaded. Having said all that, in this particular case, Sarna makes a good argument that Ps 19 does, in fact, function as a polemic against foreign religious influence within Israel. If this is the case, then the argument for a Deuteronomic reading of Ps 19 is further strengthened.

[47] Such is the association with the Dtr worldview that Sarna views this polemic as a product of the Josianic reforms (*On the Book of Psalms*, 74).

[48] See, for example, Wagner, "Psalm 19 as Prayer," 250, *contra* Kraus, *Psalms*, 276. Ultimately, this argument revolves around Ps 19:4, a verse which, as we have seen already, is rather difficult to translate (see p 90n38, above).

Because "nothing is hidden from its heat" (v 6b), the sun constantly energises the earth and makes life possible. So it is, the psalmist claims with God's *torah;* it makes life possible. In short, when vv 7–10 are heard following vv 1–6, they present *torah* on a cosmic scale. God's instruction is built into the very structure of the universe, and life depends on *torah* as much as it depends on the daily rising of the sun.[49]

The Deuteronomic background of Ps 19 is really unmistakable. No reader can reasonably contemplate the contents of this psalm without being struck by its high view of the torah. Some commentators have tried to present this as an alarming (late) legalistic redaction, but surely such an approach misses out on the poetic beauty of this psalm. This is not the commendation of legalism, this is not the law that kills—clearly the psalmist *delights* in the torah of Yahweh with great sincerity and passion.[50] This type of attitude resonates with the patterns for piety suggested by Deuteronomy and the Deuteronomistic literature. It is also strongly reminiscent of one of the central themes of the introduction to the Psalter—delighting in the torah (Ps 1:2). Here the psalmist (and the superscription, placement and content of this psalm suggest that the psalmist is the king[51]) exemplifies one who really does delight in the torah of Yahweh. Ps 19 provides *an example* of the righteous person who follows the pattern laid out in Ps 1 and offers a public hymn which expresses a joyous appreciation of the statutes and ordinances, the instruction, of Yahweh which have set Israel apart from the other nations (Deut 4:5-8, 32-40; Psalm 147:19-20). Miller puts it well:

> Delight in the torah and obedience to it stand at the beginning and end of this collection in the torah entrance liturgies, Pss 15 and 24... *But that collection also places joy in the torah at the center in the form of Ps 19. Indeed, it is that psalm that best conveys the tone of Ps 1's delight in torah as it speaks of it being sweeter than honey and offering a great reward. The sheer pleasure of the torah that is suggested in the use of* ḥepeṣ *in Ps 1 is echoed in Ps 19's valuing of it as more than fine gold and sweeter than honey.* The awareness of the good consequences of torah obedience that is present in the simile of the transplanted tree by the water, the prosperity of the torah keepers, and the Lord's preservation of their way is carried forward in Ps 19's claim of a great reward in keeping the torah. The meditation of the heart at the end of Ps 19 echoes the meditation on the torah of Ps 1 and tells us quite clearly what this meditation is. It is not a vacuous contemplation. It is the study, reflection, and

---

[49] McCann, *Psalms*, 752.
[50] Eaton, *Psalms of the Way*, 52.
[51] See the discussion of the indications of a royal background to Ps 19, p 101 below.

keeping of torah.... So this small collection takes its cue from the introduction given in Ps 1 and it centres in torah obedience, which is also the alpha and omega of these prayers.[52]

Even cursory exegetical examination of Ps 19 answers two of our questions—firstly, Ps 19 clearly draws upon Deuteronomic emphases in its content and, secondly, it is intimately linked with Ps 1 by way of deliberate thematic connection. Torah is central to this psalm, and the presentation of a high view of the importance and vitality of Yahweh's Law is the ultimate aim of this psalm, a theme which is obviously significant to any Dtr redaction of the Hebrew Bible. Also Ps 19 provides the reader with an example of that which Pss 1 and 2 commend—the king as an exemplar of the one who keeps the torah of Yahweh.

4.2.3 PRAYER OF PSALM 19 AND PERSONAL PIETY

Another, perhaps less obvious, link between Ps 19 and Dtr theology is found in the heartfelt plea of the prayer in the third strophe. Much of the theology of the psalms which we have examined may seem simplistic in its presentation of piety—"There are two ways: choose the right one!" The prayer of Ps 19 adds another dimension to this equation in acknowledging the difficulty of walking in Yahweh's paths and declaring the psalmist's dependence upon God in order to be able to do so. "Who can discern his sins?" (v 13a)... "acquit me" (v 13b)... "keep your servant from deliberate sins" (v 14). There is an acknowledgement of the psalmist's own inability to be right before his God, even given his delight in the torah. Therefore he offers a plea for Yahweh to work on his behalf in order to help him follow the command to walk in his paths. This dichotomy between a call to piety and a recognition of one's inability to be pious without Yahweh's help is echoed in the idealistic, yet realistic, theology of Deuteronomy. McConville comments:

> In both places [Deut 10:16 cf. Deut 30:6] the author uses the metaphor of circumcision of the heart to convey the idea of true inward devotion to the way of Yahweh. In 10:16 we read a simple exhortation to Israel: "Circumcise your hearts..." In 30:6, however, a shift occurs, so that now Yahweh himself declares that *he* will take an initiative in this respect: "The Lord your God will circumcise your hearts and the hearts of your descendants," resulting in Israel's ability to obey the exhortation to love him with all their heart and soul....[53]

---

[52] Miller, "Kingship," 127–28 (emphasis mine).
[53] J. Gordon McConville, *Grace in the End: A Study in Deuteronomic Theology* (Carlisle: Paternoster Press, 1993), 136–37.

Such an attitude is reflected in the prayer of Ps 19, another indication that this poetic work is shaped by a mindset which has been influenced by the teaching of the Deuteronomist.

4.2.4 PSALM 19 AND DEUTERONOMY 4

Another theological link between Ps 19 and the text of Deuteronomy is its close association with the ideas of Deut 4. Mays points out that:

> The theological basis of this description of Torah is the identification of the Sinai covenant and its teaching as the wisdom by which Israel is to live and find life (Deut 4:1–8). The terms for Torah are an eclectic list referring to whatever the poet viewed as a medium of the Lord's instruction. Four of the six are single, two are plural, indicating that the poet thinks of Torah as a comprehensive entity that is present also in particular precepts and legal sentences. The predicates as a group are those used for the qualities of what is righteous, right in relation to the LORD; note the way verse 9 [MT v 10] concludes with the statement, "They are altogether righteous." Righteousness inheres in the torah, and the righteousness of persons depends on it. The first four appended phrases recite the benefits of Torah; it bestows life, wisdom, and joy.[54]

The whole approach of Ps 19 towards the torah of Yahweh resonates strongly with Moses' exhortation to the people prior to the conquest of the Promised Land, according to Deuteronomy's self-presentation. The idea is one of the torah of Yahweh being תמימה—being all-sufficient, addressing every area of life and practice, setting God's people apart from all others. This is a concept which is closely associated with the DtrN school, and the whole thrust of this psalm resonates strongly with this type of worldview—the torah is all-sufficient when combined with prayer to Yahweh for the task of godliness.

There are probably other lesser connections which could be drawn between Ps 19 and the Book of Deuteronomy, however, such exhaustiveness appears to be unnecessary. An argument has been offered which indicates that Ps 19 is thoroughly grounded in a Deuteronomic worldview. The poem draws heavily upon the concepts which are most important to the Deuteronomic frame of mind and it also echoes the theology of Pss 1–2. Two more questions must be addressed briefly before moving on to assess Psalms 20 and 21; i.e., first, its relationship with the previous psalm in this psalm grouping; and then, secondly, closer consideration of the relationship between Ps 19 and Pss 1–2.

---

[54] Mays, *Psalms*, 98–99 (emphasis added). This idea is also supported by McCann, *Psalms*, 752, and Kirkpatrick, *Psalms*, 105.

4.3 LINK BETWEEN PSALM 18 AND PSALM 19

In order to establish that a particular theological redaction of the Psalter has taken place, one has to be able to show that psalms have been placed in *deliberate* juxtaposition. This, of course, is no easy task because it is virtually impossible to establish the practices or thought processes which resulted in the association of two or more psalms in a grouping. However, following the methodology suggested by Wilson and Howard,[55] the best way to establish the likelihood of deliberate concatenation is to examine these neighbouring psalms for lexical (key-word, *Leitwörter*) links and thematic repetition. In the previous essay, such links were indicated between Pss 1 and 2, and exegetical examination of Psalms 18 and 19 also gives reason to conclude that their juxtaposition is more than coincidental. The connections are multiple, varied, and spread throughout the psalm and the overlap is central to the *theology* of each psalm.

4.3.1 SUPERSCRIPTIONS

It may seem slightly superfluous to mention the first of these connections, given the fact that effectively all of the psalms in Book I bear a Davidic superscription,[56] but from a canonical perspective the superscriptions have a significant role to play in the establishment of editorial activity.[57] Both of the psalms begin with the לדוד superscription, not that these are identical, however. The superscription of Ps 18 is one of the few which gives an implied historical setting to the circumstances of the psalm, whereas the superscription of Ps 19 contains the more standard form of Davidic superscription. However, these superscriptions indicate the royal background to these psalms—they reflect a setting in kingship and are indicative of the importance of "Yahweh's anointed" in the religious life of Israel and in the theology of these psalms. The figures of psalmist and king merge.

4.3.2 APPELLATIVES

There are, however, more substantial correspondences between Psalms 18 and 19. One of the aspects of Ps 18 which was characterised as reflecting a deliberate link with the book of Deuteronomy was its use of appellatives. In par-

---

[55] See chapter 1 above.
[56] See chapter 2 above.
[57] See Childs, *IOTS*, 521 and Wilson, *Editing*.

ticular, we saw that the psalmist focused these predicates for God around the central concept of God as his "Rock." In Ps 18, this was reflected particularly in the words—סלעי and צורי—and the psalmist describes Yahweh as צורי again in Ps 19:15. Once more the name is used with the first person singular prefix, making clear in Ps 19 the psalmist's claim that Yahweh is *his* Rock and Refuge, just as was the case in Ps 18.

4.3.3 CHARACTERISTICS OF YAHWEH AND HIS TORAH

Another strong connection between these two psalms is the attribution of certain characteristics to Yahweh in Ps 18 and the self same characteristics to his torah in Ps 19. In fact, Allen suggests that a chiastic structure is formed by this repetition.[58] Ps 18:27 declares Yahweh to be pure/innocent (תתברר); Ps 18:29 states that Yahweh gives light (תאיר); and Ps 18:31 describes Yahweh's way as perfect (תמים). Correspondingly, Ps 19 attributes exactly the same characteristics to the torah, but in (more or less) reverse order—v 8 the torah is described as perfect (תמימה); v 9 in the torah gives light (מאירת); and v 9 also describes the torah as being pure (ברה). Whether or not the chiastic structure is justifiable (the sentence structure of v 9 means that it does not work very neatly), the repetition of these attributes in succeeding psalms is quite remarkable and provides a further indication of deliberate editorial association of the psalms.

4.3.4 SERVANT OF THE LORD

Further royal overtones are found in the use of the phrase "servant of the Lord" (עבד יהוה). At first sight, such an association may seem somewhat tenuous, as the phrase "servant of the Lord" is found very often throughout the Hebrew Bible. Of course, this is true in narrative passages, but it should be noted that up until this point in the canonical Psalter the noun form of עבד has not been used at all. It is used for the first time in the superscription of Ps 18 which describes the psalm as being of David "of the servant of Yahweh" (לעבד יהוה, Ps 18:1) and then in Ps 19:12, 14 the psalmist describes himself as "your servant" (עבדך). Once more, this is indicative of a certain attitude—the king is pointing out his own subservience towards Yahweh, and this is the sign of one who is a true follower

---

[58] Leslie C. Allen, "David as Exemplar of Spirituality: The Redaction Function of Psalm 19," *Bib* 67, no. 4 (1986): 546.

of Yahweh.[59] The noun form of "servant" does not appear again within the Psalms 15–24 collection, so it appears that this repetition can reasonably be seen as another indication of deliberate linking.

> In any case, to hear Psalm 19 as a unity is to appreciate its bold and sweeping claims about God's torah, "instruction" and to ensure that, Psalm 19 intends to teach. Its instructional intent may be emphasised by its placement within a series of royal psalms of (Psalms 18, 20–21); *that is, Psalm 19, especially verses 7–14, describes the orientation to life that faithful kings were supposed to embody and model for the people (see Psalms 18:20–30; 21:7; note especially the repetition of "blameless" in 18:23, 25 and 19:13).*[60]

4.4 Association of Psalm 19 with Psalms 1 and 2

Psalm 19, in very explicit ways, echoes the theology of the Psalter's introduction by way of the repetition of the two main themes of Psalms 1 and 2: torah and kingship.

4.4.1 Expansion of Torah Theme

An important comparison between Ps 19 and Pss 1–2 is the expansion of the concept of torah. Verse 8 introduces the torah of Yahweh as being תמימה and then the succeeding verses expand upon this statement using various synonyms for torah in order to demonstrate its completeness and perfection. These synonyms provide an expansion upon the singularity of Ps 1, where, rhetorically speaking, the simple repetition of torah (תורה, Ps 1:2) stands in contrast to the multiplicity of the ways of the wicked (Ps 1:1).[61] Ps 19 takes the concept of torah and celebrates its *fullness* by using such terms as עדות (statutes), פקודים (precepts), מצות (commands), יראת (fear) and משפטים (judgements). These are

---

[59] Miller, "Kingship," 128. Miller argues that the significance of this phrase is increased because it is applied to two figures—king and torah-keeper—effectively merging these two concepts and portraying the king as an exemplar of piety. We shall discuss this idea further in the chapter 7.

[60] Sheppard, *Wisdom*, 140–42 (emphasis mine). As Sheppard and Allen (Allen, "David as Exemplar") point out, the placement of Ps 19 amidst a group of royal psalms indicates the likelihood that this poem is meant to be read as the hymn and prayer of the king. The use of the term "your servant" (אבדך), a phrase commonly associated with the royal office, and the references to "gold" (זהב) and "pure gold" (פז) in verse 11 are also possible indications of a royal background to Ps 19.

[61] Yehoshua Gitay, "Psalm 1 and the Rhetoric of Religious Argumentation," in *Literary Structure and Rhetorical Strategies in the Hebrew Bible* (ed. L. J. de Regt et al.; Assen/Winona Lake, IN: Van Gorcum/Eisenbrauns, 1996), 235–36.

words used of the torah of Yahweh both in the book of Deuteronomy[62] and are also used extensively as synonyms for תורה in the one remaining torah psalm, Ps 119.[63] These terms reflect the holistic nature of torah being referred to in the Psalter, including all the different types of legal text and much more. It is the instruction of Yahweh as it is most broadly defined which is being celebrated in Ps 19.[64]

4.4.2 PSALM 19 AS EXAMPLE OF DELIGHT IN YAHWEH'S TORAH

It is interesting to notice that Ps 19 appears to function as a practical example of the theology of Pss 1 and 2. This is a hymn written for the express purpose of delighting in the torah of Yahweh, in accordance with the exhortation of Ps 1. The image presented by Ps 19 is of the psalmist-king, clearly *delighting* in the torah of Yahweh, just as Ps 1 commends (Ps 19:11 cf. Ps 1:2).[65]

4.4.3 CONCEPTUAL ASSOCIATIONS

There are further intellectual connections between Ps 19 and Pss 1–2: (1) The king's awareness that following in the way of righteousness, as reflected in Yahweh's revelation, brings great reward (Ps 19:12b cf. Ps 1:3). (2) The king's acknowledgement that wisdom is found in the instruction of the Lord (Ps 19:12a cf. Ps 2:10), thus contrasting the psalmist-king of Ps 19 with the rebellious kings and rulers of Ps 2 who would reject this wisdom. (3) The final strophe's emphasis upon the importance of right meditation, an idea which is central to Ps 1 (Ps 19:15 cf. Ps 1:2, the root word הגה is used in both psalms). The words of the psalm and the meditation which underpins the public proclamation of delight in the torah poem are entrusted to the Lord, seeking his acceptance and commendation, in a way which is similar to the challenge of Ps 1 that the OT believer should meditate on the word of Yahweh day and night. There are strong links between theology of Ps 19, which lies at the heart of this collection of psalms, and the theology of the introduction to the Psalter.

---

[62] See, for example, the kingship law itself. Deut 17:18–19 appears to use the ideas of התורה and החקים in such a fashion. Other examples would be Deut 30:10 and 33:10 which use the same synonyms as are found in Pss 19 and 119 in the same sort of way.

[63] As we shall see in the next chapter, each eight-line stanza of Ps 119 is dominated by the various torah synonyms.

[64] Mays, *Psalms*, 98.

[65] Ashburn, "Creation and Torah," 246.

4.4.4 KINGSHIP THEME

The superscription suggests that Ps 19 is a psalm of the king—this is his poem, his delight, his prayer. This fact obviously resonates with the dual emphases of Pss 1 and 2. Ps 1 directs the people of God to the understanding that righteousness is only to be found by way of torah-obedience and Ps 2 emphasises the importance of the "anointed one" of the Lord in his universal plans. Through the repetition of key words, the two psalms are linked intimately—the king and obedience to the torah. Once again, we see the association of these two themes in Ps 19. Perhaps in even more explicit terms, we see again the figure of the "messiah" (Ps 18:51[66]) mentioned in the same breath as this overflowing celebration of the importance of torah. Ps 19 takes up the theology of Pss 1 and 2 and presents the king in accordance with the ideal of that introduction: that is, as the torah-keeper. In the Psalms 18–21 the king is the central figure, and he is presented as the exemplar for the people, the one who keeps the torah. Gerald Sheppard picks up on this fact when he writes concerning Pss 1 and 2:

> There is a high degree of correspondence in the substance of these two psalms... [and] by his associations with Ps 2, David... is identified fully in accord with the ideals of Ps 1. The entire Psalter, therefore, is made to stand theologically in association with David as a source book of guidance for the way of the righteous.[67]

4.5 CONCLUSION REGARDING PSALM 19

As has been mentioned, it is difficult to prove conclusively that poetic texts have been deliberately placed alongside one another. However, the overlap which exists between Psalms 18 and 19 is remarkable. Wagner states that this linking between Pss 18 and 19, "involves an impressive number of connections of the vocabulary and thought."[68] Also, this association occurs at points which are central to the theology of these compositions. This seems to indicate the presence of editorial activity in juxtaposing the psalms and that they have in fact been placed alongside each other in order to reflect themes which were important to the editors. As with the introduction to the Psalter, the themes which are being emphasised are kingship and torah. This connection is further emphasised by the bracketing function of Psalms 20 and 21, giving a kingship-law-kingship

---

[66] The connection between Pss 18 and 19 is discussed more fully above.
[67] Sheppard, *Wisdom*, 140–42.
[68] Wagner, "Psalm 19 as Prayer," 257n52.

focus at the very centre of Pss 15-24. Now we shall move on to this closing bracket, by examining Pss 20 and 21 together.

5. ANALYSIS OF PSALMS 20 AND 21

BHS	Translation

Psalm 20

לַמְנַצֵּחַ מִזְמוֹר לְדָוִד:
יַעַנְךָ יְהוָה בְּיוֹם צָרָה יְשַׂגֶּבְךָ שֵׁם אֱלֹהֵי יַעֲקֹב:
יִשְׁלַח־עֶזְרְךָ מִקֹּדֶשׁ וּמִצִּיּוֹן יִסְעָדֶךָּ:
יִזְכֹּר כָּל־מִנְחֹתֶךָ וְעוֹלָתְךָ יְדַשְּׁנֶה סֶלָה:
יִתֶּן־לְךָ כִלְבָבֶךָ וְכָל־עֲצָתְךָ יְמַלֵּא:
נְרַנְּנָה בִּישׁוּעָתֶךָ וּבְשֵׁם־אֱלֹהֵינוּ נִדְגֹּל יְמַלֵּא יְהוָה כָּל־מִשְׁאֲלוֹתֶיךָ:

1 To the director of music. A psalm of David.
2 May Yahweh answer you in the day of your distress; May the name of the God of Jacob set you on high.
3 May he send help for you from the sanctuary and may he sustain you from Zion.
4 May he remember all your sacrifices and may he accept your whole burnt offerings. Selah.
5 May he give you according to your heart and fulfill all your counsel.
6 We will shout for joy in your salvation and we will raise up banners in the name of our God; Yahweh will fulfill all your requests.

עַתָּה יָדַעְתִּי כִּי הוֹשִׁיעַ יְהוָה מְשִׁיחוֹ יַעֲנֵהוּ מִשְּׁמֵי קָדְשׁוֹ בִּגְבֻרוֹת יֵשַׁע יְמִינוֹ:
אֵלֶּה בָרֶכֶב וְאֵלֶּה בַסּוּסִים וַאֲנַחְנוּ בְּשֵׁם־יְהוָה אֱלֹהֵינוּ נַזְכִּיר:
הֵמָּה כָּרְעוּ וְנָפָלוּ וַאֲנַחְנוּ קַּמְנוּ וַנִּתְעוֹדָד:

7 Now I know that Yahweh saves his anointed, he answers him from his sanctuary, with the strength of deliverance by his right hand.
8 Some in chariots and some in horses, but as for us, we will trust in the name of Yahweh our God.
9 They bow down and they fall down, but as for us, we rise up and we are restored.

יְהוָה הוֹשִׁיעָה הַמֶּלֶךְ יַעֲנֵנוּ בְיוֹם־קָרְאֵנוּ:

10 Save the king, O Yahweh. Answer us in the day when we call out.

Psalm 21

לַמְנַצֵּחַ מִזְמוֹר לְדָוִד:
יְהוָה בְּעָזְּךָ יִשְׂמַח־מֶלֶךְ וּבִישׁוּעָתְךָ מַה־יָּגֶיל מְאֹד:
תַּאֲוַת לִבּוֹ נָתַתָּה לּוֹ וַאֲרֶשֶׁת שְׂפָתָיו בַּל־מָנַעְתָּ סֶּלָה:

1 To the director of music. A psalm of David.
2 O Yahweh, in your strength, the king rejoices; And in your salvation, how greatly he rejoices.
3 You give him the desire of his heart;

Torah-Kingship Theme in Psalms 18–21

כִּי־תְקַדְּמֶנּוּ בִּרְכוֹת טוֹב תָּשִׁית לְרֹאשׁוֹ עֲטֶרֶת פָּז:
חַיִּים שָׁאַל מִמְּךָ נָתַתָּה לּוֹ אֹרֶךְ יָמִים עוֹלָם וָעֶד:
גָּדוֹל כְּבוֹדוֹ בִּישׁוּעָתֶךָ הוֹד וְהָדָר תְּשַׁוֶּה עָלָיו:
כִּי־תְשִׁיתֵהוּ בְרָכוֹת לָעַד תְּחַדֵּהוּ בְשִׂמְחָה אֶת־פָּנֶיךָ:
כִּי־הַמֶּלֶךְ בֹּטֵחַ בַּיהוָה וּבְחֶסֶד עֶלְיוֹן בַּל־יִמּוֹט:

And you have not withheld the request of his lips. Selah.
4 For you come before him with rich blessings; And you place on his head a crown of pure gold.
5 He asked for life from you and you gave it to him; Length of days forever and ever.
6 Great is his honour in your salvation; Majesty and honour are placed upon him.
7 For you have placed upon him blessing forever; You cause him to rejoice with the joy of your presence.
8 For the king trusts in Yahweh; And because of the steadfast love of the Most High, he will not be shaken.

תִּמְצָא יָדְךָ לְכָל־אֹיְבֶיךָ יְמִינְךָ תִּמְצָא שֹׂנְאֶיךָ:
תְּשִׁיתֵמוֹ כְּתַנּוּר אֵשׁ לְעֵת פָּנֶיךָ יְהוָה בְּאַפּוֹ יְבַלְּעֵם וְתֹאכְלֵם אֵשׁ:
פִּרְיָמוֹ מֵאֶרֶץ תְּאַבֵּד וְזַרְעָם מִבְּנֵי אָדָם:
כִּי־נָטוּ עָלֶיךָ רָעָה חָשְׁבוּ מְזִמָּה בַּל־יוּכָלוּ:
כִּי תְּשִׁיתֵמוֹ שֶׁכֶם בְּמֵיתָרֶיךָ תְּכוֹנֵן עַל־פְּנֵיהֶם:
רוּמָה יְהוָה בְעֻזֶּךָ נָשִׁירָה וּנְזַמְּרָה גְּבוּרָתֶךָ:

9 Your hand will find your enemies; Your right hand will find those who hate you.
10 You shall put them, as it were, in a fiery furnace, in the time of your appearing O Yahweh, in your anger you will swallow them; You will consume them with fire.
11 You shall cause their fruit to perish from the earth; Their seed from the sons of man.
12 For they incline evil against you; They plot wickedness but they will not succeed
13 You will make them turn their backs; With bows you will aim upon their faces.
14 Be exalted, O Yahweh, in your strength! We will sing and rejoice in your strength!

Whilst Psalms 18 and 19 have attracted much attention from the scholarly community, the same cannot be said for Psalms 20 and 21.[69] Like a small country located between international superpowers, Psalms 20 and 21 do not command the same sort of fascination as Psalms 18 and 19, on one side, and Psalms 22 and 23, on the other. Whilst they are probably never going to be top of the "favourite psalms" chart, a canonical approach to the Psalter does increase the significance of these psalms beyond that suggested by the attention which they

---

[69] There are no major difficulties with regard to the text of these psalms in the MT.

have received thus far.[70] The bracketing function around Ps 19 which the psalms fulfil provides added confirmation of the themes which were important to the editors of the Psalter. As with Psalms 18 and 19, there are several questions which we need to ask of these texts in order to assess whether or not they do in fact confirm the possibility of a Dtr torah-kingship redaction. First, do these psalms reflect a background in Deuteronomic theology? Secondly, are there signs of deliberate concatenation with Psalms 18 and 19? Thirdly, can these psalms be said to confirm the theological priorities suggested by Pss 1 and 2 as the introduction to the Psalter?

5.1 Association of Psalms 20 and 21

However, before we begin to discuss these questions, there is a preliminary issue which needs to be addressed. Namely, why are these psalms being discussed together? They are, after all, quite clearly separate poetic compositions? The rationale behind this is largely based upon the suggestions of Auffret and Miller that the psalm grouping, Psalms 15–24, follows a chiastic or envelope structure.[71] Their suggestion is that these psalms were treated as a unit by the editors of this collection to act as a chiastic counterbalance to Ps 18. The thematic similarity of content between these three psalms is marked. Each of them is clearly a royal psalm, each of them involves the king being faced with enemies, each of them deals with the king's total dependence upon Yahweh's strength in the face of these (probably) military challenges. Such close thematic overlap in juxtaposed psalms is somewhat unusual, which leads the reader to consider the possibility of deliberate placement and association of these psalms. Almost all of the commentators on the Psalms comment upon the similarity in content of Psalms 20 and 21[72] (as we shall see, many of the commentators also

---

[70] Interestingly, Mitchell makes a point that these psalms—like other royal psalms—should be in significant editorial positions, but are not. I would suggest that the positioning of these oft-ignored psalms is very meaningful for establishing the theological concerns of the Psalter's redactors because of the role with they play in indicating this torah-kingship link which appears to associate the eschatological hope in a coming Davidic king with the Deuteronomic Law of the King. See Mitchell, *Message*, 244.

[71] Miller, "Kingship"; Auffret, *La Sagesse*.

[72] Mays, *Psalms*, 90; McCann, *Psalms*, 757; Kraus, *Psalms*, 280–81. Kirkpatrick comments, "The 20th and 21st Psalms are closely related in structure and contents. Both are liturgical Psalms: the first is an intercession, the second a thanksgiving. In both the king, the representative of Jehovah and the representative of the people, is the prominent

link these psalms with Ps 18 and Ps 2)—not that this fact is in itself a conclusive argument for association, but this association has been widely recognised. It is difficult to say why the editors would include one double psalm in a chiastic pattern where single compositions apply in each of the other categories. Probably, the most likely reason for doing so is that, Ps 18 being one of the longest psalms in the Psalter, the editors, accordingly, felt that one short royal psalm of similar thematic focus would not provide a sufficiently lengthy counterbalance to this poem, so Psalms 20 and 21 were placed together to provide a (slightly) more substantial response. Another possibility is, of course, simply that these psalms were known to the editors as having the same type of content and, hence, all three were associated by way of close proximity of placement within the Psalter—separated only by that which they saw as being central to true kingship, the torah of the Lord. Whilst it is impossible to say conclusively why the psalms have been linked in this way, their similarity in tone, content, genre and setting makes this association a reasonable one.

5.2 Deuteronomic Content of Psalms 20 and 21

The basis in a Dtr worldview shines through in Pss 20 and 21, just as it does in Pss 18 and 19, confirming the suggestion that the primary background to Pss 18–21 is to be found in a Deuteronomic view of kingship and personal piety. There are a number of ideas within the content of Pss 20 and 21 which could be described as "classically Deuteronomic." The concept of name theology (Ps 20:2, 6, 8); the theme of total dependence upon Yahweh, particularly expressed in anti-militaristic terms which echo the limitations imposed upon the king by the Kingship Law; the theology of the two ways, and several other themes indicate Dtr allusions. We also find recurrences of motifs prominent in Pss 1–2 and in Pss 18–19, indicating the likelihood of concatenation within this psalm grouping and also of editorial association of Pss 18–21 with Pss 1–2.

5.2.1 Name-Theology

The idea of name-theology is an extremely significant one in the Book of Deuteronomy. Patrick Miller sums this up in his analysis of the third commandment in Deut 5:11 when he writes, "In Deuteronomic theology, the name of God

---

figure; and the salvation or victory which Jehovah bestows upon him is the leading thought," (*Psalms*, 106).

in a very serious way represents the presence of the reality of God."[73] The psalmist-king is the object of the prayers of the people in the first stanza of Ps 20, and the people pray for his protection in "the name of the God of Jacob" (ישגבך שם אלהי יעקב). This seems to be an appeal based upon Yahweh's real presence (in some special sense?) with his messiah (cf v 7). The same sort of concept is repeated in Ps 20:6, and finds its culmination in Ps 20:8 where the psalmist and the people[74] declare that, whilst some trust in military might, they "will trust in the name of Yahweh our God" (ואנחנו בשם־יהוה אלהינו נזכיר). The fact that it is the name of Yahweh that is being called upon sets the theology of this psalm somewhat apart from the norm. Proclamations of trust in Yahweh are common in the Psalter, yet this declaration of trust in the *name* of Yahweh adds a Deuteronomic nuance to the theology of this psalm. Kraus comments:

> Conspicuous is the heavily profiled שם-theology, which leaves the impression of a Deuteronomic slant... The שם of God is mentioned three times in Psalm 20: vv. 1b, 5a, 7b. The underlying thought here is the conception related to Deuteronomy and the Deuteronomistic writings that Yahweh himself is enthroned in heaven, while on earth only his שם is present (R. Kittel; O. Grether, *Name und Wort Gottes im Alten Testament*, BZAW 64 [1934], 46). But the שם does not, as in the heathen world round about, operate as a magic power... It is the protective power working on earth with which Yahweh, upon the king's request, can answer and prove his presence. This "name theology," which is closely connected with the central sanctuary and with the *praesentia Dei* there active, plays an important role in the Psalms: Pss. 44:5; 54:6; 118:10–12; 124:8.[75]

---

[73] Miller, *Deuteronomy*, 78. See, for example, Deut 12:5, 11, 21; 14:23–24 etc. Of course, there is much debate as to the essence of the concept's meaning in Deuteronomy studies: Why is "the name of Yahweh" such a prominent thought in Deuteronomy? What is its particular significance as compared simply to the presence of Yahweh himself? What is its particular connection with the central sanctuary? Analysis of these questions in any detail goes far beyond the remit of this thesis, but suffice it to say that this is an idea drawn from Deuteronomic theology.

[74] The role of the king in what seems to be a liturgical hymn of the community is very significant in this psalm (see Mays, *Psalms*, 101). How the "messiah" and worshipping community relate to each another will be discussed in Chapter 7.

[75] Kraus, *Psalms*, 279–80. In this quote Kraus draws upon an understanding of the "name of Yahweh" which has often been presented in the secondary literature discussing Deuteronomy: Yahweh himself really lives in heaven but his "name" (a kind of divine hypostasis) dwells on earth. I would suggest that such an understanding of "name" theology does not represent the true essence of this idea in either Deuteronomy or the Psalms. The idea of "name" seems to be most closely associated with God's presence in the midst of his people and the legitimacy of his rule over them (see J. Gordon McConville and J.

Given the battle context of these psalms it is possible that the reference to the "name of Yahweh" stands in contrast to the physical images of gods that other ANE nations would carry into battle. In this way, the Dtr emphasis on the "essential spirituality of God"[76] (as opposed to any visible form) is the essence of the usage of "name theology" in Ps 20.

5.2.2 Dependence upon Yahweh

The above declarations of trust in Yahweh are significant not simply because of the appropriation of Deuteronomic name theology, but also in their presentation of total dependence and trust in God alone, which—as we have already seen—reflects attitudes borne out of a Deuteronomic mindset. This is a strong theme in both Ps 20 and Ps 21. In Ps 21, the theological importance of dependence upon Yahweh's strength is emphasised by an inclusio where the king celebrates in "your strength, O Yahweh" (יהוה בעזך, Ps 21:2, 14). Each time the phrase "in your strength" (בעזך) is combined with the psalmist's use of the vocative in his praise of Yahweh. This bracketing device emphasises the importance of the dependence theme to the theology of Ps 21. As we have seen and mentioned above, this attitude of total trust in and dependence upon Yahweh as the sole source of victory over enemies and as the sole source of the ability to be right in God's eyes is one which finds its roots in the explicit commands and exhortations of the book of Deuteronomy and in the narrative encouragements of the DtrH. Creach points out that, "The idea [total dependence upon Yahweh as a virtue] occurs in other parts of the Old Testament, such as the holy war tradition. For example, Deut 20:1–4 declares that Israel should rely completely on Yahweh for victory.... Israel's primary role in holy war is to trust in Yahweh's ability to win the battle."[77] The idea of seeking refuge in Yahweh is central to a proper understanding of the meaning of Pss 20 and 21.

Gary Millar, *Time and Place in Deuteronomy* [JSOTSup 179; Sheffield: Sheffield Academic Press, 1994], 111–16). Certainly, Pss 20 and 21 indicate no conflict between the idea of Yahweh's real presence in heaven *and* in his Temple: Ps 20:3, for example, indicates that Yahweh (not his name) "will send help from the sanctuary and sustain [the king] from Zion." The use of "name" in these two psalms is best understood as a metaphor representing the real presence of God with his people. Hence, I make use of this quote from Kraus in support of the Dtr connection in Pss 20–21's use of name-theology, but reject his understanding of that Dtr concept.

[76] McConville, *Grace in the End*, 126.
[77] Creach, *Yahweh as Refuge*, 57n21.

5.2.3 TRUST IN YAHWEH VS. DEPENDENCE IN MILITARY POWER

Ps 20 emphasises one particular nuance of this dependence upon Yahweh which seems to be drawn directly from the kingship law of Deut 17. Ps 20:8 declares that:

אלה ברכב ואלה בסוסים ואנחנו בשם־יהוה אלהינו נזכיר

Some trust in chariots and some in horses;
But as for us, we will trust in the name of Yahweh our God.

Clearly, this declaration of the people's dependence upon Yahweh in the face of opposition is interesting in its anti-militaristic content. The worshipping community declares that their trust shall be in Yahweh rather than military technology, and this reflects one of the three limitations which are placed upon the king in the kingship law of Deut 17:14-20. Deut 17:16-17 prohibits the Israelite king from having many wives (with the accompanying dangers of apostasy), from possessing great wealth and from "acquiring great numbers of horses for himself" (רק לא־ירבה־לו סוסים). Whilst this prohibition may also be connected with the accumulation of wealth, it seems more likely that this is a distinct prohibition against the raising of a permanent army and trusting in its strength rather than Yahweh's ability to save his people. Miller comments upon the king's restricted authority:

> [T]hese restrictions and injunctions serve the main purpose of Deuteronomy, *to enjoin a full and undivided allegiance to the Lord*. The primary commandment is everywhere present in these verses. Limitation of horses and wealth had definite religious implications... where horses along with wealth (cf v 17) are seen as things that lead to pride, to loss of awareness of the need to trust in Yahweh, and so to unfaithfulness and apostasy.[78]

Other commentators pick up on the importance of this anti-militaristic tone within Ps 20:

> The liturgy of Psalm 20 is characterised by the faith that Yahweh's chosen king can endure only through the ישועה and through the protective power of the divine שם in the decisions of war. Because all human potential in weapons accomplishes nothing, the congregation—through the priestly singers—prays for the ruler. It receives the promise, and with it the certainty, that Yahweh is intervening (v 6) "from heaven above" and is helping the king.[79]

---

[78] Miller, *Deuteronomy*, 148.
[79] Kraus, *Psalms*, 282.

"These by chariots and by horses." These were the chief reliance of the ancient enemies of Israel in their wars from the earliest times. Israel, living chiefly in hilly and mountainous districts, had little use for them. The law of the king (Deut 17:16) forbids them, although Solomon and other luxurious monarchs made use of them. The sentiment of the prophets was ever against their use... Yahweh is the chief, if not the sole, author of victory to His anointed king and people.[80]

The combination of these two characteristics—total trust in Yahweh and a rejection of anything which would detract from that commitment—is, as Miller states above, typical of a Deuteronomic frame of mind. Yahweh reigns, not only in Israel, but also among the nations (i.e., the "enemies" of Pss 20–21), accordingly his people are to trust in him implicitly and without duality of trust. Such is the theology of Psalms 20 and 21, and the similarity of this theology to the teachings of Deuteronomy and especially the Kingship Law is striking.

5.2.4 SALVATION/VICTORY BELONGING TO YAHWEH

This Deuteronomic attitude of dependence upon Yahweh is seen further in the use of the ישע semantic field throughout these two psalms. ישע, or one of its derivatives, appears in Ps 20:6, 7 (twice), 10; and also in Ps 21:2, 6. Every usage of this word is to acknowledge the salvation of Yahweh, rather than to celebrate the wondrous victories of the king as was common in the ancient Near East. Once more, this "subset" of the notion of dependence on Yahweh, is one which derives its origin from the Dtr idea of the absolute sovereignty of Yahweh in all the affairs of his people, including sovereignty over other (foreign) nations, who are represented in the figure of the enemies (איבים) in these psalms.[81]

> The importance of the king in the psalm is clear. He is the LORD's anointed (see Psalm 2). He is the central person on whom the intercession of his people is concentrated and for whose prayers they seek a divine answer. It is his salvation from and victory over threatening danger that will bring them joy. They are bound into the hope of his salvation. But in the theology of the psalm, the king is not the savior but the saved. The saving victory will be God's work.[82]

---

[80] Briggs, *Psalms*, 180. See also Craigie, *Psalms*, 186–87 and Mays, *Psalms*, 102 for similar analysis suggesting that Ps 20:8 reflects the teaching of Deut 17:16.

[81] As we shall see below, this is also a significant linking feature within the psalm grouping currently under discussion.

[82] Mays, *Psalms*, 101.

This approach found in Pss 20 and 21 coincides with the Dtr theology of holy war. Whilst the signficance of holy war as a part of Dtr theology can be over-emphasised, this idea is part of the Dtr frame of mind. Holy war in Deuteronomy is "a reminder to Israel that they gain nothing in their own strength, but only as a gift of God."[83] This is precisely the emphasis of these two psalms (e.g., 20:7–8, 10; 21:2, 8, 9–13) which plead for and rejoice in the Lord's salvation.

5.2.5   COVENANT THEME IN PSALM 21

The pivotal motif of kingship in the DtrH is the Davidic Covenant of 2 Samuel 7. This notion is a constantly recurring theme throughout the historical books, much like the signature refrain of a West End musical. Many of the central theological questions which arise out of the DtrH are shaped by the Davidic Covenant: Why was the kingdom allowed to divide? Why were so many of the kings ajudged godless? Why, ultimately, was the Davidic dynasty allowed to fail? So many of the "big issues" of the DtrH are grounded in the question of Yahweh's promises made to David and his descendants. Undoubtedly, this is one of the most important themes in the Old Testament, and is central to the theology of the Deuteronomistic History.

Given the backdrop in Deuteronomic theology which we find in this psalm grouping, perhaps, it should not be surprising that we find allusion to the Davidic Covenant in Ps 21. Combined with the confession of total dependence upon Yahweh, the content of Ps 21 is strongly reminiscent of the language of covenant.[84] Add to this the presence of the king in this psalm, it seems likely that the reader was meant to make association with 2 Samuel 7. Much of the psalm revolves around the special relationship which exists between Yahweh and his messiah, and many of the commentators highlight verses 7–8 as being the focal point and structural centre of the psalm.[85]

> The language of the declaration is the language of covenant, especially notable in the words בטח and חסד, and these two words sum up, in a sense, the entire theology of the psalm. There are two partners to the covenant, God and Israel

---

[83] McConville, *Grace in the End*, 140. See also Miller, *Deuteronomy*, 158–59.

[84] This is seen particularly in vv 7–8 which speak of Yahweh's eternal blessing of the king and of the king's trust in response to Yahweh's covenant faithfulness (הסד), ideas which resonate with the presentation of the Davidic covenant in 2 Sam 7. This is later contrasted with the impermanence of the offspring of the king's enemies in v 11.

[85] McCann, *Psalms*, 757.

(represented by the king); God's fundamental character in the covenant relationship is lovingkindness (חסד), and the king's response was to be one of trust (בטח). The former is unchangeable, but the latter must be constantly maintained if the covenant relationship is to prosper. Thus, in this solemn moment in the progress of liturgy, the fundamentals of the covenant are made clear and affirmed.[86]

Psalm 21 seems to indicate that the Davidic king is still under the blessing of the Davidic Covenant, making its retention in the (post-exilic) final form of the Psalter all the more remarkable. There must have been a notable sense of dissonance for the post-exilic readers of this psalm. This would verge upon the ridiculous, were it not for the fact that there was a sense of expectation that the Davidic throne would one day be restored. Kirkpatrick points out that the Targum replaces "king" (מלך) with "king-messiah" (מלך־משיח), reflecting the sense of eschatological expectation that a new and renewed "anointed one" would be restored to rule over Israel.[87] It does appear that the final form of the Psalter retains a sense of hope concerning the figure of the Davidic king and his covenant with Yahweh. Not that the Psalter does not express its doubts about what has happened to the Davidic line (e.g., Ps 89), but the retention of the royal psalms in the canonical Psalter is significant, reflecting a hope that the covenant is not over for good, but that it shall be reconstituted. It is difficult to imagine the community of Israel singing the words, "For you have placed upon him blessings forever" (כי־תשיתהו ברכות לעד, Ps 21:7), merely as a historical relic of past glories. Rather, this is likely retained as a reflection of future hope based in the ideal of kingship and the king's relationship with Yahweh.[88]

Once more, there are perhaps other aspects of Psalms 20 and 21 which could be described as Dtr,[89] however, such exhaustive analysis seems unnecessary. The aim was to show that there is a general and readily observable Dtr milieu which shapes the presentation of reality and spirituality found in these psalms, and hopefully this has been done. Two questions remain before some conclusions should be drawn from this analysis. First, the relationship of Pss 20 and 21 with the preceding psalms of this collection (Pss 18 and 19); and, secondly, the relationship between Pss 20–21 and Pss 1–2.

---

[86] Craigie, *Psalms*, 192.
[87] Kirkpatrick, *Psalms*, 110.
[88] Seitz, *Word without End*, 165.
[89] For example, Craigie draws a link between the view of history presented in Psalm 21 and the Dtr view of history past, present and future (see his *Psalms*, 193).

5.3 ASSOCIATION WITH PSALMS 18 AND 19

Many commentators link Pss 18, 20 and 21, either because of formal similarities (they are all royal psalms) or because of similarities in their content (each of these three psalms deals with the king's reliance upon Yahweh in the face of battle).[90] We have shown above that Ps 18 is closely connected with Ps 19—the extent of the lexical connections between the two psalms is such that coincidental repetition seems more far-fetched than the idea of deliberate placement. Psalms 20 and 21 are integrally linked with Ps 18 (which is linked closely with Ps 19), therefore it seems unnecessary to analyse in great detail the similarities which exist, as this would involve much repetition of ground already covered. Perhaps it is sufficient to point out the themes which are common to all four psalms. The figure of the king—according to both the superscriptions and the content of each psalm—is common to all four psalms, as is the focus upon his (and Israel's) total dependence upon Yahweh. Beyond this, we see that a prayer motif is central to all four psalms. Over and above these themes which are found in all four psalms, we see that there are several themes which are to be found in perhaps two or three of the psalms, but not necessarily in all four: for example, the context of battle and enemies in Pss 18, 20 and 21, or the prominence of the torah theme in Pss 18 and 19. All in all, exegetical study of these four psalms indicates the likelihood that they have been deliberately placed alongside each other to serve the theological purposes of the redactors of the Psalter. It is my suggestion that the theological purpose of these editors was to point to an ideal of kingship in their presentation of the type of eschatological king the people should expect. This figure was not going to be like the kings of the past, but a king who was grounded in love for the torah of Yahweh, commitment to him and dependence upon him, as the Dtr Law of the King directs. Furthermore, this figure of the ideal king also served as an example of the ideal Israelite, an exemplar of piety—the reader is challenged by this redaction to follow "the king's" example and to truly love Yahweh his God.

5.4 ASSOCIATION WITH PSALMS 1 AND 2

In one sense, it should not be a surprise to find similarities in content between psalms of similar genre,[91] yet the links which exist between Pss 20–21

---

[90] Mays, *Psalms*, 90; Hossfeld and Zenger, *Die Psalmen I*, 138; McCann, *Psalms*, 758–59.

and Pss 1–2 go beyond merely formal considerations. The liturgical setting of the covenant community's worship may have lead to some overlap in style and (perhaps) vocabulary, however, the important question when comparing Pss 20–21 with Pss 1–2 is: "Can one observe a central *theological* connection?" Are these psalms saying the same thing about Israel's king? Do they emphasise the same characteristics? Do they stress the same priorities? Form and liturgy are important considerations which associate individual poems, but there is also a deliberate attempt to link these psalms *theologically* in the final form of the Psalter. This theological association includes their placement in relationship to one another. It is important not only to analyse what the individual psalms say but, also, to ask how they each relate to other psalms at the heart of this group.

5.4.1 KINGSHIP-TORAH THEME

Arguably the most significant connection with the introduction to the Psalter is the placement of Pss 20–21. Their association of the idea of kingship dependent upon Yahweh with the king who delights in the torah of Yahweh (Ps 19), echoes the torah-kingship association of Pss 1 and 2. Effectively Pss 18, 20 and 21 are a small group of royal psalms which has been divided by a torah psalm, and it seems that the editors of the Psalter wanted the reader to notice the close juxtaposition of ideas which echo themes found in the introductory psalms. Allen notes that, "In terms of genre it [Ps 19] interrupts a run of royal psalms, Pss 18; 20; 21. This phenomenon is suggestive in the light of Wilson's research: was Ps 19 intentionally inserted into the group by way of hermeneutical comment?"[92] Miller adds to these observations:

> [T]here are two separate matters in the introduction—delight in the torah (Ps 1) and God's activity through the king (Ps 2)—and... these separate concerns will be taken up respectively... as this particular collection in Pss 15–24 moves forward. In the midst of the explicitly royal psalms is Yahweh's torah. God's word in the torah and God's rule through the king are bound together. The witness to that single torah-shaped rule is the voice of the king here at the center.[93]

The repetition of the torah-kingship paradigm from Pss 1–2 indicates that the juxtaposition of Pss 18–21 was a deliberate attempt on the part of the redactors to associate these compositions with the book's introduction.

---

[91] Kraus points out this fact, (*Psalms*, 285).
[92] Allen, "David as Exemplar," 546.
[93] Miller, "Kingship," 128.

5.4.2 MESSIAH LINK

Another association between Pss 20–21 and the introduction is the centrality of Yahweh's "messiah." Just as the king was described as Yahweh's messiah in Ps 2:2, 6, we come across the same idea in Ps 20:7, a verse which is central to the theology of the psalm.[94] Whilst the word משיח does not appear in Ps 21, the idea the Lord's anointed is self-evident in the psalm. Clearly, Pss 18–21 focus upon the sovereign lordship of Yahweh—it is he who initiates covenant, he is the one who is able to save and offer great victories—however, the role of his anointed is significant in these psalms' presentation of the community before God. Pss 20–21 set out a type of relationship between the king and Yahweh which resonates strongly with the theological emphasis of Ps 2: God's anointed is important for the fulfillment of his plans for his people, thus the representative nature of kingship is significant for a proper understanding of both Pss 1–2 and 18–21.

5.4.3 PRAYER THEME

Connected with this idea of significant relationship between Yahweh and king, we see the repeated idea of the importance of prayer (as seen in Ps 2:8; 20:2, 3, 7; and Ps 21:3–5). In each of these psalms is the assurance that the king—or rather, to be more specific, the torah-keeping king—can offer his prayers to Yahweh in the certain knowledge that these prayers are heard and shall be answered. As we have seen in Ps 18, and is implied by the concatenation of Pss 19, 20 and 21, this assurance is dependent upon the king's "blamelessness" and commitment to Yahweh's torah.

> The situation of the song of thanksgiving is clearly pointed out in v. 2 [of Ps 21]: the king has directed a prayer to Yahweh, and that prayer has been heard. Here we should first consider that in the OT God's chosen king had the privilege of free prayer (1 Kings 3:5ff.; Pss. 2:8; 20:4; G. von Rad, *OT Theol*, 1:320). He held an exceptional priestly position (Jer. 30:21). Concerning the contents of the king's prayer we hear details in v. 4.[95]

---

[94] See the above quote from Mays, p 109n82.

[95] Kraus, *Psalms*, 285. By implication Kraus suggests that the king has a privileged prayer status over the rest of Israel. This is certainly not the necessary interpretation of these psalms, where the king especially is being called upon to pray, but in doing so he sets an example for all the people. The king's prayer is connected with his task as representative of the people, but the right of prayer is certainly not limited to him, as is seen by the fact that Ps 20 is an account of the people's prayer for the king. (See also Miller's comments on the democratised figure of the king in "Kingship.")

Torah-Kingship Theme in Psalms 18–21

Our thesis... is that the king/Israelite who is the central figure of this collection not only delights in and keeps torah—as we would expect in the light of the clues provided from the introduction in Pss 1 and 2—but demonstrates in the rest of the psalms the way of faithful prayer in trust.[96]

According to the ideal of kingship in the psalms, the king was given the privilege and power of prayer in a pre-eminent way. As the one who was son in relation to God, he could ask and hope to be answered. But what he received from God he must request. None of his gifts and endowments were inherent in his person. He was the model of the indispensable place of prayer in the human relation to God. The Old Testament basis for "Our Father in heaven" was laid in him (Pss 2:7–8; 18:6; 20:4–5; see Mark 11:23–34; Luke 11:5–13).[97]

5.4.4   THEME OF THE TWO WAYS

One of the key features of the theology of Pss 1 and 2 was the clear contrast of the way of Yahweh as opposed to the way of the wicked. This contrast was established in Ps 1 with the contrasting way of the "one who delights in the torah" leading to life and prosperity and way of "the wicked" leading to destruction (v 3 cf v 6). The idea was continued into Ps 2 with the contrasting states of "those who take refuge in Yahweh" (v 12) and the kings and rulers who rebel against Yahweh and his anointed one (vv 1–2)—the former finding happiness (אשרי, v 12) and the latter, again, finding themselves on the way of destruction (ותאבדו דרך, v 12). We see the continuation of this idea in Psalms 20 and 21 where there are, once more, two contrasting paths presented to the reader. For example, there are those who trust in military might in Ps 20:8 as opposed to those who trust in the Lord; and Ps 21 tells of those who trust in Yahweh as opposed to those who hate him.[98] However, the idea of the two ways is most clearly seen in the contrast between the king and his enemies in Pss 20–21. The former knows the daily salvation of Yahweh (20:7, 10) and his eternal blessing (21:7–8), the latter experiences his opposition and punishment (20:8–9, 21:9–13). Therefore, another prominent aspect of the didactic purpose of Pss 1–2 as a hermeneutical construct is repeated in Psalms 20–21.

So we see that the theology of Pss 1–2, which provides the reader with a hermeneutical paradigm for the reading of the Psalms, is repeated in Psalms

---

[96] Miller, "Kingship," 134.
[97] Mays, *Psalms*, 103–04.
[98] It is unclear whether the reference in Ps 21:9 refers to Yahweh or the king. However, in the Psalter, it appears that either act amounts to much the same thing (Ps 2:2).

20-21, just as it has been repeated in Pss 18–19. It appears that there has been a deliberate attempt to link these four psalms with the theology of the Psalter's introduction.

6. Conclusion

The exegetical work having been done, some final observations should be drawn from these texts, before moving on to study Pss 118 and 119. There are several observations which can be drawn from the above exegesis which are significant to the overall argument of this thesis:

6.1 Background in Deuteronomic Theology

Whilst there may also be other themes at work in these psalms, Psalms 18–21 are firmly grounded in Dtr theology. As we have seen above, themes which are prominent in Deuteronomy are also to be found in these psalms. It is widely acknowledged that the influence of Deuteronomy upon the OT canon is broad, and that influence is observable in the Psalter.[99] This fact is significant because such a background should be expected if there has been a deliberate attempt on the part of the editors of the Book of Psalms to juxtapose kingship and torah psalms in order to reflect the Kingship Law. In order to make their point, the redactors of the Psalter make use of lyrics which draw on the theological perspective which they seek to emphasise. We can observe that these individual poems are firmly grounded in the worldview of the Deuteronomist, making the allusion to the Kingship Law all the more visible to the reader.

6.2 Torah-Kingship Connection

Over and above the general Deuteronomic background to the psalms, we see a concerted effort to associate the king with the torah of Yahweh. This is seen in two ways: firstly, in the content of Ps 18 where the central strophe is a declaration of the king's devotion to Yahweh and his torah; and, secondly, in the centrality of Ps 19 within this psalm grouping. The way in which Ps 19 breaks up a run of royal psalms of similar theme makes its positioning seem all the more significant, and this setting amidst kingship compositions further accentuates the indications within Ps 19's content that the psalmist is, in fact, the king. The

---

[99] See Miller, "Deuteronomy and Psalms."

close association of kingship and torah poems functions as a red flag to draw the the reader's attention to that which they have seen before. The placement of Pss 1-2 at the beginning of the Psalter was designed to drawn the attention of the reader to themes which were important to those who had put the book of Psalms together; the intention being that awareness of these motifs should remain prominent in the mind of the reader throughout their reading or hearing of the Psalter. Therefore, when that reader comes to Psalms 18-21 and notices a kingship-torah-kingship pattern, she is reminded of the voice of the introduction to the Psalter. The Dtr background which is apparent in these psalms goes beyond a general concern for the Dtr worldview in the life of Israel: rather, the reader's attention is drawn particularly to the Kingship Law and the piety suggested by it.

6.3 DEMOCRATISATION OF THE KING

Psalms 20 and 21, through their setting in liturgy, confuse the roles of king and people. The latter pray for the king, and the king, in turn, represents the people before Yahweh acting as a "guarantor" of security for them. The king's trust in Yahweh is echoed by the same response from the people, and that blessing which the king receives is blessing for the nation. As McCann points out, there is something of a fusion of roles within these psalms—the identity of the king and the identity of the individual being merged in certain ways:

> As reflected in vv 4-5, it was the prerogative of the king to make requests of God (see Commentary on Ps 2:8-9; see also... Ps 21:4). Verse 5a indicates that the welfare and future of the people are bound up with that of the king.[100]
>
> The Hebrew reads, "O LORD, grant victory! May the king [i.e., God] answer us when we call" (so NJPS). This reading emphasizes that the LORD is the true king. It may represent a democratizing understanding that claims the right and privileges of the anointed for the people (see Psalm 2...).[101]
>
> Moreover, the presence of Psalm 19 in book one, especially juxtaposed to a psalm about kingship, seems to indicate further association of the concepts of meditating on *tôrâ* and seeking refuge in Yahweh. *Given the nature of Psalms 1-2 and these emphases in David 1, it seems possible that book one of the Psalter should be read as an extended picture of true piety, seen in total reliance on Yahweh and exemplified by David.*[102]

---

[100] McCann, *Psalms*, 755.
[101] Mays, *Psalms*, 102.
[102] Creach, *Yahweh as Refuge*, 80 (emphasis mine).

This process of democratisation emphasises the dual purpose of this kingship-torah redaction: (1) the figure of the king is important as part of the eschatological hope voiced in the Psalter, but more than that; (2) he is important as an example of piety for all of the people of Israel. These psalms seem to reflect the idea that the blessings and privileges which were available to be Lord's anointed are also available to the people of God who will walk in the ways of Yahweh, keeping his torah.

6.4 LIMITATION OF THE POWER OF THE KING

The kingship which is celebrated within these psalms is not the kingship which is found in the DtrH. As we shall see in our discussion of Deut 17:14–20, Deuteronomy and the Deuteronomic History present an image of kingship which can—at best—be described as ambivalent, if not verging on negative. The kingship which is manifest within these poetic texts is of a very different nature from even the best examples to be found within the DtrH. The characteristics of the king which are lauded within Psalms 18–21 are not the characteristics of might, power, wealth or status, but rather the king is exalted in as much as he humbles himself to accept the rule of Yahweh. The main characteristic which runs throughout these psalms is one of total dependency upon and commitment to Yahweh, trusting in him above all else for all matters of piety and polity. Such characteristics are not often found in the DtrH's portrayal of the kings of Israel and Judah, thus the presentation of the ideal of kingship found in these psalms is not one which focuses upon the trappings of wealth and power, but one which concentrates the attention of the reader upon the king's submission to Yahweh and his rule. If anything, the ideal king is presented as one who submits himself to Yahweh—limiting his own power and status—and trusts in him alone.

6.5 TORAH-PRAYER LINK

One further element of the theology of Pss 1 and 2 is greatly magnified in Pss 18–21, i.e. the importance of prayer to Yahweh (Ps 2:8). In Psalms 18–21 the prominence of prayer is combined with a piety based around the torah of Yahweh. Each of these four psalms contains an element of prayer which refers either to the psalmist's adversity in combating "enemies" (with the connotations of the "two ways," Pss 18, 20 and 21) or to the task of pursuing personal godliness (Ps 19:13-15). This increased emphasis on prayer adds to the idea that the king is being presented as an ideal of spirituality before God—the king is being portrayed as the ideal follower of Yahweh whose example all the people of Israel, in turn, should follow. Prayer and delight in the torah are two essential elements of that piety, as is further emphasised in the message of Pss 118-119.

These considerations are all significant in our task of establishing whether or not there has been a Deuteronomic redaction of the Psalter which has deliberately placed torah and kingship psalms in close proximity in order to replicate the theology of the Deuteronomic Kingship Law as part of the Psalter's presentation of the king.[103] It appears, from detailed exegetical analysis of the four psalms in question (Psalms 18-21), that these psalms have been deliberately placed alongside one another, and that the purpose of that juxtaposition was to bring the Kingship Law to mind as the reader of the Psalter considers questions of the rule of Yahweh and the life of piety. The same conclusion has been drawn from analysis of Pss 1 and 2, therefore our attention now turns to the examination of Ps 119 in its context in order to establish if this is a holistic redaction observable throughout the book of Psalms.

---

[103] Once again, this suggestion is only part of the canonical Psalter's presentation of kingship. There are other importantly placed royal psalms which reflect upon different aspects of kingship (e.g. Pss 72 and 110 which dwell more upon the eschatological dimensions of kingship).

CHAPTER 4
TORAH-KINGSHIP THEME IN PSALMS 118–119

1. INTRODUCTION

In some ways Psalms 118 and 119 appear to provide the greatest challenge towards demonstrating a redaction of the Psalter which reflects the Deuteronomic Law of the King. In the previous two chapters, we have noted the juxtaposition of royal and torah themes at the introduction to the Book of Psalms (Pss 1 and 2) and at the heart of Book I of the Psalter (Psalms 18–21). It could be said that this was a non-controversial task—almost without exception scholars recognise the torah theology found in Psalms 1 and 19 and the royal emphases of Psalms 2, 18, 20 and 21. However, it is a somewhat different story with Psalms 118 and 119. There are, for example, no superscriptions linking either of the psalms with the Davidic king and Psalm 118 is seen to be part of the Egyptian *Hallel*, thus associated with Exodus themes rather than royal themes. Whilst the torah focus of Psalm 119 is beyond question, the identity of the speaker of Psalm 119 is much debated, with many scholars placing this psalm firmly in the ranks of the wisdom psalms and associating it with the wisdom schools of post-exilic Judaism. So, it could be argued that, whilst the observations with regard to Psalms 1–2 and 18–21 may well be valid, Psalms 118 and 119 do not readily fit into this pattern of deliberately juxtaposed royal and torah psalms, thus the argument as a whole fails.

Any such conclusion, however, must be based on exegesis and not merely supposition. Indeed, it is by way of detailed exegetical examination of Psalms 118 and 119 that I hope to establish that these juxtaposed psalms represent the zenith of the Deuteronomic kingship theology of the Psalter. We shall see that Psalms 118–119 likewise are deliberately placed alongside one another in order to reflect the Deuteronomic Law of the King and to highlight the representative function of the expected, eschatological king amongst his people. Moreover, this ideal of kingship is held up before the readers of the Book of Psalms as the ideal of personal piety, as an exemplar which all those who are intent upon "walking in the ways of Yahweh" should follow. Psalm 118 reflects the theology of the Entrance Psalms (Psalms 15 and 24), and it is the king who leads the people in this antiphonal act of worship as their representative before Yahweh. It is this same king who offers up a prayer in Psalm 119, an intercession of lament to his God, which represents a spirituality firmly grounded in God's revelation. The "typical" indicators may be missing from Psalms 118–119, but the dual focus upon torah and royal themes is still present, reflecting the influence of a Deuteronomic redaction which puts the royal theology of the Psalter into a proper canonical context. Yes, the people are to expect a renewed kingship, but this is to be a kingship which is radically different from that recorded in the Deuteronomic History.

2. Selection of Psalms 118 and 119

Obviously, selection of the primary material to be studied is a vital factor in the results which any study will arrive at. Therefore, we must remind ourselves why Psalms 118 and 119 are the focus for this next stage of our study. The answer to that question is essentially the same as the answer provided with regard to the choice of Psalms 18–21: namely, the selection of primary material is dictated by the positioning of the so-called "torah psalms."[1] When one adopts a canonical approach to the Psalter, questions of ordering and placement are of great importance.[2] Thus, one of the most significant questions that can be asked of the canonical Book of Psalms is, "Why is Psalm 1 the first psalm? Why start with this psalm rather than another which is more representative of the contents of the Psalter or Book I—a lament, for example?" In asking this question, the significance of the torah psalms—whose importance was generally denigrated by form-critical scholars—is suddenly elevated.[3]

---

[1] See above, pp 72–74.

[2] See, for example, Childs, *IOTS*, 512–14, or Wilson, *Editing*, 139–41. Wilson further expands upon these ideas in such articles as "Shape" and "Understanding" among others.

[3] Mays, "Place of the Torah-Psalms."

We have seen that Psalm 1—by way of lexical interaction, lack of superscription and common themes—was deliberately juxtaposed alongside Psalm 2 (a royal psalm), and so the reader is able to observe a linking of torah and kingship themes which provides a particular hermeneutical perspective right at the start of the Psalter. This, then, raises the question about whether or not the other torah psalms reflect this same sort of torah-kingship paradigm. So our attention is turned to the remaining torah psalms: first, to Psalm 19 and its neighbours and then to Psalm 119 and the surrounding psalms.[4] Our analysis, and choice of material, is dictated by the torah psalms and their positioning within the canonical Psalter. It is because Psalm 119 is clearly a torah psalm, that we must ask the question about whether or not it too plays a role in a possible DtrN redaction of the Psalter designed to reflect the Kingship Law of Deuteronomy 17:14-20 in the theology of the Psalms.

The question then arises, "Why choose Psalm 118 and not Psalm 120? Is this a random choice? Or is there reason to do so?" Indeed, the choice of Psalm 118 is not random, but one which is indicated by the positioning of that psalm in relation to Psalm 119 and the surrounding poems in Book V. Psalm 120 is clearly part of the "Songs of Ascents" collection (שׁיר המעלות), as is indicated both by its superscription and its content. Therefore, Psalm 120 is to be associated with the ensuing psalms rather than Psalm 119. At first glance, it appears that the same argument could be made with regard to Psalm 118. Is it not part of the Egyptian Hallel and therefore more to be associated with Psalms 113-117? In the Rabbinic literature Psalm 118 is seen as part of the Great or Egyptian Hallel,[5] however, the *textual* grounds for the association of Psalm 118 with the *hallel* psalms are limited—the association is more drawn from historical praxis than canonical exegesis. Psalm 118 does not have the הללו יה introduction or conclusion shared by all of the poems in the Great Hallel (except Psalm 114[6]),

---

[4] Mays, "Place of the Torah-Psalms," 3, 11.

[5] J. Ross Wagner, "Psalm 118 in Luke-Acts: Tracing a Narrative Thread," in *Early Christian Interpretation of the Scriptures of Israel: Investigations and Proposals* (ed. Craig A. Evans and James A. Sanders; JSNTSup 148 & SSEJC 5; Sheffield: Sheffield Academic Press, 1997), 158–59; T. F. Torrance, "The Last of the Hallel Psalms," *EvQ* 28 (1956): 101–08.

[6] Ps 114 lacks the הללו יה superscription, but, exceptionally for this group of psalms, Ps 113 contains both *hallelu yah* superscription and postscript. It is likely that the *hallelu yah* postscript from Ps 113 was originally the superscription of Ps 114 (see Freedman, *Psalm 119*, 4).

nor does it readily reflect the Exodus themes which run throughout the collection. Undoubtedly, the historical evidence suggests that Psalm 118 *came to function* as part of the Great Hallel used in the liturgy of the festivals, but it is questionable whether this was the intent of the redactors in their positioning of Psalm 118. Was it meant to be associated with the Hallel? Or was the intent rather for Ps 118 to be associated with Ps 119 as a centrepiece to Book V?

First, as Patrick Miller points out, thematically, Psalm 118 does not fit well as part of the Egyptian Hallel: "It is not fully accurate to set Psalm 118 under the 'Exodus' theme.... It is centered on Zion and the temple, of course."[7] Secondly, Wilson points out that the signs of editorial activity in Books IV–V of the Psalter differ from those found in Books I–III. One of the distinctive characteristics of editorial activity within Psalms 107–150 which Wilson draws attention to is the use of *hllwyh* and *hwdw* headings to differentiate between different groups of psalms.[8] Each of Psalms 111–117 include הללו יה either as superscription or postscript; by way of contrast Psalm 118 begins with the words הודו ליהוה. Freedman suggests that it is actually Pss 111–117 which form a cohesive grouping rather than the traditional 113–118 Hallel group: "Both [Pss 111 and 112] have the same distinctive heading, shared by several others in this group from no. 111 through 117—*a group of seven psalms*, each of which begins or ends with the expression *hallelu yah*...."[9]

This would tend to indicate that the editors of the Psalter intended to disassociate Psalm 118 from the preceding *hallel* psalms, leaving Psalms 118 and 119 as an isolated pairing between two pre-existing collections (the Hallel Psalms, 111–117, and the Songs of Ascents, 120–134). Therefore, it appears that—by placing Psalm 118 alongside Psalm 119 and sandwiching them between two collections of psalms—the editors of the canonical Book of Psalms intended that these psalms should be associated together as the centrepiece to Book V. It is for these reasons that Psalms 118 and 119 form the next part of our study: firstly, as dictated by our analysis of the torah psalms as a category; and, secondly, as implied by the above indications of editorial activity within Book V.

Having established the grounds for the selection of Psalms 118–119 as the object of our study, now we must turn our attention to consideration of the ques-

---

[7] Miller, "The End of the Psalter: A Response to Erich Zenger," 104.
[8] Wilson, "Shaping," 78–79.
[9] Freedman, *Psalm 119*, 4 (emphasis added). See also Mitchell, *Message*, 87.

tion in hand. Do these psalms reflect general Deuteronomic concerns (indicating some sort of Dtr redaction); and, if so, do they echo the preoccupation with kingship and torah which we have seen in the previous torah-kingship psalm groupings? Again, if the theory of a redaction which seeks to give the Psalter's theology of kingship a Dtr slant is to be proven, then the psalms must be allowed to speak for themselves. Therefore, we must turn our attention to Psalm 118.

3. ANALYSIS OF PSALM 118

BHS	Translation
הוֹדוּ לַיהוָה כִּי־טוֹב כִּי לְעוֹלָם חַסְדּוֹ׃ יֹאמַר־נָא יִשְׂרָאֵל כִּי לְעוֹלָם חַסְדּוֹ׃ יֹאמְרוּ־נָא בֵית־אַהֲרֹן כִּי לְעוֹלָם חַסְדּוֹ׃ יֹאמְרוּ־נָא יִרְאֵי יְהוָה כִּי לְעוֹלָם חַסְדּוֹ׃	1 Give thanks to Yahweh, for he is good; for his steadfast love is for ever! 2 Let Israel say, "His steadfast love is forever." 3 Let the house of Aaron say, "His steadfast love is forever." 4 Let those who fear Yahweh say, "His steadfast love is forever."
מִן־הַמֵּצַר קָרָאתִי יָּהּ עָנָנִי בַמֶּרְחָב יָהּ׃ יְהוָה לִי לֹא אִירָא מַה־יַּעֲשֶׂה לִי אָדָם׃ יְהוָה לִי בְּעֹזְרָי וַאֲנִי אֶרְאֶה בְשֹׂנְאָי׃	5 From my straits I called out to Yahweh; Yahweh answered me with a broad place. 6 Yahweh is for me, I will not be afraid; What can man do to me? 7 Yahweh is for me, he is my help; and I will look with triumph over those who hate me.
טוֹב לַחֲסוֹת בַּיהוָה מִבְּטֹחַ בָּאָדָם׃ טוֹב לַחֲסוֹת בַּיהוָה מִבְּטֹחַ בִּנְדִיבִים׃	8 It is better to take refuge in Yahweh; than to trust in man. 9 It is better to take refuge in Yahweh; than to trust in princes.
כָּל־גּוֹיִם סְבָבוּנִי בְּשֵׁם יְהוָה כִּי אֲמִילַם׃ סַבּוּנִי גַם־סְבָבוּנִי בְּשֵׁם יְהוָה כִּי אֲמִילַם׃ סַבּוּנִי כִדְבוֹרִים דֹּעֲכוּ כְּאֵשׁ קוֹצִים בְּשֵׁם יְהוָה כִּי אֲמִילַם׃ דַּחֹה דְחִיתַנִי לִנְפֹּל וַיהוָה עֲזָרָנִי׃ עָזִּי וְזִמְרָת יָהּ וַיְהִי־לִי לִישׁוּעָה׃	10 All the nations surrounded me; in the name of Yahweh I cut them off. 11 They surrounded me again; but in the name of Yahweh I cut them off. 12 They surrounded me like bees, yet they were extinguished like a burning thorn bush; by Yahweh's name I cut them off. 13 I was pushed firmly to fall; but Yahweh helped me. 14 My strength and song is Yahweh; and he has become my salvation

קוֹל רִנָּה וִישׁוּעָה בְּאָהֳלֵי צַדִּיקִים יְמִין
יְהוָה עֹשָׂה חָיִל׃
יְמִין יְהוָה רוֹמֵמָה יְמִין יְהוָה עֹשָׂה חָיִל׃

15 Shouts of joy and salvation are in the tents of the righteous, "Yahweh's right hand is doing mighty deeds.
16 "The right hand of Yahweh is lifted high; the right hand of Yahweh has done a mighty deed."

לֹא אָמוּת כִּי־אֶחְיֶה וַאֲסַפֵּר מַעֲשֵׂי יָהּ׃
יַסֹּר יִסְּרַנִּי יָּהּ וְלַמָּוֶת לֹא נְתָנָנִי׃
פִּתְחוּ־לִי שַׁעֲרֵי־צֶדֶק אָבֹא־בָם אוֹדֶה יָהּ׃

17 I will not die, but I will live; and I will recount Yahweh's deeds.
18 Yahweh has disciplined me strongly; yet he has not given me over to death.
19 Open for me the gates of righteousness; I will enter in and give thanks to Yahweh.

זֶה־הַשַּׁעַר לַיהוָה צַדִּיקִים יָבֹאוּ בוֹ׃

20 This is the gate of Yahweh; the righteous will enter it.

אוֹדְךָ כִּי עֲנִיתָנִי וַתְּהִי־לִי לִישׁוּעָה׃
אֶבֶן מָאֲסוּ הַבּוֹנִים הָיְתָה לְרֹאשׁ פִּנָּה׃
מֵאֵת יְהוָה הָיְתָה זֹּאת הִיא נִפְלָאת בְּעֵינֵינוּ׃
זֶה־הַיּוֹם עָשָׂה יְהוָה נָגִילָה וְנִשְׂמְחָה בוֹ׃

21 I give you thanks because you heard me; and you have became my salvation.
22 The stone the builders rejected has become the capstone.
23 Yahweh has done this thing and it is wonderful in our eyes.
24 This is the day that Yahweh has made; let us rejoice and be glad in it.

אָנָּא יְהוָה הוֹשִׁיעָה נָּא אָנָּא יְהוָה הַצְלִיחָה נָּא׃

25 O Yahweh, save us, we pray; O Yahweh, prosper us, we pray.

בָּרוּךְ הַבָּא בְּשֵׁם יְהוָה בֵּרַכְנוּכֶם מִבֵּית יְהוָה׃
אֵל יְהוָה וַיָּאֶר לָנוּ אִסְרוּ־חַג בַּעֲבֹתִים עַד־קַרְנוֹת הַמִּזְבֵּחַ׃

26 Blessed is he who comes in the name of Yahweh; we bless you from the house of Yahweh.
27 Yahweh is God, and he enlightened us; Call a festival with boughs unto the horns of the altar.

אֵלִי אַתָּה וְאוֹדֶךָּ אֱלֹהַי אֲרוֹמְמֶךָּ׃

28 You are my God and I will give thanks to you; My God and I will exalt you.

הוֹדוּ לַיהוָה כִּי־טוֹב כִּי לְעוֹלָם חַסְדּוֹ׃

29 Give thanks to Yahweh because he is good; for his steadfast love lasts forever.

3.1 DEUTERONOMIC INFLUENCES IN PS 118

Once again our initial task is to ascertain whether or not there is a Deuteronomic background to this composition. Does it readily reflect the attitudes and priorities that Dtr editors would wish to promote?

3.1.1 PS 118 AS ENTRANCE LITURGY

Most commentators are agreed that Psalm 118[10] reflects an antiphonal act of worship, with the king leading the people in a public celebration of Yahweh's faithfulness towards himself specifically (possibly in providing a military victory), and also towards the people in general.[11] So, it would be reasonable to

---

[10] The text of Ps 118 itself is not particularly problematic, with only minor textual issues. The most significant issue in terms of interpretation is the division of the psalm, as an antiphonal act of worship, into "voices." The division of the text above suggests one possible rendering of this "conversation," but it is by no means the only one possible.

[11] Leslie C. Allen, *Psalms 101–150* (WBC; Waco: Word Books, 1983), 123–25; A. A. Anderson, *The Book of Psalms, Volume II, Psalms 73–150* (NCB; London: Marshall, Morgan & Scott, 1972), 797–98; Croft, *Identity*, 85; Mitchell Dahood, *Psalms III, 101–150: A New Translation with Introduction and Commentary* (AB; Garden City, New York: Doubleday and Co., 1970), 155; Eaton, *Psalms*, 271–72; Aubrey R. Johnson, *Sacral Kingship in Ancient Israel* (Cardiff: University of Wales Press, 1967), 123–24; Mays, *Psalms*, 379; VanGemeren, *Psalms*, 729 and Artur Weiser, *The Psalms: A Commentary* (OTL; trans. H. Hartwell; Philadelphia: Westminster Press, 1962), 724–25, all see the speaker as being the Davidic king. McCann (*Psalms*, 1153), sees the king as being the most likely candidate for the role of speaker in Ps 118, but is unwilling to be more emphatic than that. Oesterley (*Psalms*, 484); Kirkpatrick (*Psalms*, 697) and Briggs (*Psalms*, 402–04), all speak about some unidentified representative of Israel being the speaker of Ps 118, but none of these three explain why Yahweh's חסד towards this unidentified individual is so significant for the whole community. The one significant question-mark with regard to the kingship of the speaker is the lack of a Davidic superscription. However, such a superscription is not essential for a poem to be accepted as a royal psalm, e.g. Ps 2. Indeed, Wilson points out that such "authorship" designations are largely lacking from Books IV & V and that other editorial designations are used in these books instead ("Shaping," 73). There are several textual indications that the leader of this antiphonal worship is the king: (1) The apparent setting for the deliverance received from Yahweh is one of military conflict, thus indicating that the most likely speaker is the king who would lead the people into battle. (2) The speaker refuses to trust in men or "princes" (v 9), as we shall see in the course of our study, this is probably a reference to foreign leaders and it is likely that only the king would have the opportunity to put his trust in princes by way of international alliance. (3) Verses 10–12 speak of the opposition of the nations surrounding the speaker, again indicating a military setting, where the king would lead the people in battle against other nations. (4) The representative nature of the speaker, who leads the community into Temple worship, means that the psalmist-speaker must fulfill some sort of official function on the people's behalf—of all

expect Psalm 118 to be firmly grounded in the Priestly, cultic literature;[12] this is, after all, a psalm which focuses upon Zion and the Temple and even the altar. On the contrary, however, Psalm 118 does not find its roots in the Priestly literature, but rather is deeply rooted in the moral and legal concepts of righteousness found in the Book of Deuteronomy and the Deuteronomic literature. Zion and the temple do, indeed, provide a backdrop to Psalm 118, but this hymn is more akin to the Entrance Psalms (15 and 24) than to the psalms of the cult, *per se*.[13]

Psalm 118 is essentially a hymn of thanksgiving to Yahweh which is both individual and corporate, as is reflected by the changes from first person singular to first person plural speech throughout the psalm. Most likely, it was because of this concentration upon thanksgiving for Yahweh's salvation that Psalm 118 became associated with the *hallel* psalms and the festivals,[14] but the scene enacted in Psalm 118 reflects the theology of the Entrance Psalms rather than the cultic ideas of the sacerdotal system itself.[15] Following on from a praise introduction, the king publicly recounts the trials and difficulties which he has faced, gives thanks to God for his deliverance, and then—based upon Yahweh's mercy extended to him—he seeks entrance into the Temple to offer thanks to Yahweh. This request is met with the challenge of the priests guarding the gate that only the righteous (צדיקים) may enter into the holiness of the Temple. Ultimately, Yahweh's action in delivering the king is seen as testimony to his blamelessness.[16] The same sort of concepts apply in Psalms 15 and 24 where the ques-

---

the known offices it is most likely that the king would fulfil the role indicated in Ps 118. (5) Finally, Eaton points out that the "Blessed is he who comes in the name of the Lord" formula is one which is associated with kingship in the OT (*Kingship*, 62). Therefore, it seems most likely that it is the king who is the speaker-leader in Ps 118.

[12] See the discussion in Croft, *Identity*, 85–88.

[13] Hans-Joachim Kraus, *Psalms 60–150: A Commentary* (trans. Hilton C. Oswald; Minneapolis: Augsburg, 1989), 395, writes: "Psalm 118 therefore belongs to the area of gate liturgies, which are in greater detail recognisable above all in Psalms 15 and 24.... At the entry to the temple area each cultic participant is to give a declaration of loyalty. Only the צדיקים (v 20b; Isa 26:2) may pass through the 'portals of Yahweh' and enter the sanctuary." See also Anderson, *Psalms*, 797, and Weiser, *Psalms*, 728.

[14] James A. Sanders, "A New Testament Hermeneutic Fabric: Psalm 118 in the Entrance Narrative," in *Early Jewish and Christian Exegesis: Studies in Memory of William Hugh Brownlee* (Atlanta: Scholars Press, 1987), 180.

[15] Mays writes that the theological claims of Ps 118 are "not tied to a particular historical occasion or social setting or festival...." ("Psalm 118 in the Light of Canonical Analysis," in *Canon, Theology and Old Testament Interpretation: Essays in Honor of Brevard S. Childs* [ed. G. M. Tucker et al.; Philadelphia: Fortress Press, 1988], 310).

tion is asked, "Lord, who may dwell in your sanctuary? Who may dwell on your holy hill?" (Ps 15:1), or, alternatively, "Who may ascend the hill of the Lord? Who may stand in his holy place?" (Ps 24:3). In both of these instances, the reply to the question comes in moral terms, in concepts grounded in a Dtr understanding of righteousness.[17] The Dtr worldview dominates the whole collection of Pss 15–24 (as we saw in our analysis of Pss 18–21) and, since Ps 118 is theologically associated with Pss 15 and 24, the reader should expect to see the influence of this worldview providing the proper backdrop to Ps 118. The king is giving testimony to the goodness of Yahweh in providing salvation, and he does so in terms which reflect the theology of Deuteronomy. So, we see that, at the most fundamental level, the setting of Ps 118 as an Entrance Psalm is designed to awaken the reader's awareness of a setting in Dtr theology.

3.1.2 ETERNAL HESED OF YAHWEH

Psalm 118 begins and ends with the celebration of Yahweh's steadfast love (חסד, vv 1–4, 29). Of course, this is the concept which is found throughout the whole of the Old Testament, and, therefore, cannot in and of itself be described as Deuteronomic. However, whilst not seeking to claim the idea of חסד as being inherently Deuteronomic, it would be equally wrong to forget the intimate link between חסד and covenant—particularly since the idea of לעולם חסדו, as it is found here in Ps 118, is a usage of *hesed* which is particularly associated with the covenant.[18] The חסד of Yahweh is revealed to Israel primarily in his covenant with them. He has bound himself to a covenant relationship of חסד with Israel as a community (Ex 20:6) as well as with the Davidic king as his anointed (2 Sam 7:15). It is in this concept of covenant, or treaty, with Israel as his people that the reader is reminded of the link between the חסד of Yahweh and the Book of Deuteronomy. Deuteronomy presents itself as the written covenant between Yahweh and his people (e.g. Deut 27:1–8)—a covenant of חסד, but a covenant with binding effect nonetheless.[19]

The word חסד is found only three times in Deuteronomy, but what is significant concerning Deuteronomy's use of חסד is its association with law-

---

[16] Mays, "Ps 118," 158–59.
[17] Miller, "Kingship," 127–28, 135.
[18] See, for example, Mitchell's discussion of the link between eternal *hesed* and covenant in Ps 89 in *Message*, 254.
[19] Miller, *Deuteronomy*, 12–15; Wright, *Deuteronomy*, 2–3.

keeping.[20] It is found in the repetition of the Ten Commandments (Deut 5:10), where חסד is promised to a "thousand generations of those who *love me and keep my commandments*" (ועשה חסד לאלפים לאהבי ולשמרי מצותי). The people are reminded of this promise again in Deut 7:9, 12 where Moses challenges the people once more that Yahweh's covenant of חסד means that they are to "pay attention to these laws" (תשמעון את המשפטים האלה) and that they are to be "careful to follow them" (ושמרתם ועשיתם אתם). The association suggested by the Book of Deuteronomy is that continued enjoyment of the eternal covenant with Yahweh requires a correct attitude towards the *torah*.[21]

Given the context of Psalm 118, where its description of Yahweh's loving faithfulness (חסד) towards king and people is combined with an inherent expectation of righteousness on the part of both king and people (v 20), it appears that the usage of חסד in the introduction and conclusion of Psalm 118 is not far removed from the Deuteronomic understanding of Yahweh's covenant of חסד.[22] Yahweh does show *hesed* towards his people, but they are expected to keep the law in a response of love to the covenant promises of Yahweh. This point is particularly emphasised when one considers the deliberate juxtaposition of Psalm 118 alongside Psalm 119—Yahweh acts in salvific love for his people instituting covenant relationship with them, and the people's response should be to love him by keeping his commands. The introductory and concluding celebration of Yahweh's *hesed* cannot be divorced from the expectation of righteousness which lies at the heart of Psalm 118, and this rings true to Deuteronomy's understanding of Yahweh's covenant with his people based in חסד.

3.1.3 Fearers of Yahweh

Verses 2–4 of Psalm 118 appear to be a deliberate echo of Ps 115:9–13, where the same three groups of people ("Israel," "the house of Aaron" and "the fearers of Yahweh") are addressed twice. It is difficult to know why these three groups are mentioned specifically, but it seems likely that this form of address is somehow connected with the function of the Egyptian Hallel in the festivals,[23] with the involvement of the people of Israel in general and the priesthood in par-

---

[20] Miller, *Deuteronomy*, 113.
[21] McConville, *Grace in the End*, 20–24, 132–33; Wright, *Deuteronomy*, 117.
[22] Kraus, *Psalms II*, 395–96; Kirkpatrick, *Psalms*, 697; S. B. Frost, "Psalm 118: An Exposition," *CJT* VII, no. 3 (1961): 158–59.
[23] Sanders, "NT Hermeneutic Fabric," 181–82.

ticular, but who are "those who fear Yahweh?" This is a question which appears to go unanswered in both Ps 115 and Ps 118, but for the careful reader of the Psalms this address would probably lead her or him to certain Dtr associations. The link between Ps 118 and the Entrance Liturgies would suggest that the reader think about the יראי יהוה in terms of a righteousness based in moral propriety—a righteousness founded upon application of the torah—echoing the answers provided to the soul-searching questions of Pss 15 and 24.²⁴ These questions and their answers evoke a piety grounded in Dtr moral theology. So the reader should be inclined to understand "those who fear Yahweh" in terms that echo the Dtr conditions of access found in Pss 15 and 24.²⁵

This connection is more clearly understood by examination of the Deuteronomic presentation of the "fear of Yahweh," which is associated with torah obedience. Deuteronomy's presentation of fearing Yahweh often equates to keeping the laws and commands which he has given his people. There are many examples of this in the Book of Deuteronomy—4:10–14 sets the concept of "fearing Yahweh" alongside the concept of "learning the decrees and laws" (ללמד אתכם חקים ומשפטים לעשתכם אתם בארץ) which the people are to follow once they have crossed the Jordan (4:14). Such passages as 6:2, 24; 8:6; 10:12–13; 28:58; 32:12 etc., all make a direct correlation between keeping the torah (expressed using one synonym or another) and fearing Yahweh (e.g. 6:2, למען תירא את־יהוה אלהיך לשמר את־כל־חקתיו ומשפטיו). Furthermore, Deuteronomy makes it clear that *the Israelite king*—the central figure of Ps 118—is also meant to be a "fearer of Yahweh" (Deut 17:19).²⁶ After the king wrote out for himself a copy of the torah, he was to read it all the days of his life "so that he may learn to fear Yahweh his God and to keep all of the words of this torah and to do all of these statutes" (למען ילמד לירה את־יהוה אלהיו לשמר את־כל־דברי התורה הזאת ואת־החקים האלה לעשתם). Miller elaborates on the Dtr connection of "fearing the Lord" in the Psalms:

---

²⁴ Anderson, *Psalms*, 797; Miller, "Kingship," 131.

²⁵ The fear of Yahweh, like the theology of the two ways, is a concept which is found most commonly in the Deuteronomic Literature and Wisdom Literature. As Weinfeld argues, there does seem to be a substantial degree of overlap between these two schools, and this is borne out in our analysis of these psalms. However, Pss 118 bears characteristics in common with the Deuteronomic Psalms 15 and 24, whereas it does not bear any of the typical characteristics of Wisdom Psalms.

²⁶ Miller, *Deuteronomy*, 149; Wright, *Deuteronomy*, 209–10.

The goal of the whole, as both books inform us, is *to teach the fear of the* Lord. When the Psalmist says, "Come, O children, listen to me; I will teach you the fear of the Lord" (Ps 34:12 [Eng. 11]), one hears as well the voice of Moses in those words. In Deuteronomy, "the fear of the LORD your God" is synonymous with the demand of the First Commandment, "You shall have no other gods besides me." The positive form of that demand in Deuteronomy is "You shall fear the LORD your God." But the whole purpose of the law, of writing it down, of listening to it read, of teaching it to the children, is so that those who read and listen may learn to fear the Lord your God (e.g., Deut 4:10; 6:2, 24; 31:12-13). Even the rituals of festival and tithe are so that the people may learn to fear the Lord your God always (14:23), and the primary duty of the king is to model the aim of every citizen by reading in his copy of the law constantly ("all the days of his life") to learn the fear of the Lord his God (17:19).[27]

Clearly, Psalm 118 echoes the Dtr theology of piety and kingship, placing the king (the main speaker in this psalm) within the group of those who "fear Yahweh" and, by way of his representative function within the psalm, he serves as exemplar for the people. The only grounds for the king's admission into the Temple is righteousness (צדקה, v 20), and by implication the same conditions apply to all those who sought to enter Yahweh's "holy place." Deuteronomy's Kingship Law suggests that this is no more than should be expected of the Israelite king—he is, above all else, meant to be the example of a true Israelite for all Israel.[28] It is this principle that we see at work in Ps 118, and in the light of this Dtr understanding of "those who fear of Yahweh," we see again the significance of the editors putting Ps 118 alongside the great torah psalm, Ps 119.

> The designation "those who fear the Lord" will not be read simply as a term for public participants. The term will assume the meaning of torah-piety rehearsed endlessly in Ps 119 (see v 38), where response to and hope in Yahweh's *hesed* depend upon one's relationship to his torah.[29]

All Israel is called upon to celebrate Yahweh's steadfast love, the priesthood is called upon to celebrate that covenant commitment and, finally, those who are committed to a piety based upon the remembrance and practice of the torah of Yahweh are also called upon to celebrate his חסד. This idea is implied by the Dtr (Entrance Liturgy) background to Ps 118, and made explicit by its placement alongside Ps 119.

---

[27] Miller, "Deuteronomy and Psalms," 15.
[28] Wright, *Deuteronomy*, 209.
[29] Mays, "Ps 118," 304.

3.1.4 TRUST IN YAHWEH

The following stanza (vv 5–7) further emphasises the Dtr themes which we have seen already in our analysis of Pss 1–2 and 18–21.[30] Deuteronomy commends an attitude of trust in Yahweh, and this trust is to be displayed especially by the king. He is not to trust in wealth or military might or foreign alliances, but is to trust implicitly in Yahweh.[31] This is very much the idea which is presented in vv 5–7, and this stanza both links Pss 118–119 with Pss 18–21 and reflects a point of view which is prominent in Deuteronomy and the DtrH.

Like the king in the previous torah-kingship psalm groupings, the speaker in Psalm 118 describes how he cried out to Yahweh as a result of the distress which he was facing (v 5) and how Yahweh delivered him from that danger (the explicit nature of the distress which the king faced is unclear, although certain indicators suggest that a military conflict may provide the backdrop to Ps 118).[32] This awareness of divine deliverance results in an attitude of trust in Yahweh which echoes the ideal of Israelite leadership. As we shall consider further below, the Israelite king was not to trust in external factors of strength, the implication being that he should trust only in Yahweh.[33] In terms reminiscent of Romans 8:31, the king as speaker in Ps 118:5–6 declares confidently:

יהוה לי לא אירא מה־יעשׂה לי אדם:
יהוה לי בעזרי ואני אראה בשׂנאי:

Yahweh is for me, I will not be afraid; What can man do to me?
Yahweh is for me, he is my helper; and I will look with triumph over my enemies.

---

[30] See chapters 2 and 3 above.

[31] Miller, "Kingship," 148.

[32] Mays, *Psalms*, 375–76; Dahood, *Psalms III, 101–150*, 155. Others such as Eaton, *Psalms*, 270–71, and Sanders, "NT Hermeneutic Fabric," 181–82, see this as an example of the king's ritual humiliation during the autumnal enthronement celebration. Some scholars suggest that the nature of the distress is deliberately ambiguous so that the psalm would be applicable to many people in different settings and generations (see, for example, McCann, *Psalms*, 1156). Dahood comments that, "the psalmist's references to an encounter with death... seem to be literal," and there is a sense of urgency in the verses of this lyric which seems to suggest a literal danger as the background to this psalm.

[33] Miller, *Deuteronomy*, 148; Wright, *Deuteronomy*, 209. Miller comments: "[T]hese restrictions and injunctions serve the main purpose of Deuteronomy, *to enjoin a full and undivided allegiance to the Lord*." Wright adds: "The value of a king is assessed solely by the extent to which he will help or hinder that loyalty [i.e. the people's loyalty to Yahweh as God]. A king who will not trust in God but in his own defenses (cf. 3:21)... such a king will quickly lead the people in the same disastrous direction."

This certitude serves as a reminder of Yahweh's commissioning of Joshua with its twofold emphases—that he should not stray from the book of the torah, but should meditate on it day and night, and, secondly, that he should not *be afraid or dismayed* (Jos 1:6–9).[34] Again, this is an idea which is presented in a positive light in Deuteronomy and the Deuteronomistic History, further emphasising the Dtr mindset underpinning the king's presentation of his worldview in Ps 118:5–7. The king knows that his confession of faith is one which any faithful king of Israel should make—because Yahweh is with him, he need not fear, nor seek to find his security in any other source.[35] Although, Weinfeld's emphasis upon the quasi-regal function of Joshua implied in his commissioning seems unnecessary and misleading, his discussion of the Israelite leader's function as example of faithfulness to Yahweh for the people is helpful.[36] Weinfeld suggests that the torah obedience of the king (or lack thereof) will have a profound effect on "the fate of the people for good or ill; the righteous kings cast glory on their reigns while the wicked kings create a shadow over their period and cause their people to sin."[37] Whilst Weinfeld's presentation of kingship as a "requirement" of the book of the torah is debatable,[38] his analysis of the Deuteronomic ideal king as exemplar sheds some light on the worldview influencing the attitude of the king in his declaration in Ps 118:5–7. Deuteronomy and the DtrH present trust in Yahweh as an ideal which leaders in Israel should cling to, which in turn will positively affect the people: similarly here in Ps 118, the psalmist confesses

---

[34] We should remember that Joshua's commissioning parallels Psalm 1 and 2's joint presentation of a proper world-and-life view. See pp 46–48, above.

[35] Jos 1:6–9, Deut 17:16–17.

[36] Weinfeld, *The Deuteronomic School*, 170–71. It seems that Weinfeld's association of Joshua (and, indeed, Moses) with regal function is a result of his assumption that "kingship" is essential to the "implementation of the moral law" (p 170). This is a question which we shall discuss in more detail as part of our study of Deut 17:14–20 in its broader context (Deut 16:18–18:22). However, it seems that adherence to the torah and the ordering of one's life in accordance with the book of the law is a factor which Deuteronomy as constitution expects (either explicitly or implicitly) of *all* leaders within Israel, including the king. Therefore, Yahweh's expectation that Joshua should meditate upon the torah and not stray from it is analogous to the kingship law inasmuch as Joshua was to lead the people in the same manner as would be expected of a king in leading the people. This does not mean that Joshua himself fulfilled a quasi-regal function, but rather that he was to bear the characteristics expected of all leaders in Israel, and, indeed, of all Israelites.

[37] Weinfeld, *The Deuteronomic School*, 171.

[38] McConville, *Grace in the End*, 31–32.

that Yahweh is greater than all external circumstances, therefore he will not be afraid. This is the attitude which Moses sought to instill in the people (Deut 20:1-4) and in Joshua as the leader of the people (Jos 1:6-9) prior to the conquest of Canaan. The king's confession is that he has learnt from the experience of Yahweh's deliverance that the theology of Deuteronomy is true and applicable in reality—his public confession of the "rightness" of this attitude is designed to positively impact the worshipping community at large.

3.1.5   YAHWEH AS THE PSALMIST'S HELP

In v 7 the psalmist declares his victory over his enemies (a concept which seems to bear royal overtones[39]) and celebrates the fact that Yahweh is his "help" (בעזרי). This is a description of God which is reminiscent of the Blessings of Moses in Deut 33. Three times in this passage Yahweh is referred to as being "the help" of his people (Deut 33:7, 26, 29). In context, this assurance of help seems to function in correspondence to Yahweh's mockery of foreign gods in Deut 32:38, where he says, "Let them rise up to help you!" Aligned with the central theme of Deuteronomy—complete allegiance and commitment to Yahweh—the Song of Moses derides idolatry and trust in anyone or anything other than Yahweh. The implication is clear: gods of wood and stone cannot help. Following on from this in Deuteronomy 33, three times the tribes of Israel are assured that Yahweh, himself, will be their help. The psalmist-king of Ps 118 makes the same sort of claim in these verses. He will not put his trust in anything other than Yahweh, accordingly God himself will be the psalmist's help.[40] Once again, when this term is viewed in its proper context, we see an attitude which adopts Dtr concepts of faithfulness and commitment to the Lord.

3.1.6   TRUST IN YAHWEH—NOT IN MEN/PRINCES

The theme of explicit trust in Yahweh is further developed in vv 8-9 where two antithetical parallelisms are developed positing the greater good of taking refuge in Yahweh as opposed to trusting in man, or princes. This is a further development of the Dtr idea (explicit trust in Yahweh above all else) that has been the subject of our consideration in the previous two sections.

---

[39] Kraus, *Psalms II*, 397-98; Anderson, *Psalms*, 799-800.
[40] Mays, *Psalms*, 374-75.

טוֹב לַחֲסוֹת בַּיהוָה מִבְּטֹחַ בָּאָדָם׃
טוֹב לַחֲסוֹת בַּיהוָה מִבְּטֹחַ בִּנְדִיבִים׃
It is better to take refuge in Yahweh than to trust in man
It is better to take refuge in Yahweh than to trust in princes.

It seems that this dual parallelism is also designed to deliberately echo the Kingship Law. Firstly, we find in v 8 the statement that, "It is better to take refuge in Yahweh" (טוב לחסות ביהוה). This, as we have already seen, is a concept which is editorially significant throughout the Book of Psalms and one which is reminiscent of Deuteronomy's constant refrain that the people should find their security in relationship with Yahweh rather than in visible, external sources or the gods of the nations around them.[41] Once again this expression of trust seems to parallel the content of Deut 32 and 33. Deut 32:37 asks: Where are the gods in which the people took refuge? The implied response is that these false gods provide no refuge, and, in rejecting Yahweh, Israel rejects their one true source of security and shelter, as is made clear in the blessings of Deut 33.

Ps 118:8–9's declaration of trust in Yahweh seems to intentionally reiterate one of the limitations placed upon the king in the Kingship Law. Verse 8 contrasts taking refuge in Yahweh with trust in man in a general sense, but verse 9 develops this thought more specifically into a declaration that the king finds refuge in Yahweh to be a better option than trusting in princes (מבטח בנדיבים). Whilst it is difficult to define exactly what the psalmist had in mind when using the word "princes" (נדיבים), the context seems to suggest that he is speaking about foreign princes.[42] Accordingly, the implication of vv 8–9 is that the psalmist-king finds it better to take refuge in Yahweh than to trust in the international alliances with foreign powers. Such alliances were common practice in the ancient Near East, especially for smaller nations who saw these treaties as a means of withstanding the military opposition of neighbouring superpowers.[43]

---

[41] Creach, *Yahweh as Refuge*, 64–65.

[42] Verse 7 speaks of the psalmist's triumph over his enemies—a concept which is traditionally reserved for foreign opposition. Verse 10 speaks of the nations (גוים) surrounding the psalmist, which obviously refers to foreign nations. Therefore it appears likely that the נדיבים are foreign princes rather than some form of post-exilic Israelite nobleman. Kraus, *Psalms II*, 397–98; McCann, *Psalms*, 1153–54. Anderson considers both options to be valid possibilities in the Psalter generally, but suggests that foreign princes is a better understanding in Ps 118:9 (*Psalms*, 782).

[43] Jeffrey H Tigay, *Deuteronomy* דברים (Philadelphia: Jewish Publication Society, 1996), 167; Peter Craigie, *Deuteronomy* (NICOT; Grand Rapids: Eerdmans, 1976), 256.

Deut 17:17 specifically prohibits the Israelite king from taking for himself many wives (ולא ירבה־לו נשים), a practice which (in parallel with many other prohibitions in Deuteronomy) could lead his heart astray from devotion to Yahweh.[44] So, the Kingship Law forbids the Israelite king from finding his source of security in international alliances—he is to trust in Yahweh instead. The psalmist-king is making a similar type of confession here in Psalm 118. He has discovered from Yahweh's gracious deliverance that it is better to take refuge in him than to trust in strategic alliances with foreign princes.[45] Mays comments:

> Human strength is vulnerable to the power and threat of adversaries. It is better not to rely on it, even if it belongs to princes. The Lord's help is a power in which one can take refuge from both human weakness and human threats. "If God is for us, who is against us?" (Rom 8:31).[46]

So, again, the public confession of the king seems to be a declaration of a world-and-life view which follows the pattern of the Kingship Law.

3.1.7 SURROUNDING NATIONS, CIRCUMCISION, NAME THEOLOGY

The next stanza (vv 10–12) is an awkward one, and most of the commentators are unsure quite what to make of it. The three verses are clearly linked by the themes of the surrounding nations (כל־גוים סבבוני, v 10; סבוני גם־סבבוני, v 11; סבוני כדבורים, v 12) and the king's response; namely, to circumcise them or cut them off (אמילם) and to do so in the name of Yahweh (בשם יהוה). It is, indeed, difficult to find a point of reference for these ideas and the words of these verses seem to give rise to more questions than they answer.[47] In particular, what is the king doing in response to the (implied) threat from the nations? Is he causing them to be circumcised (by force), as suggested in Brown, Driver, Briggs?[48] Or is he, figuratively speaking, cutting them off (destroying them), as suggested by Gesenius?[49] The commentators attain no greater agreement.[50]

---

[44] As is seen in the negative presentation of Solomon in 1 Kings 11:1–13. Deuteronomy 17:17's ban on the king acquiring many wives for himself applies to the foundation of international treaty alliances (which were normally sealed by the giving of a daughter in marriage) as a source of trust which would diminish the king's trust in Yahweh.

[45] Creach, *Yahweh as Refuge*, 67.

[46] Mays, *Psalms*, 376.

[47] For example, see McCann's comment on the translation of v 12, *Psalms*, 1154.

[48] Brown et al., *BDB*, 558.

[49] H. W. F. Gesenius, *Hebrew-Chaldee Lexicon to the Old Testament* (Grand Rapids: Baker Books, 1979), 456.

It is possible that the *hifil* form of מול of Ps 118:10–12 is functioning as a parallel to the *hifil* form of כרת from Deut 12:29–13:1.[51] The contexts appear to be similar: (1) There is a situation of military conflict in Deut 12 and Ps 118;[52] (2) There is an implied backdrop of the danger of unfaithfulness from contact with these nations;[53] and (3) The corrective offered is based in torah-obedience.[54] Therefore, it may be that the action of the king in Ps 118 is a decisive military victory of the type suggested by the DtrH conquest accounts, which was significant in securing for the people a proper setting for continued devotion to Yahweh.

The other two elements common to these verses both represent Dtr themes. Firstly, the people of God surrounded by hostile foreign nations is a theme which is prominent in both Deuteronomy and the DtrH. Many of the paraenetic sections of Deuteronomy consist of Moses' appeals and challenges to the people to maintain their allegiance to Yahweh and not to succumb to the pressure to adopt the ways of the nations around them.[55] This theme of God's people surrounded by nations hostile to the ways of Yahweh is further developed in the DtrH.[56] In all of these cases the threat from the surrounding nations is presented as a threat to Yahweh's ordained way of life for his people.[57] Secondly, in each of these three verses the psalmist-king comes against the opposing nations "in the name of Yahweh" (בשם יהוה). This element of his confession, once again, emphasises

---

[50] Eaton, *Psalms*, 271, suggests that this was part of the "symbolic ordeal" of the Autumn Festival. Whereas, Kraus, *Psalms II*, 397; Mays, *Psalms*, 374–75 and Allen, *Psalms*, 124, all focus upon either the threat from the surrounding nations or the fact that the psalmist calls upon the name of Yahweh, without making any suggestion with regard to the king's action in response to this threat.

[51] EVV 12:32. The same form is also used in Deut 19:1 to describe Yahweh's work in giving over the land to Israel.

[52] The description of how the conquest is to proceed in Deut 12 and conflict with "enemies" and "nations" in Ps 118.

[53] In inquiring after the gods of the nations in Deut 12, and in forming alliances with "princes" in Ps 118.

[54] Deut 13:1 responds to this threat with the challenge that the people should do all that Moses has commanded them, and Ps 118 as an Entrance Liturgy grounds the king's right of access into the Temple in righteousness based upon torah-obedience.

[55] Deut 12:29–32; 18:9–13; 29:16–18; 32:1–43 etc.

[56] For example, the conquest accounts in Joshua; the oppression by various neighbouring nations in the Judges with its corresponding effect on the spiritual state of the people (e.g. Gideon account); the narratives relating to David's military victories etc.

[57] McConville, *Law and Theology*, 59–60.

the king's dependence upon Yahweh. "The motif [in the name of the Lord] identifies the real source of strength that enables the celebrant to resist the power of surrounding nations, a motif that continues the emphasis on human power in contrast to the Lord."[58] As we have seen before, this is a classically Dtr concept.[59] Kraus comments that:

> שׁם is here the salvific presence of Yahweh guaranteed by the promise. The שׁם is like a weapon, like a shield, that enfolds him who is surrounded by the rage of the enemy...[60]

Yet again this is indicative of the king's plea being firmly based not in his worth or ability, but in the work of God on his behalf. This attitude of humble trust in God alone is one which the text of Deuteronomy strives to inculcate in the hearts and minds of the people (Deut 7; 30:1–10), it appears that the king here desires to present his own adoption and application of this attitude as an example to the worshipping community.

3.1.8 YAHWEH AS HELP AND SALVATION

Psalm 118:13–14 continues the theme of Yahweh's aid, succour and support for the psalmist-king. He was "pushed hard to fall," but, Yahweh helped him, another evidence of his Yahweh's acceptance of him and, therefore, of the rightness of his admission into the Temple. Ps 118:14 is, of course, a direct quote from the Song of Moses in Exodus 15:2—providing, perhaps, another reason why Psalm 118 was included with the Egyptian Hallel. However, the theology of these verses, whilst obviously echoing the exodus theme of deliverance, is also reminiscent of Deuteronomy 32 and 33, where Moses warns the people that they should not to reject Yahweh, who is their help (עזר, Deut 32:38; 33:7, 26, 29 cf. Ps 118:13) and their salvation (ישׁועה, Deut 32:15 cf Ps 118:14). The king's claim is clear—he has not rejected Yahweh as his help and salvation, and this is evidenced by the fact that God is still helping him and providing him with

---

[58] Mays, *Psalms*, 374.

[59] See Kraus, *Psalms*, 279–80 and the comments in Chapters 2 and 3 above. Whether or not the theology of the Psalter presents the idea of the "name of Yahweh" in the same light as the assessment of this phrase found in the secondary literature of Deuteronomic Studies is another question entirely. It seems that the psalmic presentation of the "name of Yahweh" is associated with the idea of the real presence of God with his people as a present help on their behalf (see pp 104–5 above).

[60] Kraus, *Psalms II*, 397–98.

salvation. "Vv 13–14 assert further that the celebrant's survival and strength come from the Lord, who in his deliverance became his salvation."[61]

3.1.9 THIS DAY, PROSPERITY, NAME THEOLOGY

In the concluding verses of Ps 118 we come across some further indicators of a background in Dtr theology. First, there is a temporal sense of urgency in Ps 118:24 which reflects a theme which is commonly found in both Deuteronomy and the DtrH, especially in the Book of Joshua (e.g. Deut 26:16; 27:9–10; Jos 24:15). Secondly, the king and people pray together for salvation and *prosperity* (הצליחה) in v 25. As we saw in our analysis of Pss 1 and 2 as an introduction to the Psalter, this is a concept which has become associated with keeping the torah. Thirdly, we see, once again, that the one who is blessed as he enters into the Temple is the one who comes "in the name of Yahweh" (בשם יהוה, v 26). This Dtr concept is infused throughout the whole psalm and provides further emphasis upon the appropriateness of the king's dependence upon Yahweh, an important Dtr motif.

Following on from the proverbial account of Yahweh's vindication of the king in vv 22–23, we come to a verse well known from Sunday school songs:

זה־היום עשה יהוה נגילה ונשמחה בו:
This is the day that Yahweh has made. Let us rejoice and be glad in it.

One of the interesting features of this verse is the sense of immediacy presented in the fact that it is *this day* that Yahweh has made and therefore the people should rejoice now. There is a focus upon making the proper response *now*, which reflects the temporal emphases of the Books of Deuteronomy and Joshua especially. Ps 118:24 presents this in the predicative form (זה־היום, "this *is* the day"), whereas Deuteronomy and Joshua commonly present this in the attributive form (היום הזה, e.g. Deut 26:16 or Jos 3:7) or simply by using היום in an emphatic sense (e.g. Deut 30:15–16 or Jos 24:15), however, the temporal stress is common to both Ps 118 and Deuteronomy–Joshua. The idea appears to be one of immediate application, as opposed to procrastination. In Ps 118:24, the speaker[62] announces today as the day which Yahweh has made, therefore no time should be wasted but the people should rejoice. One can imagine that this

---

[61] Mays, *Psalms*, 374–75.

[62] It is not absolute clear whether this is the voice of the king or of the priests in vv 22–24 (see Sanders, "NT Hermeneutic Fabric," 181–82).

verse took on new meaning in the festivals of the post-exilic period when there must have been a great temptation for the people to set their hearts upon the future restoration of the king and kingdom. In its ambiguous setting and language, Ps 118 is designed to give hope in every situation, no matter how bleak, that Yahweh is still the God who delivers his people.[63] In Deuteronomy and Joshua, the temporal stress is normally connected with the presentation of choices to the people—*choose this day*, will you follow Yahweh or the foreign gods of the nations?[64] In both Ps 118 and the DtrH there is an inherent challenge: will the people stick with God as their Lord regardless of external pressures and circumstances or will they stray?[65]

Secondly, the community prays in vv 25-27 that Yahweh will "save" them (הושיעה) and "prosper" them (הצליחה). The first of these pleas in Ps 118 reflects the same type of prayer as is found in Pss 18 and 20.[66] The second of these requests redirects the reader of the Psalter to Ps 1:3 and its context within Dtr theology. As we have argued in an earlier chapter,[67] the idea of God's people prospering has become closely associated with keeping the torah of Yahweh. Ps 1:3 tells the reader that the blessed person delights in the torah of Yahweh and meditates upon it day and night; this person is like a tree planted by streams of water bearing fruit and in everything she does, she prospers (וכל אשר־יעשה יצליח). The prospering (both Ps 1:3 and Ps 118:25 use *hifil* forms of the verb צלח) is dependent upon the torah-obedience. This idea is accentuated positively in Jos 1:8, and negatively in Deut 28:29. A causal relationship between torah-obedience and prosperity is made in Joshua's commissioning—if he meditates upon and obeys the law, he will prosper in all that he does (כי־אז תצליח את־דרכך ואז תשכיל). Negatively, in the description of the covenant curses in Deut 28 the people are assured that if they reject the torah of Yahweh then they will not prosper in their ways (v 29, לא תצליח את־דרכיך).[68] So by implication this prayer

---

[63] Mays, "Ps 118," 310.

[64] J. Gary Millar, *Now Choose Life: Theology and Ethics in Deuteronomy* (Leicester: Apollos, 1998), 94–95. This could be a further echo of the Deut 30 motif in Ps 118. In the former Moses presents the ways of life and prosperity death and destruction to the people *today* (היום) and in Ps 118 the day to rejoice is today.

[65] McCann, *Psalms*, 690.

[66] See chapter 3 above,

[67] See above, pp 45–48.

[68] This loss of prosperity is the direct result of not keeping the commandments and decrees commanded by Moses *that day* (Deut 28:15, Miller, *Deuteronomy*, 197–98).

for prosperity brings with it a tacit awareness that prosperity is dependent upon a certain lifestyle of torah-obedience—the people cannot expect prosperity in answer to their prayer without a lifestyle of torah-piety and the careful reader of the Psalter would be aware of this fact.

Thirdly, we see that it is the one who enters the Temple "in the name of Yahweh" who receives the priestly blessing (v 26). Implied in this formula is the fact that the one who comes is not found righteous by his own worth, rather, in accordance with his trust in Yahweh, he secures admittance into his presence.[69] The connection between Temple (central sanctuary) and the name of Yahweh gives a strongly Dtr feel to this verse and to the poem as a whole.[70]

3.1.10 INDIVIDUAL AND COMMUNITY

One other factor which is relevant to this thesis as a whole is the close interplay between the role of the individual (king) and community in Ps 118. Many of the commentators comment upon the significance of God's deliverance of the king for the people as a whole.[71] In Ps 118:26, the blessing of the king leads to the blessing of the community. Sanders writes:

> At the conclusion of the plea, which may in the actual ceremony have been much longer, full of joy and wonder, the priests, who had earlier fulfilled their role as gate-keepers (v 20), now joyfully intone the great "Blessed be he who enters," thereby officially recognising and receiving the one arriving as indeed the king. The climax of the ceremony has been reached. The king is once more king. *It would appear, as has been noted, that Yahweh's kingship is in part expressed in the earthly Davidic king so that the very presence of the king is the divine gift of light, and so the chorus and people affirm the point (v 27).*[72]

Mays adds:

> Fourth, the "I" is understood in terms of the "we." The theological identity is corporate. Note the use of first-person songs for the people in narrative and prophetic contexts in the OT (e.g., Exodus 15; Isaiah 12). This does not cancel the function of the first-person style or eliminate the reading and the use of the psalm by individuals. Ps 56, which is similar in language and scenario, is attributed to a setting in David's life. *What happens, in the interplay of scrip-*

---

[69] Anderson, *Psalms*, 803; Kirkpatrick, *Psalms*, 699.
[70] Whilst rejecting the classical interpretation of Dtr "name theology" (where the name is seen as a divine hypostasis), there is an obvious connection between the "name of Yahweh" and the Temple in Deuteronomy 12.
[71] Mays, *Psalms*, 373–74; Mays, "Ps 118," 309; Sanders, "NT Hermeneutic Fabric."
[72] Sanders, "NT Hermeneutic Fabric," 182–83 (emphasis mine).

ture, is a correlation of corporate and individual identities. David's narrative is taken as illustration and instruction about the people's life under God. Through David and his first-person style of the psalms, individuals understand their own existence in terms of the faith of the community.[73]

The implication of the antiphonal interaction between king, priests and people is that the king must be righteous in order to enter into the Temple and receive the priestly blessing, and as such he is *exemplar* for the whole worshipping community.[74] As v 20 indicates, only those who are righteous may enter into the presence of God (not even the king is exempt from this necessity) therefore, the people too must follow his example in order to be declared right in God's eyes. The king is found righteous by the saving work of Yahweh, but also by a commitment to live in accordance with his torah. The same would be expected of the people. It appears that a major function of the torah-kingship redaction of the Psalter is to present a picture of the ideal (Dtr) king as an example for "those who fear Yahweh" to follow. This function is at work not just in the editorial juxtaposition of Pss 118–119, but also within the text of Ps 118. The Davidic king, in entering into the presence of God, is seen as the quintessential "fearer of Yahweh" and provides a pattern of piety for others to follow.

4. PSALM 118 IN THE LIGHT OF PSALMS 1–2 and 18–21

As well as assessing the Dtr background to Ps 118, we must also consider possible areas of connection with the torah-kingship psalms groupings previously analysed. Many of the lexical and thematic connections between Ps 118 and the previous psalm groupings have been mentioned above in our examination of Dtr influences upon this poem, so we need not dwell on these features in great detail once again. There is, however, evidence that Ps 118 further extrapolates the theological emphases of Pss 1–2 and 18–21.

4.1 SALVATION OF THE LORD'S ANOINTED

Much in the same way as we find in Pss 2, 18, 20 and 21, the king of Ps 118 is faced with some sort of crisis, probably military. The nature of the threat is not made absolutely explicit in any of these psalms, so that the content of the

---

[73] Mays, "Ps 118," 310 (emphasis mine).
[74] Cf. Allen, "David as Exemplar," with regard to a similar function of the figure of the king in Psalm 19.

poems will be applicable to many readers and situations.⁷⁵ However, the implicit background to these kingship psalms is one where Yahweh responds to the prayers of the king and people when his "anointed" is faced with the rebellion of enemies. It is not that the king himself is of such great import, but rather the fact that he is part of the order which God has established for his people and the nations.⁷⁶ Although the word משיח is not used in Ps 118, there is ample evidence from the text to show that the "one who comes in the name of the Lord" is the Davidic king,⁷⁷ as is seen, for example, in the significance of his deliverance for the wider community:

> The messianic use of verse 26 [in the Gospel narratives] calls attention to the messianic dimensions of the figure in the psalm. In his conflict with all the nations and in the significance of his salvation for the people of the Lord, the celebrant in Ps 118 resembles the anointed king of Pss 2; 18; 20; 21; and 89.⁷⁸

So Ps 118's setting, as the thanksgiving lyric of the anointed king faced with crisis and deliverance, connects it with the psalms examined above.

4.2 DEPENDENCE UPON YAHWEH

Another characteristic of Psalm 118 which reflects the theology of the previous psalm groupings is the king's confession of total dependence upon Yahweh. Just as it was Yahweh who established the king in Zion in Psalm 2:7 and who protected him from the rebellion of the nations, so it is Yahweh who provides deliverance for the psalmist-king of Ps 118. Psalms 18, 20–21 also reflect the same sort of attitude—the appellatives of Ps 18, for example, indicating the king's reliance upon Yahweh as "his Rock." This attitude of submission and dependence is also testified to in the significance of the name-theology in Ps 20 and Ps 118—the strength and worth of the king lies not in any inherent righteousness or ability, but in his relationship with God. It is the fact that the king comes in the name of Yahweh that is significant for his admittance and acceptance. This reflects an attitude of deliberate dependence and subordination—Yahweh is the true king of all the earth and the significance of the

---

⁷⁵ Mays, *Psalms*, 375–76.

⁷⁶ See, for example, Victor Sasson, "The Language of Rebellion in Psalm 2 and in the Plaster Texts of Deir 'Alla," *AUSS* 24, no. 2 (Summer 1986): 147–54, or Macintosh, "Consideration" for discussion of this idea.

⁷⁷ See pp 127–28n11.

⁷⁸ Mays, *Psalms*, 379.

Davidic king is found only in his relationship with the true king. The pleas for salvation (e.g. Ps 118:25, הושיעה נא) that we find in Pss 18, 20 and 118 also show this attitude of reliance upon Yahweh. Neither the king nor the people can trust in any external factor for their salvation, their confession is that Yahweh alone is powerful to save and that he has, indeed, "become their salvation." As we have seen previously, Deuteronomy and the DtrH view this attitude as a virtue.[79] The king and the people are to trust in Yahweh and to live their lives as "fearers of the Lord." Such is the attitude that we find in Psalm 118, as Eaton writes concerning this poem, "The ceremonies have taught confidence in God rather than in creaturely strength."[80] This same lesson is found in Pss 1–2, 18–21 also.

4.3 YAHWEH AS REFUGE

Connected with the above theme of dependence is the idea of Yahweh as refuge for king and, by implication, for people. As Jerome Creach has pointed out, the idea of Yahweh as refuge (חסה) plays a significant role in the theology of the Psalter,[81] and this is seen clearly in the three psalm groupings which we have examined. Psalms 2, 18 and 118 all stress the importance of taking refuge in Yahweh.[82] Ps 118:8–9 sets this act in deliberate contrast with trust in man, especially trust in princes and international alliances.

> The use of the refuge metaphor in Isaiah and Zephaniah has parallels in the Psalter (i.e. Pss 2:12; 118:8–9).... Interestingly, these two prophets seem to have a close relationship to the monarch.... The king spoke with this language to demonstrate his dependence on God in battle. The prophets, in turn, utilised similar vocabulary and figures of speech to describe proper political policy for the nation.[83]

This idea of Yahweh as refuge seems to suggest that it is better for the king and the people to take refuge in Yahweh than to place their trust in policies which may seem more tangible but which ultimately draw the people away from

---

[79] Miller, *Deuteronomy*, 157; Creach, *Yahweh as Refuge*, 57n21.

[80] Eaton, *Psalms*, 272. Eaton interprets the deliverance of the king to be part of an annual "humiliation ritual." Whilst this is possible, it could also be that some actual event of history provides the backdrop to this psalm. However, regardless of the nature of the deliverance the lesson learnt is the key issue, and that lesson is to trust in Yahweh rather than alternate sources of power.

[81] Creach, *Yahweh as Refuge*, 17–18.

[82] Pss 2:12; 18:3, 31 and 118:8–9.

[83] Creach, *Yahweh as Refuge*, 67.

Yahweh.[84] The fact that this theme appears again in Pss 118 and 119 is another indicator of the common theological perspective shared by Pss 1–2, 18–21 and 118–119.

4.4 THEOLOGY OF THE TWO WAYS

The theology of the two ways is brought back into focus in a strong way in Psalm 118 (and in Psalm 119). As our examination of both of the previous psalm groupings has shown, this Dtr/Wisdom theme plays a prominent role in these juxtaposed torah and kingship psalms.[85] Central to this antiphonal celebration is the entrance of the king and the people into the Temple and verse 20 makes it clear that not all may enter, but only the righteous.[86] This reflects the ideology of the two ways: there is a righteousness defined by the torah, and those who seek after that righteousness shall gain admittance into the worship of the Temple—by implication therefore, those who do not seek to live in accordance with Yahweh's torah shall not be allowed to enter. The same ideas are also found in the concepts of "those who fear Yahweh," "those who take refuge in Yahweh," those for whom "Yahweh has become their salvation" and also those who come "in the name of the Lord." Each of these phrases contains elements of inclusion and exclusion. A community is created of those who "fear Yahweh," but the inevitable corollary of this like-minded community is the exclusion of those who do not fear Yahweh or take refuge in him.[87] Therefore, in reality, Ps 118 is thoroughly grounded in the theology of the two ways and this provides a further connection with the previous torah-kingship psalm groupings.

4.5 PRAYER THEME

Another connection between Ps 118 and the previous psalm groupings is the setting in prayer. Whilst Ps 118 does not substantially consist of direct prayers to Yahweh, vv 5–21 are essentially an account of the king's prayerful petition for salvation and Yahweh's response to it. What is more, vv 25 and 28 *are* direct prayer to Yahweh: the first is a prayer of the community in v 25, and, secondly,

---

[84] Wright, *Deuteronomy*, 209.
[85] See above, pp 53, 65–66, 84–86 etc.
[86] Anderson, *Psalms*, 797; Kirkpatrick, *Psalms*, 697; Briggs, *Psalms*, 402–03.
[87] Mays, "Ps 118," 304.

we hear the prayer of the king in v 28. Even after the account of Yahweh's deliverance of the king—with its corresponding benefits for the people—the congregation still prays that Yahweh will "save" (הושיעה נא) and "prosper" (הצליחה נא), showing a continuing attitude of dependence upon God which follows the example set by the king in his earlier account. This prayer, although voiced by the people, very much resembles the attitude of prayer attributed to the king in Psalms 18–21.[88] Whilst the central works of the Psalms 15–24 collection focus on kingship and torah, prayer plays a significant part in that interaction;[89] and we see that prayer connection reflected again in Psalm 118.[90] The second prayer (Ps 118:28) appears to be spoken by the king[91] and this too reflects the example which we have seen in Psalms 18–21. The prayer emphasises the psalmist's personal relationship with God, his dependence upon him and his delight in relationship with God. This is seen in the attitude of praise and the use of the first person singular pronominal suffix which is so characteristic of the prayers of Pss 18–21.[92] The theme of prayer undergirds Ps 118 and links it to the previous psalm collections.

4.6 TORAH-PIETY

One final, and significant, factor which links Ps 118 with the previous psalm groupings is its subtle connection with the torah-piety which influences the final form of the Psalter. Whilst the torah content of Ps 118 may not be as explicit as we have seen in some of the other psalms, it is clearly present nonetheless. First, Psalm 118's categorisation as an Entrance Liturgy places it within a worldview which elevates the role of torah in the life of the OT believer.[93] Secondly, the covenant context of *hesed* within Psalm 118:1–4 implies a responsibility on the part of both psalmist and people to live in accordance with the torah of

---

[88] Miller, "Kingship," 134. Miller describes how in Pss 15–24 "the centrality of the king does not mean that the larger community's voice is not heard in these prayers. They are powerfully joined here." The same principle seems to be at work in Ps 118, adding a powerful democratising effect to the central lesson.

[89] Miller, "Kingship," 132 ff.

[90] McCann, *Psalms*, 1156.

[91] Sanders, "NT Hermeneutic Fabric," 183.

[92] Cf. Pss 18:3, 47–51; 19:15 etc., (see chapter 2, above).

[93] Miller discusses how the Dtr ideal of torah-piety thoroughly permeates the Entrance Liturgies, Pss 15 and 24. It seems reasonable that the same standard be applied to Psalm 118 which fulfills the same function (see Miller, "Kingship," 139–41).

Yahweh—that is their part of the deal.[94] Thirdly, assuming the temporal priority of Deut 17, according to what other standard would the Davidic king be declared righteous? The self-presentation of Deut 17:14-20 is that the king is obliged to live in accordance with the torah, and if the priests (cf. 17:18) are the ones calling him to account, prior to granting admittance into the Temple, then what other standard would they apply?[95] It may seem obvious, but the most logical source against which the righteousness of the king would be judged is the torah of Yahweh. Fourthly, a righteousness based in torah-piety is suggested by the juxtaposition of Psalm 118 alongside Psalm 119. Psalms 118-119 serve as the focal point of Book V, together they are positioned in between two larger pre-existing collections which are in turn bracketed by two Davidic collections.[96] These factors combine to suggest that the readers of this psalm would have understood the righteousness which is required of the king (and by implication, of the people) to be a righteousness based in the torah of Yahweh.

4.7 Conclusion regarding Psalm 118

Once again, exegetical examination of the text seems to indicate that Psalm 118 borrows heavily from the theology of Deuteronomy and the DtrH. Secondly, there are signs that the theology of Psalm 118 is strikingly similar to the theology represented in Psalms 1-2 and 18-21. Furthermore, the democratising tendencies which we have seen in the other royal psalms are continued in Psalm 118, indicating that the piety of the king fulfilled not so much a sacral function, but an exemplary function—the piety of the king was meant to be an example of godliness for all the people. It remains to be seen how these themes and ideas are worked out in Psalm 119.

5. Analysis of Psalm 119

BHS	Translation
אַשְׁרֵי תְמִימֵי־דָרֶךְ הַהֹלְכִים בְּתוֹרַת יְהוָה:	1 Blessed are those whose way is blameless; those who walk in the torah of Yhwh.
אַשְׁרֵי נֹצְרֵי עֵדֹתָיו בְּכָל־לֵב יִדְרְשׁוּהוּ:	2 Blessed are those who keep his statutes; with all their heart they seek him.

---

[94] See the argument outlined above, pp 130-132.

[95] Miller, "Deuteronomy and Psalms," 16. Miller writes that the rule of the king is "utterly determined by obedience to the law of the Lord."

[96] We shall discuss this in greater detail in chapter 6.

Torah-Kingship Theme in Psalms 118–119

אַף לֹא־פָעֲלוּ עַוְלָה בִּדְרָכָיו הָלָכוּ:
אַתָּה צִוִּיתָה פִקֻּדֶיךָ לִשְׁמֹר מְאֹד:
אַחֲלַי יִכֹּנוּ דְרָכָי לִשְׁמֹר חֻקֶּיךָ:
אָז לֹא־אֵבוֹשׁ בְּהַבִּיטִי אֶל־כָּל־מִצְוֹתֶיךָ:
אוֹדְךָ בְּיֹשֶׁר לֵבָב בְּלָמְדִי מִשְׁפְּטֵי צִדְקֶךָ:
אֶת־חֻקֶּיךָ אֶשְׁמֹר אַל־תַּעַזְבֵנִי עַד־מְאֹד:

3 Surely they do no wrong; they walk in his ways.
4 You have commanded your precepts; to be closely kept.
5 Oh, that my ways would be firm; to keep your decrees.
6 Then I will not be ashamed when I consider all your commands.
7 I give thanks to you in uprightness of heart, when I learn your righteous judgements.
8 Your decrees I keep; do not utterly forsake me!

בַּמֶּה יְזַכֶּה־נַּעַר אֶת־אָרְחוֹ לִשְׁמֹר כִּדְבָרֶךָ:
בְּכָל־לִבִּי דְרַשְׁתִּיךָ אַל־תַּשְׁגֵּנִי מִמִּצְוֹתֶיךָ:
בְּלִבִּי צָפַנְתִּי אִמְרָתֶךָ לְמַעַן לֹא אֶחֱטָא־לָךְ:
בָּרוּךְ אַתָּה יְהוָה לַמְּדֵנִי חֻקֶּיךָ:
בִּשְׂפָתַי סִפַּרְתִּי כֹּל מִשְׁפְּטֵי־פִיךָ:
בְּדֶרֶךְ עֵדְוֹתֶיךָ שַׂשְׂתִּי כְּעַל כָּל־הוֹן:
בְּפִקֻּדֶיךָ אָשִׂיחָה וְאַבִּיטָה אֹרְחֹתֶיךָ:
בְּחֻקֹּתֶיךָ אֶשְׁתַּעֲשָׁע לֹא אֶשְׁכַּח דְּבָרֶךָ:

9 How can a young man keep his way pure? By living according to your word.
10 With all my heart I seek you; Do not allow me to stray from your commands.
11 In my heart I store up your words; so that I will not sin against you.
12 Praise you, O Yahweh; Teach me your decrees.
13 With my lips I will recount; all the judgements of your mouth.
14 In the way of your statutes I rejoice; as *one would* concerning great riches.
15 I meditate upon your precepts; and I will consider your ways.
16 I take delight in your decrees; I will not forget your word.

גְּמֹל עַל־עַבְדְּךָ אֶחְיֶה וְאֶשְׁמְרָה דְבָרֶךָ:
גַּל־עֵינַי וְאַבִּיטָה נִפְלָאוֹת מִתּוֹרָתֶךָ:
גֵּר אָנֹכִי בָאָרֶץ אַל־תַּסְתֵּר מִמֶּנִּי מִצְוֹתֶיךָ:
גָּרְסָה נַפְשִׁי לְתַאֲבָה אֶל־מִשְׁפָּטֶיךָ בְכָל־עֵת:
גָּעַרְתָּ זֵדִים אֲרוּרִים הַשֹּׁגִים מִמִּצְוֹתֶיךָ:
גַּל מֵעָלַי חֶרְפָּה וָבוּז כִּי עֵדֹתֶיךָ נָצָרְתִּי:
גַּם יָשְׁבוּ שָׂרִים בִּי נִדְבָּרוּ עַבְדְּךָ יָשִׂיחַ בְּחֻקֶּיךָ:
גַּם־עֵדֹתֶיךָ שַׁעֲשֻׁעָי אַנְשֵׁי עֲצָתִי:

17 Deal well with your servant so that I may live; and I will keep your word.
18 Open my eyes that I may see wonderful things from your torah.
19 I was a stranger in the land; do not hide your commands from me.
20 My soul is broken with longing for your judgements at all times.
21 You rebuke the proud who are cursed; those who stray from your commands.
22 Remove from me scorn and contempt; for I keep your statutes.
23 Even though princes sit speaking against me; your servant meditates on your decrees.
24 Also your statutes are my delight; they are my counsellors.

דָּבְקָה לֶעָפָר נַפְשִׁי חַיֵּנִי כִּדְבָרֶךָ:
דְּרָכַי סִפַּרְתִּי וַתַּעֲנֵנִי לַמְּדֵנִי חֻקֶּיךָ:
דֶּרֶךְ־פִּקּוּדֶיךָ הֲבִינֵנִי וְאָשִׂיחָה בְּנִפְלְאוֹתֶיךָ:
דָּלְפָה נַפְשִׁי מִתּוּגָה קַיְּמֵנִי כִּדְבָרֶךָ:
דֶּרֶךְ־שֶׁקֶר הָסֵר מִמֶּנִּי וְתוֹרָתְךָ חָנֵּנִי:
דֶּרֶךְ־אֱמוּנָה בָחָרְתִּי מִשְׁפָּטֶיךָ שִׁוִּיתִי:
דָּבַקְתִּי בְעֵדְוֺתֶיךָ יְהוָה אַל־תְּבִישֵׁנִי:
דֶּרֶךְ־מִצְוֺתֶיךָ אָרוּץ כִּי תַרְחִיב לִבִּי:

הוֹרֵנִי יְהוָה דֶּרֶךְ חֻקֶּיךָ וְאֶצְּרֶנָּה עֵקֶב:
הֲבִינֵנִי וְאֶצְּרָה תוֹרָתֶךָ וְאֶשְׁמְרֶנָּה בְכָל־לֵב:
הַדְרִיכֵנִי בִּנְתִיב מִצְוֺתֶיךָ כִּי־בוֹ חָפָצְתִּי:
הַט־לִבִּי אֶל־עֵדְוֺתֶיךָ וְאַל אֶל־בָּצַע:
הַעֲבֵר עֵינַי מֵרְאוֹת שָׁוְא בִּדְרָכֶךָ חַיֵּנִי:
הָקֵם לְעַבְדְּךָ אִמְרָתֶךָ אֲשֶׁר לְיִרְאָתֶךָ:
הַעֲבֵר חֶרְפָּתִי אֲשֶׁר יָגֹרְתִּי כִּי מִשְׁפָּטֶיךָ טוֹבִים:
הִנֵּה תָּאַבְתִּי לְפִקֻּדֶיךָ בְּצִדְקָתְךָ חַיֵּנִי:

וִיבֹאֻנִי חֲסָדֶךָ יְהוָה תְּשׁוּעָתְךָ כְּאִמְרָתֶךָ:
וְאֶעֱנֶה חֹרְפִי דָבָר כִּי־בָטַחְתִּי בִּדְבָרֶךָ:
וְאַל־תַּצֵּל מִפִּי דְבַר־אֱמֶת עַד־מְאֹד כִּי לְמִשְׁפָּטֶךָ יִחָלְתִּי:
וְאֶשְׁמְרָה תוֹרָתְךָ תָמִיד לְעוֹלָם וָעֶד:
וְאֶתְהַלְּכָה בָרְחָבָה כִּי פִקֻּדֶיךָ דָרָשְׁתִּי:
וַאֲדַבְּרָה בְעֵדֹתֶיךָ נֶגֶד מְלָכִים וְלֹא אֵבוֹשׁ:
וְאֶשְׁתַּעֲשַׁע בְּמִצְוֺתֶיךָ אֲשֶׁר אָהָבְתִּי:

25 My soul clings to the dust; revive me according to your way.
26 I recounted my ways and you answered me; Teach me your decrees.
27 Cause me to understand the way of your precepts; and I will meditate on your wonderful deeds.
28 My soul weeps from sorrow; Establish me according to your word.
29 Cause me to turn aside from the way of deception; Be gracious to me through your torah.
30 I have chosen the way of faithfulness; I have established your judgements.
31 I cling to your statutes, O Yahweh; Do not put me to shame.
32 I run in the way of your commands; for you have enlarged my heart.

33 Teach me, O Yahweh, the way of your decrees; and as a result, I will keep it.
34 Give me understanding to keep your torah and I will keep it with all my heart.
35 Cause me to tread the path of your commands; For I delight in it.
36 Turn my heart to your statutes; and not to unjust gain.
37 Avert my eyes from seeing worthless things; Revive me in your way.
38 Establish your word for your servant; so that you may be feared.
39 Take away the scorn I dread; because your commands are good.
40 O how I long for your precepts; By your righteousness I am revived.

41 Let your steadfast love go with me, O Yahweh; your salvation according to your utterance.
42 Then I will answer the one who taunts me; For I trust in your word.
43 Do not take the word of truth utterly from my mouth; For in your commands I put my hope.
44 I keep your torah continually; forever and ever.
45 I walk in freedom because I seek your precepts.
46 I speak of your statutes before kings and I am not ashamed.
47 I delight in your commands which I love.

Torah-Kingship Theme in Psalms 118–119

וְאֶשָּׂא־כַפַּי אֶל־מִצְוֹתֶיךָ אֲשֶׁר אָהָבְתִּי
וְאָשִׂיחָה בְחֻקֶּיךָ:

48 I lift my hands concerning your commands which I love and I meditate upon your decrees.

זְכֹר־דָּבָר לְעַבְדֶּךָ עַל אֲשֶׁר יִחַלְתָּנִי:
זֹאת נֶחָמָתִי בְעָנְיִי כִּי אִמְרָתְךָ חִיָּתְנִי:
זֵדִים הֱלִיצֻנִי עַד־מְאֹד מִתּוֹרָתְךָ לֹא נָטִיתִי:
זָכַרְתִּי מִשְׁפָּטֶיךָ מֵעוֹלָם יְהוָה וָאֶתְנֶחָם:
זַלְעָפָה אֲחָזַתְנִי מֵרְשָׁעִים עֹזְבֵי תּוֹרָתֶךָ:
זְמִרוֹת הָיוּ־לִי חֻקֶּיךָ בְּבֵית מְגוּרָי:
זָכַרְתִּי בַלַּיְלָה שִׁמְךָ יְהוָה וָאֶשְׁמְרָה תּוֹרָתֶךָ:
זֹאת הָיְתָה־לִּי כִּי פִקֻּדֶיךָ נָצָרְתִּי:

49 Remember your word to your servant; by which you have given me hope.
50 This is my comfort in my suffering – that your word gives me life.
51 The proud mock me badly; but I will not turn from your torah.
52 I remember your eternal commands, O Yahweh, and I find comfort in them.
53 Great zeal has seized me because of the wicked, the ones who forsake your torah.
54 Your decrees have become my songs in my dwelling place.
55 I remember your name by night, O Yahweh; and I keep your torah.
56 This has become my *habit* for I keep your precepts.

חֶלְקִי יְהוָה אָמַרְתִּי לִשְׁמֹר דְּבָרֶיךָ:
חִלִּיתִי פָנֶיךָ בְכָל־לֵב חָנֵּנִי כְּאִמְרָתֶךָ:
חִשַּׁבְתִּי דְרָכָי וָאָשִׁיבָה רַגְלַי אֶל־עֵדֹתֶיךָ:
חַשְׁתִּי וְלֹא הִתְמַהְמָהְתִּי לִשְׁמֹר מִצְוֹתֶיךָ:
חֶבְלֵי רְשָׁעִים עִוְּדֻנִי תּוֹרָתְךָ לֹא שָׁכָחְתִּי:
חֲצוֹת־לַיְלָה אָקוּם לְהוֹדוֹת לָךְ עַל מִשְׁפְּטֵי צִדְקֶךָ:
חָבֵר אָנִי לְכָל־אֲשֶׁר יְרֵאוּךָ וּלְשֹׁמְרֵי פִּקּוּדֶיךָ:
חַסְדְּךָ יְהוָה מָלְאָה הָאָרֶץ חֻקֶּיךָ לַמְּדֵנִי:

57 My portion is Yahweh; I have promised to keep your words.
58 I seek your face with all my heart; Be gracious to me according to your promise.
59 I consider my ways; and I turn my feet to your statutes.
60 I hurry and do not tarry to keep your commands.
61 The bonds of the wicked surround me; But I will not forget your torah.
62 In the middle of the night I arise to give thanks to you for your righteous laws.
63 I am united with all those who fear you and with those who keep your precepts.
64 Your steadfast love fills the earth; Teach me your decrees.

טוֹב עָשִׂיתָ עִם־עַבְדְּךָ יְהוָה כִּדְבָרֶךָ:
טוּב טַעַם וָדַעַת לַמְּדֵנִי כִּי בְמִצְוֹתֶיךָ הֶאֱמָנְתִּי:
טֶרֶם אֶעֱנֶה אֲנִי שֹׁגֵג וְעַתָּה אִמְרָתְךָ שָׁמָרְתִּי:
טוֹב־אַתָּה וּמֵטִיב לַמְּדֵנִי חֻקֶּיךָ:

65 You do good for your servant, O Yahweh, according to your word.
66 Teach me discernment and knowledge because I believe in your commands.
67 Before I was humbled I was going astray; But now I keep your words.
68 You are good and you do good; Teach me your decrees.

טָפְלוּ עָלַי שֶׁקֶר זֵדִים אֲנִי בְּכָל־לֵב אֶצֹּר פִּקּוּדֶיךָ:
טָפַשׁ כַּחֵלֶב לִבָּם אֲנִי תּוֹרָתְךָ שִׁעֲשָׁעְתִּי:
טוֹב־לִי כִי־עֻנֵּיתִי לְמַעַן אֶלְמַד חֻקֶּיךָ:
טוֹב־לִי תוֹרַת־פִּיךָ מֵאַלְפֵי זָהָב וָכָסֶף:

69 The proud smear me with deception; But with all my heart I keep your precepts.
70 Their hearts grow fat; But I rejoice in your torah.
71 It was good for me that I was humbled, in order that I might learn your decrees.
72 It is good for me, the torah of your mouth; *Better* than thousands *of pieces* of gold and silver.

יָדֶיךָ עָשׂוּנִי וַיְכוֹנְנוּנִי הֲבִינֵנִי וְאֶלְמְדָה מִצְוֹתֶיךָ:
יְרֵאֶיךָ יִרְאוּנִי וְיִשְׂמָחוּ כִּי לִדְבָרְךָ יִחָלְתִּי:
יָדַעְתִּי יְהוָה כִּי־צֶדֶק מִשְׁפָּטֶיךָ וֶאֱמוּנָה עִנִּיתָנִי:
יְהִי־נָא חַסְדְּךָ לְנַחֲמֵנִי כְּאִמְרָתְךָ לְעַבְדֶּךָ:
יְבֹאוּנִי רַחֲמֶיךָ וְאֶחְיֶה כִּי־תוֹרָתְךָ שַׁעֲשֻׁעָי:
יֵבֹשׁוּ זֵדִים כִּי־שֶׁקֶר עִוְּתוּנִי אֲנִי אָשִׂיחַ בְּפִקּוּדֶיךָ:
יָשׁוּבוּ לִי יְרֵאֶיךָ וְיֹדְעֵי עֵדֹתֶיךָ:
יְהִי־לִבִּי תָמִים בְּחֻקֶּיךָ לְמַעַן לֹא אֵבוֹשׁ:

73 Your hands made and established me; Give me understanding that I may learn your commands.
74 Those who fear you look on me and rejoice because I have put my hope in your word.
75 I know, O Yahweh, that your commands are righteous; and in faithfulness you have afflicted me.
76 May your steadfast love comfort me according to your promise to your servant.
77 May your love go with me and I will live; For your torah is my delight.
78 Let the proud be shamed for falsely accusing me; I meditate on your precepts.
79 Let those who fear you return to me; those who know your statutes.
80 May my heart be blameless by your decrees, so that I will not be put to shame.

כָּלְתָה לִתְשׁוּעָתְךָ נַפְשִׁי לִדְבָרְךָ יִחָלְתִּי:
כָּלוּ עֵינַי לְאִמְרָתֶךָ לֵאמֹר מָתַי תְּנַחֲמֵנִי:
כִּי־הָיִיתִי כְּנֹאד בְּקִיטוֹר חֻקֶּיךָ לֹא שָׁכָחְתִּי:
כַּמָּה יְמֵי־עַבְדֶּךָ מָתַי תַּעֲשֶׂה בְרֹדְפַי מִשְׁפָּט:
כָּרוּ־לִי זֵדִים שִׁיחוֹת אֲשֶׁר לֹא כְתוֹרָתֶךָ:
כָּל־מִצְוֹתֶיךָ אֱמוּנָה שֶׁקֶר רְדָפוּנִי עָזְרֵנִי:
כִּמְעַט כִּלּוּנִי בָאָרֶץ וַאֲנִי לֹא־עָזַבְתִּי פִקּוּדֶיךָ:

81 My soul faints with longing for your salvation; For your word in which I put my hope.
82 My eyes fail for your utterance; To say, "When will you have compassion upon me?"
83 For I was like a wineskin in thick smoke; Your decrees I have not forgotten.
84 Until when *must* your servant *wait*? When will you bring my persecutors to justice?
85 The proud dig pits for me which is not in accordance with your law.
86 All your commands are faithful; Help me when the deceitful pursue me.
87 They almost wiped me from the earth;

Torah-Kingship Theme in Psalms 118–119

כְּחַסְדְּךָ חַיֵּנִי וְאֶשְׁמְרָה עֵדוּת פִּיךָ:

But I have not forsaken your precepts.
88 Be gracious to me in your love and I shall keep the decrees of your mouth.

לְעוֹלָם יְהוָה דְּבָרְךָ נִצָּב בַּשָּׁמָיִם:
לְדֹר וָדֹר אֱמוּנָתֶךָ כּוֹנַנְתָּ אֶרֶץ וַתַּעֲמֹד:
לְמִשְׁפָּטֶיךָ עָמְדוּ הַיּוֹם כִּי הַכֹּל עֲבָדֶיךָ:
לוּלֵי תוֹרָתְךָ שַׁעֲשֻׁעָי אָז אָבַדְתִּי בְעָנְיִי:
לְעוֹלָם לֹא־אֶשְׁכַּח פִּקּוּדֶיךָ כִּי בָם חִיִּיתָנִי:
לְךָ־אֲנִי הוֹשִׁיעֵנִי כִּי פִקּוּדֶיךָ דָרָשְׁתִּי:
לִי קִוּוּ רְשָׁעִים לְאַבְּדֵנִי עֵדֹתֶיךָ אֶתְבּוֹנָן:
לְכָל תִּכְלָה רָאִיתִי קֵץ רְחָבָה מִצְוָתְךָ מְאֹד:

89 Your word, O Yahweh, is eternal; It is established in the heavens.
90 From generation to generation is your faithfulness; You established the earth and it continues.
91 Your laws continue until today; for all things are your servants.
92 Had your torah not been my delight; I would have perished in my suffering.
93 I will never forget your precepts; for by them you revive me.
94 I belong to you—save me because I seek your precepts.
95 The wicked wait to destroy me; but I will consider your decrees.
96 To all perfection I see an end; Your commands are very broad.

מָה־אָהַבְתִּי תוֹרָתֶךָ כָּל־הַיּוֹם הִיא שִׂיחָתִי:
מֵאֹיְבַי תְּחַכְּמֵנִי מִצְוֹתֶךָ כִּי לְעוֹלָם הִיא־לִי:
מִכָּל־מְלַמְּדַי הִשְׂכַּלְתִּי כִּי עֵדְוֹתֶיךָ שִׂיחָה לִי:
מִזְּקֵנִים אֶתְבּוֹנָן כִּי פִקּוּדֶיךָ נָצָרְתִּי:
מִכָּל־אֹרַח רָע כָּלִאתִי רַגְלָי לְמַעַן אֶשְׁמֹר דְּבָרֶךָ:
מִמִּשְׁפָּטֶיךָ לֹא־סָרְתִּי כִּי־אַתָּה הוֹרֵתָנִי:
מַה־נִּמְלְצוּ לְחִכִּי אִמְרָתֶךָ מִדְּבַשׁ לְפִי:
מִפִּקּוּדֶיךָ אֶתְבּוֹנָן עַל־כֵּן שָׂנֵאתִי כָּל־אֹרַח שָׁקֶר:

97 How I love your torah! All day long it is my meditation.
98 Your commands make me wiser than my enemies, for they are ever with me.
99 I have greater insight than all my teachers; for your decrees are my meditation.
100 I have greater understanding than the elders because I guard your precepts.
101 I have kept my feet from all the paths of evil, in order to keep your word.
102 I have not turned from your judgements; for you yourself have taught me.
103 How pleasant are your utterances in my palate; *sweeter* than honey in my mouth.
104 I consider diligently your precepts therefore I hate all paths of deception.

נֵר־לְרַגְלִי דְבָרֶךָ וְאוֹר לִנְתִיבָתִי:
נִשְׁבַּעְתִּי וָאֲקַיֵּמָה לִשְׁמֹר מִשְׁפְּטֵי צִדְקֶךָ:
נַעֲנֵיתִי עַד־מְאֹד יְהוָה חַיֵּנִי כִדְבָרֶךָ:
נִדְבוֹת פִּי רְצֵה־נָא יְהוָה וּמִשְׁפָּטֶיךָ לַמְּדֵנִי:

105 Your word is a lamp to my feet and light to my path.
106 I swore and I confirmed that I would keep the commands of righteousness.
107 I was humbled severely; O Yahweh!

נַפְשִׁי בְכַפִּי תָמִיד וְתוֹרָתְךָ לֹא שָׁכָחְתִּי:
נָתְנוּ רְשָׁעִים פַּח לִי וּמִפִּקּוּדֶיךָ לֹא תָעִיתִי:
נָחַלְתִּי עֵדְוֹתֶיךָ לְעוֹלָם כִּי־שְׂשׂוֹן לִבִּי הֵמָּה:
נָטִיתִי לִבִּי לַעֲשׂוֹת חֻקֶּיךָ לְעוֹלָם עֵקֶב:

סֵעֲפִים שָׂנֵאתִי וְתוֹרָתְךָ אָהָבְתִּי:
סִתְרִי וּמָגִנִּי אָתָּה לִדְבָרְךָ יִחָלְתִּי:
סוּרוּ־מִמֶּנִּי מְרֵעִים וְאֶצְּרָה מִצְוֹת אֱלֹהָי:
סָמְכֵנִי כְאִמְרָתְךָ וְאֶחְיֶה וְאַל־תְּבִישֵׁנִי מִשִּׂבְרִי:
סְעָדֵנִי וְאִוָּשֵׁעָה וְאֶשְׁעָה בְחֻקֶּיךָ תָמִיד:
סָלִיתָ כָּל־שׁוֹגִים מֵחֻקֶּיךָ כִּי־שֶׁקֶר תַּרְמִיתָם:
סִגִים הִשְׁבַּתָּ כָל־רִשְׁעֵי־אָרֶץ לָכֵן אָהַבְתִּי עֵדֹתֶיךָ:
סָמַר מִפַּחְדְּךָ בְשָׂרִי וּמִמִּשְׁפָּטֶיךָ יָרֵאתִי:

עָשִׂיתִי מִשְׁפָּט וָצֶדֶק בַּל־תַּנִּיחֵנִי לְעֹשְׁקָי:
עֲרֹב עַבְדְּךָ לְטוֹב אַל־יַעַשְׁקֻנִי זֵדִים:
עֵינַי כָּלוּ לִישׁוּעָתֶךָ וּלְאִמְרַת צִדְקֶךָ:
עֲשֵׂה עִם־עַבְדְּךָ כְחַסְדֶּךָ וְחֻקֶּיךָ לַמְּדֵנִי:
עַבְדְּךָ־אָנִי הֲבִינֵנִי וְאֵדְעָה עֵדֹתֶיךָ:
עֵת לַעֲשׂוֹת לַיהוָה הֵפֵרוּ תּוֹרָתֶךָ:
עַל־כֵּן אָהַבְתִּי מִצְוֹתֶיךָ מִזָּהָב וּמִפָּז:

Revive me according to your word.
108 Look favourably upon the free-will offerings of my mouth, O Yahweh; and teach me your judgements.
109 My life is constantly in my hands; yet I will not forget your torah.
110 The wicked set a trap for me, but I will not wander from your precepts.
111 Your decrees are my inheritance forever; for they are my heart's delight.
112 I incline my heart to keep your decrees; they are my reward forever.

113 I hate the half-hearted, but I love your torah.
114 You are my hiding place and my shield; I have put my hope in your word.
115 Turn away from me, evil-doers, that I may keep the commands of my God!
116 Sustain me according to your promise and I will live; do not turn my hope to shame.
117 Support me and I shall be saved; I will lift up your decrees continually.
118 Make light of all those who stray from your decrees for their deceitfulness is vain.
119 You remove the dross of all the earth's wicked; so I love your statutes.
120 My flesh shivers in dread of you and I fear your commands.

121 I have done justice and righteousness; Do not give me over to my oppressors.
122 Ensure your servant's good; do not let the proud oppress me.
123 My eyes fail *looking for* your salvation and your righteous promise.
124 Do for your servant in accordance with your steadfast love; and teach me your decrees.
125 I am your servant – give me understanding that I may know your statutes.
126 It is time to act, O Yahweh, they are breaking your torah.
127 Because I love your commands more than gold, more than pure gold;

Torah-Kingship Theme in Psalms 118–119

עַל־כֵּן כָּל־פִּקּוּדֵי כֹל יִשָּׁרְתִּי כָּל־אֹרַח שֶׁקֶר שָׂנֵאתִי:

פְּלָאוֹת עֵדְוֹתֶיךָ עַל־כֵּן נְצָרָתַם נַפְשִׁי:
פֵּתַח דְּבָרֶיךָ יָאִיר מֵבִין פְּתָיִים:
פִּי־פָעַרְתִּי וָאֶשְׁאָפָה כִּי לְמִצְוֹתֶיךָ יָאָבְתִּי:
פְּנֵה־אֵלַי וְחָנֵּנִי כְּמִשְׁפָּט לְאֹהֲבֵי שְׁמֶךָ:
פְּעָמַי הָכֵן בְּאִמְרָתֶךָ וְאַל־תַּשְׁלֶט־בִּי כָל־אָוֶן:
פְּדֵנִי מֵעֹשֶׁק אָדָם וְאֶשְׁמְרָה פִּקּוּדֶיךָ:
פָּנֶיךָ הָאֵר בְּעַבְדֶּךָ וְלַמְּדֵנִי אֶת־חֻקֶּיךָ:
פַּלְגֵי־מַיִם יָרְדוּ עֵינָי עַל לֹא־שָׁמְרוּ תוֹרָתֶךָ:

128 Because I consider all your precepts upright – I hate all the paths of deceit.

129 Your statutes are wonders, therefore my soul obeys them.
130 The opening of your word brings light, understanding for the simple.
131 I open my mouth in longing, because I love your commands.
132 Turn to me and be gracious to me; according to your justice toward those who love your name.
133 Establish my footsteps according to your word and do not allow any sin to have mastery over me.
134 Ransom me from the oppression of men; that I may keep your precepts.
135 May your face shine upon your servant; that I may learn your decrees.
136 Tears go down my eyes; because they do not keep your torah.

צַדִּיק אַתָּה יְהוָה וְיָשָׁר מִשְׁפָּטֶיךָ:
צִוִּיתָ צֶדֶק עֵדֹתֶיךָ וֶאֱמוּנָה מְאֹד:
צִמְּתַתְנִי קִנְאָתִי כִּי־שָׁכְחוּ דְבָרֶיךָ צָרָי:
צְרוּפָה אִמְרָתְךָ מְאֹד וְעַבְדְּךָ אֲהֵבָהּ:
צָעִיר אָנֹכִי וְנִבְזֶה פִּקֻּדֶיךָ לֹא שָׁכָחְתִּי:
צִדְקָתְךָ צֶדֶק לְעוֹלָם וְתוֹרָתְךָ אֱמֶת:
צַר־וּמָצוֹק מְצָאוּנִי מִצְוֹתֶיךָ שַׁעֲשֻׁעָי:
צֶדֶק עֵדְוֹתֶיךָ לְעוֹלָם הֲבִינֵנִי וְאֶחְיֶה:

137 You are righteous, O Yahweh, and your judgements are upright.
138 You commanded your righteous statutes and *they are* fully trustworthy.
139 My zeal is putting an end to me because my enemies forget your words.
140 Your promise is exceedingly refined and your servant loves it.
141 I am insignificant and despised; But I do not forget your precepts.
142 Your righteousness is righteous forever and your torah is true.
143 Trouble and distress find me, but your commands are my delight.
144 Your statutes are righteous for ever; Give me understanding that I may live!

קָרָאתִי בְכָל־לֵב עֲנֵנִי יְהוָה חֻקֶּיךָ אֶצֹּרָה:
קְרָאתִיךָ הוֹשִׁיעֵנִי וְאֶשְׁמְרָה עֵדֹתֶיךָ:
קִדַּמְתִּי בַנֶּשֶׁף וָאֲשַׁוֵּעָה לִדְבָרְיךָ יִחָלְתִּי:
קִדְּמוּ עֵינַי אַשְׁמֻרוֹת לָשִׂיחַ בְּאִמְרָתֶךָ:
קוֹלִי שִׁמְעָה כְחַסְדֶּךָ יְהוָה כְּמִשְׁפָּטֶךָ חַיֵּנִי:

145 I call out with all my heart – answer me, O Yahweh – I keep your commands.
146 I call out to you, save me and I will keep your statutes.
147 I rise before dawn and I cry out for help; I have set my hope in your words.
148 My eyes stay open through the night-

קָרְבוּ רֹדְפֵי זִמָּה מִתּוֹרָתְךָ רָחָקוּ:
קָרוֹב אַתָּה יְהוָה וְכָל־מִצְוֹתֶיךָ אֱמֶת:
קֶדֶם יָדַעְתִּי מֵעֵדֹתֶיךָ כִּי לְעוֹלָם יְסַדְתָּם:

watches to meditate upon your promises.
149 Hear my voice in accordance with your steadfast love; O Yahweh, revive me in accordance with your justice.
150 My persecutors are near, plotting; they are far from your torah.
151 You are near, O Yahweh, and all your commands are true.
152 From of old I have known your statute; for you established them forever.

רְאֵה־עָנְיִי וְחַלְּצֵנִי כִּי־תוֹרָתְךָ לֹא שָׁכָחְתִּי:
רִיבָה רִיבִי וּגְאָלֵנִי לְאִמְרָתְךָ חַיֵּנִי:
רָחוֹק מֵרְשָׁעִים יְשׁוּעָה כִּי־חֻקֶּיךָ לֹא דָרָשׁוּ:
רַחֲמֶיךָ רַבִּים יְהוָה כְּמִשְׁפָּטֶיךָ חַיֵּנִי:
רַבִּים רֹדְפַי וְצָרָי מֵעֵדְוֺתֶיךָ לֹא נָטִיתִי:
רָאִיתִי בֹגְדִים וָאֶתְקוֹטָטָה אֲשֶׁר אִמְרָתְךָ לֹא שָׁמָרוּ:
רְאֵה כִּי־פִקּוּדֶיךָ אָהָבְתִּי יְהוָה כְּחַסְדְּךָ חַיֵּנִי:
רֹאשׁ־דְּבָרְךָ אֱמֶת וּלְעוֹלָם כָּל־מִשְׁפַּט צִדְקֶךָ:

153 Look upon my suffering and deliver me; because I do not forget your torah.
154 Defend my cause and redeem me; revive me according to your promise.
155 The wicked are far from your salvation; because they do not seek your decrees.
156 Your compassion is great, O Yahweh; Revive me according to your judgements.
157 Many are my persecutors and enemies; I have not turned away from your statutes.
158 I view the faithless with loathing; those who do not keep your utterances.
159 See how I love your precepts; O Yahweh, preserve my life according to your steadfast love.
160 All your words are true; All your commands are forever righteous.

שָׂרִים רְדָפוּנִי חִנָּם וּמִדְּבָרְךָ פָּחַד לִבִּי:
שָׂשׂ אָנֹכִי עַל־אִמְרָתֶךָ כְּמוֹצֵא שָׁלָל רָב:
שֶׁקֶר שָׂנֵאתִי וַאֲתַעֵבָה תּוֹרָתְךָ אָהָבְתִּי:
שֶׁבַע בַּיּוֹם הִלַּלְתִּיךָ עַל מִשְׁפְּטֵי צִדְקֶךָ:
שָׁלוֹם רָב לְאֹהֲבֵי תוֹרָתֶךָ וְאֵין־לָמוֹ מִכְשׁוֹל:
שִׂבַּרְתִּי לִישׁוּעָתְךָ יְהוָה וּמִצְוֹתֶיךָ עָשִׂיתִי:
שָׁמְרָה נַפְשִׁי עֵדֹתֶיךָ וָאֹהֲבֵם מְאֹד:
שָׁמַרְתִּי פִקּוּדֶיךָ וְעֵדֹתֶיךָ כִּי כָל־דְּרָכַי נֶגְדֶּךָ:

161 Rulers persecute me without cause; but my heart trembles before your words.
162 I rejoice continually in your promise; like one finding great spoil.
163 I hate and abhor deception; I love your torah.
164 Seven times a day I praise you because of your righteous commands.
165 Much peace is to those who love your torah and nothing makes them stumble.
166 I wait for your salvation, O Yahweh; and I keep your commands.
167 My soul keeps your statutes and I love them greatly.
168 I keep your precepts and your statutes; For all my ways are before you.

תִּקְרַב רִנָּתִי לְפָנֶיךָ יְהוָה כִּדְבָרְךָ הֲבִינֵנִי:
תָּבוֹא תְחִנָּתִי לְפָנֶיךָ כְּאִמְרָתְךָ הַצִּילֵנִי:
תַּבַּעְנָה שְׂפָתַי תְּהִלָּה כִּי תְלַמְּדֵנִי חֻקֶּיךָ:
תַּעַן לְשׁוֹנִי אִמְרָתֶךָ כִּי כָל־מִצְוֹתֶיךָ צֶּדֶק:
תְּהִי־יָדְךָ לְעָזְרֵנִי כִּי פִקּוּדֶיךָ בָחָרְתִּי:
תָּאַבְתִּי לִישׁוּעָתְךָ יְהוָה וְתוֹרָתְךָ שַׁעֲשֻׁעָי:
תְּחִי־נַפְשִׁי וּתְהַלְלֶךָּ וּמִשְׁפָּטֶךָ יַעֲזְרֻנִי:
תָּעִיתִי כְּשֶׂה אֹבֵד בַּקֵּשׁ עַבְדֶּךָ כִּי מִצְוֹתֶיךָ לֹא שָׁכָחְתִּי:

169 May my cry for help draw near to you, O Yahweh; Give me understanding in accordance with your word.
170 May my supplication come into your presence; Deliver me in accordance with your promise.
171 Praise pours forth from my lips because you teach me your decrees.
172 My tongue is occupied with your words because all your commands are righteous.
173 May your hand be my help for I choose your precepts.
174 I long for your salvation, O Yahweh; and your torah is my delight.
175 My soul lives and will praise you; and your judgements are my help.
176 I have strayed like a lost sheep—seek out your servant, because I have not forgotten your commands

5.1　Deuteronomic Influences on Psalm 119

Arguably, the least controversial statement of all the suggestions contained in this thesis would be to say that Psalm 119[97] is thoroughly grounded in the torah theology of Deuteronomy. Were arguments proven solely on the basis of the number of commentators who agree on any given issue, then this question would be a dead certainty—all of the commentators, as far as I am aware, make some sort of connection between Psalm 119 and the theology of the Book of Deuteronomy. However, academic accord is not a sufficient standard of evidence, the text of the Hebrew Bible must be allowed to speak for itself. Therefore, we should take some time to examine the Dtr content in Psalm 119.

5.1.1　Torah Synonyms

Perhaps the most obvious Dtr connection is Psalm 119's use of torah and its seven synonyms. Clearly, the central focus of Psalm 119 is the torah of Yahweh and its significance in the life of the speaker of the psalm. The eight-fold

---

[97] Perhaps surprisingly for a poem of this length, the text of Ps 119 is largely unproblematic. Also the acrostic pattern means that it is not difficult to determine the structure of the psalm!

acrostic structure is matched by the use of eight torah words which are used interchangeably within this massive poem.⁹⁸ The word used most commonly is torah (תורה) itself and the seven other words, in other contexts, seem to reflect particular aspects or elements of legal understanding,⁹⁹ but here they are used as synonyms of torah, to convey the same essential meaning using different words. The overall impression is not that the psalmist is trying to subtly distinguish between the various torah terms, rather that he uses them interchangeably to reflect the totality of God's revelation.¹⁰⁰

This preoccupation with torah terms is characteristic of the Book of Deuteronomy and the Deuteronomic literature. All of the terms used in Psalm 119 are to be found in Deuteronomy itself, apart from פקודים which appears to be a poetic equivalent of חקים and is only to be found in the Psalms. What is especially characteristic of Deuteronomy is the use of many of these torah terms in close conjunction:

> a) Multiple Torah Terms. We have already discussed the poetic function of the multiple terms for Torah and the fact that throughout the legal traditions dual terms for Torah are used. But it is particularly characteristic of the deuteronomic style to go even further than dual terms in its zeal for comprehensiveness where Torah is concerned.¹⁰¹

Levenson further emphasises this connection between Deuteronomy, as opposed to the Priestly literature, and Ps 119:

> The concern with commandments, under various names, is also common to Ps 119 and Deuteronomy. Indeed, in some Deuteronomistic paraenetic texts (e.g.

---

⁹⁸ Mays, *Psalms*, 382; Soll, *Psalm 119*, 38–45.

⁹⁹ I have chosen the following definitions of each of the synonyms: עדות–"statutes"; פקודים–"precepts"; הקים–"decrees"; מצות–"commands"; משפטים–"judgments"; דבר–"word(s)" and אמרה–also "word(s)." These largely follow the accepted definitions of these terms. Some scholars seek to define אמרה as "promise," and it may sometimes have this meaning in certain contexts. Generally, I have decided to follow the LXX in translating דבר and אמרה in the same way, using "word(s)" because it appears that אמרה functions as a poetic synonym of דבר, (Kirkpatrick, *Psalms*, 704), but occasionally it is translated as "promise," when the context so suggests. תורה, I have left untranslated for the moment as the proper understanding of this term as it is used in the torah psalms will be the subject of later discussion

¹⁰⁰ R. Norman Whybray, "Psalm 119 Profile of a Psalmist," in *Wisdom, You Are My Sister: Studies in Honor of Roland E. Murphy, O. Carm., on the Occasion of His Eightieth Birthday* (CBQMS 29; ed. Michael L. Barré; Washington D.C.: Catholic Biblical Association of America, 1997), 31.

¹⁰¹ Soll, *Psalm 119*, 107.

Deut 4:1-6), one can hear as many as five of the eight synonyms of Psalm 119 in only a few verses. In contrast, distinctive Priestly terminology is largely absent in the psalm.... The poet stands in the Deuteronomic tradition of repentance, not in the Priestly tradition of atonement and expiation.[102]

Although each of these terms really functions in the same way in the poem, it is likely that the poet made use of all eight terms in order to stress the fullness and diversity of divine revelation, accentuating the completeness with which the word of God addresses the life of the OT believer. Again, this concern reflects the teaching of Deuteronomy:

> Apparently the poet knew of eight principle terms in the authoritative tradition that named the subject about which he wanted to write. So he used the alphabet to signal completeness and the whole vocabulary to represent comprehensiveness.[103]

> [T]he conception associated with תורה in view of Psalms 1; 19B; and 119 is more narrow. One thinks of the canonised law of God, and especially of the norm brought about by Deuteronomy. In favour of this conception would be not only the variation of terms in Psalm 119 (and Psalm 19), which places clearly juridical terms like חק and משפט alongside of תורה, but also the inner content. Psalm 119 speaks about keeping, preserving, and not forgetting the Torah. Those are demands that constantly recur in Deuteronomy. Intensive, unremitting association with the Torah is commanded, especially in Deut 6:7ff and Joshua 1:8. Also taking the Torah to heart and its presence in one's innermost being, as is taught in Ps 119 is characteristic for Deuteronomic exhortation and theology (cf Deut 4:39; 6:6; 30:14). Worth noting, finally, is the living דבר character that clings to the תורה concept and then expresses itself also in Psalms 19 and 119. There can hardly be any doubt that there are close connections between Deuteronomic circles and the תורה piety of Psalms 1; 19B; and 119.[104]

So we see that the use of multiple torah terms in Ps 119—as in Ps 19— grounds this poem in the piety of the Deuteronomist.

5.1.2 LANGUAGE OF DEVOTION

As well as picking up on the use of multiple legal terms in the above quote, Kraus points out another Deuteronomic connection in highlighting the language of devotion used in Psalm 119 which bears marked similarities to the paraenetic challenges of the Book of Deuteronomy. Many of the activities related to the

---

[102] Levenson, "Sources," 564.
[103] Mays, *Psalms*, 382.
[104] Kraus, *Psalms II*, 413.

law of Yahweh in Ps 119 are commanded in Deuteronomy—for example, as Kraus suggests, "keeping, preserving, and not forgetting the torah"[105] are all commands which are commonly found in Deuteronomy (e.g. Ps 119:2, 4, 10 etc. cf. Deut 4:1-14; 6:1-25 etc.). Soll also argues that such language puts Psalm 119 firmly within the terms of reference of Deuteronomic theology and he goes on to add that the use of "psychophysical terms" also reflects this worldview.

> The characteristically deuteronomic phrase "with all my heart" occurs six times in Psalm 119. The only difference is that Psalm 119 employs *bĕkōl lēb*, where the deuteronomic tradition prefers *bĕkōl lĕbab*. It is used in Psalm 119, as in Deuteronomy and the deuteronomistic history, to modify verb phrases involving seeking YHWH (Psalm 119:2, 10, 58, 145; Deut 4:29 etc) and carrying out the commandments (Ps 119:34, 69; Deut 26:16; 30:2 etc).[106]

Other commentators also draw attention to Psalm 119's use of a language of devotion which is very similar to the piety encouraged in Deuteronomy:

> Commentators have called the psalm Deuteronomic in thought, and there are certainly affinities between the psalm and Deuteronomy. Deuteronomy employs seven of the key words (only *piqqûdîm* is absent), and many phrases appear in both places. Most important, Psalm 119 employs the affective language of Deuteronomy: love (*'āhab*) of *tôrâ* with all one's heart, listening and keeping *tôrâ*.[107]

---

[105] Kraus, *Psalms II*, 413.

[106] Soll, *Psalm 119*, 127–28.

[107] Freedman, *Psalm 119*, 90–91. Freedman's consideration of Ps 119 in this work is insightful and theologically rich, however, I cannot agree with the central thesis of his work. He suggests that at some point the acrostic psalms formed a group in which the number of syllables in Ps 119 exactly corresponds to the combined syllable count of all of the other acrostic psalms. There are several problems with this thesis: (1) Freedman's theory is dependent upon a degree of exactness in the analysis of the text which is not available to us (as Freedman himself must admit, e.g., "determining colon boundaries and hence the number of cola in a stanza or a poem is not an exact science... [p 18]); (2) The difference in vocalisation (which accordingly influences the number of syllables) between the original Hebrew text of these psalms and the MT is not properly taken into account (pp 59–61)—to split the difference between long and short spellings seems somewhat random and cannot guarantee a correct answer regarding the original number of syllables in each poem; (3) Other theories for assessing metre are not given proper consideration (p 77), the fact that counting syllables (as opposed to accented syllables) gives a neater result in this case is insufficient evidence in and of itself to establish that this method of syllable counting (if any) was employed by the author of Ps 119; (4) Even were this remarkable correspondence in the number of syllables to be accepted, it does not necessarily lead to the conclusion that the acrostics once formed a psalm grouping.

Torah-Kingship Theme in Psalms 118–119

The voice speaking in the psalm is that of a consciousness shaped by many influences, all of them scriptural. The psalmist knows and thinks with the theology and vocabulary of Deuteronomy. The great exhortation of Deuteronomy 6:1–9 to love the Lord by keeping and teaching his words is the central impulse of the psalmist's religion.[108]

So it can be seen that the torah synonyms are not the only key areas of lexical connection grounded in Dtr theology, the whole language of devotion found in Ps 119 borrows heavily upon Dtr concepts of a proper, worshipful, obedient attitude towards Yahweh.

5.1.3   DEPENDENCE UPON YAHWEH AND NAME OF YAHWEH

Once again we see in Psalm 119 themes which have been constant refrains in the torah-kingship psalms. One of the most prominent themes in these psalms, and also in the Book of Deuteronomy, is the idea of total dependence upon God. This concept is foundational to the very idea of personal and corporate piety within the Psalter, which makes it clear that there is no way for the believer to please God without a proper attitude of trust in him. Obviously, this theological emphasis has become are a psalmic theme—something intrinsic to the theology of the psalms themselves—yet this is a concept which would have known roots in the Deuteronomic literature. In all situations, the Israelite believer and the community of believers should trust in Yahweh over and above all else: such is the message of Deuteronomy and of the Psalms.

Many verses of Ps 119 show this attitude of absolute trust in Yahweh as opposed to other potential sources of confidence. The following verses are particular examples, but a cursory reading of the psalm will quickly reveal others:

v 23   גם ישבו שרים בי נדברו עבדך ישיה בחקיך
Even though princes sit speaking against me; your servant shall meditate on your decrees.
v 72   טוב־לי תורת־פיך מאלפי זהב וכסף
The torah of your mouth is good for me; [better] than thousands of *pieces of* gold and silver.
v 114   סתרי ומגני אתה לדברך יחלתי
You are my hiding place and my shield; I have put my hope in your word.

These three verses illustrate repeated themes in the statements of trust in Yahweh in Ps 119. Whybray observes:

---

[108] Mays, *Psalms*, 384. See also Kirkpatrick, *Psalms*, 704–05 and Kraus, *Psalms II*, 415.

A number of themes are endlessly repeated: the psalmist makes it clear that God, whose will is expressed in his torah or teaching, *is the sole guiding principle of his life*: he loves and delights in his law, which is eternal and righteous, saves him, gives him life, freedom and superior wisdom. He studies it and meditates on it and so receives illumination. Yet he recognises that his understanding of it is incomplete, and he desperately longs for a deeper knowledge. He also recognises the *danger of being led astray by a desire for wealth and unjust gain, and prays that he may avoid this*. He feels isolated from society and *prays to be delivered from his tormentors who seek his life*. He prays for life, help, comfort and grace, and speaks of his frequent turning to God in prayer and praise.[109]

These repeated themes within the Psalm 119 echo the spirit of the Kingship Law.[110] The three verses highlighted above show specifically how the psalmist declares his trust in Yahweh's torah as opposed to: 1) Princes and their mocking (corresponding to the international treaties sealed by royal marriages banned in Deut 17:17 cf. also v 46); 2) Great wealth; and, 3) Military strength (Yahweh is the psalmist's shield and hiding place, not weapons of war or armies). The three areas explicitly prohibited as sources of trust for the Israelite king are all explicitly addressed in the text of Psalm 119. This psalmist declares his absolute dependence upon Yahweh (by learning from and living in accordance with his torah), as opposed to all external factors, and in doing so he displays the type of priorities that are demanded of the king in Deut 17:14–20.[111]

This attitude of absolute dependence upon Yahweh is further solidified by the use of the "name motif" in verses 55 and 132. The idea presented by the "name of Yahweh" in Psalm 119 (as well as in the other psalms which we have examined) seems to reflect an understanding of the "real presence of God."[112] This is used as a symbol of his actual presence with his people. It is "remembered" (זכר) and "loved" (אהב) in these two verses, thus reflecting the type of personification of the name concept that we have seen in the other kingship-torah psalms. Although not a prominent theme in Ps 119, clearly the psalmist views Yahweh as being present and worthy of trust above all else.[113]

---

[109] Whybray, "Psalm 119," 40 (emphasis mine).

[110] As we shall see below, the pray-er of Psalm 119 may well be the Davidic king.

[111] Kraus, *Psalms II*, 415–16; Kirkpatrick, *Psalms*, 733.

[112] See the discussion of "name theology" at various points in chapter 3, above.

[113] Kirkpatrick, *Psalms*, 714. Kirkpatrick writes concerning the "name of Yahweh" in v 55, "The constant recollection of all that He has revealed Himself to be, is the most powerful motive to observance of His laws."

Once again we see that the psalmist reflects an attitude which is commended—even commanded—in Deuteronomy. Throughout that book emphasis upon absolute trust in Yahweh is often repeated. Deut 6–8 reminds the people of the dangers of forgetting Yahweh and trusting in syncretism, or becoming proud of their election, relying upon wealth, and so on.[114] The constant theme of these chapters concerns *that which Yahweh has done for them and the necessity of trusting in him alone*. The same principle can be seen in the Kingship Law (Deut 17)[115] and the law governing war (Deut 20)[116] and at other points throughout the book. Deuteronomy makes it clear that Yahweh is the source of all good for his people, so they should rely solely on him and not turn to any other source of empowerment—this message finds a ringing reprise in the content of Ps 119.

5.1.4 YAHWEH AS REFUGE AND TORAH

Connected with the above theme of dependence upon Yahweh, is the idea of Yahweh as refuge for his people. We have discussed the significance of this concept in terms of the editorial placement of the psalms, and examined the role that the "refuge" (חסה) semantic group plays in the torah-kingship psalms. It seems significant, therefore, that the חסה group *does not* appear in Psalm 119, but rather the reader witnesses something of a transformation with regard to the concept of Yahweh as refuge in this poem. Creach points out that *the language which is normally associated with the* חסה *group becomes associated with the torah in Ps 119*.[117] In fact, it appears that torah has become (perhaps in late psalmic literature) a focal point for the believer's understanding of refuge in God.

> Again, Ps 119 speaks of trust in the *tôrâ* like other psalms in the Psalter refer to seeking refuge in Yahweh. In contrast to this portrait of righteousness, Ps 119 presents the wicked as those who fail to depend on *tôrâ*... Thus, Ps 119 takes over language previously applied to Yahweh to describe what seems to be the tutelary function of *tôrâ*. Yahweh's instruction, which perhaps includes the content of the Psalter itself, comes to be seen as a kind of refuge, an object of hope and a source of protection.[118]

---

[114] Millar, *Now Choose Life*, 53; Miller, *Deuteronomy*, 114–18.
[115] Wright, *Deuteronomy*, 208–10.
[116] Creach, *Yahweh as Refuge*, 57n21.
[117] Creach, *Yahweh as Refuge*, 72.
[118] Creach, *Yahweh as Refuge*, 72.

This is an interesting phenomenon, and one worthy of further consideration. Just why is the language of refuge applied to the torah in Psalm 119? Creach suggests that the answer to this question is to be found in a process of democratisation:

> It is also interesting that a number of late psalms... have adopted language of the *ḥāsâ* field to describe a proper stance before Yahweh (Pss 25, 34, 37, 119). This distribution of *ḥāsâ* and related terms may indicate a development in which later writings (wisdom books and late psalms) incorporated language of royal ideology (in royal psalms) and prophetic directives to the nation... to teach personal piety.[119]

The חסה semantic field reflects the idea of God as Rock and Refuge which is rooted in Dtr theology (e.g. Deut 32:37),[120] yet the language which is typically associated with God as refuge is applied to the torah in Psalm 119. This seems to reflect a process of democratisation by which the king's function as "model Israelite" is now being presented directly to the people in order to encourage them towards a comparable type of personal piety.

> *Namely, late Psalms seemed to borrow from earlier writings that described as national policy or the piety of the king in order to express and encourage a personal devotion.* This development holds two important implications for understanding the present Psalter: (1) the incorporation of *ḥāsâ* and associated terms in some of the latest psalms of the book (i.e. Ps 119) is perhaps an indication that the ideas expressed by the *ḥāsâ* field were important for the final collection. (2) More specifically, the association of *tôrâ* with Yahweh's refuge provides a clue as to how Yahweh's instruction was understood and how the Psalter was meant to be read: the content of the Psalter seemed to be intended as a guide to a life of dependence; the most concrete way of expressing such allegiance was in the study of *tôrâ*.[121]

5.1.5 THEOLOGY OF THE TWO WAYS

Much of Psalm 119 is presented in almost adversarial tones (e.g. vv 21–23, 61, 69–70 etc.). Whilst most scholars describe Psalm 119 as a psalm of mixed genre, Soll makes a strong argument that Psalm 119 is, in fact, an individual psalm of lament. As is common with this genre of psalms, much of the content addresses issues concerning the psalmist's enemies, opposition and the

---

[119] Creach, *Yahweh as Refuge*, 68.
[120] Creach, *Yahweh as Refuge*, 72.
[121] Creach, *Yahweh as Refuge*, 73 (emphasis mine).

persecution which he faces.[122] Often psalms of individual lament present the psalmist's lifestyle in contrast to that chosen by his enemies, and this is true of Psalm 119. Thus, it could be said that this psalm bears constant witness to the theology of the two ways. Every verse makes a statement concerning a way of life in relation to the torah of Yahweh—one either accepts that way and walks in accordance with divine revelation, or, alternatively, one rejects that way and therefore chooses to walk in the way of the wicked. This is shown most clearly in the *daleth* stanza, which gives the psalmist a natural opportunity to make use of the word דרך ("way"). Here, for example, we see the psalmist speak about "the way of faithfulness" (דרך־אמונה, v 30) as opposed to "the way of deceit" (דרך־שקר, v 29). However, the idea of the two ways is not limited to the *daleth* stanza, and it finds expression throughout the whole of Psalm 119, particularly in the usage of דרך and ארח ("path"), but the concept is inherent to the poetic intent of the whole psalm. The psalmist is making a declaration that he does follow and will follow a lifestyle based in the torah. This lifestyle has its counterpoint in a lifestyle based on the rejection of torah—be that conscious rejection or simply a lifestyle which places its priorities elsewhere. The reader is aware of this fact from v 1:

אשרי תמימי־דרך ההלכים בתורת יהוה:
Blessed are those whose way is blameless; Those walking in the torah of Yahweh.

From the outset the reader sees that the psalmist is talking about a world-and-life view centred around the torah. This is shown not only by the use of way imagery but also in the idea of "walking in the torah of Yahweh" (הלך), which reflects a choice of lifestyle and worldview, rather than a one-off act or declaration of loyalty. This language sounds a note that rings loud in Deuteronomy:

> Subsequent verses introduce other terms for God's revelation. Verse 2 is reminiscent of Deuteronomy, where God's "decrees" (see Ps 19:7) are to be heard and kept (see Deut 4:45; 6:17, 20) and where God is to be sought wholeheartedly (see Deut 4:29; Ps 119:10). Verse 3 is unusual in that it does

---

[122] Obviously, in a psalm of this length, there is going to be varied content—hence, the majority opinion that Psalm 119 is of mixed genre. However, much of Psalm 119 is made up of the declarations of innocence, cries of lament and petitions for salvation, all of which are common within the psalms of individual lament. Soll points out that over half of the verses of Ps 119 fall within the categories of petition or lament, which as a percentage is comparable to the petition/lament content in psalms which are universally acknowledged to be lament psalms (see Soll, *Psalm 119*, 69–70).

not contain one of the eight major synonyms. Rather, God's "ways" indicate God's revelation in this case (see also vv 15, 37), and *the image of walking in God's ways is again reminiscent of Deuteronomy, occurring often in parallel with keeping God's commandments (see Deut 8:6; 10:12–13; 11:22; see Ps 119:6).*[123]

> The phrase itself ["walk in his ways," Ps 119:3] is a synonym of verse 1b. Deissler suggests that this expression has its home in the Deuteronomic circles, where it is usually coupled with loving Yahweh (Deut 19:9, 30:16) and keeping his Commandments (Deut 8:6, 26:17, 28:9, 30:16). Sometimes it may express one of the essential aspects of Israelite religion, as in Jeremiah 7:23: "Obey my voice... and walk in all the ways that I command you..." (cf 1 Kings 2:3; 2 Chronicles 6:31; Isaiah 48:17).[124]

Furthermore, Anderson points out that the "choose life" language of Ps 119 reflects the Dtr challenge to live in accordance with Yahweh's design rather than to choose alternatives:

> I have chosen thy precepts (v 173): cf. Deut 30:19 where Moses sets before his people the two possibilities: blessing or curse, life or death. The Psalmist has chosen to obey God's commandments by loving him and by walking in his ways (cf Deut 30:15f.), and therefore he can claim the promises of God.[125]

So, we see once again, that a prominent Deuteronomic theme, which has played a significant role in the other torah-kingship psalms, is not only present in Psalm 119 but is fundamental to a correct understanding of the psalmist's intent. The piety of Psalm 119 is presented as a lifestyle, a path to be walked in.

5.1.6 MEDITATION AND PROSPERITY

Our previous studies have shown that the torah-piety of the Deuteronomic literature has a dual focus upon attitude and effect.[126] That is, the right attitude towards torah brings positive effects. The Scriptures generally, and the Psalter specifically, make it clear that this link between torah-obedience and reward should not be understood formulaically,[127] nonetheless Deuteronomy and the DtrH seem to suggest that true and lasting reward results from obedience to

---

[123] McCann, *Psalms*, 1168 (emphasis mine).
[124] Anderson, *Psalms*, 809.
[125] Anderson, *Psalms*, 846–47.
[126] See above, pp 45–48, 99–100 etc.
[127] Walter Brueggemann and Patrick D. Miller, "Psalm 73 as a Canonical Marker," *JSOT* 72 (1996): 45–56.

Yahweh's word.[128] This dual focus upon torah-obedience and the reward of Yahweh is also observable in the text of Psalm 119.

In a very literal sense the torah of Yahweh *is* the constant meditation of the psalmist throughout Psalm 119. There are, of course, verses which speak *about* the psalmist's meditation upon torah (e.g. vv 15, 23, 27, 48, 78 etc.), however the reality is that *Psalm 119, in and of itself, is an act of meditation upon the torah of Yahweh.* Psalm 119 is not merely an ode to torah, a celebration of its beauty and worth (as in Ps 19), rather it is an example of the piety endorsed by the Deuteronomic literature and Psalm 1:3. This fact is quite significant, raising implications both for our understanding of the canonical placement of this poem and with regard to the question of the identity of the individual in Psalm 119.

> By asserting his determination to keep the statutes of YHWH, to meditate on them and delight in them, and by voicing his expectation that YHWH himself will be with him in this endeavour as teacher, the psalmist concludes his prologue with affirmations and aspirations that establish Torah not only as an expression of YHWH's revealed will, but also as the fundamental expression of his hope.[129]

Furthermore, Psalm 119 expands the reader's understanding of reward by presenting the study of the word of God as *reward in itself.* In an interesting commentary upon the idea of reward, such verses as Ps 119:72, 103, 127 present the study of the law of Yahweh as being of greater reward than much silver, gold etc. This, of course, has implications for our understanding of the concept of "reward" in the previous torah-kingship psalm groupings. Kraus picks up on both of these features in his discussion of the theological heart of Psalm 119:

> Two observations in particular about the תורה understanding of Psalm 119 must be kept in mind: (1) The fact that an individual describes his relation to the תורה is striking (cf also Psalms 1 and 19B). Surely the OT revelation of the תורה always involves the ברית, i.e., the relation of God and people (cf also Psalms 78:5, 10; 105:45), but in Ps 119 the individual emerges. (2) The valuations and effects that are ascribed to the תורה are amazing. It is best first to bring together the statements about the value and the effect of the תורה. In Ps 119 the תורה (cf. also the substituted terms) counts as the "highest good," more valuable than gold or silver (v 72); it is the essence of all that is reliable and

---

[128] As can be seen in the paraenetic passages of Deuteronomy (e.g. Deut 6:4-9) and the commissioning of Joshua (Jos 1:8). Similar attitudes are to be found in Pss 119 (e.g. vv 18-19 etc.). At the very least, this relationship can be understood negatively, i.e. one should not expect to receive reward from Yahweh if one does not delight in the law.

[129] Soll, *Psalm 119*, 93.

lasting (v 142).... It is the צדיק who enjoys a particularly intimate relation to this תורה. Psalm 119 is filled with elements of lament and petition. The צדיק prays for a proper attitude to the Torah (v 34). He pleads: "Bless me with your instruction!" (v 29). But then there are, in addition to the laments, numerous confessions that witness to the right relation of the צדיק to the תורה: "Your instruction I do not forget" (vv 61, 109). I do not retreat from it (vv 61, 157). I keep it, walk in it (vv 34, 44, 55, and often). I love the Torah (vv 97, 113, 160, 165). I find joy and pleasure in it (vv 70, 77, 174). The צדיק constantly meditates upon the Torah (Ps 1:2), he carries the Torah in his heart (Ps 37:31).[130]

Once again, the conclusion seems clear: The Dtr teaching which focuses upon the vital importance of meditation on the law of God and the concomitant rewards of this act is echoed in Ps 119. Indeed, Psalm 119 adds to the reader's understanding of what is meant by the concepts of meditation and torah.

5.1.7 CONTINUOUS TORAH MEDITATION

This Dtr emphasis upon torah-meditation is further underlined by the psalmist's confession of the *constancy* of his meditation. Deuteronomy attests that the people of God should seek to apply the divine law in a constant manner (Deut 4:9-10; 6:1-2; 17:19, also seen in the DtrH e.g. Jos 1:8). This constant meditation should also be applied in a consistent and comprehensive manner—that is, not only should the law be the constant subject of the meditation of the people of God but it should also play a role in every area of area their lives. Psalm 119 echoes the ethos of these recommendations as the psalmist seeks to call upon the torah in every life situation and also to meditate upon it day and night with the type of constancy commended in Deuteronomy.[131]

> Very noteworthy is the Psalmist's enthusiastic love for the law. The love which the Israelite was bidden to cherish for Jehovah (Deut 4:5 etc.) is kindled by the manifold revelation of His Will in the Law. "O how I love thy law: it is my meditation all the day" (97). It is no irksome restraint of his liberty, but his delight, his joy, his treasure, his comfort, *the subject of his meditations by day and by night, the source of trust and hope amid all the perplexities and troubles of life.* "Thy word is a lamp unto my feet and the light unto my path."[132]

---

[130] Kraus, *Psalms II*, 412–13.

[131] See Ps 119:44, 55, 97, 117 etc., regarding temporal constancy in meditating upon the torah and vv 11, 23, 46, 50, 95 etc., regarding the comprehensive situational application of the torah.

[132] Kirkpatrick, *Psalms*, 704–05 (emphasis added).

Reflective self-observation is significant for the torah-piety of Ps 119 (v 59). It is required in view of the snares and traps that are set up by the רשעים (v 61). The entire life—by day and by night—is determined by obedience and praise (verse 62, cf Psalms 1:2; 42:8; 63:6).[133]

This constant meditation upon the torah and the psalmist's desire to apply the law in every situation provides the reader with yet another link between Psalm 119 and Deuteronomy.

5.1.8 GRACE ENABLING OBEDIENCE

Whilst obedience to the torah is clearly central to Psalm 119, there is also a strong awareness of this psalmist's need of the assistance of Yahweh if he is going to be able to be obedient. This is a concept which is prevalent throughout much of the OT, but it plays an important role in the theology of Deuteronomy.[134] Running alongside the constant call to obedience, the reader witnesses a strong sense of probability that the people are going to be unfaithful in Deuteronomy. This is implied in the closing paraenetic framework of the book: Deut 30:1–10 basically declares that the curses of Deut 28 will take place because of the people's unfaithfulness (30:1); Moses angrily states the likelihood of rebellion in Deut 31:24–29; and the Song of Moses in Deut 32 also implies that the people risk falling into apostasy. However, there is a constant thread of grace which weaves its way subtly through these passages: counterbalancing the sense of the inevitability of disobedience is the hope that Yahweh himself will work on the people's behalf in order to help them to be obedient. We see this in Deut 30:6, the verse that is central to Deut 30:1–10,[135] where Moses assures the people that, following their faithlessness, *Yahweh himself* will "circumcise their hearts so that they may love him." This is Yahweh's gracious response to the people's failure to meet the challenge (Deut 10:16) to remain faithful by "circumcising their hearts." They were incapable of doing so themselves so Yahweh works in them to do that which they could not do for themselves. This divine grace on the people's behalf is also seen in the promise of restoration in Deut 32:36–43 and the promise of salvation for the tribes of Israel in Deut 33:26–29.

---

[133] Kraus, *Psalms II*, 417.
[134] McConville, *Grace in the End*, 135–37.
[135] Wright, *Deuteronomy*, 289.

This same theme is important to the theology of Psalm 119, where—alongside this psalmist's declarations of obedience to the torah of Yahweh—we witness his pleas for help *that he may be* obedient to the torah of Yahweh. This dependence upon God for the ability to keep the torah in the reality of the psalmist's own life is often seen throughout the psalm; for example, in the *gîmel* stanza (vv 17–24) the psalmist prays that God will "deal well" with him *so that* he may live and keep Yahweh's word.[136] There is also the constant prayer that Yahweh himself will teach the psalmist his law (vv 12, 27, 33 etc.)—as Whybray writes: "Nowhere else in the OT is there such a constant appeal to God to instruct the writer as in this psalm."[137] Over and above these prayers, the reader witnesses a sense of passion, bordering on desperation, in the psalmist's prayers that God will keep him *from* the way of the wicked and walking *in* right ways (vv 28–29, 31, 35, 37, 81, 117 etc.). Perhaps the clearest expression of the psalmist's dependence upon the grace of God comes in the closing *tāw* stanza, where v 176 presents an interesting echo of the teaching of Ps 1:

תעיתי כשה אבד בקש עבדך כי מצותיך לא שכחתי:
I have strayed like a lost [perishing] sheep;
Seek out your servant, for I have not forgotten your commands.

McCann points out the possible connection with the way of the wicked in Ps 1:6:

> The word "lost" (אבד *'ōbēd*) is more literally "perishing." Thus, just as Ps 119:1 was reminiscent of the first verse of Psalm 1, so also Ps 119:176 recalls the final verse of Psalm 1. But—and this is the remarkable thing—in Ps 1:6, it is the wicked who are to perish! The final verse of Psalm 119 is, therefore, the final reminder of what the psalmist has affirmed along: *The faithful are saved by grace*.[138]

The ideas of "straying" and "perishing" are commonly associated with the rejection of the law in Deuteronomy. Whilst תעה ("to err or wander") is largely to be found in the wisdom and prophetic literature, the same sort of idea is conveyed by the Dtr usage of סור ("to turn aside"). Not wandering from the law is commonly held out as a challenge to Israel (e.g. Deut 4:9; 5:32; 11:16 etc.), and, more specifically, the life of the king is to be so focused around the torah that he does not stray from it (17:17, 20). אבד ("being lost" or "perishing") is the alterna-

---

[136] I have taken the link between the two cola to be a causative one.
[137] Whybray, "Psalm 119," 34.
[138] McCann, *Psalms*, 1174 (emphasis mine).

tive to "life in the land in Deuteronomy," it is the result of rejecting God's law or worshipping other gods (Deut 4:26; 8:19; 30:18).[139]

It is, indeed, interesting that the psalmist chooses to conclude his epic work on this note, with a confession of his natural tendency to stray from the torah and an appeal to Yahweh for restoration. *The psalmist is entirely focused upon a piety based in torah-obedience, yet his confession is clear—apart from the grace of Yahweh, he is wholly incapable of such obedience.* This echoes the central idea of Deut 30:1–10. Other commentators have noticed this theme of the centrality of the grace of Yahweh towards the psalmist:

> In the *beth* strophe Yahweh is celebrated as the wisdom teacher *par excellence* (vv 9, 11, 12b; cf. Prov 7:1). He affirms the joy afforded by preoccupation with his moral teachings, and declares his desire to set his mind on, and to govern his life by, Yahweh's revealed standards. *But he confesses that he cannot cope unaided and prays for God's personal help in his moral endeavour.*[140]

> [The psalmist's] promises of piety do convey assurances in a manner similar to the vow of praise. That is, they express not only the psalmist's willingness to respond to deliverance in an appropriate manner, but also imply that *YHWH will in fact provide the conditions that make this response possible.*[141]

> This psalm may be characterised as a prayer for salvation, the various supporting elements (testimony, profession of trust and loyalty, vows etc.) being built upon one great theme—the word of God.... Such written deposits [the Pentateuch or proto-Pentateuch] were no doubt important for our author, but here and with all the other forms of the divine word *he is chiefly thinking of communion with God, the God who hereby touches him with the breath of grace and power.*[142]

Once again, the careful reader of Ps 119 observes a type of piety that is rooted in a Dtr worldview—the psalmist bases the practice of his religion around torah-meditation and obedience, yet at the same time confesses his inability to keep the law and his great need for Yahweh's grace.

5.1.9 THE "I" OF PSALM 119 AS THE DTR KING

Whilst the above list of Dtr features in Psalm 119 is far from exhaustive, it is probably sufficient to establish the Dtr background to the theology of this

---
[139] Miller, *Deuteronomy*, 214–15.
[140] Allen, *Psalms*, 142 (emphasis mine).
[141] Soll, *Psalm 119*, 82 (emphasis).
[142] Eaton, *Psalms*, 273 (emphasis mine).

psalm. There is, however, one further connection which deserves examination: namely, the identity of the speaker in Psalm 119. Psalm 119, like Psalm 118, is without superscription, so there is no explicit editorial indication of who the pray-er might be, but the language used in Psalm 119 does provide the reader with some indication of the most likely identity of the speaker. Some commentators associate the speaker in Psalm 119 with some sort of wisdom figure (a wisdom teacher or pupil),[143] but there is good reason to question this suggestion.

Firstly, there are serious grounds to question the genre classification of Psalm 119 as a wisdom poem: 1) Whilst there are wisdom themes apparent in Psalm 119, it would be difficult to argue that these themes necessarily dominate the text. In fact, as Soll has argued, the presence of wisdom themes should not automatically lead to a wisdom classification:

> These themes [fear of God, praying for wisdom, God as Creator, the dichotomy between the righteous and the wicked etc.] cannot be said to be "wisdom themes" in any exclusive sense. At best, they become wisdom themes when discussed in a wisdom context. They cannot be assumed to be "wisdom themes" when simply assumed or affirmed in the course of a prayer.[144]

2) We have already noted the apparent connection between the piety of the wisdom tradition and that of the legal tradition, so it could be argued that many of the so-called "wisdom" themes are in fact legal emphases.[145] 3) Ps 119 is not treated as a wisdom poem by experts in the wisdom literature. The wisdom link seems to have derived from Mowinckel's classification of Ps 119 as an example of late, nomistic poetry used as a didactic tool in the wisdom schools.[146] The repetition of this idea over the years, however, does not add weight to its original basis in textual evidence, and it appears that the text of this psalm points the reader in a different direction. Two of the most influential studies on the wisdom psalms both exclude Ps 119 from the list of psalms of this genre.[147]

---

[143] Croft, *Identity*, 167, 181; Anderson, *Psalms*, 806–07.

[144] Soll, *Psalm 119*, 122.

[145] Soll writes, "Of course, according to Deuteronomy, to speak of Torah is to speak of wisdom in some sense. The Torah is marked by YHWH's wisdom, and the people are wise for having received it (Deut 4:6)," *Psalm 119*, 124 (see also Weinfeld, *The Deuteronomic School*, 244–247).

[146] Mowinckel, *PIW*, 113–14.

[147] R. E. Murphy, "A Consideration of the Classification 'Wisdom Psalms,'" *Studies in Ancient Israelite Wisdom* (ed. J. L. Crenshaw; New York: Ktav Publishing House, 1976) and J. K. Kuntz, "The Canonical Wisdom Psalms of Ancient Israel: Their Rhetori-

Secondly, the internal indicators found in Psalm 119—especially the use of language and imagery—point the reader towards identification of this poem with the king.[148] Psalm 119 displays many of the classic signs of a background in a royal setting: for example, we see the psalmist contrast his commitment to the torah with the attitude of princes and kings (Ps 119:23, 46).[149] Other indications of a royal background would include the comparison of the worth of God's law over silver and gold, even fine gold (Ps 119:72, 127); the psalmist's use of "your servant" (עבדך, Ps 119:17, 23, 38 etc.) is common in a royal setting where the king is speaking (especially as it seems to be used in antithetical correspondence to the "princes" of v 23); enemies, plotting and persecution (Ps 119:23, 98, 167) are also often associated with the psalms of individual lament, especially in Book I where they frequently have a Davidic superscription implying a royal background; the fact that Yahweh himself is the speaker's teacher seems to set the psalmist apart also (see the emphatic use of אתה in the v 102); and it is at least possible that the word אמרה functions in the sense of "promise" in certain verses and is intended to reflect the covenant between Yahweh and the Davidic king (see, for example, Ps 119:116).[150] Whilst these indicators may be open to alternative interpretations, given the fact that the king is associated with many of the psalms of individual lament, it seems most likely that the pray-er of Ps 119 is to be understood as the king.

Although this argument is slightly circular, supposing the "I" of Ps 119 to be the king makes good sense in the light of the Deut 17:14–20. In the previous pages we have been able to observe Psalm 119's setting in Dtr theology—this epic poem is grounded in the worldview and teaching of Deuteronomy and the Deuteronomistic History. Given that such is the theological setting of Psalm

---

cal, Thematic and Formal Dimensions," *Rhetorical Criticism: Essays in Honor of James Muilenburg* (eds. J. J. Jackson and M. Kessler; Pittsburg: Pickwick Press, 1974).

[148] It must be said that none of these indicators are absolutely conclusive (hence the continuing debate over the identity of the central figure in Ps 119), however, the combination of these various elements bears marked similarities to the psalms of Books I and II which are associated with the Davidic king (see Bruce K. Waltke, "Theology of the Psalms," in *New International Dictionary of Old Testament Theology and Exegesis, Volume 4* [W. A. VanGemeren, gen. ed.; Carlisle: Paternoster Press, 1997], 1101–02).

[149] It is possible that a wisdom teacher associated with the royal court may have such opportunity also, but the complete set of circumstances described in Ps 119 seem most suited to the figure of the king himself.

[150] Soll, *Psalm 119*, 39.

119, which other individual would be expected to place such a strong emphasis upon the law of God? Deut 17:14-20 indicates that the king is to devote himself to meditation on the torah, so that he will live in accord with its teaching. It is this very notion that dominates the expression of the psalmist-speaker in Ps 119.

> The tradition of the Deuteronomistic History and the royal psalms which we have just surveyed makes an excellent context for understanding the relation of the speaker in Psalm 119 to Torah. In both the deuteronomistic history and the Psalms, the king emerges as the individual with the greatest cause for preoccupation with Torah due to the role Torah plays in the royal ideology. Given Psalm 119's close associations with the Deuteronomic tradition, the king emerges as the one most likely to frame his prayer with continual reference to the law which is to be his constant meditation, his responsibility to promulgate, and on which his office depends.[151]

Soll develops this argument further in his discussion of the setting of Ps 119:

> The Deuteronomistic History's conception of the king's relation to the law is therefore of great importance for our investigation [of Ps 119]. This relation may be summarised in the following points. 1) Observance of Torah, fostered by study and meditation, is a special duty of the king. 2) The Davidic dynasty's durability is conditional upon its obedience to Torah. 3) The king should lead his people in compliance with Torah; indeed, Torah requires a king for its full implementation.... No doubt this law stems from the deuteronomistic desire to have the king carry out Torah, but for more than obedience to its explicit demands. The emphasis on continual study and absorption seems to indicate the Deuteronomist's recognition of the personal character of the king's leadership and the decisions he would have to make beyond Torah's stated requirements. These, while not legally prescribed should nonetheless be informed by Torah, to which end the Deuteronomistic History wants Torah to be not only upheld by the king but continually on his lips.[152]

Soll's argument is helpful for a proper understanding of Psalm 119. Deut 17 commands, not simply that the king obey the torah, but rather that he *steep himself* in the torah of Yahweh. The idea is that he should live not only in accordance with the express legal requirements, but that he comes to view life and the world around him from the perspective of divine revelation. This is precisely the type of attitude that the psalmist of Psalm 119 portrays.

---

[151] Soll, *Psalm 119*, 135. See also Dahood who suggests that, "[T]he psalm was composed for a ruler—even, perhaps, a Davidic king who stood in special relation to God's law (cf. Deut 17:18ff; Ps 40:6-8))...." *Psalms, vol. 3*, 173 and Eaton, *Psalms*, 274.

[152] Soll, *Psalm 119*, 128–29. Whilst agreeing with the general thrust of this statement, I do not accept (*contra* Soll and Weinfeld) that the Torah requires a king for its full implementation. Rather the Torah *allows for* a king as part of its implementation.

The canonical placement of Ps 119 alongside Ps 118 further emphasises this (slightly circular) association of the "I" of Ps 119 with the Davidic king.[153] In Ps 118, we see the image of the king seeking entry into the Temple and being challenged by the priestly gate-keepers that only the righteous may enter. The king replies with his account of Yahweh's vindication in Ps 118, and it is in Ps 119 that the reader of the Psalter is presented with a fuller account of the nature of the piety which has led to his acceptance by Yahweh. We have seen a similar pattern in both of the previous torah-kingship psalm groupings: the anonymous איש of Ps 1 is set in parallel with the משיח of Ps 2,[154] suggesting that they are one and the same; the psalmist of Ps 19 is identified by a Davidic superscription, and his identity is further confirmed by the placement of his hymn and prayer amidst three royal psalms where the king seeks and receives Yahweh's deliverance.[155] We have already argued that Pss 118 and 119 form the joint-centrepiece of Book V of the Psalter, placed between two larger collections—the *hallel* psalms (111–117) and the Songs of Ascents (120–134).[156] Here, we see the significance of that placement, both of these psalms are about the king—his righteousness is challenged in Ps 118 and the nature of that righteousness is explained in Ps 119. Whilst these arguments will definitely not be the last word regarding the identity of the speaker in Ps 119, it is at least possible (perhaps more than possible) that the one whose prayer is soaked in the piety of the torah is the Davidic king.

6. Links between Psalms 118 and 119

Some of the canonical, lexical and theological links apparent in Pss 118 and 119, have been discussed above, so we shall not dwell on them at length.

6.1 Canonical

There are two main canonical reasons why these two psalms should be treated as having been deliberately juxtaposed in the position where they lie: (1) Their canonical position between two larger groupings of psalms; and, (2) Their lack of superscription. Each of these factors serves to link these two poems,

---

[153] This suggestion cannot be seen to serve as a proof of royal background to Ps 119, rather my argument is to suggest that positing the king as the psalmist in Ps 119 makes good sense of the content of the psalm.
[154] Miller, "Beginning," 91–92.
[155] Allen, "David as Exemplar," 546.
[156] See pp 122–25, above.

whilst separating them from the neighbouring compositions. Regardless of praxis in the post-canonical Jewish festivals, which would see Psalm 118 as part of the Great Hallel, a canonical reading would lead one to a different conclusion—namely, that Psalm 118 is separated both from the preceding hallelujah psalms and the succeeding Songs of Ascents. Psalm 118 is dislocated from the surrounding psalm groupings and therefore is associated with its neighbouring work which also cannot reasonably be adjoined to either of the bracketing groups of psalms.

As with Psalm 1 and 2, neither Psalm 118 nor Psalm 119 bears a superscription of any kind, which is somewhat unusual in Book V of the Psalter. Whilst Wilson points out that there are fewer authorship designations in the superscriptions in Books IV–V,[157] still the lack of superscription is somewhat unusual within this section of the Psalter. Only Psalms 107, 118, 119, 136 and 137 lack any form of superscription.[158] All of the other psalms bear either a superscription or postscript.[159] Therefore, due to the rarity of psalms without headings within Book V, the fact of Psalms 118 and 119's juxtaposition seems to be significant, associating these two psalms whilst, at the same time, differentiating them from the collections with headings on either side.

6.2 LEXICAL

There are lexical connections between Pss 118 and 119 which also point to deliberate concatenation of these texts. It can, of course, be argued that whenever a psalm as lengthy as Psalm 119 is placed alongside any other text there is bound to be lexical overlap based on sheer volume (i.e. there are so many words in Psalm 119 there is bound to be some overlap with the words of Psalm 118). Whilst this is true, the significant factor in terms of the lexical links between Psalms 118 and 119 is that there are certain concepts which are central to both psalms that are expressed using the same words or closely related synonyms. The main lexical links revolve around the words חסד ("steadfast love"), ירא ("fear"), ישועה ("salvation"), חיה ("living"), אשרי/ברך ("blessing") and אור ("to

---

[157] Wilson, "Shape," 131–32.

[158] I am inclined to agree with Zenger that Wilson overstates the significance of the use of *hôdû* at the beginning of Psalms 107, 118 and 136. This does not appear to function as a means of editorial division or an attempt to link these three psalms, therefore they should be treated as being without superscription (see Zenger, "Composition," 87).

[159] See the above discussion of Psalm 114, p 123n6.

enlighten"). Each of these words represents a concept which is somehow important to each psalm. The significance of the juxtaposition of two poems using these words is not necessarily found in the number of times that these words are repeated but rather in the centrality of the concepts which they express.

It is perhaps not surprising that the חסד of Yahweh is one of the central themes of both psalms as celebration of Yahweh's *hesed* is a constant theme in the Psalter (Ps 118:1, 2, 3, 4, 29; Ps 119:41, 64, 76, 88, 124, 149, 159). However, it is clear that the gracious, covenant love of God is important to the speaker in both Ps 118 and Ps 119. This is not some theoretical or formulaic celebration of Yahweh's *hesed*, rather in both cases we see a heartfelt delight in Yahweh's covenant love. In both poems the speaker realises that, without this *hesed*, he is lost. It is the speaker's awareness of his absolute dependence upon the steadfast love of Yahweh in all things that strikes the common note between these two psalms.[160]

We noted above the significance of the address to "those who fear Yahweh" (יראי יהוה, v 4) in our assessment of Psalm 118:4, 6[161] and this is a concept which is also central to the theology of Psalm 119 (Ps 119:63, 74, 79, 120). The speaker in Psalm 119 declares himself to be part of a *community of Yahweh-fearers* (יראוך, v 63) and he goes on to make it clear how this community is defined: the fearers of Yahweh are those who "keep his precepts." Therefore we see that the concept of fearing Yahweh from Ps 118:4 (יראי יהוה) is, as was suggested, rooted in the ideas of torah obedience. This community aspect of fearing Yahweh is also emphasised in Ps 119:74 and 79.[162]

Associated with the theme of absolute dependence upon Yahweh, which is central to both psalms, we find a lexical link in the word ישועה (Ps 118:14, 15, 21; Ps 119:123, 155, 166, 174). In each psalm we find strong expressions of the psalmist's reliance upon salvation from Yahweh, the speaker is keen to confess his own inability and to stress his reliance upon a salvation which comes from

---

[160] Anderson writes concerning Ps 119, "Whatever may have been the historical details of these key events, the basic truths illustrate the pre-eminence of God's grace," (*Psalms*, 808). See also Kraus, *Psalms II*, 420, and McCann, *Psalms*, 1174, for similar sentiments with regard to Ps 119. Frost, "Psalm 118," 161, Sanders, "NT Hermeneutic Fabric," 181–82 and Mays, "Ps 118," 303–04, present similar analyses of the significance of *hesed* to the theology of Ps 118.

[161] Pp 130–32, above.

[162] Mays, "Ps 118," 304.

Yahweh alone. This dependence upon God seems to be grounded in the speaker's relationship with him (Ps 118:14; 119:166, 174). Trust in Yahweh's salvation is, of course, related to the trials and circumstances which the psalmist faces, however there appears to be a very real sense in which dependence upon Yahweh for provision of salvation is an expression of the speaker's piety and priorities. Certainly the idea of Yahweh's salvation is central to the theology of both psalms and this is indicated by lexical as well as thematic links.[163]

Perhaps the most significant lexical connection between Psalms 118 and 119 is the use of the verb חיה (Ps 118:17; 119:17, 25, 37, 40, 50, 77, 88, 93, 107, 116, 144, 149, 154, 156, 159, 175). This is the climatic declaration of the king in Ps 118:17 and is the constant subject of the king's prayer in Ps 119. There appear to be two different contexts in which חיה is used in Psalm 119: first, the psalmist prays for life in order that he may continue to keep the torah of Yahweh (vv 17, 77, 88); and, secondly, the psalmist extols the reviving, life-giving power of Yahweh through his torah (vv 25, 37, 40 etc.). In each case there is a connection between keeping the law of God and choosing life, resonating with the king's central and emphatic declaration in Ps 118:17 that he has been saved from death because he was found "righteous" before Yahweh.[164]

The idea of "blessedness" also provides a lexical link between Psalms 118 and 119. The priestly response to the entrance of the king into the Temple, having been declared righteous, is to declare him "blessed" (ברוך, v 26) and, interestingly, Psalm 119 begins with two verses which align "blessedness" (אשרי, vv 1–2) with keeping the torah, seeking Yahweh and walking in blamelessness. Whilst it is not the same Hebrew word that is used in each case, we have already seen that (although there may be some difference in the contexts of their usage), the words ברוך and אשרי effectively function as synonyms within the Psalter.[165] In this way the reader is left with a clearer understanding of why the entering king is blessed by the priestly gatekeepers—Psalm 119:1–2 indicates that the reason for his blessing is to be found in his attitude towards the torah.

---

[163] Mays, *The Lord Reigns*, 133–34; Kraus, *Psalms II*, 398; Seybold, *Introducing*, 24.

[164] McCann, *Psalms*, 686–87; Anderson, *Psalms*, 846–47.

[165] Kraus, *Psalms*, 115; Mays, *Psalms*, 41. Mays's suggestion is that ברוך is used when the blessing of God is actually being evoked, and אשרי is used in beattitudes where a certain type of behaviour is being set up as an example for others. This seems to fit well with the usage of the respective terms in Ps 118:26 and Ps 119:1–2.

The king giving account of Yahweh's deliverance also seems to be of importance in both psalms. The ספר verb ("to recount") is found in Ps 118:17 and in Ps 119:13, 26, but it is particularly the connection between the "narrative" account of Ps 118 and 119:26 that seems to be significant:

Ps 119:26   דרכי ספרתי ותענני למדני חקיך:
I recounted my ways and you answered me; Teach me your decrees.

The significance of Ps 119:26 is that it seems to recount the same sort of experience as took place in Ps 118. In the preceding antiphonal psalm we see the king give an account of his prayer and of Yahweh's saving deliverance from distress in response to that prayer. It is this account of prayer and answer which is seen as a justification of the king's righteousness by the Temple gate-keepers in v 20. Ps 119:26 indicates an act of similar nature: the king recounts his ways (ספרתי) and is rewarded with an answer to his prayer.

There is one final lexical repetition worthy of note; namely, the use of אור (Ps 118:27; Ps 119:105, 130, 135). This particular connection is worthy of note because the use of the verb אור (Ps 118:27) seems slightly incongruous in the context of Psalm 118. This is a concept which is normally associated with teaching and learning, as is seen by its common usage within the Wisdom Literature.[166] However, Psalm 118 does not bear any of the typical characteristics of a wisdom psalm: the act of "enlightenment" referred to in v 27 may be the realisation that the one rejected is actually accepted by Yahweh and important to him. Almost by way of explanation, Psalm 119:105 and 130 make it clear that enlightenment comes from the word of God. So, in a manner analogous to the idea of "blessedness" mentioned above, we read of how the people give thanks to God that he has enlightenment them to see that the rejected one is actually Yahweh's chosen one in Psalm 118 and then Psalm 119 goes on to tell the reader that enlightenment comes from the word of Yahweh. Ps 119:105, 130 almost provide a corrective for the situation of Psalm 118. Yahweh's chosen one goes unrecognised and rejected until God's deliverance of him is recognised as a sign of blessing, the question therefore arises: How can the people of God avoid such a lack of awareness, failing to recognise the one whom Yahweh blesses? The answer is provided by the speaker in Psalm 119: The word of Yahweh brings light and understanding to the people of God.[167]

---

[166] Job and Psalms alone account for over one third of the occurrences of this word.

There are many other lexical repetitions to be found in Psalms 118 and 119: ידה (Ps 118:1, 19, 21, 28, 29; Ps 119:7, 62); טוב (Ps 118:1, 8, 9, 29; Ps 119:39, 65, 66, 68, 71, 72, 122); עולם, where the eternity of God's *hesed* is paralleled with the eternity of God's word (Ps 118:1, 2, 3, 4, 29; Ps 119:44, 52, 89, 93, 98, 111, 112, 142, 144, 152, 160); עזר (Ps 118:7, 13; Ps 119:86, 173, 175) etc. However, these are words which are commonly found in the Psalter, so their repetition may not be so significant. The repetitions examined above are probably sufficient to show lexical, as well as canonical, association.

6.3 THEOLOGICAL

Most of the theological connections between Pss 118 and 119 have been more fully discussed above. Therefore it should be sufficient to merely draw attention to the theological points of contact that we have already highlighted. Theological concerns found in Ps 118 which are repeated in Ps 119 include: dependence upon Yahweh for salvation (including the idea of rejecting dependence upon other sources of power), name theology, Yahweh as refuge, the "two ways" (including the link between obedience and prosperity) and the importance of a proper piety before Yahweh (the king's righteousness in Ps 118 and the torah-obedience of Ps 119). Each of these theological concepts is significant to a proper understanding of both texts.

Therefore, it seems that these three types of connection—canonical, lexical and theological—were designed to point the reader towards the association of Ps 118 with Ps 119, so that she would treat these two psalms as a nexus reflecting the interpretative hermeneutic established by the Psalter's introduction.

7. PSALM 119 IN THE LIGHT OF PSALM-GROUPINGS 1–2 and 18–21

Given the theological interconnections which we have already observed, it is perhaps not surprising to find that most of the emphases which we have observed in the previous psalm groupings are also apparent in Psalm 119. Many of the Deuteronomic themes which lie at the heart of Pss 1–2 and 18–21 also play a part in the king's prayer in Psalm 119.

---

[167] Mowinckel observes regarding Ps 119: "The value of the law, because it enlightens the ignorant and admonishes the faltering, is particularly emphasised," *PIW*, 113–14.

7.1 TORAH-PIETY

Most obvious of these connections is the torah-piety, abundantly present in Psalm 119, which is also to be found in Psalms 1, 18 and 19. It is as a result of this emphasis on the torah of Yahweh that the suggestion has arisen that Psalms 1 and 119 at some point represented the beginning and end of the Psalter.[168] The type of piety based around the study of Yahweh's word that is common to these psalms is reflected in several features observable in Psalm 119.

First, from a linguistic perspective, we see a particular emphasis on the singular form torah, as is the case with Psalm 1;[169] yet, at the same time, Psalm 119 echoes the comprehensiveness of the five torah synonyms which are used in Psalm 19, and indeed, goes beyond this in adding three further synonyms.[170] The emphasis on torah in Psalm 119—this word is only used in the singular (the others all use singular and plural forms)[171] and occurs more often than all of the other words[172]—reflects the singular focus of Psalm 1 where torah is seen as the proper, singular response to the multiplicity of the ways of the wicked.[173] At the same time, however, Psalm 119 seeks to emphasise the holistic nature of torah and its applicability to every situation of life, just as does Psalm 19 through the use of multiple torah terms.[174]

Secondly, we see that the torah—so emphasised throughout Psalm 119—is clearly the psalmist's *delight*, an attitude which is also idealised in Psalm 1:2 and Psalm 19:11–12. Psalm 119:35 makes this statement explicitly, using the same Hebrew word as in Ps 1:2 (חפץ) and v 92 makes the same point using a synonym (שעשעים). However, essentially the whole psalm testifies to the fact that the psalmist truly does delight in the torah of Yahweh. The whole, massive poem is a celebration of a lifestyle grounded in God's law and clearly reflects the type of attitude which Psalm 1 commends to the readers of the Psalter. This is seen in the psalmist's favourable comparisons of the torah to "silver and gold" (זהב וכסף,

---

[168] Westermann, *Praise and Lament*, 253; Smith, "Use and Influence," 11. We will discuss this more fully in chapter 6.

[169] "The term *tôrâ* is used twenty-five times in Psalm 119. The eight terms for 'law' in Psalm 119 are used almost interchangeably, but there is good reason for regarding the term torah as *primus inter pares*. It is the term employed in the first verse, and it is used a total twenty-five times in the psalm, the most of any term," (Soll, *Psalm 119*, 35).

[170] Allen, *Psalms*, 139; Kraus, *Psalms II*, 412–13.

[171] Whybray, "Psalm 119," 35.

[172] Soll, *Psalm 119*, 35.

[173] Gitay, "Psalm 1," 235–36.

182   *The King as Exemplar*

v 72), "gold and fine gold" (מזהב ומפז, v 127), etc. This favourable comparison of the torah of Yahweh to the finer things of life also reflects the theology of Psalm 19:11-12, and is a further indication of the likelihood that the speaker in Psalm 119 is in fact the king, who is much more likely to have experienced these luxuries than is a cultic prophet or wisdom teacher. Mays writes:

> Ps 119 is the sequel to Psalms 1 and 19 in topic and outlook. Like the first, it knows the delight of the law of the Lord and the importance of the constant study of it. Like the nineteenth, it shows the inestimable value of the law in all its forms as a life-enhancing power. But in its design it has taken the topic to the limits of literary expression.[175]

7.2 MEDITATION

Another aspect of torah-piety which is clearly to be seen in Pss 1 and 19, and which is re-emphasised in Ps 119, is the importance of meditation upon torah. The thrust of Pss 1 and 19 is that the torah, in all its forms, is to be internalised by way of prayerful reflection upon it. This is expressed clearly in Ps 1:2's description of the blessed person as one who "meditates upon the torah day and night" (ובתורתו יהגה יומם ולילה). Ps 119 has a similar emphasis, although it uses slightly different vocabulary. Rather than using the verb הגה (as in Ps 1:2), the psalmist uses שיח (vv 15, 23, 27, 48, 78, 148) which is also best translated "to meditate" and which reflects the same type of practice.[176] The following quote from McCann describes the similar passionate meditation upon torah which exists in both Ps 119 and Ps 1:1-2:

> As is always the case with the beloved person or thing, the psalmist has God's revelation always in mind (v 97b). The word "meditates" (שיח *śiaḥ*) occurs several times in Psalm 119 (see also vv 15, 23, 27, 48, 78, 99, 148), but this is the only place where the meditation is "all day long" (see also the chronological references in vv 55, 62, 147-148, 164). Thus v 97 is reminiscent of Ps 1:1-2 (although the Hebrew words translated "meditate" are different), where those who meditate on God's instruction are pronounced "happy." The psalmist in Psalm 119 exemplified such happiness; it is not a superficial cheeriness

---

[174] McCann, *Psalms*, 752, 1168.

[175] Mays, *Psalms*, 381.

[176] Gesenius, *Hebrew Lexicon*, 789. It is interesting that שיח and הגה seem to have the similar connotation of meditation by way of talking or muttering to oneself. Gesenius describes הגה as "*to meditate* (prop. to speak with oneself, murmuring and in a low voice, as is often done by those who are musing" (p 215). In a similar vein, he describes שיח as "*to talk with oneself,* i.e. *to meditate,* especially on divine things" (p 789). BDB contains similar definitions on p 211d and p 976c, respectively.

(see vv 81–88) but the happiness of a person who is in love with the one who truly offers life. Not surprisingly, v 103 employs the sensual language of the Song of Solomon (see 2:3; 4:11; 5:1, 16; 7:9; see also Ps 19:10; Prov 24:13–14). The psalmist has an emotional attachment to God's word that is indicative of his or her love for and commitment to God.[177]

Secondly, as this quote also indicates, the temporal elements apparent in Ps 119 emphasise the same *type* of torah-piety, based on *constant* meditation, as is seen in Psalms 1 and 19. The reader of the Psalter is told in Psalm 1:2 that the blessed person meditates on Yahweh's torah "day and night" (יומם ולילה), emphasising the benefits of the constant study of Yahweh's law.[178] Whilst the torah section of Psalm 19 does not explicitly give such a recommendation, this same emphasis upon constant reflection is implicit to the prayer content of Ps 19.[179] (This piety, founded upon consistent reflection, is also expressed in Ps 119:55, 62, 97, 148 etc.). The psalmist makes it quite clear that God's word is his permanent preoccupation—he prays and meditates upon it all day long and throughout all the days of his life. The psalmist clearly expresses a type of piety which is firmly rooted in the ideas of Psalms 1 and 19.[180]

7.3 Blessedness and Prosperity

Another train of thought which is characteristic of the torah psalms is the idea of meditation on the law leading to "blessedness" or "happiness" and "prosperity." This is reflected in the opening words of the Psalter: אשרי האש אשר. The person who rejects the way of the wicked (Ps 1:1) in favour of the way of Yahweh's torah is described as אשרי—"blessed" or "happy." Ps 1:3 goes on to tell the reader how the person who makes the torah their first priority will be fruitful like a tree planted by streams of water and this is summarised by the declaration "in everything he does he prospers" (וכל אשר־יעשה יצליח). This idea is echoed again in Ps 19:11–12 where the psalmist-king describes Yahweh's judgements as being more desirable than pure gold and honey and indeed "in keeping them there is much reward" (בשמרם עקב רב).[181] This same concept of the "happiness" as a consequence of torah loyalty is obvious in Ps 119. It is perhaps for-

---

[177] McCann, *Psalms*, 1172.
[178] McCann, *Psalms*, 684–85; Craigie, *Psalms*, 60.
[179] Miller, "Kingship," 127–28; Wagner, "Psalm 19 as Prayer," 253.
[180] Mays, *Psalms*, 381.
[181] Again we have a different word for "reward" cf. Ps 1:3, but the ideas reflected by these terms seem to be very similar.

184   *The King as Exemplar*

tuitous that the word אשרי begins with an *aleph* as this gives the psalmist the ideal opportunity to begin the first two verses of his mammoth poem with this same word. Ps 119:1 certainly seems to be a deliberate attempt to connect the lessons of Ps 1 with the message of Ps 119. This verse uses many of the concepts of Ps 1—"happiness" (אשרי cf. Ps 1:1), "way of blamelessness" (תמימי־דרך cf. דרך צדיקים, Ps 1:6), "walking" (ההלכים cf. לא הלך באצת רשעים, Ps 1:1) and "in the torah of Yahweh" (בתורת יהוה cf. בתורת יהיה, Ps 1:2). From the outset, the psalmist seeks to frame his poem within the context of the theology of Ps 1. This is further underlined by the inclusion of ideas which also reflect the concept of reward as a result of torah-obedience (e.g. Ps 119:112).[182] Whybray offers this consideration of the author's purpose in linking Ps 119 with the theology of Ps 1:

> Like Psalm 1, Ps 119:1–3 pronounces "happy" (*'ašrê*) those who are sincerely devoted to the observance of God's law. This similarity perhaps suggests the kind of readership for whom Psalm 119 was composed. The use of the term *'ašrê* in vv 1 and 2 implies that the kind of spirituality displayed in the rest of the psalm is not something that is exclusive to the psalmist: that the psalm is, in a real sense, addressed to others who, whether or not they have reached the "happy" state of the author, "seek him (Yahweh) with the whole heart" (v 2b). The purpose of the author is to encourage them in that search.[183]

7.4 THE TWO WAYS

Reflecting the ideas of Deuteronomy and the Wisdom Literature, the classic maxim of the "two ways" is found in common to each of the torah psalms, and their companion kingship psalms. This theme is constantly in the mind of the psalmist in making his public profession of priorities in Ps 119, as is witnessed by two repeated themes—the psalmist's declaration of commitment to Yahweh and his torah (e.g. vv 1, 2, 3, 11 etc.)[184] and the opposition of the "proud," "rulers," "the wicked" (e.g. vv 21–23, 42, 53 etc.).[185] These themes represent the contrasting ways of Ps 1, the way of the righteous/happy person contrasted with the way of the wicked/perishing person (Ps 1:6). Interestingly, the idea of

---

[182] The idea of benefit from keeping the law is implicit throughout much of Ps 119, but is phrased differently from Ps 1 and is more in line with Ps 19. The psalmist positively compares torah-obedience to great wealth (v 72), to the sweetness of honey (v 103), he speaks of its reviving, life-giving power (vv 50, 93 etc.).

[183] Whybray, "Psalm 119," 32–33. See also McCann, *Psalms*, 684–85, 1168; Kraus, *Psalms II*, 116–17, 121.

[184] Anderson, *Psalms*, 809.

[185] Kirkpatrick, *Psalms*, 702.

the two ways can be observed to one degree or another in all of the psalms that we have examined. Apparently, therefore, this notion is to be seen as central to the purpose of the redactors in shaping the Psalter in this way. The kingly example of commitment to Yahweh based on torah-observance is meant to function as an encouragement to the readers of the Psalter that they too should choose to walk in this way, regardless of their surrounding circumstances.[186]

7.5 PRAYER

Psalm 119 continues the theme of prayer which plays a strong part in many of the psalms which have been the subject of our consideration. Apart from the first three verses, the entirety of Psalm 119 *is* a prayer addressed directly to Yahweh, hence the eight torah synonyms used throughout the poem always bear a second person, masculine, singular pronominal suffix—"your torah," "your statutes" etc.[187] This theme of prayer functions as a corollary to the emphasis upon torah-piety in the psalms groups which we have examined; the implication being that without Yahweh's intervention in response to prayer neither the psalmists nor the readers are actually able to live in accordance with divine revelation. This prayer theme runs throughout the three psalm groupings: from the Lord's anointed being encouraged to pray so that he would be granted the nations as an inheritance in Ps 2:7[188] to his prayers for deliverances of various types in the remaining psalms (Ps 18:4, 7; Ps 19:13–15; Ps 20:2, 7; Ps 21:3; Ps 118:5).[189] The link between torah and prayer finds its ultimate expression here in Ps 119 with 176 verses celebrating the torah of God and 173 of these verses consist of prayer to him. Soll points out that this torah-based prayer is most appropriate coming from the lips of the Dtr king: "Given Psalm 119's close associations with the Deuteronomic tradition, the king emerges as the one most likely to frame his prayer with continual reference to the law which is to be his constant meditation, his responsibility to promulgate, and on which his office depends."[190]

---

[186] The purpose of this redaction will come under discussion in chapter 7.

[187] Soll comments: "[T]he psalmist seeks to relate his prayer to Torah, and uses the eight Torah words to establish a basis for his petition," *Psalm 119*, 148.

[188] McCann, *Psalms*, 689.

[189] See Miller, "Kingship," 132–33, for consideration of prayer in the psalm grouping 18–21; and Mays, "Ps 118" for discussion of prayer in Ps 118.

[190] Soll, *Psalm 119*, 135.

7.6 Dependence upon Yahweh and the Kingship Law

An integral part of the prayer theme which so dominates Psalm 119 is the idea of the psalmist's complete dependence upon Yahweh rather than upon alternative sources of security, which is a significant idea in Pss 1–2 and 18–21 also. As we saw above, the dependence theme in Ps 119 is seen in such verses as 23, 72 and 114 which intentionally reflect the limitations placed upon the power of the king in the Kingship Law. Such expressions of dependence upon Yahweh can be found in the refuge idea of Ps 2:12b;[191] in the appellatives of Ps 18, all of which explicitly reflect trust in Yahweh;[192] in the prayer for protection from sin in Ps 19:13–15;[193] in the anti-militaristic ideas of Ps 20:8;[194] and in the concept of salvation belonging to Yahweh in Ps 21:2, 6.[195] In reflecting the Kingship Law's rejection of all other sources of power and security, Ps 119 picks up on themes already apparent in the previous torah-kingship groupings.

7.7 Name Theology

In his recent work on Ps 119, Freedman writes: "Another major difference between Deuteronomic theology and Psalm 119 is the absence of the Deuteronomic 'name theology' associated with the Temple."[196] Whilst Ps 119, indeed, does not emphasise name theology specifically "associated with the Temple," Freedman's statement does beg a question: "Is Dtr name theology necessarily to be associated with the Temple?" Whilst this is not a dominant theme, Ps 119 does contain elements of name theology in vv 55 and 132. These verses use the concept of the name of Yahweh to represent the spiritual essence or personship of God—his real presence with the pray-er. This type of understanding is consistent with the name theology apparent in the other torah-kingship psalms where the particular emphasis is upon Yahweh's protective presence with his anointed and his people. Pss 18:50; 20:2, 6, 8; and 118:10–12, 26 all refer to the name of Yahweh in the context of his real presence and protection.

---

[191] Creach, *Yahweh as Refuge*, 18.
[192] Berry, *Psalms and Readers*, 93.
[193] Mays, *Psalms*, 99; Miller, "Kingship," 132–33.
[194] McCann, *Psalms*, 756; Kraus, *Psalms*, 282.
[195] Mays, *Psalms*, 103–04.
[196] Freedman, *Psalm 119*, 90–91.

7.8 BLAMELESSNESS OF THE KING

At their deepest level the torah-kingship psalm groupings seem to be preoccupied with a particular type of piety, an attitude towards life and spirituality which is focused upon divine revelation and prayer. This is reflected in the repeated theme of "blamelessness" (not legalistic perfection but a total orientation of life towards God and his ways) throughout these psalms. The word תמים is used explicitly in Ps 18:24, 26, 31, 33; Ps 19:8 and Ps 119:1 and 80, but, in fact, this concept seems to be the (sometimes unstated) aim of each of these psalm groupings. Ps 1's way of torah-obedience is essentially the way of blamelessness.[197] The psalmist's declarations of blamelessness in Ps 18:21–25 are to be held in tension with the psalmist's prayer for Yahweh's help to be blameless in 19:13–15.[198] The king is, by implication, declared blameless in Ps 118 in that only the "righteous" may enter the Temple.[199] The focus of Ps 119 as a prayer is also an appeal to Yahweh for his help and enabling so that the psalmist may fulfill his desire to be blameless.[200] Again, a theme central to the torah-kingship psalms finds its fullest expression in Ps 119, what is more, this is a theme which borrows heavily from the theology of Deuteronomy.[201]

7.9 CONCLUSION

Central to this thesis is the question: "Is there evidence of deliberate editorial association in these three groups of psalms?" One of the factors which seems to confirm this deliberate arrangement theory is the fact that Ps 119 takes into account most of the main theological emphases which are found not only in the other torah psalms (as one might expect), but also in the royal psalms juxtaposed alongside them. Psalm 119 could be described as a very lengthy summary statement drawing together the ideas of Pss 1–2 and 18–21. The lexical and theological overlap is such that one may reasonably be led to the conclusion that Psalm 119 could have been composed in order to echo the piety of Pss 1 and 19, and their associated psalms, in the concluding book of the Psalter. Certainly it reflects the same Dtr school of thought observable in the psalm groupings which we have previously considered.

---

[197] McCann, *Psalms*, 1168.
[198] Allen, "David as Exemplar," 546; McCann, *Psalms*, 752–53.
[199] Mays, "Ps 118," 304.
[200] Whybray, "Psalm 119," 40.
[201] Miller, "Kingship," 130.

8. Conclusion regarding Torah-Kingship Psalm Groupings

Based on detailed exegetical examination of the psalm groupings 1–2, 18–21 and 118–119 we can make three general observations:

1. There has been a deliberate attempt on the part of the editors of the Psalter to juxtapose torah and kingship psalms, following the pattern established in the introduction to the Book of Psalms.

2. These juxtaposed royal and torah psalms bear marked similarities in the Dtr overtones in their use of language and theological content.

3. The editorial placement of royal psalms alongside torah psalms seems to be an attempt to bring the theology of the Kingship Law to the forefront of the Psalter's call to piety and its eschatological expectation of a renewed Davidic kingship.

One more exegetical task remains, however, if we are ultimately to confirm these observations: namely, examination of the Kingship Law and its function within the Book of Deuteronomy. We have been able to present a plausible *prima facie* case that Pss 1, 2, 18, 19, 20, 21, 118 and 119 are intended to reflect Deuteronomy's Law of the King in their association one with the other. By studying Deut 17:14–20 in more detail we should be able to establish more definitely the actual similarities that exist between these psalms and this passage. The torah-kingship psalms seem to suggest two things to the reader of the Psalter: (1) the ideal characteristics of the eschatological king, expected at the time of the book's closure; and (2) the type of piety which the reader should apply in his own life lived *coram Deo*. The question which we should now ask is: Are the concerns of these psalm groupings also to be found in Deuteronomy's Kingship Law?

CHAPTER 5
THE KINGSHIP LAW AS A PARADIGM

1. INTRODUCTION

"The 'Law of the King' has, as those familiar with the controversies over Deuteronomy in general will recognise, occasioned extensive debate."[1] Such is the somewhat understated assessment of Baruch Halpern concerning the state of academic debate surrounding Deuteronomy's Law of the King (17:14–20).[2] In common with most of the major areas of debate in Deuteronomy, the Kingship Law has proven to be the source of much discussion and no small amount of disagreement. Indeed, the complexities of interpreting this passage reflect many of the crux issues which fuel the debate with respect to the theology and historical setting of Deuteronomy.

Some of the contentious issues regarding this passage are historical: for example, does the Kingship Law reflect the royalist ideology of the Judean Court at the time of Josiah?[3] Or, on the contrary, do the limitations placed upon the power of the king point the reader towards an anti-monarchic agenda in Israelite

---

[1] Baruch Halpern, *The Constitution of the Monarchy in Israel* (HSM 25; Chico, CA: Scholars Press, 1981), 226.
[2] Lopez acknowledges that, "Dt 17,14–20 a été et continue à être l'objet de nombreuses polémiques," ("Le Roi d'Israel: Dt 17,14–20," in *Das Deuteronomium: Entstehung, Gestalt und Botschaft* [ed. N. Lohfink; Leuven: Leuven University Press, 1985], 277).
[3] One example, amongst others, would be Moshe Weinfeld, "Deuteronomy: The Present State of Enquiry," in *The Song of Power and the Power of Song: Essays on the Book of Deuteronomy* (ed. D. L. Christensen; Winona Lake: Eisenbrauns, 1993), 28. Weinfeld attributes this "positive" view of the monarchy to the "scribes of the courts of Hezekiah and Josiah" (p 34).

society?[4] Other questions are more theological in nature: for example, do Deuteronomy and the DtrH speak with the same voice regarding the monarchy? Or could it be said that one is pro-monarchic whereas the other is anti-monarchic, and if so which is which?[5] As well as such issues, there is also the challenge of the complex question of the origins of the text of Deut 17 and the succeeding influences of redactors, be they exilic or post-exilic?[6]

Much effort could be put into the discussion of these questions. However, such discussion is somewhat beyond the scope and remit of this thesis. Rather, our desire it is to ask the question, "Could the Kingship Law have functioned as a paradigm for the organisation of the psalm groupings considered in the preceding chapters?" This line of enquiry requires investigation more from a textual and literary perspective than from a historical perspective. Our quest is not to prove that Deuteronomy 17 is sufficiently ancient,[7] rather it is to establish that the literary indicators are such that it seems convincing that the editors of the Psalter had the Law of the King in mind when juxtaposing torah and kingship psalms as part of their eschatological programme of kingship in the Psalms. The message of the canonical Psalter seems to be that a restored, Davidic king is to be expected. This is emphasised by the placement of royal psalms at key points throughout the book.[8] The linking of kingship and torah psalms in Pss 1–2; 18–21; and 118–119, adds nuance to this sense of royal expectation, however. Namely, the king who is to come shall not be a king in the mould of the often bitter and disappointing experience of the DtrH, instead he shall be a king who functions as an exemplar of proper piety before Yahweh in accordance with the Deuteronomic Law of the King.

---

[4] Chiefly Martin Noth, *The Deuteronomistic History* (trans. H. G. M. Williamson; JSOTSup 15; Sheffield: JSOT Press, 1981), 91; Gerhard von Rad, *Deuteronomy: A Commentary* (trans. Dorothea Barton; OTL; London: SCM Press, 1966), 120; E. W. Nicholson, *Deuteronomy and Tradition* (Oxford: Basil Blackwell, 1967), 49–50. There are others who follow this view, as will become clear in the course of this study.

[5] Knoppers, "Deuteronomist and Deuteronomic Law of the King."

[6] See the discussion in Mayes, *Deuteronomy*, 271, regarding possible additions to an "original" law.

[7] Not that this would be a contentious question. There is almost universal agreement that the canonical text of Deuteronomy (even were one to posit the latest suggested date for the formation of Deuteronomy) was closed prior to the final formation of the text of the Psalter.

[8] Wilson, "Use of Royal Psalms," passim; *Editing*, 209–14.

Of course, emphasis upon textual and literary connections does not make historical questions obsolete. On the contrary, the ordering of these royal and torah psalms is most likely part of a (perhaps much broader) Deuteronomistic redaction of the Psalter. If this is the case, then it would be reasonable to expect the view of kingship which is displayed in the Psalter to broadly reflect the DtrH's presentation of kingship. If the same hand lies behind both, then there should be some degree of observable overlap between these texts. We shall seek to answer this broader question in chapter 7.

For now, our focus must be upon the exegetical examination of Deut 17:14–20. As throughout this thesis, our primary objective must be to allow the text to speak for itself. In order to establish the central argument of this thesis, it must be shown that there is substantial overlap between the content of Deuteronomy's Kingship Law and the content of the psalm groupings examined above. If we are to accept that the Law of the King functioned as the paradigm for the canonical placement of Pss 1–2, 18–21 and 118–119 then exegetical examination of the text must show that there are textual, thematic and theological similarities which may be observed in the Law of the King and in these psalm groupings. This is the task to which we now turn.

2. ANALYSIS OF THE LAW OF THE KING (DEUT 17:14–20)

BHS	Translation
כִּי־תָבֹא אֶל־הָאָרֶץ אֲשֶׁר יְהוָה אֱלֹהֶיךָ נֹתֵן לָךְ וִירִשְׁתָּהּ וְיָשַׁבְתָּה בָּהּ וְאָמַרְתָּ אָשִׂימָה עָלַי מֶלֶךְ כְּכָל־הַגּוֹיִם אֲשֶׁר סְבִיבֹתָי: שׂוֹם תָּשִׂים עָלֶיךָ מֶלֶךְ אֲשֶׁר יִבְחַר יְהוָה אֱלֹהֶיךָ בּוֹ מִקֶּרֶב אַחֶיךָ תָּשִׂים עָלֶיךָ מֶלֶךְ לֹא תוּכַל לָתֵת עָלֶיךָ אִישׁ נָכְרִי אֲשֶׁר לֹא־אָחִיךָ הוּא:	14 When you enter the land which Yahweh your God is giving you—when you take possession of it and dwell in it—and you say, "Let us set a king over ourselves like all the nations which surround us."[9] 15 Be sure that you set a king over yourselves whom Yahweh your God chooses. You shall appoint a king over youselves from amongst your brothers. You must not place a foreigner, who is not one of your brothers, over you.

---

[9] As is characteristic of this passage concerning the offices, and other sections, of the Book of Deuteronomy, the people are addressed using a second person singular form of address. Accordingly the first person deliberations of the people (translated above "Let us...") are actually written in the first person singular in the Hebrew text (effectively "Let me..."). I have used the plural throughout in the English translation of this text in order to facilitate a more "readable" working translation.

רַק לֹא־יַרְבֶּה־לּוֹ סוּסִים וְלֹא־יָשִׁיב
אֶת־הָעָם מִצְרַיְמָה לְמַעַן הַרְבּוֹת סוּס
וַיהוָה אָמַר לָכֶם לֹא תֹסִפוּן לָשׁוּב בַּדֶּרֶךְ
הַזֶּה עוֹד: וְלֹא יַרְבֶּה־לּוֹ נָשִׁים וְלֹא יָסוּר
לְבָבוֹ וְכֶסֶף וְזָהָב לֹא יַרְבֶּה־לּוֹ מְאֹד:

16 Only he must not multiply for himself horses and he must not send the people back to Egypt in order to multiply horses, for Yahweh said, "Do not return that way ever again." 17 And he must not multiply wives for himself so that his heart does not stray. Also he must not multiply much silver and gold for himself.

וְהָיָה כְשִׁבְתּוֹ עַל כִּסֵּא מַמְלַכְתּוֹ וְכָתַב לוֹ
אֶת־מִשְׁנֵה הַתּוֹרָה הַזֹּאת עַל־סֵפֶר מִלִּפְנֵי
הַכֹּהֲנִים הַלְוִיִּם: וְהָיְתָה עִמּוֹ וְקָרָא בוֹ
כָּל־יְמֵי חַיָּיו לְמַעַן יִלְמַד לְיִרְאָה
אֶת־יְהוָה אֱלֹהָיו לִשְׁמֹר אֶת־כָּל־דִּבְרֵי
הַתּוֹרָה הַזֹּאת וְאֶת־הַחֻקִּים הָאֵלֶּה
לַעֲשֹׂתָם:

18 When he takes the throne of his kingdom, he is to write out a copy of this torah for himself—taken from the priests who are Levites—into a book. 19 And he is to keep it with him and read it aloud all the days of his life, so that he will learn to fear Yahweh his God and to keep all the words of this torah and to follow [lit: to do] all these decrees.

לְבִלְתִּי רוּם־לְבָבוֹ מֵאֶחָיו וּלְבִלְתִּי סוּר
מִן־הַמִּצְוָה יָמִין וּשְׂמֹאול לְמַעַן יַאֲרִיךְ
יָמִים עַל־מַמְלַכְתּוֹ הוּא וּבָנָיו בְּקֶרֶב
יִשְׂרָאֵל: ס

20 He must not exalt himself over his brothers and he must not turn aside from the commandment, neither to the right or to the left, so that he and his sons may reign in Israel for many days.

The Law of the King is, without question, quite an extraordinary document in its context within the ancient Near East. Whilst Israel was not the only ANE society to provide written advice for rulers,[10] we find no other ancient texts which seek to limit the power of the king in this way. Knoppers writes, "In placing a series of major constraints upon the powers of kingship, the Deuteronomic law of the king is highly unusual. The powers of the monarchy, so dominant in the civilizations of the ancient Near East, are greatly circumscribed in Dtn 17,14–20."[11] McConville emphasises this same point, "Deuteronomy evidently intends somehow to circumscribe or restrict the powers of the king. The king as

---

[10] "Advice to a Prince" (W.G. Lambert, *Babylonian Wisdom Literature* [Oxford: Clarendon, 1960] 110–115) bears some similarities to the Kingship Law, but does not explicitly limit royal powers: rather it discusses the possible consequences of the abuse of royal prerogatives. It certainly does not present itself as having binding authority over the king.

[11] Knoppers, "Deuteronomist and Deuteronomic Law of the King," 329–30.

presented here differs enormously from that of the usual ancient Near Eastern concept of the king as the chief executive in all aspects of the nation's life."[12]

The unusual nature of Deuteronomy's "take" on kingship is further accentuated by its position within the laws dealing with the distribution of power within Israel (16:18–18:22). One would think that, whilst the law concerning the king seeks to limit his power, surely he is for all that still the central and most important figure in the power structure of ancient Israel. The DtrH indicates that this was how the office of king developed in practice, however, the legal framework of Deuteronomy presents kingship as being of secondary importance to an impartial judiciary.[13] So the reader—aware of the typical role of kingship in the ancient Near East—is confronted with a double challenge to his perception of kingship: the king is subject to legislation limiting his power (just like any other citizen of the land); and, secondly, his office is presented as secondary in significance to the function of judge. These unexpected perspectives lead one to formulate questions concerning the essence and function of the law of the king: just what is its purpose, what does it seek to achieve?

It is in answering these fundamental questions about the Kingship Law that the reader is led to certain conclusions about the theological quintessence of Deut 17:14–20. I would suggest that in examining the essential nature of this law our attention is drawn to certain themes and foci which, as we have already seen, are central to the meanings and purposes of our psalm groupings. The Kingship Law, following the unusual but important introductory verse 14,[14] splits into four units dealing with four themes:

1. King as chosen by Yahweh (v 15).
2. King as one of the Hebrew brothers, i.e. democratising effect (vv 15, 20).
3. Limitations of royal power, stressing dependence on Yahweh (vv 16–17).
4. Centrality of *torah* in the life of the king (vv 18–19).

These key motifs, of course, require further elaboration, but first we must look at the question of whether or not the Kingship Law is inherently anti-

---

[12] McConville, "King and Messiah," 276. See also Wright, *Deuteronomy*, 209, and Tigay, *Deuteronomy*, 166, for further discussion of the unusual nature of the Kingship Law in its ancient Near Eastern context.

[13] Lohfink, "Distribution," 347; Wright, *Deuteronomy*, 207–08; Miller, *Deuteronomy*, 147.

[14] Deut 17:14 is unusual in that it presents a scenario in which a leadership office is created at the behest of the people rather than at the command of Yahweh.

194   *The King as Exemplar*

monarchic, as this would fundamentally affect the interpretation of this text and its possible application as a paradigm in the Psalter.

3. KINGSHIP LAW AS INHERENTLY ANTI-MONARCHIC?

The best way to seek to answer this question is by way of detailed analysis of the text itself. The first two verses of the Law of the King speak to the question of whether or not this text is explicitly against the idea of kingship.

3.1 INTRODUCTION TO THE KINGSHIP LAW

Verse 14, by way of introduction, puts the following stipulations regarding the king into their proper context. Firstly, it stresses the absolute kingship of Yahweh and, secondly, it shows the "non-essential" nature of kingship within the Hebrew constitution and power structures. The land is Yahweh's to give (הארץ אשר יהוה אלהיך נתן לך, "the land which Yahweh your God is giving you"), not the king's to allot which was one of the traditional functions associated with ANE kingship.[15] Also the office of king is not commanded by Yahweh in the same manner as the judicial office, rather kingship is *allowed* to come into being following a time-delayed, and somewhat dubious request from the people. Compare "you shall appoint judges and rulers" (שֹׁפְטִים וְשֹׁטְרִים תִּתֶּן־לְךָ, Deut 16:18), with "let us place a king over us, like all the nations that surround us" (וְאָמַרְתָּ אָשִׂימָה עָלַי מֶלֶךְ כְּכָל הַגּוֹיִם אֲשֶׁר סְבִיבֹתָי, Deut 17:14). The former is clearly ordained and commanded by Yahweh,[16] the latter reflects an origin in the people rather than God and the reasons given run contrary to the basic theology of Deuteronomy.

So how are we to understand the kingship law in the light of its introduction? First of all, v 14 starts by accentuating the *kingship of Yahweh*. Human kingship is permitted but only in the context of the *ultimate* kingship of Israel's God. Wright expresses this idea:

---

[15] McConville writes, "The limits on [the king's] power are adumbrated by the formulaic introduction of the law, which reaffirms that it is Yahweh who has given the land (17:1); there is no sign here of the king as the one who makes land grants," ("King and Messiah," 276).

[16] Whilst the verb used in Deut 16:18 is a Qal, imperfect, 2ms form, rather than an imperative, the simple future translation of the verb gives it the imperative sense of an act commanded by Yahweh ('You shall appoint...'). This is reflected in the EVV: NIV, KJV, NKJV, RSV, NRSV, ESV & NASV all translate this verse in this way.

The supreme authority is Yahweh himself, whose theocratic focus of power and authority in a vertical sense effectively flattens and disperses power at the horizontal level. The constitutional aspects of human authority are thus set firmly in the context of God's transcendent authority and revealed will and word.[17]

McConville makes a similar point:

> [Deuteronomy's] covenantal theology is that of all Israel, and its covenantal story will lead in time to a monarchy in relationship with Yahweh. The law of the king itself anticipates something that is not yet a fact in Israel's life. Its stress is on constraint, and its aim to ensure the true primacy in Israel of Yahweh and his Torah (or law). It neither promotes nor criticises any actual dynasty, but certainly has the potential to do the latter.... [A]ny human kingship in Israel is seriously qualified by Deuteronomy's theology of Yahweh's kingship. This is implicit in the structure the book, which, as is well-known, closely resembles the form of a vassal-treaty, contracted between a greater and a lesser king. In terms of this metaphor, it is Yahweh who is the "Great King."[18]

Secondly, the office of king is portrayed as being *optional* by the way in which it is introduced. Speaking more specifically of the Kingship Law, Wright adds: "This section, therefore, is permissive rather than descriptive legislation. It does not command monarchy but allows for it."[19] Similarly Craigie writes, "This section, containing laws relating to kingship, is the only one of its kind in the Pentateuch. It takes the form of permissive legislation, rather than positing a requirement."[20] Von Rad accurately sums up the overall impression given by the tone of v 14: "the law concerning the king almost gives us the impression of being merely an 'optional arrangement.'"[21]

Thirdly, the *reason* given from the people's request places kingship in a distinctly negative light when viewed from the perspective of the overall message of the Book of Deuteronomy. "A king over ourselves *like all the nations which surround us*," is a term which has unequivocally negative connotations in Deuteronomy. Tigay writes, "Deuteronomy, by mentioning only this motive for wanting a monarchy, characterises the institution as unnecessary and unworthy."[22] For Nicholson this formulation is sufficient, in and of itself, to indicate that these stipulations are basically anti-kingship:

---

[17] Wright, *Deuteronomy*, 203.
[18] McConville, *Grace in the End*, 31.
[19] Wright, *Deuteronomy*, 208.
[20] Craigie, *Deuteronomy*, 253.
[21] von Rad, *Deuteronomy*, 120.
[22] Tigay, *Deuteronomy*, 166.

Indeed the law on kingship in Deuteronomy 17:14f makes it quite clear that the authors of the book had little regard for the institution of monarchy. The expressions "like the nations that are round about" in verse 14 is itself polemical (cf. 1 Sam 8:5–9, 19–20). For Deuteronomy kingship is essentially an institution of foreign importation.[23]

Certainly, the other occurrences of comparison with the surrounding nations are to be found either in the context of Israel being distinct from their practices (6:14, 13:7) or simply describing these nations as enemies from which Yahweh will give them rest (12:10, 25:19). Deuteronomy stresses the fact that Israel is given the land in the first place, not because of her inherent worth, but because of the wickedness of the nations (9:4). Clearly, the motivation for requesting a king is meant to be read in a negative light—whatever other factors may be at work in this request, *the reasons given* should be understood negatively.

In summary, Deut 17:14 as an introduction to the law of the king leaves the reader with a rather negative view of human kingship. It stresses the ultimate kingship of Yahweh, the optional nature of the office of human king and the people's wrong reasons in making the request for a king in the first place. Were this the end of the legislation, there would be little doubt about the Dtr view of kingship. However, the author's perspective on the office of king is not so one-dimensional and the remaining verses of the statute leave the reader with competing information concerning the human king. These views of kingship are to be held in creative tension.

3.2 KINGSHIP AND YAHWEH'S CHOICE

The transparently negative overtones regarding kingship in v 14 are immediately confronted with a quite different approach to kingship in v 15. The people are told to be sure that the king whom they install is the one chosen by Yahweh, that he is one of the Hebrew brothers and that he should not be a foreigner but (again) a brother. So the reader moves from the negative impression of the people's choice (based in an apparently inappropriate desire to be like the nations) to Yahweh's choice, implying divine approval of king and kingship?

The contrast is stark and indicative of the complexities involved in trying to establish a single Dtr view of kingship. Inherent to the act of Yahweh's

---

[23] Nicholson, *Deuteronomy and Tradition*, 49–50.

choosing is an implication of divine approval,[24] thus a different light is shed upon the ambivalent tones of v 14.

> The concept of Yahweh's choosing is an important one in the OT especially in Deuteronomy and the Deuteronomistic History. When Yahweh chooses a people, or place for worship, or a king, he has determined the direction, and given his blessing on the choice. With this grace kingship is thus immediately placed under Yahweh's rule.[25]
>
> The common element in the "choosing" contexts seems to be an insistence on Yahweh's prior or sovereign action in the arrangement of Israel's affairs. When it is said that Yahweh chooses the people, the king and the priests, it is clear enough in each case that the dominant idea is simply that of Yahweh's choice... Other occurrences of the choosing motif are also expressions of this grand truth. In 17:14f, the people's resolve to have a king... is fundamentally changed in character by the qualification that that king shall be one whom Yahweh, as opposed to the people themselves, will choose. In this, according to Deuteronomy, the Israelite monarchy is to be distinct from that of the surrounding nations.[26]
>
> The effect of v 15 upon the Kingship Law is marked. An initially sceptical approach to kingship—based in the optional nature of kingship and the questionable motives lying behind the request for a king—is qualified by Yahweh's sovereign act of choosing. The implications of this reversal should be read back into verse 14 as well as forward into the remainder of the statute.[27]

As part of Yahweh's kingship, he is sovereign over the choice of any particular king and over the royal office in general. This reversal in tone, as McConville points out above, leads us to the very heart of the matter in terms of the Kingship Law. The central issue, in fact, is not the question, "Should there be a king in Israel?" This is taken somewhat for granted in the text. Rather the key question is, "What should Israel's king be like?" The ensuing verses take up this question and make it clear that Israel's king is to be radically different from all other ANE models of kingship. The tension with regard to the "rightness" of kingship in Deut 17 is nonetheless real and should not be explained away too easily. However, I would argue that the dubiety of v 14 is not sufficient to lead one to the conclusion that the voice of Dtr in the Law of the King is anti-

---

[24] B. E. Schafer, "The Root *Bḥr* and Pre-Exilic Concepts of Chosenness in the Hebrew Bible," *ZAW* 89, no. 1 (1977): 20–42.
[25] Gerbrandt, *Kingship*, 110.
[26] McConville, *Law and Theology*, 30–31.
[27] Gerbrandt, *Kingship*, 109–10.

monarchic, *per se*.²⁸ Rather, I would suggest that this verse sounds a strong note of caution with regard to the office of king. For it is, arguably, with regard to kingship that the risk of lapsing into the abuse of power is greatest and the effects of such abuse would be furthest-reaching.²⁹ This cautionary note, however, does not automatically indicate divine rejection of human kingship as inherently incompatible with the kingship of Yahweh, as is testified by Yahweh's insistence that he choose the candidate for king. Furthermore, Yahweh does allow kingship as part of this "polity of the covenant people."³⁰ The king *has* a role to play: the main content of the Kingship Law is made up of discussion of what that king should be like—what should characterise Israel's king? If the Psalter reflects a redaction which seeks to reflect the Kingship Law then we should expect some similarity between the characteristics of the king as presented in the torah-kingship psalm groupings and the ideal king of Deut 17:14–20. Therefore, we now turn to consideration of the Dtr presentation of what the ideal king is to be like.

4. CHARACTERISTICS OF THE KING

As mentioned above, we perhaps do the text of Deut 17:14–20 a disservice in asking whether it is pro- or anti-monarchic.³¹ Kingship is posited as future

---

²⁸ *Contra* von Rad, Nicholson *et al*. At the same time, the Kingship Law should not necessarily be seen as pro-monarchic in a royalist sense. The Law of the King is typically Deuteronomic in its content, i.e. it is more concerned with the worldview, humility and piety of the king as a leader of the covenant people and facilitator of covenant obedience, than it is with an abstract discussion of the pros and cons of monarchic rule.

²⁹ Tigay, *Deuteronomy*, 166.

³⁰ S. Dean McBride, "Polity of the Covenant People: The Book of Deuteronomy," in *The Song of Power and the Power of Song: Essays on the Book of Deuteronomy* (ed. D.L. Christensen; SBTS, Vol. 3; Winona Lake: Eisenbrauns, 1993), 62. Wright summarises this tension well when he writes: "Kingship in Israel is immediately set in an ambivalent light. On the one hand, if it comes it will be by the people's own request (v 14), but on the other hand, the individual king is to be Yahweh's choice (v 15).... Though the literary account of the request in 1 Samuel obviously echoes the Deuteronomic phraseology, *the Deuteronomic law is not itself negative or hostile to the people's request*. There is no harm in asking. The people ask other things of God that meet with approval (e.g., 12:20, 18:16f.). If the request for a king had been intrinsically incompatible with theocracy, it would doubtless have received a resounding rejection in the language of chapter 7. Yahweh is Israel's supreme judge, but that does not rule out human judges as his agents. Likewise, Yahweh is the true king in Israel (cf Exodus 15:18; Numbers 23:21; Deuteronomy 33:5; Judges 8:23), but that does not totally exclude human kings...." (*Deuteronomy*, 208, emphasis mine).

The Kingship Law as a Paradigm

fact, not a point of debate, within the text.[32] The question which the text itself elaborates upon is, "What should the king be like? What should typify his person and his office?" Craigie writes that the Law of the King "anticipates a time when, for practical and pragmatic reasons, kingship might become a necessity. But the legislation does not expound in detail the character of the kingly office; rather it specifies the attitudes and characteristics that would be required of the king in a state that was primarily a theocracy."[33] The focus of Deuteronomy 17 is not a detailed delimitation of the tasks, rights and responsibilities of the king, rather it focuses throughout on *character and attitude*. As mentioned above, the text of Deut 17:14–20 breaks into four units, following the introduction, and the remaining sections emphasise three additional themes.[34] Let us examine these sections in detail allowing these central themes to speak for themselves.

4.1 ESSENTIAL EQUALITY: DEMOCRATISATION

Following on from the injunction that the appointed king must be the one chosen by Yahweh. The law emphatically stipulates that the king should be appointed from within the covenant community (מקרב אחיך תשים, "from amongst your brothers you shall appoint..." 17:15). The emphatic positioning of the source from which the king is to be drawn (מקרב אחיך), placed before the verb underlines the importance of this command. The king is to be drawn from within the covenant community, the implication being (as will become clear) that he too is subject to the covenant and does not stand above it as a law unto himself. Most of the commentators pick up on this point:

---

[31] Gerbrandt, *Kingship*, 39–41, esp. 41. This view finds support in Howard, "The Case for Kingship in Deut," 101.

[32] From the DtrH (e.g. the Book of Judges and the Samuel narratives), we see from a historical perspective, that there was a strong debate within Israel surrounding the monarchy. Several commentators pick up on this fact and read this back into the Kingship Law (e.g. von Rad, *Deuteronomy*, 118–120; Nicholson, *Deuteronomy and Tradition*, 49–50). However, despite the similarities in the language of Deut 17:14 and 1 Sam 8:5, we should not impose this debate upon the text of the Law of the King. Although the initial comments give rise to questions about the appropriateness of the office of king, the remainder of this passage moves on from there to treat kingship as a political fact. The only remaining question is with regard to the type of kingship which should be found in Israel.

[33] Craigie, *Deuteronomy*, 253.

[34] In addition to the important theme of Yahweh's choosing of the king.

> Fellows: Literally, "brothers," underscoring the essential equality of the king and the other citizens. He is not their master.[35]

> The deuteronomistic historian supplemented the law of the king through the addition of vv 18f., and the later deuteronomistic editor added a note in v 16, and a phrase in v 20, by which he drew out what was for him the consequence of the king being simply a fellow-Israelite, viz. that just as his people so the king was subject to the divine law.[36]

> In Deuteronomy, this [democratising effect] is especially seen in the law of the king. He is chosen by the people from among his brothers, is not to acquire things that would either turn him away from Yahweh or exalt him above his brothers, and is not to exalt himself above other members of the community (his brothers).[37]

> Finally the theme of brotherhood of the members of the people of Israel deserves mention. The term 'aḥîm, "brothers," is Deuteronomy's characteristic expression for a referring to fellow-Israelites, regardless of social status or tribal divisions (e.g. Deut 1:16; 3:18, 20; 10:9; 15:3, 7, 9, 11). In 3:12–20 the point is made expressly that members of other tribes are also brothers. Even the king is to be "one from among the brothers" (17:15). *Its use, therefore, has a levelling function in Israel.* Allied with this is the tendency to speak of Israel as a single whole, and what seems like a deliberate disregard for divisions within the people... The theme of brotherhood, like the other themes, serves Deuteronomy's deeper concern to express the need for Israel to respond to Yahweh's action on its behalf. On the one hand the law of the king (17:14ff) draws on the idea of brotherhood in connection with the theology of election (v 15). The king's election and his status as a brother in Israel become a twin motivation not to use his office for self-aggrandisement.[38]

This emphasis adds a strong democratising element to the Law of the King. That is, the king is not to be set apart from the people because of his status, quite to the contrary, he is to be intimately associated with them, being constantly reminded that he is one of them.

The essential equality of the king with all Israelites is further stressed in v 15 by the direction that he should not be a foreigner, "who is not one of the brothers" (אשר לא אחיך הו). Whilst it is not easy to reconstruct a historical situation in which a foreigner would be appointed king in the pre-exilic period,[39] the

---

[35] Tigay, *Deuteronomy*, 169.
[36] Mayes, *Deuteronomy*, 270–71.
[37] Miller, "Kingship," 131.
[38] McConville, *Law and Theology*, 19. Emphasis added.
[39] David Daude, "One from Among Your Brothers Shall You Set over You," *JBL* 90 (1971): 480–81, suggests a backdrop in the narrative concerning Abimelech in the Book

key factor in this prohibition seems to be that a non-Israelite would not be subject to the covenant, and the king—as with all Israelites—*must* be subject to the covenant.[40] So, from v 15 we can observe, first and foremost, an essential equality between king and people. He and they alike are subject to the covenant with Yahweh—subject, as we shall see, to the *torah* of Yahweh (Deut 17:18-19). This emphasis on democratisation is further elaborated upon throughout the remainder of the Law of the King.[41]

4.2 Restrictions on the Power of the King

Perhaps the most immediately extraordinary fact concerning the Law of the King, given its ANE setting, is its focus on the restriction of the king's powers and privileges. Ancient Near Eastern kings were, generally speaking, the epitome of autonomy—laws unto themselves. As McConville notes, however, the king in Israel "would be conspicuously less powerful than the common run of oriental kings."[42] Wright observes the starkness of contrast between the stipulations governing the king in Israel and the royal practices common to that time and location:

> These three restrictions (vv 16f.) are remarkable because they quite explicitly cut across the accepted pattern of kingship throughout the ancient Near East. Military power, through the building up of a large chariot force (the point of having great numbers of horses), the prestige of a large harem of many wives (frequently related to international marriage alliances), and the enjoyment of great wealth (large amounts of silver and gold)—these were the defining marks of kings worthy of the title. Weapons, women, and wealth: why else be a king?[43]

---

of Judges (8:29-9:57). There is, however, insufficient indication of any specific historical setting in the Kingship Law to make such a concrete association. Tigay suggests that the scenario of a foreigner becoming king could result from a *coup d'état* where the military leader involved was a foreign mercenary (*Deuteronomy*, 167). Others see this as an exilic/post-exilic refusal to accept Babylonian or Persian imperial rule.

[40] Schafer, "Concepts of Chosenness," 40; Gerbrandt, *Kingship*, 148; Wright, *Deuteronomy*, 209; Craigie, *Deuteronomy*, 254–55; Tigay, *Deuteronomy*, 167.

[41] This theme is mentioned in v 15 and again in v 20, so we shall return to further consideration of the democratising effect of the king's association with the covenant community later in this chapter.

[42] McConville, "King and Messiah," 271.

[43] Wright, *Deuteronomy*, 209.

What lies at the heart of these limitations placed upon the power of the king? Why is Israel's king *not* to be characterised by weapons, women and wealth? The text of the Kingship Law seems to suggest a two-fold answer to this question: First, the sole source of the king's power is to come, not from these external factors, but rather from absolute trust in Yahweh himself; and, secondly, the king is not to exalt himself over his brethren, over the covenant community, re-emphasising the democratising effect of v15. The limitations on the power of the king seem to be fundamentally based in the concept of covenant—the king is to be entirely dependent upon Yahweh's promise and he is to be equal in status with all Israelites as he and they are under the same covenant.

4.2.1 ABSOLUTE DEPENDENCE UPON YAHWEH

Key to the concept of "polity"[44] in Deuteronomy is the fundamental theological message of the book as a whole—the sovereignty of God.[45] Yahweh reigns. It is the "task" of the covenant people to respond to that sovereignty in obedient devotion to him. A. D. H. Mayes writes that, "it should be noted that the task of the Deuteronomic law is not to pass judgement on the monarchy..., but rather to put over the characteristic Deuteronomic view of Israel as a whole...."[46] Part of that "characteristic Deuteronomic view" which is made apparent in the Law of the King is the notion of the people's absolute dependence upon Yahweh for all things. Just as the people are to place their trust in God entirely, so the king must do the same.

The people's dependence upon Yahweh is made clear in such passages as Deut 6:10–12 where the people are charged not to forget Yahweh once they enter Canaan. When cities and homes and wells and fields are provided for the people, Israel is no longer as explicitly dependent upon Yahweh for the provision of food and drink as was the case in the desert. Deuteronomy 6 warns that this new found comfort should not become the people's alternative source of strength or comfort or dependence—they must not forget that their real hope lies with Yahweh alone.[47] A similar message is repeated again for the people in

---

[44] Borrowing the term adopted by McBride in referring to *torah* in Deuteronomy as a "national 'constitution'"—*politeia* as opposed to *nomos*, ("Polity," 62).

[45] McConville, *Law and Theology*, 32.

[46] Mayes, *Deuteronomy*, 271.

[47] Wright, *Deuteronomy*, 101–03; Tigay, *Deuteronomy*, 80; Craigie, *Deuteronomy*, 173; von Rad, *Deuteronomy*, 64; Mayes, *Deuteronomy*, 178.

Deuteronomy 8—just as the people were absolutely dependent upon God in the desert, they should remember that they are no less so now, despite the fact that they live in a land of plenty. Mayes describes this constant appeal not to lose sight of one's dependence upon Yahweh as "a regular theme of Deuteronomy."[48] Such is the context within the theological understanding of the Book of Deuteronomy. In Deut 17:14-20 we see how these principles were to be applied by the king as leader and exemplar for the people.[49]

Just as the people are warned that they are not to forget Yahweh once they are settled into the relative comfort of the land, so the king is warned that he is not to allow his kingship to be marked by the typical overindulgences of oriental kingship. Why not? Within the context of Dtr theology the answer is clear: trust in the multiplication of weapons, wives and wealth as a source of power leads to apostasy, to forgetfulness of Yahweh.

"Horses" (סוּסִים) most probably represent the power of chariotry, the greatest of military strengths in the Near East at that time.[50] The Law of the King plainly states that the king is not to put his trust in military might. "Wives" (נָשִׁים) represent the power of international diplomacy through political alliances cemented by marriage.[51] The Kingship Law makes it clear that the king's power does not lie in his skills as an international power-broker. "Silver and gold"

---

[48] Mayes, *Deuteronomy*, 178.

[49] Mayes, *Deuteronomy*, 272–73. One could add here that the people and the king are both subject to the torah of Yahweh (Deut 6:1-2 cf. Deut 17:18-20). This responsibility to keep the law is a clear expression that Yahweh is the "Great King" of all Israel.

[50] In the OT possession of horses is also a symbol of wealth (Craigie, *Deuteronomy*, 255), but given that "silver and gold" (וכסף וזהב) are used in v 17 as clear representations of wealth, it seems most likely that reference is made to the temptations of placing one's trust in military might. See also Miller, *Deuteronomy*, 148; Wright, *Deuteronomy*, 209; J Ridderbos, *Deuteronomy* (trans. E. M. van der Maas; BSC; Grand Rapids: Zondervan, 1984), 199–200. The ban on the multiplication of horses as a source of military strength is further accentuated by the call not to send the people back to Egypt in order to purchase these horses. The basic function of this prohibition within the text seems to serve as a reminder of God's sovereign work in the salvation history of Israel (no chariots were needed at the Exodus, indeed they did the Egyptians no good at all). For further discussion of this aspect of v 16 see D. J. Reimer, "Concerning Return to Egypt: Deuteronomy XVII 16 and XXVIII 68 Reconsidered," in *Studies in the Pentateuch* (ed. J. Emerton; VTSup 41; Leiden: Brill, 1990).

[51] Tigay, *Deuteronomy*, 167; Wright, *Deuteronomy*, 209. A reason is given for this prohibition: the clear implication is that many wives (presumably of foreign origin cf. Deut 7:3-6) may lead the king towards the forbidden religious practices of these wives.

(וְכֶסֶף וְזָהָב), quite obviously, serve to represent great wealth.[52] Neither is the king to find self-sufficiency through the gathering of great wealth.

The essential meaning of the prohibitions placed upon the power of the king is that he is to place his trust entirely in Yahweh and his ability to provide for king and people, not in the typical sources of royal power:

> Israel might admire the kings of the nations. But the king they are to have is to be as unlike the kings of other nations as one can imagine. *Clearly the issue is not merely if Israel should have a king or not, but what kind of king that should be.* What matters fundamentally for Deuteronomy is whether or not *the whole covenant people of Israel will remain wholly loyal to Yahweh their God.* The value of a king is assessed solely by the extent to which he will help or hinder that loyalty. A king who will trust not in God but in his own defences (cf 3:21f.); a king whose heart turns away because of many wives (cf 7:3f.); a king whose great wealth leads to this snares of pride (cf 8:13 f.)—such a king will quickly lead the people in the same disastrous directions. History proves the point with depressing regularity, as the deuteronomistic historians show.[53]

> The important aspect is the religious one, for multiplying horses (in the context of establishing and strengthening a professional army) had definite religious implications. These are drawn out by the prophets, particularly Isaiah 2:7–9 and Micah 5:10ff., where horses along with wealth (cf. v 17) are seen as things which *lead to pride, to a loss of awareness of the need to trust in Yahweh, and so to unfaithfulness and apostasy....* But the intention is the same here as with the prophets, for, as the verse goes on to indicate, the danger of many wives is precisely that it *leads to apostasy from Yahweh to the religions of the wives....* [N]or shall he greatly multiply for himself silver and gold:... this represents the application to the king of the deuteronomic parenesis in 8:13f.[54]

> Second, these restrictions and injunctions serve the main purpose of Deuteronomy, *to enjoin a full and undivided allegiance to the Lord.* The primary commandment is everywhere present in these verses. Limitation of horses and wealth had definite religious implications, drawn out by the prophets... where horses along with wealth (cf. 17) are seen as the things that lead to pride, to the loss of awareness of the need to trust in Yahweh, and so to unfaithfulness and apostasy (Mayes, p 272). The danger that foreign wives will turn the king's heart away from following after the Lord is explicitly stated in verse 17 and echoed by the historical example of Solomon in 1 Kings 11:1–8 and Ahab in 1 Kings 16:29–33.... *The law of the king is, like all Deuteronomic instruction, a guard against apostasy and idolatry.*[55]

---

[52] Miller, *Deuteronomy*, 148–49; Craigie, *Deuteronomy*, 256; Tigay, *Deuteronomy*, 168.

[53] Wright, *Deuteronomy*, 209 (emphasis added).

[54] Mayes, *Deuteronomy*, 272–73 (emphasis mine).

[55] Miller, *Deuteronomy*, 148 (emphasis added).

The aim of the law is to show how the monarchy, if established, is to conform to the same theocratic principles which govern other departments of the community; and *how the dangers with which it may threaten Israel's national character and Israel's faith, may be most effectually averted*.[56]

It seems quite clear that the law's purpose in limiting the power of the king is to emphasise *the king's absolute dependence upon Yahweh* in the broader scheme of things. The proliferation of weapons or diplomatic alliances or wealth would incline the king towards an attitude of self-sufficiency. The Law of the King serves as a salient reminder that the king, like the people, is a recipient of benefits according to Yahweh's grace. The land with its bounty was a gift to the people (6:10–12). The king is such only by Yahweh's choice (17:15). The Kingship Law stresses, therefore, that God is sovereign in all the affairs of monarch and nation and without his gracious, sovereign intervention into the lives of king and people they would never have reaped the benefits on which they now set their store. The limitations of power placed upon the king are set as reminders of the "really real." The king is not to become caught up with the trappings of royalty, he is rather to be one who excels first and foremost in his devotion to Yahweh and trust in him. *Trust in anything other than Yahweh will lead to apostasy*: such is the message of Deuteronomy and this message finds specific application in the Kingship Law.[57]

4.2.2 DEMOCRATISING EFFECT

As well as reminding him of his need to trust completely in Yahweh, the limitations placed upon the power of the king are a further reminder that he should not exalt himself above his brothers. As well as being a source of military strength, chariotry was seen as a means of self-aggrandisement of the king in the ANE. Tigay notes with regard to the prohibition of the multiplication of horses, "In the king's personal entourage these [chariots] represent royal self-aggrandisement, as indicated by the would-be kings Absalom's and Adonijah's use of them."[58] Similarly with regard to a large harem, this too would set the king apart from the ordinary Israelite for whom the Dtr law forbade such inter-

---

[56] S. R. Driver, *Deuteronomy* (ICC; Edinburgh: T&T Clark, 1978), 210 (emphasis added).

[57] This point is further emphasised in the discussion of the king's relationship to the *torah* in vv 18–19, see below pp 206–10.

[58] Tigay, *Deuteronomy*, 167.

marriage (Deut 7:3–4). A large harem of foreign princesses would imply one law for the king and another for the people. As Wright puts it, "Functional authority must be exercised in a context of covenant equality...."[59] The same would, obviously, be true of the silver and gold which the king could amass for himself. Huge wealth would set the king apart from his fellows. Mayes writes that the prohibition on the king's gathering great wealth "represents the application to the king of the deuteronomistic parenesis in 8:13f."[60] That is, the same rules regarding wealth and comfort are applied to both king and people with a view to preventing apostasy.

This second function of the limitation of the powers of the king reminds the Israelite who sits on the throne that he is an Israelite. Therefore, he is subject to the stipulations of the covenant in the same way that all other Israelites are subject to them. Gerbrandt discusses this issue in his consideration of the 1 Samuel 8–12 narrative in the light of the Kingship Law:

> The assumption behind this warning is that the king, although the supreme leader of Israel, *is still subject to the covenant and its law, and in this respect on equal footing with all other Israelites*. That the king also needs to follow the law is brought out clearly in 12:14. As we earlier noted, *this is also central to the law of the king in Deuteronomy 17*. There the king was told to study the law so that he would obey it. The same point was made by emphasising that the king was to be a brother (i.e. not a foreigner who was outside of Israel's law).[61]

Miller adds that, "The democratising tendency of Deuteronomy restricts even, if not especially, the king, whose heart must not be lifted up above his brethren."[62]

So the limitations upon the power of the king serve a two-fold purpose: First, reminding the king of his complete reliance upon Yahweh as opposed to any alternative source of power; and, secondly, as a reminder of the essential equality of status that exists between the king and his subjects.

4.3 TORAH-PIETY OF THE KING

The third essential component in the Kingship Law's presentation of what the king of Israel should be like is the vital significance of the torah of Yahweh to the king's character and his exercise of office. The clear implication of vv

---

[59] Wright, *Deuteronomy*, 210.
[60] Mayes, *Deuteronomy*, 273.
[61] Gerbrandt, *Kingship*, 148 (emphasis added).
[62] Miller, *Deuteronomy*, 148.

18–19 is that the king of Israel is to immerse himself in the divine teaching in order to learn "the fear of Yahweh." The reader, it appears, is meant to assume that this study will impact both the king's character (as is implied by the quest to "learn the fear of Yahweh") and his exercise of office, as there are no other proactive stipulations in the kingship law apart from this one.[63] How, then, does the king learn to be king? By diligent study of the torah of Yahweh, is the answer indicated by the Law of the King.[64]

The picture painted in vv 18–19 is one of educational endeavour, but even more than that, it is an image of an individual whose whole world-and-life view is thoroughly shaped by and grounded in the teaching of Yahweh. The educational process is aided by two "classical" teaching strategies: first, the king writes out the torah himself from the copy kept by the Levites; and, secondly, he reads it (aloud) daily.[65] Both of these practices indicate a strong teaching function—the increased impact resulting from visual and audio memorisation, seeing the words written out and hearing them read.[66] It is a powerful image of one who is committed to do more than learn from his "assigned text"—he seeks to shape and form his whole life and outlook based around that text.[67]

Torah, according to Deut 17:14–20, is vital to the king's vertical and horizontal relationships. If the king is to know the blessing of Yahweh (v 20), he is to live by the torah. If he is to relate properly to his fellows (v 20), he must live by the torah. So we see that the instruction of Yahweh is absolutely essential to every aspect of the king's exercise of monarchic rule. In fact, we can observe a principle of intensification at work here. The king is to be characterised by a typically Dtr attitude towards the torah, reflecting that which is to be expected of all Israelites.[68] According to Deuteronomy, *all of the people* are to absorb the divine instruction into their inner beings so that their lives and attitudes are shaped by it (e.g. Deut 6:1–9). In fact the whole nation is set apart as different from all others because of it possession of such fine governing principles (Deut 4:5–14). The king is to be no different. He too is to allow God's word to govern

---

[63] McBride, "Polity," 74.
[64] Craigie, *Deuteronomy*, 257; Ridderbos, *Deuteronomy*, 201.
[65] Sarna, *On the Book of Psalms*, 37–38.
[66] Tigay, *Deuteronomy*, 168.
[67] Driver, *Deuteronomy*, 212; Wright, *Deuteronomy*, 209.
[68] In a similar manner to the expectation that the king trust fully in Yahweh, just as is to be expected of all Israelites.

his inner being and outer actions. However, the essence of the kingship law is that the king is expected to do so *all the more*—this is the principle of intensification. The people are to follow the torah, to keep the torah, not to forget the torah, but the king is to *excel* in these areas. The people are to learn and treasure the torah, but the king is to learn from it and treasure it to an even greater extent. Such is the implication of the added responsibilities placed upon the king to write it out for himself (וכתב לו את־משנה התורה הזאת) and to read it aloud daily (וקרא בו כל־ימי חייו).[69] Such practices were not expected of the rest of the covenant community—not even of the judges, priests or prophets[70]—only of the king. Therefore it seems that the king is being set apart as *an exemplar* of torah-piety for all the people in the awareness that his example would have an effect on the torah-obedience of the whole nation.[71]

> Finally, the law of the king places upon that figure the obligations incumbent upon every Israelite. In that sense, Deuteronomy's primary concern was that the king *be the model Israelite*. This is seen especially in the fact that the essential responsibility of the king is to read and study the law constantly (cf 6:7 and 10:19), "that he may learn to fear the Lord his God, by keeping all the words of this law and these statutes, and doing them" (v 19). This is the word that Moses constantly places on all Israel throughout his speeches.... *The fundamental task of the leader of the people, therefore, is to exemplify and demonstrate true obedience to the Lord for the sake of the well-being of both the dynasty and the kingdom. King and subject share a common goal: to learn to fear the Lord* (v 19).[72]

---

[69] Tigay suggests that, "[s]ince reading in ancient times was normally done audibly (the Hebrew term for read, *kara'*, literally means 'call out'), reading included reciting," (*Deuteronomy*, 169). This seems to echo the concept of הגה in Ps 1:2 (see pp 45–48 above). He also notes that, "According to Philo, the king is required to make his own copy because writing makes a more lasting impression than does merely reading" (p 168). See also Sarna, *On the Book of Psalms*, 37–38 and the discussion of the practice of meditation on torah in chapter 7, *Torah, Kingship and Democratisation*.

[70] The laws dealing with the official offices of Israel (16:18–18:22), however, do make it absolutely clear that all officials are subject to the *torah* of Yahweh both in terms of their character and practice. See Lohfink, "Distribution," 350, who argues that, "the Torah always has pride of place" and that, "all offices are subordinate to the Torah."

[71] The DtrH indicates, as a general rule of thumb, that "as the king so the people." In the Dtr presentation of Israel's history, a king committed to Yahweh and life according to the torah headed a nation that followed the same standards. Conversely, the Deuteronomists indicate that royal apostasy and national apostasy go hand-in-hand (Gerbrandt, *Kingship*, 98–99).

[72] Miller, *Deuteronomy*, 148–49 (emphasis mine).

The Kingship Law as a Paradigm

As is so often the case, Deuteronomy mentions only what matters. In this case, it avoids the small print of an exhaustive job description for royalty and concentrates on the fundamental priority. *The law is to permeate the king's behaviour in every sphere, whether political, administrative, judicial, or military. He should be a model of what was required of every Israelite* (v 19b).[73]

Torah was a divine constitution for a theocratic monarchy. The king was to study and "meditate" on... the law in order that he might carry out its dictates and that his personal leadership might be informed by it as well. The sovereignty of his dynasty depended on his adherence to Torah, which adherence, *by example and set policy, would involve the adherence of the entire nation.*[74]

The only positively specified task of the Israelite monarch is to study the written Deuteronomic polity throughout his reign and *to serve as a national model of faithful obedience to its stipulations* (17:18–20). Therefore the executive neither makes the law of the land nor stands above it.[75]

But the point of the Deuteronomic law of the king is that the king's responsibilities are the same as those of the people. He is to keep the torah continually and completely. *Thus he embodies faithful Israel and models Israel's way with the Lord.*[76]

The king is to serve, once again, as an exemplar in a two-fold sense. Primarily his example is to be one of a life lived in commitment to Yahweh through torah-obedience. However, once again this devotion and subjection to the torah has a levelling effect in the king's relationship with the people. He is not subject to some special law but to the same law as are all the people.[77] Clearly, in being an exemplary covenant-keeper, the king shows that he too is bound to Yahweh in the same way that the people as a whole are bound to Yahweh, thus indicating an essential equality of status before God. Indeed, the importance of keeping the torah is directly linked with the kingship of Yahweh.

---

[73] Wright, *Deuteronomy*, 209 (emphasis mine).

[74] Soll, *Psalm 119*, 133 (italics are mine).

[75] McBride, "Polity," 74 (emphasis added).

[76] Miller, "Kingship," 130 (emphasis added).

[77] It is unclear as to what exactly הַתּוֹרָה הַזֹּאת represents. The commentators offer three main options: the Kingship Law itself (this is not a popular choice amongst recent commentators); the Book of Deuteronomy (von Rad, *Deuteronomy*, 120; Mayes, *Deuteronomy*, 273); or the legal section of Deuteronomy in chs 12-26 (Tigay, *Deuteronomy*, 168; Driver, *Deuteronomy*, 212). Craigie discusses this issue (*Deuteronomy*, 256) and suggests that "this law" may even have been the Book of the Covenant from Exodus. Given the usage of this phrase throughout Deuteronomy and the DtrH (e.g. Jos 1), it seems most likely that "this torah" refers to Deuteronomy itself, or at least part thereof. This is the subject of further discussion in chapter 7 below.

He is the true King over the people including the human king, therefore all as one are subject to his revelation.[78] Wright observes that, "In his submission to the law, the king must not consider himself better than his brothers (v 20), even though he has been set over them in political terms (v 14). Functional authority must be exercised in a context of covenant equality...."[79] Further:

> This book was to be the king's *vade mecum*, his life-long companion and source of wisdom and strength. By reading and learning, he would express true reverence for his God, exemplified by his keeping of the law and statutes of God. True reverence for God would in turn keep the king mindful of his true relationship to his fellow Israelites (so that his heart is not exalted above his brothers, v 20). He would avoid being cut off from his fellows by virtue of his position or wealth (cf v 17).[80]

> The fact that the king was the administrator of the covenant did not imply that the king stood over the covenant. Rather, for the Deuteronomist the king was clearly also subject to the covenant. The king, like any other Israelite, was expected to obey the law as it was found in Deuteronomy.[81]

So we see that the king's commitment to Yahweh via the diligent study of his torah has a dual effect: 1) The king is to serve as an example for the people of commitment to Yahweh and his word; and 2) Submission to the torah puts the king on an equal footing along with all of the people before Yahweh. This focus reflects the broader theology of the Book of Deuteronomy—a people subject to the kingship to God, living in a just society in the land. The king is to play an integral part in securing both aspects of this equation: He is to be an example of devotion to Yahweh and oneness in brotherhood with the rest of the covenant people. In essence the human king's submission to the torah manifests the ultimate kingship of Yahweh: he (like all Israelites) is subject to the sovereign rule of the Great King as expressed in his revelation.[82]

4.4 ESSENTIAL EQUALITY

The egalitarian emphases which we have seen throughout this study of the Kingship Law find further expression in the closing verse of this text. Verse 20 states that the king must refrain from two things: 1) exalting himself above his

---

[78] Gerbrandt, *Kingship*, 101.
[79] Wright, *Deuteronomy*, 210.
[80] Craigie, *Deuteronomy*, 256–57.
[81] Gerbrandt, *Kingship*, 100.
[82] We shall consider this in more detail in chapter 7 below.

brothers (לבלתי רום־לבבו מאחיו) ; 2) straying from the commandment (ולבלתי סור מן־המצוה). This verse functions as a summary statement for the whole the Law of the King, drawing attention once again to these repeated themes of equality and torah-obedience, each of which is an expression of the true kingship of Yahweh.[83] Regarding this equality, Miller writes: "The king is 'set over' (v 15) the people, but his heart may not be lifted above his compatriots (v 20)."[84] Tigay puts it even more forcefully in stating, "Fellows: Literally, 'brothers,' underscoring the essential equality of the king and the other citizens. *He is not their master*."[85] Driver adds that "the same principles of loyalty towards God, and of sympathetic regard for men, which Deuteronomy ever inculcates so warmly, are to rule the life both of the king and of his subjects; he is not therefore to treat those who after all are his 'brethren' (5:15) with arrogance, or to forget the obligations towards them which his office involves."[86]

As before, there is a democratising effect in this reminder. The tension between the tendencies towards arrogant elitism which seem to be inherent in (ANE) kingship, on the one hand, and the covenant obligations of the king, on the other, is spelt out bluntly and not glossed over in the Kingship Law.[87] The DtrH makes it clear that elitist, royalist tendencies (Brueggemann's "disorder") won out far too often and the king neglected his covenant responsibilities (Brueggemann's "order") which, the Kingship Law was designed to preserve.[88] However, the ideal presented in this Law of the King is different from the observable practices of the royal lines described in the DtrH.[89] According to Deut 17:14–20, the king is like the people, not exalted over them. Equally, in as much as the king fulfills the role of torah-keeper, the people are meant to be like the king... subject to the rule of Yahweh.[90]

---

[83] J. Gordon McConville, *Deuteronomy* (Leicester: Apollos, 2002).
[84] Miller, *Deuteronomy*, 147.
[85] Tigay, *Deuteronomy*, 169 (emphasis added).
[86] Driver, *Deuteronomy*, 212.
[87] Walter Brueggemann, "Imagination as a Mode of Fidelity," in *Understanding the Word: Essays in Honour of Bernard W. Anderson* (JSOTSup 37; ed. J. T. Butler et al.; Sheffield: JSOT Press, 1985), 26.
[88] McConville puts it thus, "DtrH wants to show that the history of kingship, even in its heroes, departs from the royal ideal of Deuteronomy." ("King and Messiah," 292).
[89] As Wright reminds us, "The failure of so many of Israel's kings to abide by [the Kingship Law's] standards does not invalidate its moral force. We know how much they failed only and precisely because of the presence of a law like this," (*Deuteronomy*, 210).
[90] Miller, *Deuteronomy*, 149; Wright, *Deuteronomy*, 209.

The reminder with regard to the keeping of "the commandment" bears typically Dtr overtones. The king must not "turn from the commandment either to the right or to the left" (cf. Jos 1:6–9). The question which springs to mind is, "Which commandment?" What exactly does *the* commandment" represent? Mayes suggests that "the commandment" is "used in the later parts of Deuteronomy comprehensively for the whole law."[91] Tigay adds that "the commandment" is related to keeping the law generally and, more specifically, to the prohibition against idolatry.[92] Wright sees this as a reference to the "whole substance of the law referred to as a single entity, i.e., the fundamental principle of covenant loyalty."[93] Similarly, Millar notes that, "the noun *miṣwâ* occurs regularly as the lone singular... rather like the more familiar uses of *tôrâ* and *derek*. Along with the variety of verbal forms used, the 'commandment' and other nominal forms combine in Deuteronomy to represent an overall response which Yahweh deserves and demands."[94] The usage of this term throughout the Book of Deuteronomy lends support to these interpretations, which are essentially very similar.[95] "This commandment" refers to the essence of the law—covenant loyalty to Yahweh as True King—which encompasses all of the details of that law. The king is to keep the spirit of covenant loyalty by obeying the details of the torah, the subject of his daily meditations (vv 18–19).

4.5 CONCLUSION REGARDING THE CHARACTERISTICS OF THE KING

Detailed examination of the Kingship Law leads the reader to certain conclusions about king and kingship in Israel. First, by way of overview, the Kingship Law is not a detailed consideration of the office in its every aspect. Therefore, we ask the wrong question of the text when we ask, "Is the Law of the King pro- or anti-monarchic?"[96] Rather Deut 17:14–20 is an appeal for a certain type of kingship—for kingship in accordance with the Dtr agenda of a people wholly devoted to the sovereign rule of Yahweh. The king is to serve this end.

---

[91] Mayes, *Deuteronomy*, 174, 274.
[92] Tigay, *Deuteronomy*, 169.
[93] Wright, *Deuteronomy*, 92. Craigie takes a similar view (*Deuteronomy*, 164–66).
[94] Millar, *Now Choose Life*, 51.
[95] 5:31; 6:1, 25; 7:11; 8:1; 11:8, 22; 15:5; 17:20; 19:9; 27:1; 30:11; 31:5.
[96] "This law has been used repeatedly to argue for either a pro-monarchical (usually southern) or anti-monarchical (either northern or demythologizing) agenda in Deuteronomy. But a theologically sensitive reading of the text justifies neither.... The law is for godly kingship and against ungodly kingship,"(Millar, *Now Choose Life*, 127).

Secondly, regarding the character of the king, we observe that:

1. The king is to be chosen by Yahweh. This is an important part of the validation of the office of kingship, which is initially presented as optional and at the behest of the people, but the act of divine choosing places kingship firmly within the remit of God's plan and polity for his people. Not just any king will do, only the one chosen by God to lead his people.

2. The king, again like the people, is to be entirely dependent upon Yahweh as his source of power and security. He is not to place his trust in other external factors—military might, international alliances or great wealth—and he should not allow the trappings of kingship to cause him to forget Yahweh as his sole source of security.

3. In serving this end, the king is to be an exemplar of torah-based devotion to Yahweh. He, like all the people, is to be obedient to the law. However, he is called to go further and deeper in his commitment to internalising the torah. He is to serve the people as a paradigm of one who is faithful to the covenant with Yahweh, and he is to attain to this state of devotion by way of constant meditation upon the torah. By way of this commitment to the torah, the king expresses his commitment to the True Kingship of Yahweh.

4. The king is not to exalt himself over his brothers. The Kingship Law strongly and repeatedly emphasises the essential equality of king and people as partners in the covenant with Yahweh. This democratising principle accentuates the king's function as example for the people—he is to be wholly devoted to Yahweh's covenant rule and, thus, an example to the people; they are able to follow that example because the king is essentially the same as they are.

The Law of the King paints a picture for the reader, an image of the role and character of the king within Israel according to God's plan. He is to be entirely devoted to Yahweh through torah-meditation, humble and to lead the people in covenant obedience. So now we must turn to the question, "Is this the image of kingship which is presented in the psalm groupings 1–2, 18–21 and 118–119?"

5. THE KINGSHIP LAW AS A PARADIGM IN THE PSALTER

As we have argued above, the placement of psalms within the canonical Psalter plays an important role in assessing the theological concerns of the editors of the Book of Psalms. We have highlighted the particular significance of the torah psalms throughout the Psalter—why is this the opening voice of the

Book of Psalms, and the dominant voice of the closing book of the Psalter?[97] We have also noted the "coincidence" that each of the torah psalms (Pss 1, 19 and 119) is placed alongside a kingship psalm (Pss 2, 18, 20–21 and 118). Throughout this thesis we have been asking the question, "Why is this the case?" When asked to consider the duet of torah and kingship voices, the reader's attention is drawn quite naturally to the Law of the King where these two themes play such an important role, as we have just seen.[98]

Accordingly, our quest has been to examine these psalms groupings in order to ascertain whether or not they bear the hallmarks of Dtr theology, and, more specifically, to ascertain whether their juxtaposition is designed to reflect the Law of the King (Deut 17:14–20). Having examined the exegetical content of these psalms and, now, the Kingship Law the next step is to discuss similarities and differences which exist between these respective texts. The question which we should bear in mind is, "Was the Kingship Law the paradigm for the juxtaposition of these torah and kingship psalms?" In order to address this question, we shall take Deut 17:14–20 as our conceptual starting point, as (if our argument is correct) the original editors might have done. Then we must compare the content of the psalm groupings examined above in the light of theological priorities of the Law of the King. The four summary statements with which we concluded the discussion of the "Characteristics of the King"[99] will provide the basis for our examination of the three psalm groupings. Interestingly, each of these four fundamental characteristics of the Dtr king is echoed in either one or more of the psalms within each of the highlighted psalm groupings.

5.1 KING AS CHOSEN BY YAHWEH

Fundamental to the theological basis of the Kingship Law is the idea that the king must be chosen by Yahweh. As we have seen above, Yahweh's act of choosing transforms the initial impression of kingship as being an ignoble demand of the people and places it firmly under his sovereign control as part of

---

[97] Mays, "Place of the Torah-Psalms"; J. Clinton McCann, "The Psalms as Instruction," *Int* 46, no. 2 (April 1992): 117–28 and *Theological Introduction*, passim; Miller, "Kingship."

[98] As has been observed by a number of commentators. See, for example, Miller, "Kingship," and "Beginning"; Craigie, *Psalms*, 60; McCann, *Psalms*, 684–85; Mays, *Psalms*, 92–93 etc.

[99] See above p 212–13.

The Kingship Law as a Paradigm 215

the polity of his people. The king must be Yahweh's king. He cannot be a foreigner, someone without the covenant—he must be one of the Hebrew brothers and what is more he must be Yahweh's selection from within the covenant community.[100] The idea of kingship in the Psalms is also intimately linked with Yahweh's choosing, as we see from Ps 89:3, "I have made a covenant with my chosen one; I have promised my servant David." So in the psalmic idea of kingship is implied the idea of divine choice.

5.1.1   CHOSENNESS IN PSALMS 1–2

The concept of chosenness in the first psalm grouping is inferred from the figure of the "son" in Ps 2.[101] The central figure in Ps 2 is variously described as Yahweh's "anointed one" (מְשִׁיחוֹ, v 2), "my king" (מַלְכִּי, v 6) and "my son" (בְּנִי, v 7 and possibly v 12[102]) and it is clear that he plays an important, if subordinate, role in Yahweh's rule over the nations (v 3). Each of these three terms is intimately connected with the idea of being chosen by Yahweh. The anointed one, set apart for Yahweh's purposes of ruling over kings and nations. The king whom Yahweh has installed in Zion, by divine, sovereign act. The son whom, this day, Yahweh has begotten. These notions are strongly linked with the act of divine choice, an essential component of the Kingship Law's portrayal of kingship.[103]

5.1.2   CHOSENNESS IN PSALMS 18–21

Similar motifs are also observable in Pss 18–21, particularly through the powerful use of possessives throughout these psalms. The vivid use of appellatives in Psalm 18 (in which the king refers to God as "my rock" [צוּרִי, v 47], "my stronghold" [מְצוּדָתִי, v 3], "my shield" [מָגִנִּי, v 3]) indicates—from the perspective of the psalmist—a special and intimate relationship with Yahweh. This "chosen" relationship is confirmed in v 51 where the psalmist is referred to as Yahweh's

---

[100] See above, pp 199–201.

[101] In the editorial linking of Pss 1 and 2 a parallel is drawn between the figure of the "blessed person" of Ps 1 and the "son"/ "messiah"/ "king" of Ps 2. See above, pp 67–68.

[102] Ps 2:12 is notoriously difficult to translate. It may include the command to "kiss the son," where the Aramaic word בַּר is used instead of the normal Hebrew בֵּן. The question is why the psalmist would use the Hebrew form in v 7 and then switch to the Aramaic in v 12? This is difficult to explain, but none of the alternative translations offered are entirely convincing either. See the commentaries for further discussion and p 57–58n43.

[103] Kraus, *Psalms*, 126–27; McCann, *Psalms*, 668–69; Craigie, *Psalms*, 64–65 etc.

"messiah" (מָשִׁיחַ) the first occurrence of this term in the Psalter since its usage in Ps 2:2. Again, Ps 18 emphasises that the king is chosen and set apart by Yahweh.[104] The same emphasis is seen in Pss 20–21, where the king is once again referred to as Yahweh's מְשִׁיחַ (Ps 20:7) and the recipient of Yahweh's "perpetual blessing" (כִּי־תְשִׁיתֵהוּ בְרָכוֹת לָעַד, Ps 21:7).[105] Pss 18:1 and 19:12, 14 also refer to the psalmist-king as Yahweh's "servant" (עַבְדְּךָ[106]), once more suggesting that the central figure in these psalms is chosen by Yahweh to serve his purposes.[107]

5.1.3 CHOSENNESS IN PSALMS 118–119

We witness a similar pattern in Pss 118–119. The theme of chosenness is, perhaps, slightly more oblique in Ps 118, but it is nonetheless present in the imagery of the psalm. We read, for example that Yahweh is "for" the central figure of this entrance liturgy (יְהוָה לִי, vv 6–7); that Yahweh has "become his salvation" (וַיְהִי־לִי לִישׁוּעָה, v 14); and he is accepted into the Temple courts as "the one who comes in the name of Yahweh" (הַבָּא בְּשֵׁם יְהוָה, v 26). All of these phrases, in the context of the "narrative" of the psalm, combine to make it clear that the "hero" of this poem is chosen by Yahweh to serve a special purpose within the community of "those who fear Yahweh" (v 4 cf. Deut 17:19).[108] In the psalmist's prayer of Ps 119, he constantly refers to himself as "your servant" (vv 17, 23, 38 etc.), a phrase which, as we have seen above, has royal overtones in the Psalter. Indeed, there are other indicators within the text of this lengthy prayer which indicate that the speaker was, in fact, the king—Yahweh's chosen one.[109]

5.2 KING'S DEPENDENCE UPON YAHWEH

It is interesting that each of the Psalter's torah psalms is paired alongside a kingship psalm, but even more interesting is the fact that in each of these kingship psalms we witness a situation where the king faces difficulties beyond his ability to cope and seeks the aid and assistance of Yahweh.[110] In one form or

---

[104] See above, pp 88–89 etc.
[105] See above, pp 110–11.
[106] Which Ps 89:3 implies is a sign of being chosen by Yahweh.
[107] See above, pp 101, 114.
[108] See above, pp 130–32.
[109] See above, pp 171–75.
[110] Sometimes the king pleads for this assistance himself (e.g. Ps 18), or he recounts Yahweh's salvation in response to his plea (e.g. Ps 118). On other occasions there is a third party plea on behalf of the king in his inability to cope (e.g. Ps 20) or celebration of

another, each of Pss 2, 18, 20, 21 and 118 we see a confession of the king's weakness and his dependence upon Yahweh. In no case is this state of dependence hidden behind a plea of capability, rather the king openly professes his complete trust in Yahweh for deliverance.

5.2.1 DEPENDENCE THEME IN PSALMS 1–2

The dependence theme is explicit in Ps 2 where we are party to a rebellion of the nations and peoples, their kings and rulers, against Yahweh and his anointed one (vv 1–3). It is difficult to definitively determine the various voices in Ps 2,[111] but regardless of who is speaking the emphasis in vv 4–9 is clear. It is Yahweh who mocks the rebellion of the nations (v 4); it is Yahweh who speaks terror to them (v 5); Yahweh has set his king in Zion (v 6); Yahweh has given the nations to him as an inheritance (v 8); and it is Yahweh who will strike the rebellious nations (v 9). The central idea is the activity of Yahweh in response to this rebellion. The focus of the king's "strength" (v 7) is his trust in the fact that Yahweh has declared him his "son." The king is co-regent with Yahweh, but it is clear that his rule is dependent upon the might and authority of God rather than any strength or power of his own.[112]

5.2.2 DEPENDENCE THEME IN PSALMS 18–21

The theme of the king's dependence upon Yahweh as his source of deliverance is abundantly apparent in Pss 18, 20 and 21. The appellatives alone in Ps 18 illustrate where the king believes his real source of power to lie.[113] The psalmist goes on, however, to express his absolute inability to save himself (vv 4–7) and recounts in terms of theophany how Yahweh came to his rescue (vv 8–25). There is no attempt to hide this state of absolute dependence upon divine assistance, indeed this is the focus of the whole psalm. Pss 20 and 21 echo similar themes from a different perspective. Ps 20:7–9 tells us that "Yahweh

---

that assistance (e.g. Ps 21). The exact nature of the threat with which the king is faced is (typically) unclear in these psalms. The imagery used often gives the appearance of a military threat, but this type of language may be applied to other dangers as well. However, on each occasion we see God coming to the aid of the king, rather than the king asserting his own authority. In each kingship psalm we see this free expression of the king's dependence upon Yahweh.

[111] See above, pp 57–58n43.
[112] See above, pp 58–60.
[113] See above, pp 78–80, 85 etc.

saves his anointed one" (הוֹשִׁיעַ יְהוָה מְשִׁיחוֹ) and then offers an explicit link with the Law of the King, where v 8 celebrates the fact that "some trust in chariots and some in horses, but we will trust in the name of Yahweh." This verse echoes the command that the king should not "multiply for himself horses" (Deut 17:16), but that his trust should be in Yahweh.[114] This confession of dependence is echoed in the inclusio which brackets Ps 21 rejoicing in the strength of Yahweh (בְּעֻזְּךָ, Ps 21:2, 14).[115] Over and above this, the psalmist's prayer at the end of Ps 19 expresses his incapability of living life in accordance with the torah, even although it is "more desirable than gold... and sweeter than honey" (v 11). His prayer confesses that if he is going to "walk the walk," he needs Yahweh's gracious help in order to do so.[116]

5.2.3 DEPENDENCE THEME IN PSALMS 118–119

Once again the idea of dependence on God is central to the message of Ps 118. In this entrance liturgy the king stands before the Temple gates seeking admittance (v 19) and the reply of the priestly gatekeepers is that only the righteous may enter (v 20). The king's public account of his deep distress when surrounded by hostile nations (vv 5, 10–13) and his total reliance upon Yahweh for his deliverance (vv 6–7, 13–14) is accepted by the priests as evidence of his acceptability to Yahweh, therefore of his right to enter and offer sacrifice. The confession of trust in Yahweh and dependence upon him is central to the theology of Ps 118.[117] This same trust in Yahweh is expressed in terms of the psalmist's reliance upon Yahweh for help in the face of the opposition of the wicked in Ps 119,[118] and also the need for divine intervention if he is going to be obedient to the torah which he delights in.[119]

5.3 KING AS EXEMPLAR OF TORAH-PIETY

The significance of the torah is a theme readily apparent in each of the psalm groupings because of the torah psalms themselves. As we have examined this aspect of the theology of the psalms in some detail, I will do no more that

---

[114] See above, pp 108–10.
[115] See above, p 107.
[116] See above, pp 95–96.
[117] See above, pp 133–135.
[118] See above, pp 161–63.
[119] See above, pp 169–71.

The Kingship Law as a Paradigm

mention where these torah emphases are to found and provide cross-references to our previous discussions of this topic.

5.3.1 TORAH-PIETY THEME IN PSALMS 1–2

Psalm 1, as part of the introduction to the Psalter as a whole, guides the reader towards a life-style in accordance with the theology of the psalms. That "first word" on how the reader should live is clear—the "blessed person" (אַשְׁרֵי־הָאִישׁ, v 1) is the one who "delights in the torah of Yahweh" (בְּתוֹרַת יְהוָה חֶפְצוֹ, v 2). The message is not one of simplistic legalism, but commends to the believer a world-and-life view based around divine revelation.[120] The "blessed man" of Ps 1 is paralleled with the king/son/anointed one of Ps 2, thus painting a picture which bears remarkable similarities to the above study of the king according to the Kingship Law.[121]

5.3.2 TORAH-PIETY THEME IN PSALMS 18–21

The idea of a kingly figure who devotes his life to Yahweh through the study and application of his Word is expressed twice in this second psalm grouping. Firstly, central to Ps 18 is the stanza in which the king declares his righteousness before God (vv 21–25), and central to the chiastic structure of that stanza is the king's declaration of the importance of Yahweh's torah in his life. In these verses, again we see a clear reflection of the Kingship Law upon the lips of the psalmist-king.[122] Secondly, the poetic celebration of the holistic good of God's law in Psalm 19 points the reader, once again, to the vitality of revelation in the life of the believer. The psalmist describes himself as "Yahweh's servant" (vv 12, 14) and favourably compares the torah to gold (v 11), subtle indicators that the speaker himself is actually the Davidic king, delighting in the torah, as commanded by the law governing his office.[123]

5.3.3 TORAH-PIETY THEME IN PSALMS 118–119

Psalm 119, as a prayer offered to Yahweh is the prime example of a life devoted to God through meditation upon his revealed word.[124] Over and above

---

[120] See above, pp 45–48.
[121] See above, pp 66–70.
[122] See above, pp 81–83.
[123] See above, p 101 etc.
[124] See above, pp181–84.

the fact that Psalm 119 functions as an example of the type of piety commended by the Kingship Law, the reader is struck by the fact that, although the psalm is without superscription, the psalmist could well be none other than the king himself.[125] So we see in Ps 119 a vibrant example of the type of piety which the Law of the King commands.

5.4 Humility of the King

This particular characteristic of the Dtr king is also reflected in the psalm groupings studied, in a similar way to the humility theme in the Kingship Law. The Dtr picture of the king's humility in Deut 17:14–20 is very much focused on the king's brotherhood with all of the covenant people and the fact that he is not to "exalt his heart above his brothers" (v 20), and this is expressed through dependence upon Yahweh—like the people—and subjugation to the same torah as all the people. These expressions of a proper humility on the part of the king are found in the two characteristics of kingship which we have just studied: the psalmist, openly celebrates both his dependence on God and his submission to the torah, as part of his confession of the ultimate kingship of Yahweh.

In each of these psalm groupings we witness the king's public confession of his own inherent inability to do the one thing that kings at that time were supposed to do; namely, lead the nation militarily.[126] This in itself, even if expressed in ceremony, must have been an act of some humility. The king confesses his incapability to save even himself from peril, let alone the people, and the capability of Yahweh alone to provide such salvation. The second sign of royal self-denial is seen in the king's delight in the law: he too is subject to the same torah as are all the people of God. He is no different from all others, his obligations are no different. If anything there is a sense in which the king is expected to excel in keeping the law as an example for the people. This is a public expression of brotherhood with all Israelites in the covenant.[127]

---

[125] See above, pp 171–75.

[126] This seems to be the characteristic most associated with kingship in an ANE setting. Indeed, this may have been the feature which most inspired the people to ask for a king "like the nations which surround us" (Deut 17:14 cf. 1 Sam 8–12). See Gerbrandt, *Kingship*, 98–102.

[127] Gerbrandt, *Kingship*, 100–01.

6. Conclusion

The Law of the King gives clear guidelines regarding the *character* of the king, even if it does not express the responsibilities of his office in great fullness. He has a part to play in the polity of the community, but it is a role which is not to be abused. He has powers, but is to limit his exercise of them. He has status, but is to use this for good, as an example of obedience to Yahweh. He is subject to the law, not above it. He is one of the people, not above them. Such is the Dtr picture of kingship.

Our question at the start of this chapter was, "Is this view of kingship reflected in Pss 1–2, 18–21 and 118–119?" Having examined in detail these psalms and the Kingship Law, it seems reasonable to conclude that there is a remarkable overlap in the expression of theological concerns found in Deut 17:14–20 and that found in the psalm groupings in question. Does this "prove" that the editors of the Psalter used the Law of the King as their paradigm for the juxtaposition of these psalms? That would over-state the case. However, the confluence of themes in these juxtaposed kingship and torah psalms does seem to indicate that the Dtr Law of the King could have played some part in the editors' decision to group these psalms together.

In the post-exilic period which saw the closure of the canonical Psalter, the expectation of a renewed Davidic monarchy featured highly in the religious life of the community. Indeed, the Psalter itself seems to emphasise this theme through the placement of kingship psalms at important places throughout its books. However, in juxtaposing these kingship and torah psalms, the editors of the Book of Psalms are sending out a particular message. Yes, the people are to expect a renewed kingship, but this is not to be represented by the worst excesses of the DtrH. Rather, this new kingship is to follow the ideal pattern of Deut 17.

As well as putting a particular slant on the eschatological expectation of a renewed kingship, the editors also point the readers of the Psalter to a particular lifestyle, a particular worldview, a particular type of piety. According to Deut 17:14–20, the king was meant to be an example of commitment to Yahweh through immersion in his instruction. By placing these psalms together, it seems that the editors wanted to remind those who would read their book of this Dtr teaching on how to live. There may no longer have been a king to act as an example for the people to imitate, but the pattern of life reflected in the Kingship Law was to be their example anyway.

We have, therefore, been able to show that there is some repetition (perhaps even substantial repetition) of ideas between these psalms and the Kingship Law. We see that three major themes influence both the torah-kingship psalm groupings and the Law of the King: the role of the torah, the figure of the king and the idea of democratisation. However, the analysis until now remains at a descriptive level, pointing out textual repetition and correspondences. There are still *theological* questions that need to be answered. These texts are all part of broader theological programmes, so the question remains: "Does this textual correspondence reflect the same theological agenda in both the torah-kingship psalms and the Deuteronomy's presentation of the king?" In speaking about these topics, do the Psalms and Deuteronomy speak with the same voice? When the psalms celebrate the torah of Yahweh, for example, are they are speaking about the same thing as in Deuteronomy 17? Both passages speak about the king, but surely the expansive psalmic celebration of David and Zion is far removed from Deuteronomy's approach to kingship which can (at best) be described as cautious. Could the juxtaposition of kingship and torah psalms possibly have resulted from the same theological agenda that was at work in the Kingship Law? This is a question to which we shall return in chapter 7. However, before we take up this point we must look at the significance of the placement of these psalm groupings within the Book of Psalms.

CHAPTER 6
THE EDITORIAL PLACEMENT OF THE TORAH-KINGSHIP PSALM GROUPINGS

1. INTRODUCTION

Hossfeld and Zenger provide a concise, helpful discussion of the levels at which a canonical analysis of the Psalter functions:

> Im einzelnen muß diese "kanonische" Psalmenauslegung folgende Schritte durchführen:
> a) Sie achtet auf die Stichwortbeziehungen zwischen nebeneinander stehenden Psalmen und prüft, ob derartige sprachliche und motivliche Gemeinsamkeiten einfach Zufall sind, ob sie der Anlaß waren, die betreffenden Psalmen hintereinander zu stellen, ob bei der Nebeneinanderstellung nachträglich semantische Angleichungen vorgenommen wurden, ob einzelne Psalmen für ihren jetzigen literarischen (!) Zusammenhang geschaffen wurden und ob die so gezielt miteinander verketteten Einzelpsalmen sich gegenseitig auslegen wollen.
> b) Sodann stellt sich die Frage, ob es im Psalter erkennbare "Psalmengruppen" bzw. "Teilgruppen" gibt, innerhalb derer einzelne Psalmen einen hermeneutisch besonders relevanten Ort einnehemen. Die Bezeichnung "Psalmengruppe" bezieht sich in diesem Falle nicht auf unter inhaltlichen und formalen Gesichtspunkten selektierte Einzelpsalmen (also wenn die Exegese z.B. "Königspsalmen," "Geschichtspsalmen," "Weisheitpsalmen" oder "Klage-psalmen," "Hymnen" nachträglich zu Gruppen bündelt und untersucht), sondern auf Reihungen von Nachbarpsalmen im vorliegenden Endtext des Psalters.
> c) Da diese "Teilgruppen" ihrerseits wieder im Zusammenhang eines der fünf Psalmenbücher stehen, ist auch diesbezüglich zu fragen, ob sich daraus auslegungsrelevante Gesichtspunkte ergeben, sei es hinsichtlich der Verhältnisses dieser "Teilgruppen" zueinander, sei es hinsichtlich von strukturell herausgehobenen Einzelpsalmen innerhalb der Gesamtkomposition.[1]

---

[1] Hossfeld and Zenger, *Die Psalmen I*, 24.

With regard to the torah-kingship psalm groupings, chapters 2–4 of this thesis have discussed the connections between the psalms under discussion in terms of the first two of the above-mentioned levels. There has been detailed discussion, firstly, of the shared vocabulary, themes and theology which link the individual compositions within the three torah-kingship psalm groupings (*Stichwortbeziehungen*). Secondly, as a natural progression from this task, discussion has focussed on how these connected psalms form sub-groupings (*Psalmengruppen/Teilgruppen*) within the final form of the Book of Psalms: that is, Pss 1 and 2 function as a sub-group in their own right providing a hermeneutical construct for the interpretation of the whole book;[2] Pss 18–21 function as the pivotal centre of a pre-existing collection of psalms arranged in a chiastic structure;[3] and Pss 118–119, in a manner similar to that observed with Pss 1–2, also function as a sub-group in their own right, separating the *hllwyh* collection (Pss 111–117) from the *Songs of Ascents* collection (Pss 120–134).[4] The third level of canonical analysis suggested by Hossfeld and Zenger still needs to be addressed, however. Namely, how do these sub-groupings now function when read in the light of the final, five-book structure of the Book of Psalms? Why are they to be found where they are, and how does their position impact the reader's interpretation of the Psalter? It is to this level of analysis that we now turn our attention.

In order to set about answering this question of how the torah-kingship psalm groupings influence psalm interpretation on a macro-level, we shall look first at how each psalm grouping functions within its respective Book of the Psalter and then how they influence the interpretation of the whole Psalter. However, before turning to this question, there is one issue of method which needs to be more clearly defined: that is, how does one go about defining what constitutes a psalm grouping?

2. Assessing Psalm Groupings: Conjunctive and Disjunctive Features

As discussed in chapter 1, an important element in the canonical approach to the study of the Psalms is the question of linked groups of psalms and their

---

[2] Sheppard, *Wisdom*, 136–44; Miller, "Beginning," 84–87. See above, chapter 2.
[3] Hossfeld and Zenger, *Die Psalmen I*, 12–13, 105ff; Miller, "Kingship," 127–28; Auffret, *La Sagesse*, 407–38. See above, chapter 3.
[4] Freedman, *Psalm 119*, 4; Mitchell, *Message*, 87. See above, chapter 4.

placement within the Psalter.⁵ Scholars point out how keywords (*Leitwörter* or *Stichwortbeziehungen*) or shared theological themes run through groups of juxtaposed psalms indicating the creation of a psalm grouping through deliberate concatenation.⁶ Wilson, to take just one example, points out that before the emergence of canonical readings of the Psalms, "Few have considered the relation of groups of psalms to the books in which they reside, or to the final-form of the Psalter itself."⁷ The implication is that the editorial association of psalms into groups sheds light on the theological priorities of the compilers of the Psalter and provides a broader context for the interpretation of individual compositions.⁸ However, whilst there is general acceptance of the fact that analysis and understanding of the function of psalm groupings is vital if we are to truly understand the "message" of the Psalter, one finds relatively little methodological discussion of how one defines "a psalm grouping."

The key factor in discerning "groups of psalms" seems to be the abovementioned principle of concatenation through the use of keywords or the repetition of themes.⁹ Obviously, this is an essential feature indicating the deliberate association of juxtaposed psalms: where there is no repetition of words, ideas and motifs the reader makes no connection between neighbouring psalms. There is, however, an element of subjectivity in the definition of keyword linking. When does the concatenation come to an end? Where did it begin? Sometimes linked groups of psalms have a very clear beginning and end,¹⁰ but often this linking is more difficult to define.¹¹

---

⁵ See the discussion of method in chapter 1.
⁶ Howard, *Structure*, 100–02; Wilson, *Editing*, 182–97; Wilson, "Understanding," 48; Mays, "Question of Context," 16–17.
⁷ Wilson, "Understanding," 43.
⁸ Mays, "Ps 118"; "Question of Context," 21–28; Childs, *IOTS*, 518; David M. Howard, "A Contextual Reading of Psalms 90–94," in *The Shape and Shaping of the Psalter* (ed. J. Clinton McCann; JSOTSup 159; Sheffield: JSOT Press, 1993); Murphy, "Reflections."
⁹ Hossfeld and Zenger, *Die Psalmen I*, 24, 45, 51, passim; VanGemeren, *Psalms*, 20–21; Mitchell, *Message*, 56; McCann, *Psalms*, 653; Wilson, "Understanding," 48; Howard, *Structure*, 100; Mays, *The Lord Reigns*, 120–21; Murphy, "Reflections," 21.
¹⁰ For example, the Songs of Ascents (Pss 120–134) in Book V or the Kingship of Yahweh psalms (Pss 93–99) in Book IV (see Howard, *Structure*).
¹¹ For example, how does the preponderance of laments in Book I relate to the question of groupings?

If a proper understanding of psalm groupings is key to the canonical approach to the study of the Psalter, then the method of delimiting groups of psalms needs to be more clearly expressed than it is at present. I would suggest that concatenation via keyword linking is not *always* sufficient to define a psalm grouping.[12] As well as looking for linking, the reader should also look for indicators of editorial separation of groups of psalms from their setting. The whole idea of a psalm grouping implies both a *conjunctive* and a *disjunctive* literary function. On the one hand, the idea of a "psalm grouping" implies a degree of connection between the psalms within that grouping, and, logically, it in turn implies a degree of separation from the other neighbouring psalms which are *not* part of this psalm grouping. To date psalm groupings have been defined largely by focussing on the factors that link the psalms under examination. Little consideration has been paid to the factors which separate a group of psalms from its near neighbours.[13] This seems to be a methodological weakness and clearer definition must be given to this important factor within the canonical approach.

With regard to the torah-kingship psalms, we have already looked in some detail at the factors which link these groups or pairings.[14] However, we must also consider the disjunctive functions at work in each of these psalm groupings: that is, how are these groups of psalms distinct from their surroundings? It seems reasonable to expect that both of these characteristics are present if one is to describe a set of juxtaposed psalms as a "psalm grouping." Where only one of these characteristics is observable (be that conjunctive or disjunctive function), the evidence of that single function must be weighty if we are to accept that these juxtaposed compositions were, indeed, designed to function as a group. Therefore, throughout this discussion of how the torah-kingship psalms influence the reading of their respective Books and, indeed, of the whole Psalter, we shall assess both conjunctive and disjunctive features which delineate the extent of these groupings.

---

[12] Murphy, for example, expresses the need for caution in the association of psalms due to linguistic repetition ("Reflections," 22–23, 28).

[13] To be fair to Wilson, in the presentation of his method he speaks of the "'separating' and 'binding' functions of author and genre groupings,'" (*Editing*, 199). However, in the literature which has subsequently adopted Wilson's canonical method, considerably more attention has been paid to the discussion of "binding functions" than has been paid to the discussion of "separating functions."

[14] Chapters 2–4 show evidence of linkage via shared vocabulary and theology etc.

3. PSALMS 1–2: BOOK I, THE DAVIDIC PSALTER(S) AND THE PSALTER

It is widely acknowledged that Pss 1–2 form the introduction to the Book of Psalms, indeed, this is often cited as one of the main indicators of purposeful, editorial activity in the compilation of the Psalter.[15] Seldom are the implications of this theory discussed in detail, however.[16] This first psalm grouping does give rise to a number of questions. For example, in what ways is this psalm grouping conjoined to the succeeding psalms and in what ways is it set apart as a pairing separate from the rest of Book I? Also, is this an introduction the whole Psalter, to Book I or to both? And, how does this affect our reading of the Psalms?

The first two psalms are linked by substantial internal linguistic, conceptual and theological repetition—that they are meant to be read together seems highly likely.[17] However, these two works can be described as a "psalm grouping" not only because of the internal linking factors, but also because of the unusual characteristics which separate them from the general content of Book I of the Psalter.

3.1 DISJUNCTIVE: LACK OF SUPERSCRIPTION

One of the most striking features of Books I–III of the Psalter is the almost universal presence of "authorship"[18] designations within the superscriptions of

---

[15] Childs, *IOTS*, 513–14; Sheppard, *Wisdom*, 142; Howard, *Structure*, 202–05; Miller, "Beginning," 84–85; Mays, "Place of the Torah-Psalms"; McCann, *Psalms*, 664.

[16] This is one of the reasons given by Whybray for his critique of the canonical approach (see Whybray, *Psalms as a Book*, 78–81).

[17] See the discussion in chapter 2, above.

[18] The significance of these designations is a complex question. Traditionally, the named superscriptions were treated as signs of authorship, i.e. לדוד was understood to signify that David had written any work headed by such a superscription. Critical scholarship, however, rejected this thesis for various reasons (linguistic and historical), instead suggesting that the superscriptions were late additions which bore no real similarity to the original *Sitz im Leben* of the text. This led to some modern English translations of the OT omitting the superscriptions entirely, despite the fact that they are part of the Hebrew text (e.g. NEB, the GNB included the s/ss only as footnotes, and of the EVV only the NASB follows the MT's verse numbering which includes the s/ss). Recent developments in the study of the Psalter have reframed the discussion somewhat (Wilson, *Editing*, 9–11, passim; Childs, *IOTS*, 521 and Howard, *Structure*, 103–04). Rather than discussing the historical implications of such designations (i.e. does a Davidic superscription imply Davidic authorship?), scholars now seek to discuss the literary functions of the s/ss (i.e., how does this particular heading relate to the s/ss or the content of neighbouring psalms?). For helpful discussion of the role and functions of superscriptions within the Psalter, see Brevard S. Childs, "Psalm Titles and Midrashic Exegesis," *JSS* 16, no. 2 (Autumn 1971): 137–49 and Nogalski, "From Psalm to Psalms."

each psalm. Of the 89 psalms in Books I–III, all but four of them (ignoring Psalms 1–2 for the time being) bear named superscriptions—the exceptions being Psalms 10, 33, 43 and 71. Wilson has argued that the placement of an untitled psalm immediately after a titled psalm is an editorial device to indicate the connection of these two compositions.[19] This argument is given added credence in the treatment of the above-mentioned psalms in various ancient texts. The Septuagint, for example, joins Psalms 9 and 10 as a single composition and adds Davidic superscriptions to Psalms 33 and 71. The textual apparatus of the BHS itself acknowledges that Psalms 9–10 and 42–43 are probably to be read together, the first of these pairings likely forming some sort of incomplete acrostic composition.[20] Howard comments that, "[T]here is good evidence that the juxtaposition of an untitled psalm with a preceding titled one is an editorial device to signal the latter psalm's association with the preceding one. In some cases—most notably Psalms 9–10 and 42–43—the second psalm was originally almost certainly a unified part of the preceding psalm. In several cases, however, psalms that are almost universally judged to have been originally independent compositions now appear in the MT as 'pairs' in which the first is titled and the second is untitled."[21]

Therefore, taking into account the fact that almost all of the psalms in Books I–III are headed by a superscription and that the few which are not are linked with preceding titled psalms, the omission of superscriptions in Psalms 1 and 2 is a marked disjunctive feature, separating this psalm grouping from its immediate context. This effect is accentuated when read in the light of the prominence of David in the superscriptions of Psalms 3–72.[22] The combination of this disjunc-

---

[19] Wilson, *Editing*, 173–77.

[20] Freedman, *Psalm 119*, 15.

[21] Howard, *Structure*, 103–04.

[22] If we accept the above hypothesis linking Pss 10, 33, 43 and 71 with their preceding Davidic psalms, then the figure of King David truly dominates Books I–II. Separated only by Pss 42–50 (the superscriptions of which refer to the sons of Korah and Asaph), the reader is confronted with two lengthy Davidic collections (Pss 3–41 and 51–72, Ps 72 is a Solomonic psalm rather than Davidic, however the content of this psalm is often taken to be a prayer of David for his son who is about to succeed him as king, [deClaissé-Walford, "Canonical Shape," 103]). Hence, these two collections are often referred to as the first and second Davidic psalters. This Davidic dominance is further emphasised by the postscript found in Ps 72:20: כלו תפלות דוד בן־ישׁי, "Thus end the prayers of David, son of Jesse." See Mays, *The Lord Reigns*, 123ff; Sheppard, *Wisdom*, 144 and Allen, "David as Exemplar," for further discussion of the figure of David in the Psalter.

tive device and the conjunctive intertextual associations which link these two works indicates clearly that Pss 1 and 2 were meant to be understood as a subgroup within the broader context of the Psalter. Thus, in one sense, Pss 1 and 2 are set apart from their immediate context in Book I and we shall discuss the implications of this effect below.

3.2 CONJUNCTIVE: THE DAVIDIC KING IN PSALMS 1–2

The disjunctive evidence found in the lack of Davidic superscriptions would tend to suggest that the function of this introductory psalm grouping is related more to the Psalter as a whole than it is to Book I or, more broadly, to the first and second Davidic psalters (Pss 3–41 and 51–72). However, such a conclusion would be to ignore the *content* of Psalms 1 and 2. The figure of the king is prominent in the joint message of these two psalms. The "blessed man" of Psalm 1 and the "king/son/messiah" of Psalm 2 are figures which become linked by way of shared vocabulary and theology.[23] This association between the righteous one who delights in Yahweh's torah and Yahweh's regent installed in Zion alerts the reader of the Psalter to the torah-kingship theology of Deut 17:14–20.[24] As this reader immerses herself in the text of the Book of Psalms, moving from introduction into the first and second Davidic psalters, punctuated only by nine psalms which bear no immediately apparent royal association,[25] it would be hard for her not to read the figure of King David back into the anonymous, righteous ruler of the introduction. As Zenger comments, "Wahrscheinlich denken die Redaktoren die Ps 1 und den Anfang des dem David zugeschriebenen Psalmenbuchs setzen, bei dem seliggepriesenen "Mann" zunächst an David als Psalmdichter und abgeleitet davon dann an alle, die in der Nachfolge Davids 'seine' Psalmen beten."[26] Therefore, it seems fair to suggest that Psalms 1–2 are also meant to be associated with the figure of David who so dominates Books I and II of the Psalter, thus also associating the introduction with Book I.

---

[23] Miller, "Beginning," 91–92.

[24] See chapter 5 above.

[25] Although it may well be that the Asaphite and Korahite psalms are also meant to be associated with David and a royal setting (see Eaton, *Kingship*, 21).

[26] Hossfeld and Zenger, *Die Psalmen I*, 47. Miller makes a similar point in "Beginning," 91–92, as does Sheppard in *Wisdom*, 142–44.

3.3 CONJUNCTIVE: PSALMS 1–2 CF. PSALM 41

Another feature which reconnects Psalms 1–2 with Book I is the linguistic and conceptual association of Psalms 1 and 2 with Psalm 41 which concludes the first section of the Book of Psalms. Whilst this association is not quite as strong as the internal linkage between Psalms 1 and 2 themselves, the shared vocabulary between introduction and conclusion is substantial and suggests that their placement within Book I is not accidental.

	Psalms 1–2		Psalm 41
Ps 1:1/2:12	אשרי	Ps 41:2	אשרי
Ps 2:10	השכילו	Ps 41:2	משכיל
Ps 1:2	חפצו	Ps 41:12	חפצו
Ps 1:6	תאבד	Ps 41:6	ואבד
Ps 1:5	לא יקמו	Ps 41:9	לא־יוסיף יקום

As well as this lexical repetition, there are also conceptual connections between Psalms 2 and 41. "Together, they plot against me, all those who hate me" (v 8, יחד עלי יתלחשו כל שנאי) bears marked similarities to the kings and leaders of the nations plotting in vain against Yahweh and his anointed one in Ps 2:1–2. Similarly, the protection, preservation, blessing and deliverance from enemies in Ps 41:3 echoes the idea of Yahweh's protection and exoneration of Ps 2's king in the face of his enemies. Mitchell points out that, "There are also lexical links between Psalms 1 and 41, which form an inclusio demarcating the boundaries of Book I of the Psalter."[27] Wilson has, also, noted that Psalm 2, "finds echoes in the concerns of Psalm 41, which concludes the first book. There David as the author speaks of the assurances of YHWH's protection and security in the face of the malicious murmuring of his enemies."[28]

3.4 CONCLUSION REGARDING PLACEMENT OF PSALMS 1–2

What conclusions then can be drawn from this observation of both conjunctive and disjunctive features at work in Psalms 1–2 in relation to the opening book of the Psalter? It seems apparent that Psalms 1–2 are indeed a late addition to a pre-existing "psalter," added at some stage in the canonical book's development.[29] The disjunctive effect of the lack of Davidic superscription tends to sug-

---

[27] Mitchell, *Message*, 74.
[28] Wilson, *Editing*, 209–10.
[29] It is difficult to say with any degree of certainty when Pss 1–2 were added to the Psalter. Miller's comments reflect this uncertainty when he writes, "We are not making

gest that this introduction is meant to be applied beyond the immediate context of the Davidic psalters (Books I-II). Indeed, the desire of the editors not to associate these introductory psalms too closely with their immediate context—despite the fact that their content would readily lend itself to the addition of Davidic superscriptions[30]—tends to suggest that Psalms 1-2 were designed to function as a hermeneutical construct for the whole Book of Psalms at whatever stage they were added, "Together they form a joint preface to the *entire* Psalter."[31]

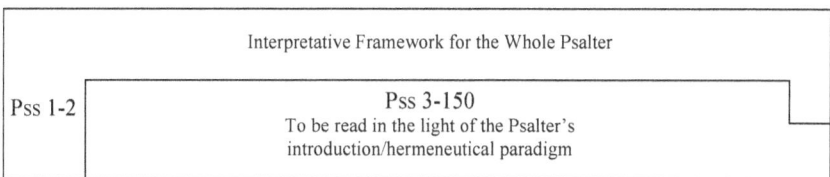

Figure 1. Pss 1-2 re. Whole Psalter

---

any effort to decide at what redactional stage Psalms 1 and 2 were added to the beginning of the Psalter as an introduction. As Sheppard has noted, this combined prologue may have been added at the latest stage in the redactional history of the Psalter or to an earlier smaller collection ending with either Psalm 119 or Psalm 41. Once the redactional move has been made, the introductory function works on all levels. We are attempting to show that is particularly the case with the first book of the Psalter without assuming necessarily that the Prologue was added at that point or is to be confined to that book in its function," ("Beginning," 87). See also S. R. A. Starbuck, *Court Oracles in the Psalms: The So-Called Royal Psalms in Their Ancient Near Eastern Context* (SBLDS 172; Atlanta: Scholars Press, 1999), 110, who is similarly unsure of the chronology of when the introduction was added. This issue shall be discussed further below, pp 246–50.

[30] This is seen most clearly in the fact that Acts 4:25 introduces the citation of Ps 2:1-2 with the words, "You spoke by the Holy Spirit through the mouth of our father, David, your servant..." (ὁ τοῦ πατρὸς ἡμῶν διὰ πνεύματος ἁγίου στόματος Δαυὶδ παιδός σου εἰπών). It appears that, by the first century C.E., Psalm 2 had come to be seen as a Davidic psalm. This probably occurred partially, because of its content and, partially because of the broader association of the whole Psalter with David. Sheppard comments that, "In this regard, it is striking that Ps 2 lacks a title because, unlike most psalms, it presumes Davidic authorship by internal evidences. This statement, "the Lord said to me," and what follows recall the oracle of Nathan to David. Furthermore, the absence of a title for Ps 2 is highly significant because it offers internal evidence to invite such a titular designation, even during a time when untitled psalms were progressively gaining them," (Sheppard, *Wisdom*, 139). See also Mays, *The Lord Reigns*, 121–27.

[31] Sheppard, *Wisdom*, 141. See also Mitchell, *Message*, 73–74, 87; McCann, *Theological Introduction*, 40–41; Mays, *The Lord Reigns*, 121–23 etc.

Yet, at the same time, there are indeed observable links between Psalms 1–2 and the first and second Davidic psalters. What is more there also seems to have been an attempt to link Psalms 1–2 with Psalm 41 forming an inclusio which delimits Book I of the Psalter. Therefore, the literary function of Psalms 1–2 is perhaps more complex than simply saying that it functions as an introduction to the Book of Psalms. This introduction is linked to Book I by its linguistic and content associations with Psalm 41 and it is linked to Books I–II by way of the figure of David.[32] Miller writes that, "Pss 1 and 2 provide a kind of interpretive key to the Psalter and particularly to the first book, Pss 3–41."[33] DeClaissé-Walford arrives at a similar conclusion:

> Another explanation [of the change from third to first person address in Ps 41] is that the community which shaped the Psalter added verses 2–4... to the beginning of the first-person psalm to tie Book One securely with Psalms 1 and 2. These verses are, then, another "footprint" of the shaping community. The end of Book One brings the reader back to the Torah, the instruction, at the beginning of the Psalter: "Happy is the one who trusts in YHWH."[34]

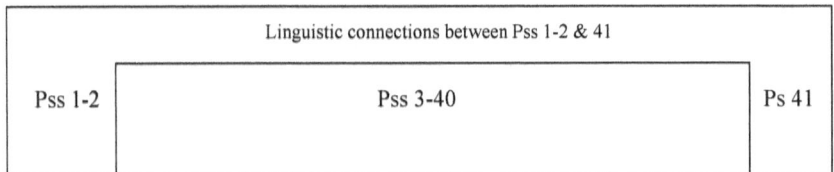

Figure 2. Pss 1, 2, & 41 as Book I Inclusio

---

[32] It should be pointed out that this Davidic association comes to be read with an idealised tone. The superscriptions which add a historical setting to Davidic psalms place the figure of David within its DtrH context, and in doing so they provide a rubric for the interpretation and application of these psalms by the reader (Childs, "Psalm Titles," 148). This association adds to the eschatological tone of the Psalms. Miller suggests with regard to Psalms 1–2 that, "the king, indeed David, is a representative figure, and never more so than as the one who lives by the Lord's Torah," ("Beginning," 91). Similarly, Mays writes, "The David in the psalms is the king of the Lord, the servant of the Lord, the chosen one, the anointed one (messiah), with whom the Lord has made covenant by solemn oath that his dynasty will last forever.... The 'messiah' or the 'king' or God's 'servant' are textual directions to think of David. When the psalms attributed to David are read in light of what is said in the psalms about him, a messianic construal is cast over the collection. It was inevitable that the psalms would be read in the light of promises of a future Davidic messiah. The role of Psalm 2 as introduction to the canoni-

The combined effect of these two phenomena on the interpretation of the Psalter is very interesting. On the one hand, as discussed above, the disjunctive function of the lack of superscriptions indicates that the introduction functions as a hermeneutical paradigm for the interpretation of the whole Psalter. In effect, this places the agenda reflected in the introduction beyond strict association with the Davidic psalters to incorporate *all* of the rich theological veins found in the complete book. Yet, on the other hand, the association of the introduction with Book I and the figure of David, is also clear to the reader of the Psalms. The net effect of this two-fold interaction is that the figure of David is read back *into* the introduction which is applied to the whole Psalter, leaving a decidedly Davidic flavour to the complete Book of Psalms—going beyond the obvious Davidic dominance in Books I–II.

> In sum, Ps 1 and 2 have been redactionally ordered in a combined prologue to the Psalter.... Ps 1 and 2 correlate the study of the Torah collection with the goal of attaining sacred wisdom like that found in the wisdom traditions, and perhaps in a set of biblical wisdom books. *By his associations with Ps 2, David, who is, in canonical terms, the chief architect of the Psalter, is identified fully in accord with the ideals of Psalm 1. The entire Psalter, therefore, is made to stand theologically in association with David as a source book of guidance for the way of the righteous.* In this fashion, the Psalter has gained, among its other functions, the use as a source for Wisdom reflection and a model of prayers based on such a pious interpretation of the Torah.[35]

> David has become firmly associated with the whole book of Psalms. Despite the presence of many psalms assigned to other figures before and after his time, the presentation of David within the book and elsewhere in Scripture provides the key sign of the book's coherence, as well as the context of its interpretation as a part of a larger Scripture. We begin to realise that the pre-scriptural hymns can be heard scripturally only when they are heard in just this association with David.[36]

> Thus the hermeneutical clues given for interpreting the Psalms by those who provided the headings say that it was primarily David's voice that has to be

---

cal book is only one piece of evidence that prophecy has become a rubric in terms of which all the psalms may be read." He goes on to add, "In turn, David's life becomes an illustration for those who use the psalms, of the way in which a life whose hope is in the reign of God is to be lived," (*The Lord Reigns*, 96, 98).

[33] Miller, "Kingship," 127.

[34] deClaissé-Walford, *Reading from the Beginning*, 56.

[35] Sheppard, *Wisdom*, 142 (emphasis added).

[36] Gerald T. Sheppard, *The Future of the Bible: Beyond Liberalism and Literalism* (Toronto: United Church Publishing House, 1990), 84.

heard in the Psalter. This one voice, which makes audible the *cantus firmus* of all the Psalms, is the voice of the promised king of Israel, the Messiah.[37]

What then can one conclude from the function of this psalm grouping as an introduction to the Psalter? The reader is invited to follow an example in his interpretation and application of the psalms. The exemplar is David—presented as the ideal of kingship following the idealistic Kingship Law—and the example which he sets is one of torah obedience and trust in Yahweh.[38] The editorial function of this psalm grouping is marked, it sends out a clear signal to the reader: namely, the promotion of two key Dtr theological priorities, that is, to live life in accordance with the torah of Yahweh and to trust entirely in God—just as David did.

> The effect of this linking [of torah and kingship psalms]... is to present David as the model Israelite whose relationship with Yahweh and obedience to Torah are the ideal to which every worshipper of Yahweh should aspire.[39]

4. Psalms 18–21 within Book I of Psalter

The local function of the psalm grouping in which Pss 18–21 are found is, perhaps, more readily understandable than was the case with Pss 1–2. Clearly the chiastically-structured grouping of Pss 15–24 is part of Book I of the Psalter. The question, however, remains as to the significance of this fact: what role does psalm grouping 15–24 (and therefore the kingship-torah grouping 18–21) play within Book I? Also, how does its function within Book I relate this grouping to the rest of the Psalter?

Whilst Auffret, Miller and others helpfully discuss the internal—that is, conjunctive—features of the psalm grouping 15–24, there is little discussion of how this grouping relates to the rest of Book I.[40] As far as I am aware, the only broader discussion of how Pss 15–24 fit within the first book of the Psalter is to be found in Hossfeld and Zenger's commentary *Die Psalmen*. They suggest that Pss 15–24 form one of four psalm groupings which together make up Book I.[41] Hossfeld and Zenger's division of Book I as suggested by follows this pattern:

---

[37] Hans-Joachim Kraus, *Theology of the Psalms* (trans. K. Crim; Minneapolis: Augsburg, 1986), 176.
[38] Gerbrandt, *Kingship*, 173; Allen, "David as Exemplar," 545.
[39] Wagner, "Psalm 19 as Prayer," 257n52.
[40] Auffret, *La Sagesse*, 407–38; Miller, "Kingship."
[41] Hossfeld and Zenger, *Die Psalmen I*, 12.

The Editorial Placement of the Torah-Kingship Psalm Groupings   235

Book I divides into four sub-groups			
Pss 3-14	Pss 15-24	Pss 25-34	Pss 35-41

Figure 3. Hossfeld/Zenger on Book I

This observation is based on two factors: first, the use of psalms of the same type as corner psalms (*Eckpsalmen*) delimiting the extent of each grouping; and, secondly, the inclusion of a central psalm in each collection which is markedly different in type/content from the neighbouring psalms within that sub-group.[42]

> Die stark anthropologisch orientierte Sammlung, die als Komposition eine umfassende Deutung der condition humaine bieten will, ist in die vier Teilgruppen 3-14, 15-24, 25-34, 35-41 gegliedert. Diese Gliederung ist zum einen durch die jeweiligen Eckpsalmen angezeigt, die vielfältig aufeinander hingeordnet sind. Zum anderen zind die Teilgruppen durch Psalmen im Zentrum markiert, die ihrerseits inhaltlich und formal aus ihrer Umgebung herausragen (Ps 8 – ein Hymnus inmitten von Klagen; Ps 19 – ein Gotteslob unter Königsgebeten; Ps 29 – ein JHWH-Hymnus im Kreis von Bitt- und Dankgebeten; Ps 38 – ein Bittgebet mit Konzentration der Hauptthemen der Nachbarpsalmen wie Krankheit, Feinde, Sünde, Südenbekenntis). Darüber hinaus sind sie motivlich-theologisch aufeinander bezogen.[43]

The question which must now be raised is whether one observes similar conjunctive and disjunctive features at work in each of these proposed sub-groups to indicate that they are indeed designed to function as a psalm grouping? Psalms 15-24 seem to exhibit both conjunctive and disjunctive functions as a result of the chiastic structure employed in this sub-group. We have already discussed the conjunctive features which unite these individual psalmic compositions into a collection—the chiastic structure of Entrance Liturgies (Pss 15 and 24), psalms of comfort (Pss 16 and 23), psalms of lament (Pss 17 and 22), kingship psalms expressing dependence upon Yahweh (Pss 18 and 20-21), and the pivotal torah-psalm (Ps 19).[44] The repetition of Entrance Psalms at the beginning and end of this collection sets the limits of this sub-group, delimiting the boundaries by use

---

[42] Hossfeld and Zenger, *Die Psalmen I*, 12.
[43] Hossfeld and Zenger, *Die Psalmen I*, 12.
[44] See chapter 3 above, pp 72-74. This chiastic structure is further accentuated by linguistic and thematic correspondences between the psalms of this grouping.

of this inclusio.[45] However, one must ask oneself the question, would the inclusio marked by Pss 15 and 24—a disjunctive function—be sufficient in and of itself to indicate that Pss 15–24 function as a sub-group? I would suggest not. Rather, the disjunctive function marked by the inclusio of Entrance Liturgies is combined with the conjunctive function of linguistic concatenation and chiastic structural association, thus linking the psalms throughout the collection to indicate that Pss 15–24 are, indeed, a sub-group in their own right.

The same question must be asked of the suggested sub-groups posited by Hossfeld and Zenger—can the reader discern both disjunctive and conjunctive features which would set these groupings apart as collections or sub-groups in their own right? Their observation concerning the corner psalms (*Eckpsalmen*) in these suggested collections is an astute and interesting one, possibly indicating disjunctive function.[46] Pss 3 and 14 are both laments in which the psalmist beseeches Yahweh for deliverance from his enemies; Pss 15 and 24, as we have seen above, are both Entrance Liturgies; Pss 25 and 34 are both acrostic petitions with marked Wisdom elements;[47] and, in the lament Pss 35 and 41, the psalmist again calls upon Yahweh to deal with his enemies. This phenomenon could indicate that these psalms mark the borders of previous groupings which were incorporated together to form Book I of the Psalter. It should be noted, however, that *at best* this phenomenon indicates only the possibility of *disjunctive* function. It seems reasonable to suggest that, before these groups of psalms can truly be classified as groupings, there should be some indication of features which *link* the psalms within the boundaries set by these corner psalms.

---

[45] An inclusio, by definition, indicates disjunctive function. Compositions on either side of the bracketing poems are automatically understood to lie beyond the collection.

[46] Hossfeld and Zenger, *Die Psalmen I*, 12.

[47] This association requires further discussion, however. As is acknowledged by Hossfeld and Zenger, there are also marked similarities in content between Pss 25 and 37 (also an acrostic) particularly in terms of the discussion of guidance, (*Die Psalmen I*, 162). It is debatable, therefore, as to which psalm would best correspond to Ps 25 in forming an inclusion. The prayer elements of Pss 25 and 34 lead Hossfeld and Zenger to associate these two psalms, however, the Wisdom elements of Pss 25 and 37 indicate association as well. Another question which requires more detailed consideration is the relationship between Pss 34 and 37—how are they associated? The answers to these questions influence the analysis of the "middle" psalms as suggested by Hossfeld and Zenger, and, indeed, the notion of Pss 25–34 as a grouping.

The Editorial Placement of the Torah-Kingship Psalm Groupings   237

Part of the difficulty in assessing the content of psalm groupings within Book I is the general dominance of lament psalms with in the first Davidic psalter.[48] This is a feature which has often been noted in canonical studies of the Psalter—the movement from a preponderance of lament psalms in Books I–III (especially in Pss 3–41) to a majority of hymns of praise and thanksgiving in Books IV–V.[49] This general predominance of laments makes it difficult for the reader to ascertain, based either on content, type or superscription (all of which are Davidic), whether or not neighbouring psalms have been deliberately placed alongside one another to form a specific sub-group or are they simply part of a larger collection dominated by laments? Can these *Eckpsalmen*[50] truly be described as demarcating groups of psalms, or are they merely representative of the dominance of lament in Book I?[51] Also, it is difficult to know what to make of Hossfeld and Zenger's suggestion that the centre psalm in each of these "collections" is markedly different from the surrounding psalms.[52] This is clearly the case with regard to Psalm 19, as one would expect of the pivotal composition in

---

[48] J. Clinton McCann, "Wisdom's Dilemma: The Book of Job, the Final Form of the Book of Psalms, and the Entire Bible," in *Wisdom, You Are My Sister: Studies in Honor of Roland E. Murphy, O. Carm., on the Occasion of His Eightieth Birthday* (CBQMS 29; ed. Michael. L Barre; Washington D.C.: Catholic Biblical Association of America, 1997), 25–26; Miller, "Current Issues," 141; William H Bellinger, "Portraits of Faith: The Scope of Theology in the Psalms," in *An Introduction to Wisdom Literature and the Psalms: Festschrift Marvin E. Tate* (ed. H. W. Ballard and W. D. Tucker; Macon, GA: Mercer University Press, 2000), 121; Mays, *Psalms*, 16, 51–54; deClaissé-Walford, "Canonical Shape," 96–97.

[49] Sheppard, *Future of the Bible*, 74–75; Miller, "Current Issues," 141; Westermann, *Praise and Lament*, 252, 257–58. Westermann writes that, "Book One contains almost exclusively Psalms of the individual and, even at first glance, in the entire first book LI (the lament of the individual) is absolutely predominant...." (p 252).

[50] Two of the four suggested sub-groups of psalms are marked by laments as their *Eckpsalmen*.

[51] In a similar vein, Vincent comments with regard to McCann's observation that the seam psalms in Books I–III which are not royal, are laments: "Second, the observation that Pss 3, 42 and 73 are laments is uninteresting, since most of the other psalms in these books are laments also. Psalm 3 does not stand out from any of the psalms which follow it as a lament; neither does Ps 42. In no way can these psalms be said to betray a clue about the organisational shaping of the Psalter; they are merely typical of the psalms that are to follow later in the respective book," ("Shape of Psalter," 72–73). A similar conclusion could be offered with regard to the suggestion that Pss 3, 14, 35 and 41 indicate the beginning and end of collections of psalms.

[52] Hossfeld and Zenger, *Die Psalmen I*, 12.

a chiastic structure. However, the evidence with regard to the other possible psalm groupings is mixed: Psalm 38, for example, does not appear to be *markedly* different from the other psalms in that "grouping." Even were we to accept that each of these groups of psalms did have a central composition substantially different in content from the others, one must ask oneself about the significance of this fact? What exactly does this establish? Is this an indicator of conjunctive function within each of these "sub-groups" or, indeed, between "sub-groups?" It is unclear whether the central psalms of these groupings really are so very different from their neighbours, and, even were this the case, the significance of this phenomenon is unclear.

What conclusions then can be drawn from the Hossfeld/Zenger suggestion that Book I divides into four sub-groups? Certainly, disjunctive functions *may* be at work in accordance with their thesis. The similarity in type and content of each of the psalms which begin and conclude these "groups" could be described as distinctive with regard to two of the suggested groupings (Pss 15–24 and 25–34) and they could be said to bracket prior collections of compositions.[53] Other than this, the general preponderance of laments in Book I makes it difficult to suggest how Psalms 3–41 divide up into collections. Apart from the case of Psalms 15–24, there appears to be a lack of obvious conjunctive editorial activity linking the psalms within the boundaries suggested by the corner psalms. That is not to say that there is no evidence of linking between the psalms in these groups, however, further research seems to be required in order to establish clear indications of concatenation between the individual compositions of the remaining three suggested collections.

Therefore, the reader is left with a situation in which she may be able to observe the placement of psalms which seem to indicate a disjunctive function, separating Book I into four sub-groups. Yet, with the exception of psalm grouping 15–24, there are no obvious signs of the conjunctive association of psalms within these "groups." So we are left with (somewhat debatable) signs of disjunctive activity and no real signs of conjunctive activity in the three other suggested sub-groups. What conclusion is the reader to draw from this? On balance, it seems unlikely that Book I divides into four defined sub-groups of psalms.

---

[53] However, please note the above-mentioned caveat with regard to the associations between Pss 25, 34 and 37.

4.1 PSALMS 18–21: CENTRAL TO BOOK I

An alternative, tentative thesis regarding the broader composition of Book I and the function of the Pss 15–24 subgroup within that collection would be to suggest that they make up a prior collection which has been placed in a roughly *central* position within the first Davidic psalter. The above consideration of the Pss 1–2 psalm grouping suggests that it functions as an introduction both to the whole Psalter and also to Book I, and, including these two compositions as part of Book I, the Pss 15–24 sub-group is preceded by 14 compositions and succeeded by 17 poetic works. Whilst, of course, this does not mean that Pss 15–24 are exactly central to Book I from an arithmetic point of view, it does tend to show that this collection dominates the heart of Pss 1–41.[54]

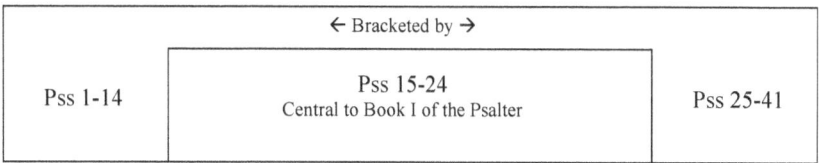

Figure 4. Pss 15-24 as Central to Book I

Even were we to accept Hossfeld and Zenger's theory about the division of Book I into four sub-groups, at the very least one could say that Pss 15–24 function as one of the central collections within the first book. Clearly, the incorporation of this collection, into the first Davidic psalter, makes a strong impact on the theological message of Book I as a whole. In Pss 1–41 we see a preponderance of psalms of lament, pleas, prayers for deliverance from enemies, sickness, trouble and despair. Whilst we do see elements of these themes within Pss 15–24 (e.g., Pss 17 and 22 are both laments), the dominant message of this collection is quite different from the overall tone of Book I. It is a message which points the reader towards the importance of Deuteronomic views of righteousness based in the law.[55] Psalms 15 and 24, at the beginning and the end of this

---

[54] Mathematical permutations do not appear to have been the guiding principle for the editorial activity which has taken place within the canonical Book of Psalms. This is seen, for example, by the varying (and apparently random) lengths of the five books of the Psalter—Book I contains 41 compositions, whereas Book IV consists of only 17. There is no indication that the ordering which has taken place in the Psalms is based around mathematical considerations. See, for example, McCann's discussion of the canonical centrality of Ps 73 (*Theological Introduction*, 143).

[55] Miller, "Kingship," 131; Brueggemann and Miller, "Psalm 73," 54–55.

collection, make it clear to the reader of the psalms that access to the Living God is to be found by living a life of righteousness with "clean hands and a pure heart."[56] This message is compounded by the central psalm's delight in the torah of Yahweh and the psalmist's prayer to be kept from sin that he too may walk in righteousness (Ps 19:13–15).[57] Such is the message that lies at the heart of Book I—amid the laments and the pleas borne out of despair—righteousness and relationship with God are to be found in the keeping of his torah.[58] This is the central message of the first Davidic psalter and we shall see a similar message lying at the heart of Book V of the Psalms.

5. Psalms 118–119: Central to Book V

Various solutions have been offered regarding the structure of Book V.[59] Each of these differs slightly from the others, yet each analysis shares one feature in common: somehow Psalm 119 is central to the structure of the Book, or, alternatively, Psalm 119 simply does not fit within the structure of the Book. Wilson, for example, writes: "The positioning of these three segments provides a collection characterised by a Davidic frame and *a center focused on the massive acrostic Psalm 119.*"[60] Similarly, Krantz sees Psalm 119 as having a special place within this Book of the Psalter "on the basis of his theory that the Psalter is the 'Torah of David' without defining it more closely in terms of its structure."[61] For Koch, Psalm 119 (together with Psalm 137) breaks the pattern which he proposes regarding the structure of Book V and its connections with Chronicles, and, therefore, he describes these psalms as "post-compositional additions."[62] Psalm 119 so dominates the landscape of Book V that—almost intuitively—the reader comes to the conclusion that somehow it must be the focal point of the Psalter's final addition.[63]

---

[56] Kraus, *Psalms*, 119–20.

[57] Wagner, "Psalm 19 as Prayer."

[58] Wagner, "Psalm 19 as Prayer," 257; Miller, "Kingship," 128; Creach, *Yahweh as Refuge*, 103; McCann, *Psalms*, 752; Bellinger, "Portraits of Faith," 116.

[59] See, for example, Zenger's analysis of the compositional theories of Wilson, Koch and Krantz, to which he adds his own suggestion, in his article "Composition."

[60] Wilson, "Shaping," 79 (emphasis mine).

[61] Zenger, "Composition," 88.

[62] See Zenger, "Composition," 84.

[63] Creach, *Yahweh as Refuge*, 102; Seybold, *Introducing*, 21–23.

The Editorial Placement of the Torah-Kingship Psalm Groupings   241

Erich Zenger also suggests a structural breakdown of Book V which places Psalm 119 at the heart of this collection.[64] He sees five sections within this Book: a Davidic, eschatological framework which brackets beginning and end (Pss 107–112 and 138–144/145); a festal framework referring, first, to the Exodus (Pss 113–118) and later to Zion (Pss 120–137); and, finally, Psalm 119 stands central to these collections in celebration of the Torah of Yahweh.[65]

R A	A			R A
107, 108-110, 111 & 112	113-118	119	120-136/137	138-144/145
David (eschatological/ messianic)	Exodus (Pesach)	Torah (Shabuoth)	Zion (Sukkoth)	David (eschatological/ messianic)

(R= royal psalm; A = acrostic psalm)
Figure 5. Zenger's Structural Analysis of Book V

Whilst I find myself in substantial agreement with Zenger's analysis of the content of Book V, there are some details which suggest a slightly different overall structure to Pss 107–145.

Zenger correctly highlights the function of both Davidic and festal frameworks in Book V,[66] however, there does appear to be a third framework which also plays a significant role in the breakdown of the overall structure of this book: namely, a "historical" framework. This is seen in Psalms 107, and then again in Psalms 135–137. Why so? First, contrary to the suggestion of Wilson and in line with Zenger, Ps 107 is not part of the Davidic framework, rather, its position appears to be an attempt to link Book V with Book IV as an extension to the previous form of the Psalter.[67] Psalms 105–106 provide a lengthy, poetic account of the history of Israel, and the repetition of Ps 106:1 in the first verse of Ps 107 is an attempt to connect these psalms[68] and, consequently, the "new" Book V to the previous version of the Book of Psalms. It must be said, however, that Ps 107 is not a historical psalm in precisely the same sense as are Pss 105–106, rather, it is a "typical" historical setting with wisdom overtones. Yet,

---

[64] Zenger, "Composition," 98.
[65] Zenger, "Composition," 98.
[66] Zenger, "Composition," 90, 98.
[67] Wilson, "Shaping," 79; Zenger, "Composition," 88. However, when Zenger comes to plot the overall structure of Book V, he does not seem to distinguish Ps 107 markedly from the first part of the Davidic collection ("Composition," 98, see Figure 5.)

the presentation of the psalm is as history—dealing with the past events of four types of people selected to make the psalmist's point (travellers returning from exile, prisoners suffering in chains, fools rebelling against God and sea-farers caught in a storm). The theological essence of the psalm is the same as that seen in Pss 105–106, namely, that Yahweh has looked after his people regardless of their circumstances, their rebellion, their stupidity or the depths of their plight.[69] Long before the canonical approach to the study of the psalms became popular, Kirkpatrick wrote regarding the doxology at the end of Ps 106, "It came to be regarded as marking the end of the fourth book, although Pss 106 and 107 are closely connected together, and the division of the fourth and fifth books does not correspond to any difference of source or character, as is the case in the other books."[70] Much more recently, Nancy deClaissé-Walford echoes this thought, writing: "Book Five opens with Ps 107, unquestionably placed at its beginning in answer to the request of the people at the end of Book Four."[71] Ps 107 does not naturally belong to the Davidic collection of Psalms 108–110,[72] on the contrary, it seems more closely connected with Pss 105–106 and its function is to link Book V into the Psalter as a continuum from Book IV.

Secondly, Pss 135–137 do not naturally belong with the Songs of Ascents (Pss 120–134), as Zenger suggests,[73] nor to the Davidic frame as Wilson suggests.[74] Again, the content of the psalms in question makes it clear that they are historical psalms, similar in content to the compositions which end Book IV and begin Book V. Zenger is correct in pointing out that the repetition of content from Ps 134:1–2 in Ps 135:2 does indicate linking,[75] however, this should not result in the inclusion of these psalms along with the Psalms of Ascents in terms of structure. On the contrary, the superscriptions which head each of Psalms 120–134 fulfil both conjunctive and disjunctive functions—the extent of the psalm grouping in question is made clear not, primarily, by the content of the

---

[68] Mays, *Psalms*, 344.
[69] Mays, *Psalms*, 342–47.
[70] Kirkpatrick, *Psalms*, 634.
[71] deClaissé-Walford, *Reading from the Beginning*, 93.
[72] As well as the content differences between Ps 107 and Pss 108–110 and content similarities between Ps 107 and Pss 105–106, it should also be pointed out that Ps 107 bears no Davidic superscription.
[73] Zenger, "Composition," 92.
[74] Wilson, "Shaping," 79.
[75] Zenger, "Composition," 92.

psalms, but by their superscriptions.[76] The inclusion of elements from Ps 134 at the beginning of Ps 135 appears, once again, to be an attempt to link and legitimate, the addition of other psalmic material to a previously existing version of the Book of Psalms.[77] Psalms 135–137 function as the second bracket of the historical frame within Book V. This historical frame combines with the Davidic and festal frames, which Zenger and Wilson have pointed out, to bracket the torah-kingship grouping (Pss 118–119) which lies at the structural centre of Book I, as the diagram below shows.

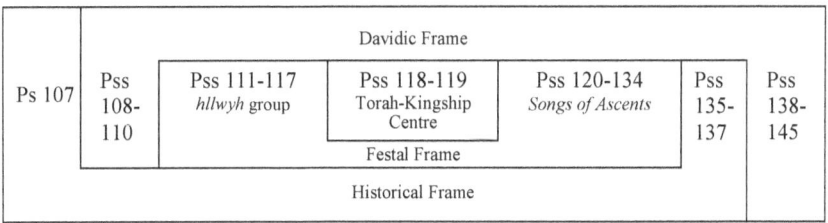

Figure 6. Pss 118-119 Central to Book V

We have already discussed at some length the reasons for linking Pss 118 and 119.[78] The historical frame, together with the Davidic and festal frames, form an altered chiastic structure centering around the torah-kingship sub-group. The reader observes both conjunctive and disjunctive factors in each of these psalm groupings based upon either superscription or content. Psalm 107 is linked with the content of Pss 105–106 and the reason that it comes first (altering the chiastic structure) is in order to link Book V with the pre-existing "Psalter" which previously ended with Book IV. Then follows the first part of the Davidic frame, as is clearly indicated by Davidic superscriptions, which, again, both link the three psalms within that grouping and set it apart from the neighbouring col-

---

[76] Westermann writes, "Psalms 120–134 constitute a self-contained book of Psalms which was later added to the collection framed by Pss 1 and 119" (*Praise and Lament*, 255).

[77] Westermann suggests that, at some point in the development of the canonical Psalter, Psalms 1 and 119 began and ended the book as a whole. His suggestion is that another pre-existing collection of psalms, the Songs of Ascents, was later added to this earlier form of the book and, yet later, further material was added to the Songs of Ascents giving us the final canonical form of the Psalter. See *Praise and Lament*, 253; Nogalski, "From Psalm to Psalms," 51–53 and Seybold, *Introducing*, 27–28.

[78] See chapter 4, above.

lections.⁷⁹ Following on from the Davidic collection comes the first element of the festal frame—the *hllwyh* group. Once again, the extent of this group is marked by the psalms' superscriptions/postscripts, each psalm is headed or concluded by a הללו־יה command.⁸⁰ Then, lying at the very heart of Book V, comes the torah-kingship pairing of Pss 118 and 119, which is followed by the correspondent sections of the festal (Pss 120–134), historical (Pss 135–137), and Davidic frames (Pss 138–145) respectively. As mentioned above, the שיר־המעלות superscriptions demarcate the extent of the second festal collection.⁸¹ The second part of the historical frame is indicated by their common lack of superscription and similarity of content. Finally, the second part of the Davidic frame is clearly indicated by the Davidic superscriptions in Pss 138–145.⁸²

Therefore, I would suggest that the Deuteronomic torah-kingship theology which marks the introduction to the whole Psalter and lies at the centre of Book I is also central to the message of Book V. This, in effect, results in a bracketing function encompassing the whole Book of Psalms.

6. Bracketing Function of Torah-Kingship Groupings

The net effect of the central positioning of the torah-kingship psalm groupings within Books I and V is to indicate a type of inclusio, a bracketing function encompassing the whole spectrum of the Psalms.⁸³ This effect is further accentuated by the over-arching influence of Pss 1–2 as the hermeneutical paradigm for the whole Psalter.⁸⁴ The message of the introduction is that the reader

---

⁷⁹ Seybold, *Introducing*, 18.
⁸⁰ Regarding Ps 114 and its superscription, see above p 123n6.
⁸¹ McCann, *Psalms*, 658.
⁸² Seybold, *Introducing*, 18.
⁸³ McCann, *Psalms*, 1167–68; Mays, *Psalms*, 381.
⁸⁴ Westermann, Seybold and others discuss the possibility that the Psalter once opened and closed with Pss 1 and 119 (Westermann, *Praise and Lament*, 253 and Seybold, *Introducing*, 27). Whilst this is possible, there is no diachronic evidence to support this hypothesis. However, their observation regarding the similarity of content and theology which led Westermann and Seybold to this conclusion can be applied in reading the final form of the text, leading to a slightly different conclusion. A formation-critical approach leads to the suggestion of a redactional layer where Pss 1 and 119 bracketed the psalms entirely, a synchronic analysis of the final-form leads to the idea of a torah-kingship bracketing function of Pss 1–2 and Pss 118–119. The introduction applies the theological priorities of Pss 1 and 2 to the whole Psalter and the repetition of these same themes at the centre of Books I and V has the same sort of effect. A syn-

The Editorial Placement of the Torah-Kingship Psalm Groupings   245

should have a heightened awareness of its dual themes—the practice of torah-piety and complete dependence upon Yahweh for the governance of all events, no matter how great the scale—throughout their reading of the Psalms, following the example of the kingly figure in Pss 1 and 2.[85] These dual themes make two further prominent appearances at the heart of Books I and V respectively. That is, the torah-kingship theme reappears in the middle of the first and last books,[86] and this repetition acts as a type of inclusio bracketing the whole Psalter within the same agenda as is presented by the introduction.

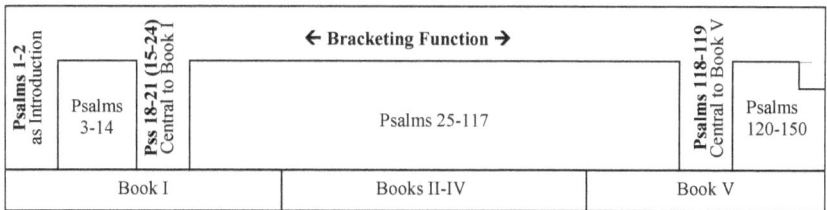

Figure 7. Bracketing Function of the Torah-Kingship Groupings

Returning to Hossfeld and Zenger's quote concerning the levels at which a canonical approach to the Psalms functions,[87] the evidence suggests that the positioning of these groups of psalms within the Psalter on a macro-level is as significant as their positioning within their respective books. The voice of the hermeneutical preface of the Psalms is reprised twice—once in the middle of the first book and again in the middle of the last book—further emphasising the fact that this theological programme is to have bearing upon the interpretation of the whole of the Book of Psalms.

---

chronic approach may be different from the diachronic suggestions of Westermann and Seybold, but the conclusion is similar: torah and kingship are important to the theology of the Psalms and this is accentuated by reading the structure of the Psalter.

[85] Mays comments, "The two psalms together call for a piety composed of obedience and trust that is fostered by the entire book. Delight in the torah and taking refuge in the Lord to constitute the faith nurtured by the psalms. The psalms offer a way and a refuge in the midst of the wickedness and power of the world," (*The Lord Reigns*, 123).

[86] Mays, "Place of the Torah-Psalms," 10; Creach, *Yahweh as Refuge*, 16.

[87] See above, p 223.

7. Excursus: A Brief Word about History

Whilst this study employs a synchronic approach throughout, as this chapter has also touched upon questions of formation, it seems appropriate to address the question of when these three psalm groupings were added to the Psalter. Most theories regarding the formation of the Book of Psalms take a strictly diachronic approach to this question, however, the problem with diachronic assessment of the composition of the Psalms is that the researcher is given so few internal, textual, historical reference points,[88] leaving assessment largely dependent upon external evidences. This problem is further compounded by the fact that the external evidence is scant and far from easy to interpret.[89] Shepherd comments

---

[88] For example, there are superscriptions which refer to events in the life of the historical David (e.g. Ps 3:1, Ps 18:1 etc.) but the self-presentation of these titles is as later additions so it is difficult to know what weight (if any) to attribute to these comments. Childs suggests that these titles may indicate that the superscriptions were added in a period when Midrash was becoming common in Israel (Childs, "Psalm Titles" see also, Nogalski, "From Psalm to Psalms"), but, again, does this add much to our understanding of when and how the various stages of the Book of Psalms developed? Other possible historical points of reference may be derived from the content of individual psalms aiding the diachronic task, e.g. references to the Temple (Pss 15, 24, 118 etc.); the demise of the Davidic kingship (Ps 89) or the return from exile (Ps 126), all place the Psalter in specific historical settings. However, at best this tells us little more than the fact that the final form of the Psalter was reached at some point in the post-exilic period—hardly an epiphany. Internal textual signs are few and far between because of the nature of the psalms. These compositions are meant to be generic (i.e. not tied too closely to specific historical events), so that as many people as possible are able to relate the expression of prayer or praise therein to the circumstances of their own lives (see Miller, *Interpreting*, 8, 48–52; "Trouble and Woe: Interpreting the Biblical Laments," *Int* 37 [1983]: 34–35 and Wilson, "Shape," 138). As the Psalms are not easily identifiable with historical events which sparked their writing, it becomes difficult even to find a starting point for a diachronic assessment of the formation of the Psalter.

[89] For example, one can see that the Psalms in some ways reflect a common ancient Near Eastern practice of gathering poetic anthologies (often with prominent royal themes). Sumerian, Akkadian and Babylonian hymns of a similar nature are often compared to Hebrew psalms (Wilson, *Editing*, 6). However, the relationship between the Psalms and these other ANE hymnic materials is a complex one and it is difficult to know just what significance to draw from these similarities, other than the fact that a common type of hymnic tradition existed in the ANE throughout the period when the psalms were written and gathered (Joel F. Drinkard, Jr., "The Ancient Near Eastern Context of the Book of Psalms," in *An Introduction to Wisdom Literature and the Psalms: Festschrift Marvin E. Tate* [ed. H. W. Ballard and W. D. Tucker; Macon, GA: Mercer University Press, 2000], 92). Another example would be Mowinckel's influential theory regarding the Autumn Festival where the Israelite king undergoes some element of ritual humilia-

that, "the available historical evidence allows for only a bare skeleton of this development [of the formation of the Psalter]. One searches largely in vain for solid biblical or extra-biblical evidence by which to trace the real causes and motivations behind many of the crucial decisions."[90] It goes beyond the remit of this thesis to enter into detailed diachronic discussion, however, the ideas mentioned above regarding the canonical placement of the torah-kingship psalm groupings may have a few implications for those engaging in historical research on the question of formation. Can the synchronic speak to diachronic? Yes, but only in a limited, broad brush-stroke manner. Some of the above observations may be of a little help with regard to the discussion of formation.

Which of the above sub-groups of psalms was the first to appear in the Psalter? Textual indications would suggest that Pss 18–21, as part of the prior collection of Pss 15–24, were probably the first to appear in the initial stages of formation as part of the first Davidic psalter.[91] The fact that the Pss 15–24 subgroup is part of the collection of Davidic compositions which have not

---

tion, suffering or battle (as reflected in the laments), before being ceremonially vindicated (enthronement psalms), an idea largely based on the Babylonian ’*akîtu* festival (Mowinckel, *PIW*, vol. 1, 106–92). Whilst this idea enjoyed some popularity for a considerable period of time, the lack of any evidence that such a festival took place in Israel has led to its rejection as an interpretative paradigm by most scholars in recent years (Brevard S. Childs, "Reflections on the Modern Study of the Psalms," in *Magnalia Dei: The Mighty Acts of God: Essays on the Bible and Archeology in Memory of G. Ernest Wright* [ed. F. M. Cross et al.; Garden City, N.Y.: Doubleday, 1976], 379–80; McCann, *Psalms*, 650; Mays, "Place of the Torah-Psalms," 12 etc., all speak of the movement away from cult-functional interpretation towards literary readings of the psalms). These are just two examples from many possible illustrations of the same point—it is notoriously difficult to build a conclusive theory regarding the formation and use of the psalms from diachronic evidence. A further example of this difficulty in interpreting historical evidence related to the Psalter would be the discussion surrounding the Qumran psalms manuscripts and the formation of the Psalter (see footnote 97, below).

[90] Shepherd, "The Book of Psalms," 85–86. Childs adds: "the Jewish canon was formed through a complex historical process which is largely inaccessible to critical reconstruction. The history of the canonical process does not seem to be an avenue through which one can greatly illuminate the present canonical text. Not only is the evidence far too skeletal, but the sources seem to conceal the very kind of information which would allow a historian easy access into the material by means of uncovering this process' (*IOTS*, 68).

[91] "We may assume that the group Pss 3–41, numerically the largest group, forms the basis of the whole collection," (Seybold, *Introducing*, 19). Westermann comes to similar conclusions (*Praise and Lament*, 254, 257), as does Wilson (*Editing*, 210).

undergone the later Elohistic redaction indicates that this was, most likely, the initial "Book of Psalms" to which was later added the Korahite collection and the second Davidic psalter (which has undergone Elohistic revision).[92] These (diachronic) observations find support in this chapter's analysis of the canonical placement of the torah-kingship psalm texts. As argued above, the Book I collection of Davidic psalms gives the impression of having functioned as a unit, to which Pss 1–2 were added as an introduction at some later stage.

Whilst it is really impossible to determine conclusively at what point the Pss 1–2 introduction was added to the Psalter,[93] the synchronic evidence would suggest that this most likely occurred either before or after (but not as part of) the Elohistic redaction as both psalms make prominent use of the divine name. The Elohistic psalter seems to have been added at the second stage of the organic expansion of the Book of Psalms, which was then followed by the addition of the second Korahite collection and Ps 89, to complete Book III.[94] This indicates that the addition of the introduction would have occurred either at the time of the inclusion of the second main section of the proto-psalter or after the closure of Book III. Such is the general homogeneity of material in Book I, it would seem unnecessary to add a hermeneutical paradigm to the Pss 3–41 collection alone, and, broadly speaking, the same could be said with regard to the inclusion of the second Davidic psalter and associated smaller collections.[95] However, by the

---

[92] Nogalski, "From Psalm to Psalms," 53. Seybold, taking a slightly different approach, suggests that "David 1 and David 2" made up the first collection (as reflected by the Ps 72:20 postscript) to which were added the Asaphite and Korahite collections, then followed the Elohistic redaction (*Introducing*, 19–28). Whilst this is possible, Seybold does not effectively explain why the Elohistic redaction did not touch Book I, the first Davidic psalter. In line with Nogalski's suggestion, it seems more likely that the Elohistic redaction was applied to the second Davidic psalter prior to its inclusion in the proto-canonical Book of Psalms, if, indeed, the Elohistic psalter is a redaction at all.

[93] "Exactly when Ps 1 was added as an introduction to the Psalter remains elusive," (Starbuck, *Court Oracles*, 110).

[94] Seybold, *Introducing*, 21–24; Westermann, *Praise and Lament*, 254–55. It is difficult to know at what stage the additional groups were added to the second Davidic psalter and how the Elohistic psalter (EP, Pss 42–83) relates to Books II and III as this redaction (if that is what happened) crosses between these two books of the Psalter. McCann suggests that the EP was not a redaction, but rather the association of original compositions where the use of *elohim* was preferred over Yahweh (see his *Psalms*, 658).

[95] Books I and II are both dominated by psalms of the individual, laments and Davidic superscriptions (Westermann, *Praise and Lament*, 254–55). Therefore, it seems unlikely that a hermeneutical paradigm for interpretation was necessary at that stage.

The Editorial Placement of the Torah-Kingship Psalm Groupings   249

"closure" of Books I–III the reader is confronted with a much broader canvas of authorship, type and content—as well as the crisis of the collapse of the Davidic monarchy in Ps 89—making the introductory guidelines for the understanding of the Psalter all the more necessary.[96] Therefore, it seems most likely that Pss 1–2 were added, chronologically speaking, as an interpretative aid to Books I–III.

Wilson points out that Books IV and V bear signs of editorial techniques that are different from those found in the first three books and that they were probably added at a later time to Books I–III.[97] Book IV was possibly added to Books I–III as a single unit, although other theories suggest the addition of a larger grouping which crosses over between Books IV and V.[98] The limitations

---

[96] "As already suggested, Psalms 1–2 are a fitting introduction to Books I and to Books I–III as a unit," McCann, *Psalms*, 664.

[97] Wilson, "Shaping," 73. This distinction is largely based on different editorial techniques—greater use of author and genre designations in Books I–III cf. use of *hllwyh* and *hodu* headings in Books IV–V etc. However, some scholars also base this distinction on the evidence suggested by the Qumran manuscript 11QPs^a, which contains all or part of 41 psalms from the last third of the Psalter plus some additional hymnic/poetic material, however the ordering of the biblical psalms varies considerably from the MT, (Smith, "Use and Influence," 16). Some scholars (generally basing their conclusions on the extensive work of James Sanders in the Qumran Pss Mss) interpret this as evidence that the shape of the canonical Book of Psalms was still in flux at the period of the Qumran community and that 11QPs^a represents an "alternative" canonical Psalter (Wilson, *Editing*, 88–92; Wilson, "Shape," 132; McCann, *Psalms*, 658 *et al*). However, as is the case with most diachronic evidence relating to the Psalter, it is difficult to know what weight to attribute ms 11QPs^a in the discussion of the formation of the canonical Book of Psalms. Miller, Howard, Skehan, Goshen-Gottstein, Tov and others argue that because we have no idea how 11QPs^a functioned within the Qumran community we cannot say conclusively whether this was, in fact, a variant form of canonical psalter, or whether it was merely a liturgical collection of poetic works for use within the community (see, for example, Miller, "Current Issues," 141–42 and Howard, *Structure*, 26–27). "[W]e cannot learn anything from the Qumran texts about 'the formative period of the building up of the standard collection of 150 Psalms,'" (Miller, "Current Issues," 142).

[98] Wilson, *Editing*, 214–19) suggests Book IV functions as a unit. Seybold, however, suggests that Pss 90–119 were added as a prior collection, resulting in Pss 1 and 119 opening and closing this version of the Book of Psalms (*Introducing*, 19–28). Whilst he does not deal with the stages of development of the Psalter in much detail, Westermann too suggests that: "We can say therefore that there was once a psalter which began with Ps 1 and ended with Ps 119. Moreover this framework bears witness to an important stage in the 'traditioning' process in which the psalter, as a collection, no longer had a cultic function primarily, but rather circulated in a tradition devoted to law. The psalms have now become the word of God which is read, studied and meditated

of a strictly synchronic approach are shown in the fact that the analysis found in this chapter cannot speak to such details, other than to confirm that Book V was most likely a later addition to the Psalter. However, the synchronic study of the final form does point out something which is often lost in the diachronic. Namely that, whilst Book V (along with Book IV) is undoubtedly a later addition, theologically it picks up on themes central to Books I–III. The theological voice which speaks in the introduction and at the heart of the first collection of psalms, is echoed at the very centre of Book V. So the late addition of Book V does not mean that it is in any sense divorced from the previous collections which were at one point viewed as the "Book of Psalms." On the contrary, Book V picks up on some of the central themes of the earlier collections as well as adding its own distinctive voice of praise.[99]

8. CONCLUSION

Whilst there are many diachronic questions which remain untouched in this brief survey, discussion of the formation of the Psalter is not the goal of this thesis. However, some light may be shed from the analysis of the final form of the MT's Book of Psalms. It is likely that the first example of psalmic torah-kingship theology based on the Kingship Law is to be found at the heart of Book I in Pss 18–21, the focal point of the chiastically ordered collection Pss 15–24. Thus the idea of a torah-piety by which the reader of the Psalms is to live, is set in a Davidic context. It is David, therefore, who functions as a type and exemplar of the righteous individual who is faithful to Yahweh throughout experiences which result in both lament and praise. Pss 1 and 2, in turn, apply this

---

upon," (*Praise and Lament*, 253). The problem with Seybold's suggestion is that it does not take into account the disjunctive function of the book divisions. Why would Pss 90–119 be divided between two books if they were a single redactional layer known to the editors of that stage in the development of the Psalter? Perhaps the book divisions happened at a later stage entirely, but Wilson's suggestion seems the more likely. This does not *necessarily* deny the fact that Pss 1 and 119 could, at some point, have begun and ended the Psalter, however, it seems more likely that Book IV was added as a unit and, perhaps, Book V was added by the piecemeal addition of smaller collections. Having said that, there is no historical evidence to indicate that a psalter concluding with Ps 119 ever existed. It seems more reasonable simply to conclude that the themes of Book I and the introduction to the Psalter were being repeated at the end of the Psalter, resulting in "torah-brackets" around the whole collection. See above, pp 244–45.

[99] Walter Brueggemann, "Bounded by Obedience and Praise," *JSOT* 50 (1991): 63–92; Seybold, *Introducing*, 27–28; Miller, "Current Issues," 141.

Davidic motif to the whole of the Psalter. Then, finally, the voice of this idealised David is heard again at the centre of Book V in Pss 118–119, as the king leads the people in worship and sets an example of piety based in Yahweh's instruction. At the beginning and end, the theological concern of the Psalter is repeated:

> The faithful reader of the Psalter will do as the king is supposed to do: study and meditate on YHWH's disclosure of himself in both the Torah *and* the Psalter (Dt 17:18–19, Ps 1).[100]

---

[100] Howard, *Structure*, 207.

CHAPTER 7
TORAH, KINGSHIP AND DEMOCRATISATION

1. INTRODUCTION

This thesis has considered the possibility that the placement of kingship psalms alongside the three torah psalms of the Psalter is not merely an accidental phenomenon, but one which results from deliberate editorial activity, designed to reflect the theology of Deuteronomy's Kingship Law. Moreover, this deliberate juxtaposition of kingship and torah psalms, it has been argued, reflects the theological concerns of the editors of the Psalter with regard to two particular issues: first, the editors wish to encourage a particular type of piety amongst the readers of the Book of Psalms; and, secondly, the editors wish to refine the Psalter's eschatological view of kingship in the post-exilic period. In considering these questions, the present thesis has given detailed attention to the exegetical examination of the torah-kingship psalms groupings (Pss 1–2; 18–21; 118–119)[1] and particularly to the Dtr themes which are apparent in these psalms. Secondly, the results of this exegetical examination have been compared, on a largely descriptive level, with the content of Deut 17:14–20;[2] and, thirdly, the significance of the canonical placement of these psalm groupings within the Book of Psalms has been considered.[3] There remains, however, one final task in order to bring a sense of completion to this study: namely, a comparison of the key *theological* concepts of the torah-kingship psalms and the Kingship Law.

Both the psalm groupings which have come under consideration and the Law of the King appear to deal with the same issues—the significance of Yah-

---
[1] See chapters 2–4, above.
[2] See above, chapter 5.
[3] See above, chapter 6.

weh's torah, the role of the king in Israel's society and the presentation of the king as exemplar for the people—yet, the question must be asked, "Do these passages speak *with the same voice* regarding these issues?" Even were one to accept that torah, kingship and democratisation are matters of primary concern both in Deut 17:14–20 and in the torah-kingship psalm groupings, attention must be paid as to whether these passages are actually speaking about the same things and to the same end? When the Law of the King speaks about torah is it speaking about the same thing as Ps 1? Or, does the Psalter's view of kingship bear any resemblance to the Dtr ideal?[4] It is not sufficient merely to point out that similar concerns are observable in the Psalter and Deuteronomy, rather, one must ask the question: Are these various texts of the Old Testament addressing the same issues *in the same way*? How are they similar? Where do they differ?

It would not be possible to examine in detail all of the Dtr concepts that have been drawn from the exegetical examination of the psalms in chapters 2–4.[5] So, this chapter will focus its attention upon the main concepts aired in the torah-kingship psalms and the Law of the King, namely: torah, kingship and democratisation. The aim of this analysis is to seek to ascertain whether or not the editors of the Psalter were using the Kingship Law as their paradigm in juxtaposing kingship psalms alongside torah psalms. Whilst these major concepts are clearly present in both the Kingship Law and the highlighted psalms, if they are

---

[4] This is a question posed by McConville in his consideration of the Kingship Law (*Deuteronomy*, 293–96, 306): is not the Dtr view of kingship far removed from the David-Zion view of kingship in the Psalter?

[5] For example, such concepts as the name of Yahweh, the two ways of life and death etc., which have been highlighted in the study of the torah-kingship psalms as part of their more general background in Dtr ideas. Examination of all of these concepts would require a much lengthier study than space and time allow. This seems to be an area worthy of further study; that is, to discuss the broader issue of Dtr influences within the Book of Psalms. Patrick Miller has suggested that there is ample scope for such dialogue between Deuteronomy and the Psalms ("Deuteronomy and Psalms"), and this present study picks up on one of the areas of confluence highlighted in Miller's works (i.e. the Kingship Law; see also "Kingship," 140–41 and "Beginning," 91–92]. However, one is left with the impression that there are many other Dtr influences in the Psalter and that these too are worthy of further study. Deuteronomy has influenced (to one degree or another) large sections of the OT, it should not be too surprising to find such influences in the Psalter as well.

being used in markedly different ways then one must question whether the Kingship Law did, in fact, function as the guiding principle for the placement of the psalms examined in this thesis. However, if there is a substantial degree of correlation between Deuteronomy's understanding of these key concerns and the use of these ideas in the torah-kingship psalms, then it would be reasonable to postulate that the Kingship Law did, indeed, function as the organisational paradigm for the placement of kingship psalms alongside the psalms which celebrate the torah of Yahweh.

2. Torah

Most scholars who have adopted a canonical approach to the study of the Psalms acknowledge that the placement of the torah psalms is of great significance.[6] The previous chapter discussed why this is the case: the Psalter is headed by a torah psalm in Psalm 1, and Psalms 19 and 119 dominate the first and last books of psalms respectively. Yet, despite the substantial agreement concerning the significance of the torah psalms, the question of what "torah" *means* within these psalms is somewhat more contentious. Many psalms scholars stress that torah cannot be simply understood as "law"[7] but that it refers to the "instruction, teaching" of Yahweh in its broadest sense.[8] They suggest that this torah does not simply refer to "law proper," according to our contemporary understanding of that word, but also to narrative, prophecy, history and even poetry—torah is the instruction of Yahweh by, in and through any and all possible means.[9] Therefore the word תורה is often defined by scholars as "instruction" or simply "teaching."[10] Other scholars see in the Psalter's references to torah a reflection of the sense of derivative authority which is,

---

[6] Mays, "Place of the Torah-Psalms," passim; Brueggemann, "Bounded," 64; Wilson, "Shape," passim; Creach, *Yahweh as Refuge*, 16, 73; McCann, *Psalms*, 650.

[7] As תורה is universally translated in the EVV, except the JPS *Tanakh* (1985) which translates תורת יהוה as "the Teaching of the Lord."

[8] McCann, *Psalms*, 684–85; deClaissé-Walford, *Reading from the Beginning*, 42; Allan M. Harman, *Psalms* (Mentor Commentary Series; Fearn, Ross-shire: Christian Focus Publishers, 1998), 72; Sarna, *On the Book of Psalms*, 27.

[9] McCann, for example, writes referring to torah: "'Instruction' here refers not to a particular corpus of stipulations, but more broadly to the whole sacred tradition of God's revelation," (*Psalms*, 684–85).

[10] Whybray, "Psalm 119," 40–41; Mays, *The Lord Reigns*, 121–22; Sarna, *On the Book of Psalms*, 27, 37–38.

arguably, inherent to the Writings.[11] Whether this derivative authority is accepted or not, some scholars see torah in the Psalms as referring to the Pentateuch, the Mosaic Torah, the authoritative source upon which their teaching is based.[12]

Similarly, and perhaps not surprisingly, there is in Deuteronomy studies an even greater degree of disagreement with regard to the definition of the word "torah." For some this is a reference to the Pentateuch (Torah) as a whole;[13] for others, it seems clearly to be a reference to the Book of Deuteronomy itself;[14] still others would limit the extent of this reference to the Dtr law code in Deut 12–26;[15] some would even suggest that the reference in the Kingship Law (Deut 17:18-19) which commands the king to meditate upon the torah is self-referent, i.e. referring to nothing more than the Kingship Law itself.[16] It is also not uncommon for scholars to associate "torah" as it is used in Deuteronomy with "its closest cousin,"[17] the Book of the Covenant, as found in Exodus.[18] The diversity of opinion as to the definition of torah both in the Psalms and in Deuteronomy is marked. The question must be asked therefore, are the torah psalms and the Kingship Law referring to the same thing when they speak of torah?

2.1 TORAH IN THE PSALMS

The main area of debate with regard to "torah" in the torah psalms is precipitated by the unspecified, generic usage of this term in these psalms. Nowhere in

---

[11] Erhard S. Gerstenberger, "Canon Criticism and the Meaning of 'Sitz Im Leben,'" in *Canon, Theology and Old Testament Interpretation: Essays in Honor of Brevard S. Childs* (ed. G. M. Tucker et al.; Philadelphia: Fortress, 1988), 24–25; John J. Collins, "Before the Canon: Scriptures in Second Temple Judaism," in *Old Testament Interpretation: Past, Present and Future, Essays in Honour of Gene M. Tucker* (Edinburgh: T&T Clark, 1995), 638.

[12] Sheppard, *Wisdom*, 141–42; Sheppard, "Theology," 153–54; T. N. D. Mettinger, *King and Messiah: The Civil and Sacral Legitimation of the Israelite Kings* (ConBOT, Vol. 8; Lund: CWK Gleerup, 1976), 289; Whybray, "Psalm 119," 39.

[13] See Sonnet's discussion in *The Book Within the Book*, 1–3.

[14] J. A. Thompson, *Deuteronomy: An Introduction and Commentary* (TOTC; Leicester: IVP, 1974), 206.

[15] Ridderbos, *Deuteronomy*, 201; Tigay, *Deuteronomy*, 168; Driver, *Deuteronomy*, 212; Miller, *Deuteronomy*, 148.

[16] See discussion in Craigie, *Deuteronomy*, 256–57.

[17] J. Gordon McConville, "Law and Monarchy in the Old Testament," in *A Royal Priesthood: The Use of the Bible Ethically and Politically* (ed. C. Bartholomew et al.; Carlisle/Grand Rapids: Paternoster/Zondervan, 2002), 78

[18] Craigie, *Deuteronomy*, 256–57.

Pss 1, 19 or 119 does the psalmist offer an explanation of what this "torah" actually is, making it difficult to pinpoint precisely the referent of this term.[19] Eaton writes, "We have seen that some commentators pointed to teachings revered by the Deuteronomists, others to the whole Pentateuch, and others again to a wider collection. But the remarkable fact remains that none of these psalms gives a specification or an example of such Scripture."[20] Speaking of torah in Ps 119, for example, Freedman writes, "In Psalm 119 *tôrâ* is a monolithic presence, consisting of individual laws and teachings to be sure, but described in only the most general terms, namely the eight interchangeable *tôrâ*-words."[21] This lack of clear definition with regard to the subject matter of the torah psalms is further accentuated by the apparent inadequacies of the English word offered by way of translation—"law." The meaning of the Hebrew word is clearly broader than our *contemporary* understanding of law proper.[22] Craigie puts the case clearly:

> Although the term *Torah* can be used of the law, or of the Pentateuch, or even (at a later date) of the Old Testament, its significance here is the most fundamental one. Basically, the word *Torah* means "instruction"; specifically, it is the instruction which God gives to mankind as a guide for life. Thus it may include that which is technically law, but it also includes other more general parts of God's revelation.[23]

Despite the broad agreement that "law" is an inadequate translation, much of the scholarly writing is still taken up with establishing the fact that a torah-based piety does not equate to legalism. Some scholars seem at such pains to point out that the torah-piety of the Psalter has nothing to do with nomism, in any sense, and as a result reject or limit the idea that torah in the Psalms is connected with a written text.[24] Torah is not "law," but "teaching," the argument goes, and

---

[19] "[W]hen *tôrâ* is used without further specification, it is often difficult to say with certainty precisely what the content of this *tôrâ* is," (Peter Enns, "Law of God," in *New International Dictionary of Old Testament Theology and Exegesis, Volume 4* [W. A. VanGemeren, gen. ed.; Carlisle: Paternoster Press, 1997], 896).

[20] Eaton, *Psalms of the Way*, 56.

[21] Freedman, *Psalm 119*, 89.

[22] On this point there is (almost) universal agreement in commentaries and lexica.

[23] Craigie, *Psalms*, 60. See also Dahood, *Psalms III, 101–150*, 173; Kirkpatrick, *Psalms*, 104; Kraus, *Psalms*, 273–74; Sarna, *On the Book of Psalms*, 37.

[24] The rationale behind the rejection of a book-based torah-piety is based on the conclusion that such religious observance inevitably leads to nomism—a conclusion, perhaps, drawn from observing some brands of Judaism. Obviously, this is not the necessary result of a book-based piety.

clearly the psalmic ideas of torah-piety are quite different from Dtr (nomistic?) ideas of a book-based law code. Levenson, for example, states concerning torah in Ps 119:

> Nothing in the psalm hints that the author considers his own pneumatic experience inferior to Moses' and only corroborative of it. In fact, in contradiction to all the Deuteronomic tradition (including Jeremiah), Psalm 119 lacks any trace of book-consciousness. In contrast, the Deuteronomistic History, in language reminiscent of the our psalm, commends conformity to the Torah of Moses (by which is meant Deuteronomy).[25]

Similarly, McCann writes concerning torah in Ps 1:

> Verse 2b is reminiscent of Jos 1:8. As Joshua succeeds Moses, he is told by God that "this book of the law" is something he is to "meditate on... day and night" in order to "make your way prosperous" (NRSV; cf. "prospers" in Ps 1:3). The king of Israel also is to have "a copy of this law" and is to "read... it all the days of his life" (Deut 17:18–19 NRSV). It is likely that "law" in these two texts does, indeed, designate the Deuteronomistic code; however, such need not be the case in Ps 1:2. There is no mention of a book or a copy of the law.[26]

Thus one could be led to the conclusion that the torah of the psalms is something quite *different* from the torah of the Kingship Law. Levenson and McCann (and others) seem to imply that the torah of the torah psalms is a concept more amorphous, general and directly experiential than the idea of torah in Deuteronomy or the DtrH. Deuteronomy and the DtrH clearly refer to a book-based piety,[27] but the psalms make no reference to ספר התורה הזה (הזאת) or, for that matter, even to התורה with the definite article.[28] Therefore it may be argued that torah in the torah psalms is very different from the understanding of torah in Deuteronomy—one is book-based and legalistic, the other is understood as being much more direct, holistically-experienced and refers to every possible aspect of divine revelation (including, it must be said, proto-canonical books but by no means limited to them or centering upon such).[29] So does the theory of linkage

---

[25] Levenson, "Sources," 564.

[26] McCann, *Psalms*, 694–85.

[27] As is indicated by the repeated phrases "the book of this law" (הספר התורה הזאת, Deut 28:61), "this book of the law" (ספר התורה הזה, Deut 29:20; 31:26; Jos 1:8), and implied in the phrase "the words of this law" (דברי התורה הזאת, Deut 17:18; 27:3, 8, 26 etc.).

[28] Sarna, *On the Book of Psalms*, 37.

[29] Whilst Levenson seeks to limit the connection between torah in Ps 119 and the Dtr ideas of torah, he does also acknowledge that this connection cannot be entirely

Torah, Kingship and Democratisation

between Deuteronomy and the Psalms fail before it starts because in referring to torah the respective passages are speaking about different concepts entirely?

2.1.1 READING TORAH IN THE TORAH PSALMS

Whilst the torah psalms do not speak explicitly about a "book of the torah," the vocabulary which is used by the psalmists to describe a proper attitude towards Yahweh's revelation indicates a practice grounded in reading and recitation—actions which cannot be performed without a book. Sarna gives detailed consideration to this issue with regard to "torah" in Ps 1:2:

> Such a notion [that Psalm 1 is not a devotional text] obscures a fundamental principle that the psalmist wishes to highlight by according the theme of Torah a pre-eminent position in the Psalter. It is that the *study of the sacred and revered text* itself constitutes a pious act, a profoundly religious experience, and is an important mode of worship. This seminal idea is emphasised and elaborated in Psalm 119 and it finds powerful expression in later Judaism.[30]

Sarna then goes on to point out that, whilst the exact connotation of the reference to torah is uncertain, the verb which is used (הגה) clearly implies reference to a fixed text.[31] He then goes on to elaborate on this conclusion, agreeing that torah does, indeed, refer to Yahweh's instruction generally, but also explaining that the psalmist does have a book in mind:

> Our text makes no mention of a "book" of the Torah. In fact, the word "book" never appears in any reference to Torah in the Psalter; nor is the definite article ever attached therein to torah. Torah must here mean simply "teaching," "instruction." Nevertheless, as noted above, "the Lord's Teaching" must define a recognisable, established, and crystallized text that can be committed to memory and recited. This is so because the Hebrew verb, usually mistranslated

---

removed: "We have seen that the author of Psalm 119 recognizes three sources of *tora*: (1) received tradition, passed on most explicitly by teachers (vv 99–100) but including perhaps some sacred books now in the Hebrew Bible, (2) cosmic or natural law (vv 89–91), and (3) unmediated divine teaching (e.g., vv 26–29). The importance for him of books we consider 'biblical' must not be minimized. They hold a kind of normative status for him; they provide the language with which to formulate a significant statement. Nonetheless, he never identifies *tora* with the Pentateuch. His own perspective is too close to that of the older wisdom tradition for him to do so," ("Sources," 570).

[30] Sarna, *On the Book of Psalms*, 28–29 (emphasis added).

[31] "It is not possible to determine what exactly was comprehended by that phrase [torah] in this context. From the second half of the verse—"and he recites His *torah* day and night"—it seems that it must pertain to a fixed text that can be memorised," (*On the Book of Psalms*, 36).

"meditates," carries a decidedly oral nuance, as anyone who consults a concordance of the Hebrew Bible for this stem *h-g-h* will soon discover. The verbal form is used for the moaning of a dove, and the growl of a lion; it takes as its subject the mouth, the tongue, and the palate. The action of the verb obviously has an acoustical effect because the throat can be its instrument... Moreover, the verb many times appears in a parallel relationship with another verb denoting sound. Finally, there are three nouns from this stem, all of which are used in contexts which suggest sound or tonality.

This understanding of the action of verse 2b as being recitative, not meditative, is reinforced by other biblical passages. A strikingly similar one is in God's address to Joshua upon his assumption of the leadership of Israel following Moses' death. Its reads: "Let not this book of Teaching [*torah*] depart from your mouth, but recite [*vehagiyta*] it day and night" (Joshua 1:8). The mouth, of course, is here the organ of speech. This emphasis on the oral nature of the obligation is repeated several times.

In short, what all this means is that the person described in our Psalm is not one engaged in meditation and contemplation, such as is required in some mystical systems or traditions. *Rather, this individual studies a sacred text which is the object of intense focus and concentration; and the method of study is reading aloud, rote learning, and constant oral repetition.*[32]

Sarna's conclusions with regard to Psalm 1 are reinforced by the use of the verb שׂיח with regard to the act of meditation[33] in Ps 119.[34] As with הגה in Ps 1, שׂיח indicates a vocal activity based around reading and recitation. The Brown, Driver, Briggs Lexicon defines this verb as meaning "to meditate upon, study" or "to talk about."[35] Similarly, Gesenius offers the definition "to talk with oneself,

---

[32] Sarna, *On the Book of Psalms*, 37–38 (emphasis added). Kraus comes to the same conclusion in vol. 1 of his commentary, where he writes, "In any case, however, the תורה in this sense is the authoritatively valid 'Sacred Scripture,'" (Kraus, *Psalms*, 116) and Mays comes to the same conclusion when he writes concerning the effects of Ps 1 on our reading of the Psalter: "The book [of Psalms] is torah of the Lord. Torah means instruction, teaching, direction that can be given *in various literary forms*. The psalms provide torah that can be learned by study and meditation," (*The Lord Reigns*, 121 [emphasis mine]). Freedman, in his detailed analysis of Ps 119 comes to the same conclusion with regard to the nature of torah: "[Torah] is the sacred, authoritative written revelation of God.... Whatever its identity, *tôrâ* is the definitive sacred text," (*Psalm 119*, 91–92).

[33] Or, to adopt Sarna's terms, "rote learning." Sarna is correct in pointing out that this is not the type of meditative contemplation practiced in many other religious, however, it should be pointed out that the desired end result of this practice is an internalisation and application of the torah of Yahweh. As long as "meditation" is understood in these terms (rather than anything more ethereal) it does seem to be an appropriate translation of both הגה and שׂיח.

[34] Psalm 119:15, 23, 27, 48, 78, 148.

[35] Brown et al., *BDB*, 967c.

Torah, Kingship and Democratisation 261

i.e. to meditate."[36] The *New International Dictionary of Old Testament Theology and Exegesis* suggests that the verb שיח is an action "fluctuating between the act of speaking and thinking."[37] Again, whilst the eight torah synonyms of Ps 119 are non-specific, the verb used to encourage individual interaction with the torah of Yahweh implies that the psalmist is calling upon a written text.[38] So, from the exhortations found in Pss 1 and 119,[39] the reader of the Psalter is expected to delight in the torah of Yahweh by way of reading, reciting and, thus, learning and internalising the divine teaching as it is found in a text. This, of course, begs a question: which text? To which text is the hearer of the psalms supposed to devote his attention?

2.1.2   TORAH IN THE TORAH PSALMS AND THE PENTATEUCH

If the torah psalms are encouraging a piety based around the study of a sacred text, as is suggested above, then the identity of that text is of some significance if we are to come to proper understanding of the message of these three psalms. So which text(s) do the torah psalms refer to? There are, of course, various possible answers to this question and much depends on the period in which the torah psalms were originally written.[40] As a result of structural parallels, Rabbinic scholars have traditionally linked the Psalter, with its five-book struc-

---

[36] Gesenius, *Hebrew Lexicon*, 789.

[37] A. R. Pete Diamond, "שיח," in *New International Dictionary of Old Testament Theology and Exegesis, Volume 3* (W. A. VanGemeren, gen. ed.; Carlisle: Paternoster Press, 1997), 1234–35. Whybray comments, "However, of the many verses in which the psalmist speaks of this 'law' of Yahweh and of his personal relationship to it, some make it plain that it is a written document (or documents). He frequently states that he has 'kept' it or will keep it, does not forget it or does not turn away from it.... He speaks of his delight in it, his love of it, and his trust in it (v 66). He declares or recounts (*sippēr*) it (v 13); he clings (*dābaq*) to it (v 31); he has chosen it (v 173). He seeks guidance from it (*dāraš*, vv 45, 94). That it is, at least sometimes, a written document of which he has access to a copy is also probably implied by the use of the word *śiaḥ*, 'meditate' (vv 15, 23, 48, 78, 99)," ("Psalm 119," 34–35).

[38] Sarna, *On the Book of Psalms*, 28.

[39] Ps 19 is a slightly different type of text when compared to the other two torah psalms. It is (probably) an older text and, rather than serving as an exhortation to torah-piety *per se*, it is a hymn which celebrates the perfect nature of Yahweh's teaching. Therefore, it contains neither הגה or שיח as part of its text. The strong lexical connections with Ps 119 and the final prayer in vv 13–15 imply, however, that the torah which is the focus of the psalmist's celebration in is indeed meant to be studied and internalised.

[40] Obviously, torah in the torah psalms cannot refer to the Pentateuch, for example, if the Pentateuch has not been written by the time of the psalm's writing.

ture, and the Pentateuch as a whole;[41] however, the torah synonyms found in Pss 19 and 119 are very reminiscent of the legal codes of Exodus and Deuteronomy, so others have linked the torah psalms more specifically with one or other collection of laws;[42] still others ask whether the "torah" of the torah psalms might not be a reference to the Book of Deuteronomy itself.[43] So which text is to be the subject of torah-meditiation?

1. Five Book Structure

From the perspective of a canonical approach to the Book of Psalms, the five-book structure of the Psalter seems to be telling.[44] Whilst the reasons for this division are nowhere made explicit,[45] the most likely reason for this structure seems to be as a deliberate echo of the Pentateuch. Otherwise, the division of the Psalter is difficult to explain. Neither length, genre, authorship designations, or content demand this division. Each book varies in length and has a mix of genres, authorship and theological emphases. Indeed, there is no absolutely compelling reason to divide the Book of Psalms at all.[46] It seems unlikely that this division is the result of previous collections which had functioned separately as a unit. Each individual book of the Psalter seems to have absorbed smaller groups of psalms that had an existence prior to their inclusion in the Psalter[47] and

---

[41] Nogalski, "From Psalm to Psalms," 48. The *Mid. Tehillim* states that, "Moses gave Israel five books of the Torah, and David gave Israel five books of the Psalms," thus highlighting the ancient talmudic links between Psalter and Pentateuch. Some scholars link the 150 Psalms with the Palestinian triennial lectionary cycle, with a reading from the psalms accompanying a reading from the Torah (Sarna, *On the Book of Psalms*, 18).

[42] Anderson, *Psalms*, 812; Briggs, *Psalms*, 168–69.

[43] Miller, for example, suggests: "What the conversation between these two books makes even clearer, however, is that for the Psalter, *the law is Deuteronomy*," ("Deuteronomy and Psalms," 11). See also Kraus, *Psalms*, 116.

[44] This five-book division is one of the key indicators of editorial activity in the Psalter (see Wilson, *Editing*, 182–86; Childs, *IOTS*, 512).

[45] In rejecting a link between the Pentateuch and Psalter based upon the five-book structure, Nogalski writes, "In short, the doxologies clearly divide the Psalter into five books, but the purpose of that division has not been ascertained with any degree of certainty," ("From Psalm to Psalms," 48).

[46] "The pentateuchal division of the Psalter is very strange, considering that, unlike the Torah, this work is not so large as to require transcription onto several scrolls for ease of handling and convenience of study," (Sarna, *On the Book of Psalms*, 17).

[47] For example, the Songs of Ascents (Pss 120–134) within Book V.

at least one group of psalms appears to transcend the book divisions.[48] Thus it seems unlikely that the five-fold division of the Psalms corresponds to the existence of prior collections.

Why then five books of the Psalter? Whilst it is impossible to know for sure, the most likely reason is that the Book of Psalms was divided in this way as a deliberate echo of the Pentateuch. The editors of the Psalter in giving it a five-book structure were drawing a deliberate parallel with the Mosaic Torah:

> The fivefold division of the book continues the identification. It gives the book a form that corresponds to the five books of the Mosaic Torah. The Psalter is a "Davidic Torah," which corresponds to and responds to the first one.[49]

> It is quite possible, therefore, that the fivefold division of the Psalter was intentionally created with that parallel in mind [i.e. with the five books of the Pentateuch].[50]

> According to Psalm 1, the Psalms stand in the shadow of the Torah, which announces the principle subject matter of the Psalms and scripture as a whole. *The Torah finds its anchor in the Torah of Moses so that the Psalms, as do the Prophets, purport to be illuminating commentary on it.* Moreover, we see in the Psalms themselves that obedience to the law and trust in God as a "refuge" is a response of loyalty to God's prior, free, and merciful claim upon Israel, rather than an effort to secure God's favour through "works righteousness."[51]

The five-book structure is a key indicator of editorial activity in the Psalms, and the message of the redactor(s) draws the reader's attention to the parallels which exist between the Psalter and the Pentateuch.

2. Internal Indicators within Torah Psalms

Over and above the five-book structure indicating the likelihood of a connection with the Pentateuch, there are internal indications within the torah psalms themselves (particularly Pss 19 and 119) which point towards a background in Deuteronomy, and hence, the Mosaic Law. Whybray, for example, points out regarding torah in Ps 119 that, whilst the psalmist may have a broader notion of torah in mind, he definitely draws parallels with the Pentateuch:

---

[48] That is the Elohistic Psalter which spans Pss 42–83 covering all of Book II and part of Book III.
[49] Mays, *The Lord Reigns*, 121.
[50] Sarna, *On the Book of Psalms*, 17.
[51] Sheppard, "Theology," 153 (emphasis mine).

He does not speak of the "covenant" (*bĕrît*); but the "law" (*tôrâ*) with its various equivalents, though its contents are not specified, *is certainly related in some way to the written laws of the Pentateuch*: this is indicated inter alia by the occurrence of words characteristic of Deuteronomy and the priestly laws: *tôrâ, dĕbārîm, miṣwôt, mišpāṭîm*.[52]

Similar conclusions may be drawn from analysis of Ps 19, as Mays suggests: "The theological basis of this description [of torah in Ps 19] is the identification of the Sinai covenant and its teaching as the wisdom by which Israel is to live and find life (Deut 4:1-8)."[53] In the same vein, Kraus concludes that, "In this expression of the will of God, which above all contains the law of God, also the historical proclamations are included (Deut. 1:5; Ps. 78:1; Neh. 8:13ff.). But the Law of God transmitted through Moses (Mal. 4:4) is and remains the real center of the תורה."[54] Primarily, the internal indicators linking the torah psalms with the Mosaic Torah are the torah synonyms found in Ps 19 and 119.[55] As we have seen in chapters 3 and 4, these terms link the torah psalms firmly with Deuteronomy and thus with the Pentateuch.[56]

However, the Pentateuchal connection is not solely limited to the torah terms of Pss 19 and 119: Schaefer points out that the concept of torah found in Ps 1 encapsulates both narrative and law, linking "torah" with *the* Torah:

> The word *tôrâh* (translated "law," v 2) refers to the story of God's actions to create a people and guide them into the future, as described in Genesis and the first chapters of Exodus. Likewise it refers to the obligations, precepts and guidelines that shape the people's live, as in the rest of the first five books of the Bible, the Torah. These two dimensions, narration and obligation, or, in the Jewish tradition, *hagaddah* and *halakah*, are complementary.[57]

---

[52] Whybray, "Psalm 119," 39 (emphasis mine). Similarly with regard to the *tôrâ* referent in Ps 119, Freedman asserts that, "The logical assumption is that the psalmist has the Pentateuch in mind," and goes on to add that, "the *tôrâ* that the psalm exalts includes at least the Pentateuch," (*Psalm 119*, 89, 91).

[53] Mays, *Psalms*, 99.

[54] Kraus, *Psalms*, 273.

[55] Kirkpatrick, *Psalms*, 102, 704.

[56] Kraus, *Psalms*, 273. We should remember that the torah synonyms in Pss 19 and 119 also provide a link with the Pentateuch via Exodus and the Book of the Covenant (Sarna, *On the Book of Psalms*, 84–85) and via the priestly legislation as well (Whybray, "Psalm 119," 39). So, whilst the primary Petateuchal connection is by way of Deuteronomy, the torah synonyms do connect the psalmic concept of torah with the Mosaic Torah more broadly.

[57] Konrad Schaefer, *Psalms* (ed. David W. Cotter; Berit Olam; Collegeville, MN: Liturgical Press, 2001), 3. Hossfeld and Zenger also see torah in Ps 1 as being linked

There does, therefore, despite the protestations of some scholars, seem to be a strong link between the torah psalms and the Pentateuch. Whatever else the psalmists had in mind in their references to the torah of Yahweh,[58] it seems that the basis and backbone of the piety which they sought to promote is to be found in meditation upon and application of the Pentateuch, probably with a particular (but not exclusive) emphasis on Deuteronomy in mind.[59]

2.2 TORAH IN DEUTERONOMY

Torah is a significant concept within Deuteronomy. Of all the books of the OT, only the Psalter makes greater use of the term. Clearly, within Deuteronomy torah has several meanings,[60] ranging from law proper[61] to teaching (cate-

---

with the Pentateuch: "In Ps 1:2b geht es also um das halblaute Rezitieren der "Tora," damit daß Leben in Gottesfurcht (als Anfang der Weisheit: Spr 1:7) gelingt, genauer um das Begeisterung, Glück und Lust über "die Tora JHWHs" als der grundlegenden Welt- und Lebensordnung, die in der Tora des Mose geoffenbart wurde, (vgl. Sir 24), geschieht," (*Die Psalmen I*, 37).

[58] As mentioned above, the exact extent of the sacred text to which the psalmists referred cannot be known for sure and depends on the time period in which the psalms were written. If, as seems likely, Ps 19 is the earliest of the torah psalms it may be the case that the psalmist celebrates some proto-pentateuchal text such as the Book of the Covenant or the Deuteronomic Book of the Torah (see Sheppard, *Wisdom*, 142). However, if Pss 1 and 119 are substantially later texts, it is highly likely that the psalmists' understanding of torah included *more* than just the Pentateuch (Vincent, "Shape of Psalter," 65; Allen, *Psalms*, 141–42; Childs, *IOTS*, 104–05 etc.). My point here is not to suggest that the Pentateuch is the *only* source of divine revelation which the psalmists revered. Freedman, for example, suggests that the torah piety of Ps 119, as a late text, may refer to the Pentateuch, the Primary History "or even to the entire Hebrew Bible essentially as it exists today (minus Daniel)," (*Psalm 119*, 91–92). Equally, it should be pointed out that there are strong Wisdom overtones in Pss 1, 19 and 119, so it seems likely that the Wisdom books may also have been treated as "torah" by the psalmists (Sheppard, "Theology," 153–54; Mays, *Psalms*, 98–99 etc.). Indeed, the inclusion of Ps 1 as introduction, implies that the Psalter itself is to be read as "torah" (Hossfeld and Zenger, *Die Psalmen I*, 47; Childs, *IOTS*, 513–14). However, the Pentateuch does seem to underlie all other revelatory sources. The piety being endorsed is a book-based one, and whatever other sources of inspiration are included in their reckoning, the psalmists create a strong link with the Pentateuch as the source by which to arrive at the proper worldview according to which one lives a life of devotion to Yahweh.

[59] Miller, "Deuteronomy and Psalms," 11.

[60] Enns, "Law," 896.

[61] S. Dean McBride, "Perspective and Context in the Study of Pentateuchal Legislation," in *Old Testament Interpretation: Past, Present and Future, Essays in Honor of Gene M. Tucker* (Edinburgh: T&T Clark, 1995), 47–48.

chesis)[62] to constitution (polity).[63] Commonly, torah is referred to with the definite article in Deuteronomy and also as a book, giving raise to the conclusion that reference is being made to some sort of fixed text. However, one of the key texts with regard to a proper understanding of torah in Deuteronomy is our text from the Kingship Law (Deut 17:14–20). It is in Deut 17:18 that, for the first time, the text of Deuteronomy makes reference to *itself* as a coherent entity to be studied.[64] This self-reference has sparked much debate as to the content of the torah which the king is to write out for himself and study. Does this refer to Deuteronomy as a whole, or to the legal codex, or to the kingship law itself, or to some altogether more ethereal concept? It is to this particular question that we now turn our attention.

2.2.1 "THIS TORAH" IN THE KINGSHIP LAW

Most of the debate concerning the content of the reference to "this torah" in Deut 17:18 circles around two possibilities: first, that this phrase refers to the Book of Deuteronomy itself; or, secondly, that it refers to the legal codex found in chapters 12–26.[65] In favour of the latter view are the legal overtones of the idea of torah, including the use of "torah" alongside the various legal synonyms which were analysed in our study of Pss 19 and 119.[66] In favour of the former view that "this torah" refers to the whole of the Book of Deuteronomy is the fact that the phrase often occurs in the framework of the book, seemingly denoting that the paraenetic passages which bracket the legal code are to be considered

---

[62] Dennis T. Olson, *Deuteronomy and the Death of Moses* (Minneapolis: Fortress Press, 1994), 10–11; B. Lindars, "Torah in Deuteronomy," in *Words and Meanings: Essays Presented to David Winton Thomas* (P. R. Ackroyd and B. Lindars; Cambridge: CUP, 1968), 117.

[63] McBride, "Polity," 62.

[64] Sonnet, *The Book Within the Book*, 71; Crüsemann, *Torah*, 273.

[65] As mentioned above (p 252) there are other possible interpretations, however, for various reasons these prove to be problematic, so attention shall be focussed on the two main interpretative possibilities, and the third (more recent) view offered by Sonnet.

[66] For example, תורה, משפט and חקים are all used in close proximity in Deut 4:1–8, and on various occasions each of the seven other legal terms used in Ps 119 is used in conjunction with torah in Deuteronomy, leaving a strongly "legal" impression in the mind of the reader. Levinson writes concerning the concept of torah in the Kingship Law that, "the reference seems in this context self-reflexive, and refers to the legal corpus of Deuteronomy 12-26," ("Reconceptualization," 523). Many other commentators would share this view: Miller, *Deuteronomy*, 148; Driver, *Deuteronomy*, 212; Ridderbos, *Deuteronomy*, 201 etc.

Torah, Kingship and Democratisation 267

"torah" as well.⁶⁷ How can this debate be resolved and what are the implications for our comparison with the torah-kingship psalm groupings? In recent years something of a *via media* has arisen in the form of Jean-Pierre Sonnet's work *The Book within the Book: Writing in Deuteronomy*.⁶⁸ This re-working of Sonnet's doctoral thesis considers in detail the Deuteronomic self-references to a written work and his conclusions are especially helpful with regard to the definition of "this torah" in Deut 17:18. It seems appropriate, therefore, to devote some more attention to consideration of Sonnet's argument.

2.2.2 SONNET ON "THIS TORAH" IN THE KINGSHIP LAW

Sonnet describes his examination of writing in Deuteronomy as "'a wheel within a wheel...' an act of communication about an act of communication,"⁶⁹ and he goes on to attest that, "in the Pentateuchal canon Deuteronomy is the book that tells about the rise of the (Torah) 'book.'"⁷⁰ This is pertinent to our examination because we seek to answer the question: what is the referent of "this torah" in the Kingship Law and what similarity—if any—does it bear to the concept of torah in the torah psalms?

Sonnet's basic thesis is that there are two "acts of communication" going on within Deuteronomy—the voice of the narrator and the voice of Moses—and that confusion about the content of the "Book of the Torah" often stems from the confusion of these two communicative acts.⁷¹ The narrator begins his account of the people on the plains of Moab, about to enter the land but "almost immediately hands it over to its *dramatis persona*, whose direct speech gives the book its distinctive ring."⁷² The voice of the narrator is not heard again until 4:44–5:1 where, following Moses' retelling of the historical setting which had led the

---

⁶⁷ E.g., Deut 1:5; 4:8; 30:10; 31:9 etc. (see Olson, *Death of Moses*, 10–11, 15, 139). His reasoning is different, but Mayes also adopts the view that "this torah" refers to the whole of Deuteronomy (*Deuteronomy*, 273); as does Thompson (*Deuteronomy*, 206).

⁶⁸ Jean-Pierre Sonnet, *The Book within the Book: Writing in Deuteronomy* (BIS, Vol. 14; Leiden: Brill, 1997).

⁶⁹ Sonnet, *The Book within the Book*, 1.

⁷⁰ Sonnet, *The Book within the Book*, 3.

⁷¹ Sonnet, *The Book within the Book*, 1–3.

⁷² Sonnet, *The Book within the Book*, 1. This is significant because this introduction sets the proper parameters for understanding the text of Deuteronomy: "Deuteronomy is to be read within the poetic parameters established in its opening. It is not a prophetic work, but a narrative about Moses' prophetic communication in Moab; its shares the historiographical claim made in the previous Pentateuchal narrative," (p 11).

people to the plains of Moab, he provides an introduction to "the law which Moses set before the Israelites," (וזאת התורה אשר־שם משה לפני בני ישראל). This interaction between narrator and Moses is significant to a proper understanding of what is being expected of the king, because the content of the "torah" upon which the king is to meditate is what follows from 5:1b–26:19.[73] In other words, Deut 17:18 proleptically projects the reception of the speeches and laws of Moses into a book and *this* is to be the subject of the king's meditation.[74]

> The demonstrative "this" is thus used as an anaphoric, referring to a previous mention of "Torah" in the text, or to a previous stretch of discourse representing "this Torah." Back-reference suggests that "this Torah (התורה הזאת)" is that which the reader perused within a definite part of the book of Deuteronomy, starting with 4:44, וזאת התורה, "This is the Torah." The anaphoric phrase התורה הזאת, "this Torah," in 31:9 is thus presumably the counterpart of the cataphoric (i.e. forward-looking) one וזאת התורה [sic], "This is the Torah" in 4:44 (the occurrence of "this Torah" in 31:9 is the first use of the phrase *by the narrator* since 4:44). Whatever its exact extent, the Torah, now transcribed by Moses, is thus found between the two markers. By combining the deictic use of "this" ("this Torah book") by Moses and its anaphoric use by the narrator ("this Torah"), Deuteronomy 31 points to the overlapping between the record on the narrative stage and a foregoing portion of the Book of Deuteronomy.[75]

Therefore, Sonnet suggests that whilst the exact extent of "this torah" as refered to in Deut 17:18 is difficult to define (i.e., is it 5:1–26:19 or 5:1–28:58)

---

[73] Sonnet suggests that Deut 27–28 should be added to this section as an addenda outlining the writing of Moses speech-act in Deut 5–26 for the benefit of the people who will live "beyond the river" in the land, following on from Moses' death (pp 101–103).

[74] "In casting the king's reception of (a copy of) 'this Torah,' Moses' speech projects its own reception—via the representativity of an exceptional reader. The producing and reading by the king of the Torah's duplicate (משנה) in a particular 'book' (ספר) therefore functions as what has been called in modern literary theory a *mise en abyme* or 'duplication intérieure,' that is, the embedding in a work of a representation of this work. The royal duplicate on a particular scroll book is, within Moses' Torah speech, an embedded representation of 'this Torah' (in its future written form). The integrity of 'this Torah' is thus anticipated and represented to the audience. 'A condensed image of the overall design,' the *mise en abyme* is somehow chronologically disturbing, since its totalizes at one point what the linguistic message spells out discursively. The 'duplication intérieure,' however, catalyses the addressee's hermeneutic task in varied ways according to its place within the whole that it mirrors. In the projected 'duplicate' of Deut 17:18, the audience (and, behind it, the reader) learns that Moses' communication will eventuate in a written corpus, the standard copy that underlies the royal duplicate. The operations enjoined on the people in Deut 6:4–9 and 11:18–21 now have the background of a future, though not yet explicit, *Urschrift*," (Sonnet, *The Book within the Book*, 79–80).

[75] Sonnet, *The Book within the Book*, 248.

Torah, Kingship and Democratisation

the basic content is clear: the torah which is to be the guide for the life of the king refers to the speeches of Moses from chapter 5 through until the end of the law code (and possibly beyond).[76] So the subject matter for the king's meditation is to be a book—neither the Book of Deuteronomy (although ultimately this would become the case)[77] nor the legal code of chapters 12–26, but "this torah" was a text made up of Moses' speeches, containing both exhortative and legal material, and this book (which was to be placed beside the ark in the tabernacle) was to be copied by the king and he was to read from it daily as his life-guide.

Sonnet's thesis with regard to the Kingship Law's challenge to the king (Deut 17:18) is similar to Sarna's suggestion with regard to the piety encouraged by the torah psalms. Both indicate a practice of book-based recitation and meditation.[78] The king in Deuteronomy is to be "the Torah's arch-reader"[79] and this is to lead him to fear Yahweh in every area of practice:

> The mediation of the Torah book warrants the presence of the totality of the covenant regulations next to the king; the same mediation also enables the king to have permanent access to this totality, as is required from him: וקרא בו כל ימי חייו, "and he shall read in it all the days of his life" (17:19). This injunction features, in Moses' speeches (as in Deuteronomy), the first occurrence of the verb קרא, "to call," in the specific meaning of "to read."[80]

Sarna suggests that the piety of the torah psalms is based in the reverent study of a sacred text (at least the Pentateuch, but in later periods the expanding canon). Sonnet alludes to a similar idea; namely, that the king in the Kingship Law is called upon to live a life of fear of Yahweh, and is to do so also by the study of a sacred text. So it seems that there is some justification in coming to the conclusion that the "torah" of the torah psalms and the "torah" of the Law of

---

[76] One of the other interesting features of Sonnet's work is that it suggests a cohesive approach towards understanding the interaction between narrative and legal texts within Deuteronomy, which has often been seen as a problematic issue within Dtr studies.

[77] Sonnet, *The Book within the Book*, 260–62. For succeeding generations, the only access by which this original "book of the torah" made up of Mosaic speeches was available to the reader was via *Deuteronomy as a book*. So, it appears that there is merit in the suggestion that "this book of the torah" effectively equates with Deuteronomy.

[78] Sonnet points out the significance of the verb קרא, namely that the king in Deut 17:18 is also expected to internalise the torah by means of reading aloud (*The Book within the Book*, 76). Sarna makes a similar point with regard to the practice of torah reading encouraged by Ps 1 (*On the Book of Psalms*, 38).

[79] Sonnet, *The Book within the Book*, 82.

[80] Sonnet, *The Book within the Book*, 76.

the King are indeed referring to the same concept: the importance of the study of Yahweh's sacred text in order to develop a worldview that is pleasing to him.

2.3 TORAH AND RELATIONSHIP WITH YAHWEH

Another common feature when considering the similarities between the attitude towards torah in the Law of the King and in the torah psalms is the aim which both Psalter and Deuteronomy share: the exhortation towards absolute devotion to Yahweh.[81] In some ways, although this overstates the case, the torah is treated almost as a manifestation of Yahweh, similar to Wisdom (חכמה) in Prov 8.[82] Certainly there is a close association between Yahweh and his torah in both Deuteronomy and the torah psalms and strong indication that devotion to the written torah has become an indispensable component for the true expression of devotion to Yahweh.[83] As Eaton points out with regard to the content of the torah psalms, "The centre of interest... remains the Lord himself, and the relation

---

[81] Crenshaw ("Deuteronomist," passim) rejects any substantial degree of Dtr influence in the Psalter based on linguistic connections and suggests that the links which do exist are unsurprising because these are similar discourses. This seems a somewhat curious argument, as if the fact that we should expect to find similarities between the Psalms and Deuteronomy somehow mitigates against or dilutes the significance of these associations. The point, however, is that, as even Crenshaw points out, there are similar paraenetic functions at work in these two books, each encouraging devotion to Yahweh. The fact that we expect such ties ought to be a spur to examine these links in greater detail.

[82] This is Freedman's suggestion: "In short, Psalm 119 gives *tôrâ* virtually the status of a divine hypostasis, like wisdom (*ḥokmâ*) in Proverbs 8. Psalm 119 and Proverbs 8 share vocabulary and theology. Neither *tôrâ* nor *ḥokmâ* can be separated from Yahweh, who created them; yet each embodies an essential aspect of Yahweh that nevertheless can be addressed, invoked, and appealed to itself as the object of devotion. Each has the power to order and bless the worshipper's life," (Freedman, *Psalm 119*, 89–90). Whilst the attribution of "divine hypostasis" to torah goes too far, Freedman's general point is helpful: the psalmist sees devotion to divine revelation as a very direct means of devotion to the Lord himself.

[83] Such is the extent of this association that Briggs goes too far in his criticism of the poet who penned Ps 119: "It is not true that this author has the Deuteronomic spirit. The personal allegiance to Yahweh of D has become a legal allegiance.... Love to the Law is characteristic of this poet: in the form of commands; of testimonies; of precepts.... The love to the Law takes the place of the earlier Deuteronomic love to Yahweh.... The object of the praise is the Law; but a later editor makes the God the object by a change of text at the expense of the measure," (*Psalms*, 418–19, 424–25, 436). It is not that the Law itself has become the object of devotion, rather the psalmist sees it as the *essential means* for the expression of proper devotion to Yahweh.

to him."[84] Allen likewise comments regarding the psalmist's attitude towards torah in Ps 119: "There is no hint of legalism in any of its twenty-two strophes. It breathes a spirit of devotion and celebrates the closest of relationships between the psalmist as 'your servant' and Yahweh as 'my God.'"[85] A similar idea is apparent in the calls to live by the torah of Yahweh throughout the Book of Deuteronomy. Sonnet points out that it is through the written torah stipulations that Yahweh's voice continues to be heard by the people.[86] Also Deut 4:1–8 makes it clear that it is in the observance of Yahweh's ordinances Israel enjoys the nearness of God.[87]

2.4 CONCLUSION REGARDING TORAH

The idea of torah in the torah psalms and the Kingship Law is grounded in the same notion: a sacred text by way of which one comes to know the Lord and his ways through meditative recitation. Therefore it appears that, with regard to the concepts of "torah" at least, the Kingship Law could have been the paradigm which inspired the placement of kingship psalms alongside torah psalms.

2.5 EXCURSUS: TRANSLATION OF TORAH

The commentators devote considerable attention to explaining that the Hebraic understanding of "torah" (תורה) is much broader than our contemporary English understanding of "law." A modern English-language understanding of law equates the word with legislation, judicial declaration and the like: that is, with "law proper." The Hebrew understanding is much broader than that, denoting holistic divine revelation: that is, law and narrative, poetry and prophecy—teaching in its widest sense. This has led some commentators to suggest that the English translation for torah would be better as "instruction" rather than "law."[88]

---

[84] Eaton, *Psalms of the Way*, 52.

[85] Allen, *Psalms*, 141–42. See also Schaefer, *Psalms*, 47 and Kirkpatrick, *Psalms*, 701 for similar conclusions.

[86] "In the perspective opened in 30:10, Moses' oral mediation gives way to the written document's: 'since you will be hearing the voice of YHWH your God and keeping his commandments and his statutes which are written in this record of the Torah.' The concept of obedience includes now the reference to the divine voice as well as the reference to the written record. God's voice that could not be heard except through Moses' is now mediated by the written stipulations of 'this record of the Torah,'" (Sonnet, *The Book within the Book*, 110).

[87] Craigie, *Deuteronomy*, 128–31; Miller, *Deuteronomy*, 53–57.

Undoubtedly, there is much merit in this suggestion, as the Hebrew concept is clearly broader than that which is found in "law" as understood in Western society today. On the other hand, however, it seems that to follow this course of action in the translation of EVV would ultimately require as much, if not more, scholarly explanation than the present translation does. The problem with the translation "instruction" is that contemporary Western society also lacks any concept of God's instruction within the context of binding covenant. "Instruction" or "teaching," according to modern understanding, implies a "take-it-or-leave-it" educative function. We can accept or reject instruction as we please. "Instruction" captures the didactic nature of the torah of Yahweh, but not its covenantal aspect. The torah *is* didactic, educational material and it *does* include much more than law. However, to adopt this as a translation in the EVV would require the added explanation that this "instruction" is not an optional extra, but is absolutely binding on the people of God. McBride's comments are telling:

> Although modern commentators often remark that the typical rendering of *tôrâ* as "law" in English translations is misleading, the alternatives usually proposed on the basis of etymological considerations, "teaching" and "instruction," are scarcely an improvement as far as the Deuteronomic usage is concerned. Conception of *tôrâ* as "teaching" or "instruction" has promoted a much too facile understanding of Deuteronomy itself as essentially a didactic, moralizing, or homiletical work. More importantly, neither term conveys the normative, prescriptive force of *tôrâ* in Deuteronomy. The "words" or "stipulations" of "this torah" are not simply admonitions and sage advice offered in the name of Moses to guide the faithful along a divinely charted path of life; they are set forth as sanctioned political policies, to be "diligently observed" by Israelite king and common citizen alike (17:19; 31:12; 32:45), and on their strict observance hangs the fate of the entire nation (e.g., 28:58–68). What speaks against the rendering "law" is not some inchoate threat of legalism that might diminish the theological vitality of the Hebrew term, for while *tôrâ* in Deuteronomy is theologically cogent, it remains no less decidedly a jurisprudential concept. Rather, the problem is that neither our English word "law" nor its Greek counterpart, *nomos*, is sufficiently discrete to express at once the distinctiveness and the scope which *tôrâ* exhibits, especially in Deuteronomic usage but also elsewhere. On the one hand, *tôrâ* in this usage is not an abstraction or umbrella term covering every rule, decision, and act that Israelite social authority might choose to acknowledge and enforce; on the other hand, it does connote the totality of particular categories of legislation and judicial practice appropriate to it. It is the type of law connoted by *tôrâ* that is at issue. We can

---

[88] Lindars, "Torah."; Olson, *Death of Moses*, 10–11; deClaissé-Walford, *Reading from the Beginning*, 42; Basil de Pinto, "The Torah and the Psalms," *JBL* 86 (1967): 155; Mays, *Psalms*, 41–42, and many others.

name it most easily with reference to its self-declared function: "This torah" is covenantal law, the divinely authorized social order that Israel must implement to secure its collective political existence as the people of God.[89]

As McBride points out, the translation "instruction" would be equally inadequate and would require clarification of a different type, explaining that this instruction is binding and essential to proper relationship with Yahweh.

What conclusions can be offered? First, it seems that the translation "instruction" may accentuate antinomian tendencies which are all too prevalent in contemporary Christian (at least Western) churches. Secondly, this translation would not do away with the need of further explanation, it would merely require a different type of clarification. Neither "law" nor "instruction" encompasses all aspects of the Hebrew "torah." Ultimately, there is no single English word which adequately conveys the various aspects of torah.[90] The best solution seems to be the one suggested by the recently published ESV[91] which adheres to the traditional translation "law" (thus indicating the binding nature of this divine revelation) but offers clarification, by way of footnotes, that this term also includes the nuance of "instruction" (thus pointing out the didactic nuance).

3. KINGSHIP

If there is an area where one's first reaction would be to say that the Psalms and Deuteronomy certainly speak with different voices, it would be the area of kingship. First impressions seem to indicate that Deuteronomy is—*at best*—cautious about kingship,[92] whereas the Psalms are overwhelmingly positive about kingship.[93] As McConville points out, the Dtr view of kingship (as expressed in the Kingship Law) and David-Zion view of kingship (as found primarily in the Psalms) are different and we should not attempt to explain these differences away lightly.[94] However, this issue is relevant to the underlying

---

[89] McBride, "Polity," 65–66.

[90] Of course, there are instances of contextual usage where the word תורה does mean precisely "law" or "instruction" and in such cases the word should be translated accordingly. This discussion is pertinent to the many occasions where the context does not lead the reader to a specific understanding of this word.

[91] English Standard Version (Wheaton, IL: Crossway Bibles, 2001).

[92] Halpern, *Constitution*, 226–31.

[93] Howard, "Case for Kingship in Psalms."

[94] McConville, *Deuteronomy*, 306. My thanks to Prof. McConville for making the proofs of his now published AOTC commentary available prior to publication.

thesis of this work: does *the juxtaposition* of kingship and torah psalms influence the reader's understanding of kingship in the Psalter? Could it be that the editorial placement of psalms within the canonical Psalter subtly redefines the psalmic view of monarchy?[95] It must also be admitted that Deuteronomy's view of king and monarchy is not straightforward either: much scholarly discussion focuses upon the issue of whether the book is pro- or anti-monarchic. Therefore, we must be careful to define the extent of the discussion in this section. The central question which will be addressed is: how do *the texts in question* view the concept of kingship and, again, could the Law of the King reasonably have acted as the paradigm for the juxtaposition of kingship and torah psalms in the Psalter?

3.1 KINGSHIP IN THE TORAH-KINGSHIP PSALM GROUPINGS

One of the effects of a canonical approach is that individual poetic texts are to be read and interpreted within a broader context: the macro context of the Psalter; the context of the book within which the poem is found; the context of a collection, perhaps; and the context of its placement alongside neighbouring psalms. This style of interpretation within various contexts has marked implications for the understanding of any given text.[96] For example, certain psalms, when read as individual texts, can seem to advocate a simplistic (almost formulaic) doctrine of "health and wealth" for God's people, yet when these same texts are read in the broader canonical context of neighbouring laments and imprecations, their interpretation is modified and nuanced by that context.

Ps 2 is a classic example of a "royal" psalm.[97] As such it seems to celebrate the kingship of Yahweh's anointed unequivocally and without restraint.[98] Such

---

[95] It should be remembered that the examination of kingship in the psalms in this section, focuses attention on the torah-kingship psalm groupings. This is not an attempt to provide a definitive discussion of the whole Psalter's view of the king, as such a task would go well beyond the remit of this thesis, taking into account many more psalms (including the remaining royal psalms and many, if not most, of the "I" psalms).

[96] Mays, "Ps 118," 302–03; Mays, *The Lord Reigns*, 126–27; Schaefer, *Psalms*, xxi.

[97] Gunkel's definition of "royal" psalms as a form or type does seem fundamentally flawed, as most of the psalms classed "royal" do, in fact, vary greatly in terms of generic type (Eaton, *Kingship*, 20–26; Waltke, "Psalms," 1103). Rather than being classified according to genre, these texts are defined by the fact that they mention the king or David or anointed one or Zion etc. Ps 2 is a good example of this type of psalm because it mentions "king," "anointed," "son" and "Zion" along with other pointedly royal images (e.g. "scepter"). As far as I am aware the commentators all agree (with the exception of Gerstenberger who sees this, and other royal psalms, as late and eschatological in origin,

wholehearted affirmation of king and Zion could not seem further from the guarded approach of the Kingship Law with its limitations on the power of the monarch. In Ps 2 the king need merely ask to receive the nations as his inheritance; in Deut 17 he is instructed not to hoard silver and gold. On a *prima facie* level, these passages seem to reflect two entirely different views of kingship.

Such an interpretation results from reading Ps 2 as a text without a context.[99] Within the context of the Psalter as a whole, as we have seen in previous chapters, Ps 2 forms the second part of the introduction, and it is closely linked to Ps 1. Reading Ps 2 in the broader canonical context of its association with Ps 1 radically changes the interpretation of that text. How so? The king-anointed-son (בן-משיח-מלך) of Yahweh in Ps 2 is to be read in the light of the anonymous "person" (איש) of Ps 1.[100] The chosen ruler is, like all Israelites, called to live life under the rule of Yahweh's torah. The implication being that, for the king to enjoy the support of Yahweh as indicated by Ps 2, the king, like the "blessed person," must delight in Yahweh's torah.[101] The monarchic power and privilege of Ps 2 cannot be divorced from the covenant obedience of Ps 1.

So, when reading Pss 1 and 2 in conjunction, the reader is left with a fused image of individual and king subject to the rule of Yahweh (by obedience to his torah) and taking refuge in him (dependent upon him).[102] This image, suggested by a canonical reading of Pss 1 and 2, is echoed in the other torah-kingship psalm groupings. In the kingship psalms (Pss 2, 18, 20–21, 118) the psalmist

---

Psalms, Part I: with Introduction to Cultic Poetry [FOTL, Vol. XIV; Grand Rapids: Eerdmans, 1988], 48–49) that this psalm is connected with the Davidic monarchy.

[98] Oesterley, *Psalms*, 123.

[99] Not that it would be hermeneutically inappropriate to examine Ps 2 as a text in its own right. The point is, however, that a canonical reading does make a difference to the interpretation of individual texts. Texts that have traditionally been understood in certain terms take on a more nuanced interpretation when read in the light of their neighbours: Ps 2 is a classic example of this principle at work. See, for example, Mays, "Question of Context," 19–20 and Brueggemann responds in kind suggesting, "The question of context is in the end, I believe, the invitation to try the literature as a whole, and *to interpret each of the parts in terms of the whole*," ("Response to Mays," 36, emphasis mine).

[100] Miller, "Beginning," 91–92.

[101] Indeed, Creach points out that the concept of "taking refuge in Yahweh" (הוסי בו, Ps 2:12) becomes intimately linked with the idea of torah-obedience when read in the context of the whole book (*Yahweh as Refuge*, 73). The king, in taking refuge in Yahweh, is expected to do so through living in accordance with his law.

[102] Creach, *Yahweh as Refuge*, 67, 80; Miller, "Beginning," 19–20; Mays, *Psalms*, 48–49.

paints a picture of the ruler as one dependent upon Yahweh for deliverance.[103] The torah psalms, in turn, emphasize the importance of the written revelation of God for king/individual to live righteously before him.[104] This constant juxtaposition of a monarch depending not on his own strength but on Yahweh and the importance of the individual's response to the torah of Yahweh echoes the main thrust of the Kingship Law. Miller writes concerning this type of juxtaposition in Pss 1 and 2:

> At this point, therefore, one recognizes a major link between Psalms 1 and 2 that is provided by Deuteronomy in its latest editorial stages. In the Deuteronomic law of the king, the ruler is given only one responsibility, one assignment. It is to have "a copy of this law" (*mišnēh hattôrâ hazzō't*, Deut 17:18) with him always, to read in it all the days of his life, and to learn to fear the Lord by keeping all its words. In the Deuteronomic ideal of human rule, the *'îš* or "one" whose delight is in the law of the Lord, and who meditates on it continually, is the king. The ideal ruler therefore is the model Israelite.[105]

Miller develops this connection further with regard to Pss 18–19, where he observes that, "the term 'servant,' according to the book in general, but more particularly in this collection, is to be associated with two figures, the ruler and the torah lover, *two figures who here merge into one*."[106] He goes on to suggest that, "the collection in Psalms 15–24 may be seen as defining proper kingship at the beginning of the Psalter. Obedience to torah and trust in Yahweh's guidance and deliverance are the way of Israel and the way of kingship."[107] These observations lead Miller to the conclusion, noted in the introduction, that, "we are once more before the Deuteronomistic theology of kingship. It may be that all of this in fact reflects a Deuteronomistic influence on the redaction of the Psalter. I do not know. If it does, then we are made even more aware of the centrality of that particular stream in biblical theology and its influence on the theology of kingship and the royal ideal."[108]

---

[103] This content has been discussed in some detail in chapters 2–4, above.

[104] See also chapters 2–4, above.

[105] Miller, "Beginning," 91. Miller goes on to add that, "The *'îš* of Psalm 1 is as much a ruler as the ruler of Psalm 2 is an *'îš*," thus showing that the instruction of Pss 1 and 2 applies as much to covenant individuals as it does to kings, we shall consider this further in our discussion of "Democratisation," where we will also consider the idea of the king as "brother" from the Kingship Law, which is also relevant to this point.

[106] Miller, "Kingship," 128 (emphasis mine).

[107] Miller, "Kingship," 140.

[108] Miller, "Kingship," 141. The main emphasis of this thesis examins the rhetorical

Finally, with regard to Pss 118 and 119, the reader is also aware of this same pattern of royal dependence upon Yahweh and the centrality of torah, thus pointing once again towards the Law of the King in the juxtaposition of these two texts. The king leads the people in worship and his central confession, which secures admittance to the Temple (118:22) refers to the deliverance of Yahweh in response to the king's empassioned plea (vv 5–14). The royal figure of Ps 118 makes clear his dependence upon Yahweh[109] and the royal figure of Ps 119 makes clear his devotion to Yahweh by way of an archetypal example of devotion to his torah.[110]

3.1.1 CONCLUSION REGARDING KINGSHIP IN THE TORAH-KINGSHIP PSALM GROUPINGS

This examination of the view of kingship presented in the torah-kingship psalm groupings reveals that these particular psalms consider the king to be characterised by two features: dependence upon Yahweh and devotion to his torah. These features, as we shall discuss presently, clearly resonate with the Dtr presentation of the ideal king in Deut 17:14–20. Interpretation of these psalms in their canonical context adds nuance to the Psalter's presentation of the monarchy. Obviously, the psalmic view of kingship is broader than the psalms which have been considered, therefore, this conclusion must be held in tension with the presentation of the king found in, for example, Pss 72 and 110.[111] The suggestion being proposed here is not that David-Zion theology is absent from the Psalms, but, rather that this theology—when the royal psalms in question are read from a canonical perspective—is, perhaps, not as far removed from the Dtr ideal of kingship as one might expect because it has been influenced by the theological ideas of the Law of the King.[112]

---

question which Miller poses, and, indeed, it does appear that the Dtr theology of kingship influences the Psalter's concept of "the theology of the king and the royal ideal."

[109] Mays, "Ps 118," 306; Creach, *Yahweh as Refuge*, 67; Harman, *Psalms*, 377.

[110] For full discussion of the royal background to Pss 119 see chapter 4, pp 168–172. See also Soll, *Psalm 119*, 133–35; Eaton, *Psalms*, 274; Dahood, *Psalms vol. III, 101–150*, 173; Schaefer, *Psalms*, 10–11.

[111] It should be added that these kingship psalms which seem, at first reading (like Ps 2), to express royal prerogatives strongly must also be read in the light of their context within the Book of Psalms. Such a reading may also lead to a slightly different understanding of the theology of these psalms.

[112] McConville, *Deuteronomy*, 366.

278   *The King as Exemplar*

3.2 KINGSHIP IN THE KINGSHIP LAW

The debate concerning kingship in Deuteronomy and the DtrH rages on unabated. In recent years Knoppers has suggested that Deuteronomy's view of kingship and DtrH's take on the same topic differ: the former being anti-monarchic and the latter pro-monarchic.[113] Levinson has suggested that torah has been elevated above the monarchy at some late stage (possibly during Manasseh's reign) as a controlling ideal seeking (unrealistically) to limit the power of an ANE monarch.[114] Both of these articles (and other scholarly works) point out differences between Deuteronomy and the DtrH in their presentation of kingship. This may well be the case, yet in a certain sense these works seek to answer a question not asked by the text. The question is not one of Deuteronomy being for or against the monarchy: rather the "correct question" should be, as Gerbrandt puts it, "to ask what kind of kingship he [the Deuteronomist] saw as ideal for Israel, or what role kingship was expected to play for Israel?"[115] Such is the purpose of the Kingship Law, to tell the reader, not whether there should be a king, but *what type* of king the community should seek to appoint.[116]

To summarise the findings of chapter 5, there appears to be one over-arching principle which dictates the tone of the Kingship Law, and this is manifest in two particular emphases of that law. The over-arching principle, as in the whole of Deuteronomy, is that Yahweh is the true King. Therefore he is Lord over all his people, including the king.[117] This over-arching principle finds

---

[113] Knoppers, "Deuteronomist and Deuteronomic Law of the King."
[114] Levinson, "Reconceptualization," 527–28.
[115] Gerbrandt, *Kingship*, 41.
[116] Chapter 5 of this thesis gives due consideration to this very question. It should be stressed, however, that the presentation of a theology of kingship in Deut 17 is only one of many voices throughout the OT concerning monarchy in Israel and Judah. Prophetic and historical accounts may, indeed, present kingship in a different light. One of the key issues in any such comparative study (viewing kingship from the perspective of Deut cf. DtrH, for example) is to have the right starting point. Both Knoppers and Levinson assume an anti-monarchic message in the Law of the King and this, obviously influences their conclusions. The desire here is not to try to reduce these voices into one, but rather to let the Kingship Law speak for itself uninfluenced by the various narrative traditions of the DtrH. The suggestion made above (chapter 5) is that the Kingship Law is, in fact neutral, if cautious, concerning the idea of kingship (not anti-monarchic), but is quite explicit about the *type* of kingship which should function in Israel.
[117] This principle is readily observable the content of the Book of Deuteronomy and also in its structure. The constant theme of the book is that Yahweh rules the people whether they are in the wilderness or in the land, (Wright, *Deuteronomy*, 208; Craigie,

manifestation in two particular aspects of the Law of the King: the limitation of royal powers (forcing an attitude of dependence) and the king's submission to the torah of Yahweh.[118]

These two emphases of the Kingship Law point the reader to conclusions similar to those observed with regard to the concept of kingship in our selected psalms. The king's powers are limited—neither military might, nor international treaties, nor wealth shall be the source of his strength—and the purpose of those limitations is to keep the monarch entirely dependent upon Yahweh, and not upon his own might or external factors.[119] Over and above this, the king (like the people) is subject to the rule of Yahweh's torah. He is not above the law, but subject to the same strictures of the covenant as are all Israelites.[120] These limitations, however, are not entirely negative. They do have a positive corollary: namely, the king becomes the archetypal follower of Yahweh.[121] The king was meant to be an example of these two factors for the people of Israel: (1) com-

---

Deuteronomy, 523 etc.). It is also inherent to the suzerain-vassal treaty structure of Deuteronomy. The message of the structure of Deuteronomy is clear: Yahweh is the Great King and Lord over his people (Thompson, *Deuteronomy*, 205–06; Olson, *Death of Moses*, 128–29).

[118] McBride, "Polity," 74; McConville, "King and Messiah," 276–78; Tigay, *Deuteronomy*, 166.

[119] Gerbrandt, *Kingship*, 89. Gerbrandt particularly emphasizes the fact that the king is not to serve the primary function of military leader as this is Yahweh's remit. It is for this reason that Samuel and Yahweh react so negatively to the request for a king in 1 Sam 8. Gerbrandt submits that it was not the request for a king *per se* that provoked the divine reaction, but rather the fact that the people sought a king like the other nations "to go before us and fight our battles" (8:20) that particularly provoked the divine and prophetic displeasure (p 101).

[120] As Lohfink points out, in the polity of Israel "the Torah always has pride of place," ("Distribution," 350–51). He goes on to add regarding the king that, "First, the law concerning kings subordinates the king completely to the Torah. According to 17:18–20, he must possess a copy of the Torah and keep it always by him, reading from it daily, so that he learns to fear Yahweh and to observe all the words of the Torah. Like every other Israelite (17:20), he is thus totally subject to the Torah."

[121] Scholars use a variety of phrases for this highly symbolic role of the king as an example for the people. For Sonnet, the king becomes "arch-reader" of the Mosaic torah speeches when they attain written form (Sonnet, *The Book Within the Book*, 71). For Gerbrandt, the king becomes "covenant administrator": "This is then our proposal for how the Deuteronomist understood kingship. It could be summarised by saying that the Deuteronomist expected the king to lead Israel by being the covenant administrator; then he could trust Yahweh to deliver. At the heart of this covenant was Israel's obligation to be totally loyal to Yahweh," (*Kingship*, 104).

plete reliance upon Yahweh; and (2) excellence in devotion towards Yahweh by meditating on and living in accordance with Yahweh's torah.

3.3 CONCLUSION REGARDING KINGSHIP

Two features are central to the Dtr presentation of the king. First, the king is not to place his trust in anything or anyone other than Yahweh. He is to depend entirely upon God. Such total trust in Yahweh is echoed in the prayer, confessions and praises of the kingship psalms considered above (Pss 2, 18, 20–21 and 118). In each of these psalms Yahweh is the main protagonist on the monarch's behalf. In no case does the king every suggest self-sufficiency or trust in any other source—in fact, he frequently denies trust in alternative sources of power. Equally, the king according to the Deuteronomist is to learn to fear Yahweh by way of torah-meditation and application in his life (Deut 17:18, 20). Correspondingly, the royal psalms are placed alongside torah psalms (Pss 1, 19, 119), implying the same conclusion: the king in the Psalter is also subject to the torah of Yahweh. The Dtr ideal of kingship does, indeed, find expression in the Book of Psalms by way of the juxtaposition of torah and kingship poems.

> One of the most interesting observations is that Psalms 1, 19, and 119 all occur in juxtaposition to a psalm about kingship. This pairing, Mays concludes, suggests that, in the thinking of the editors of the book,
>> life under the Lord must be understood and recited in the light of the reign of the Lord and that all psalms concerned with the kingship of the Lord must be understood and recited with the Torah in mind.
>
> Within the matrix of meditation on *tôrâ* and submission to Yahweh's rule the whole Psalter is to be read and understood.[122]

This matrix follows the pattern of the Kingship Law and became a paradigm for the redactors of the Psalter. This twofold message of torah-obedience and dependence on Yahweh provided a rubric for the encouragement of a similar devotion to Yahweh amongst the readers of the Psalter, thus influencing also the picture of the king of eschatological hope found in the Psalms.

4. DEMOCRATISATION

The conclusions of this chapter so far indicate that there are, indeed, similarities between the psalmic view of torah and kingship, as found in the torah-kingship psalm groupings, and the view of these concepts presented in

---

[122] Creach, *Yahweh as Refuge*, 16, citing Mays, "Place of the Torah-Psalms," 10.

Torah, Kingship and Democratisation 281

Deuteronomy's Kingship Law. There is, as we have seen in the discussion throughout chapters 2–5, one further area of apparent correspondence between these texts which needs to be addressed: that is, the idea of democratisation. The Kingship Law explicitly speaks to the king, but it is also part of the Mosaic torah speeches which were ultimately to take the form of sacred text for the whole community in Israel.[123] What, then, does this text mean for the people? Is it no more than a yardstick by which to judge the actions of the reigning monarch? Or do the strictures and exhortations addressed to the king somehow speak to the community as a whole also?[124] Equally, within the Psalter the reader is placed in the somewhat unusual position of trying to understand a poetic book dominated in various ways by the figure of the king, yet, at the time of the book's closure there was no king in Jerusalem. Indeed, most likely, there had been no king in Jerusalem for some considerable time. How was it that these psalms survived?[125] How then is the reader to view these kingship psalms? Are they no more than historical curiosities?[126] Or have they taken on some new meaning for the reader of the Psalter?[127]

It seems that, in both Deuteronomy and the Psalms, the teaching concerning the king has come to mean more to the people than was originally the case, as succeeding generations—in changed historical settings—approach these texts afresh. The texts concerning the king speak also to the people.[128] So we now turn our attention to this question of the democratisation of royal texts in the torah-kingship psalms and the Kingship Law.

4.1 DEMOCRATISATION OF TORAH AND KINGSHIP PSALMS

There is a sense in which the generic nature of all psalms means that they are democratised material. That is, the psalms were written by an individual with regard to a particular situation (be it factual or typical), yet they are expressed in such a way that the lessons learned or the prayers and praises offered may be adopted by *any* individual in *any* similar circumstance.[129] However,

---

[123] Sonnet, *The Book within the Book*, 79–82.
[124] Miller, *Deuteronomy*, 148–49.
[125] Barth, *Introduction*, 23.
[126] McCann, *Psalms*, 649–50.
[127] Starbuck, *Court Oracles*, 61.
[128] Miller, "Beginning," 91–92.
[129] As Waltke puts it: "Most of the psalms, including those whose author is identif-

there is a particular sense of interpretative movement with regard to the royal psalms. Poems which were at one point connected with the ceremonial, cultic, political or military activities of the Davidic king are, in the post-exilic (and therefore post-monarchic) period, interpreted differently.[130] This change of interpretative understanding manifests itself in two ways: in terms of eschatological re-reading and in terms of community adoption of royal texts.[131]

4.1.1 REINTERPRETATION OF ROYAL PSALMS

As the question of the eschatological re-reading of royal psalms has been dealt with in chapter 1,[132] the second of these strategies for the re-reading of the royal psalms shall here be the focus of our attention. The pre-exilic compositions written by or about the king are re-interpreted more broadly in the post-exilic period as dealing with situations that are common to all people. Starbuck describes how this process of re-interpretation came about:

> The one-time representative for all of Israel is now represented through all Israel. It is not so much that the people collectively become "king," but rather, that the oracular promises pledged of old are now re-interpreted as promises to the entire community. This reappropriation and reinterpretation is a most significant development of Israel's theological-anthropology. It is also inexplicable from the standpoint of court-sponsored royal ideology. At the same time, the understanding that any Israelite could become a faithful office bearer was already implicit in the traditions which combined an unconditional royal-grant of "office" and "dynasty" with a conditional approval of the individual filling the office.[133]

---

ied, are written in abstract terms, not with reference to specific historical incidences, so that others could use them in their worship," ("Psalms," 1103). See also Miller, "Current Issues," 138; Childs, "Psalm Titles."

[130] Sheppard, *Future of the Bible*, 64–66; Vincent, "Shape of Psalter," 66.

[131] The first of these strategies for the re-interpretation of the Psalter's royal psalms has been dealt with in some detail in chapter 1 of this thesis (pp 32–38 above). Clearly, the post-exilic reader of the psalms would feel as strong sense of dissonance concerning the content of the royal psalms and the historical reality of his or her day (in fact this would probably be true of the reader throughout much of the monarchic period also). Rather than rejecting these psalms in the final form of the book the editors retained them and placed them in prominent positions throughout the Psalter. One of the main reasons for doing so was the eschatological expectation of a renewed Davidic kingdom which seems to have been fairly prevalent around the time of the closure of the Psalter. See the quote from Vincent, pp 37–38n120, above.

[132] See previous footnote.

[133] Starbuck, *Court Oracles*, 211–12.

As Starbuck points out, a significant part of this process of reinterpretation is based in the fact that even during the monarchic period the king as "office bearer" was meant to act as an example of commitment to Yahweh for the people. Failure to follow the divine instruction would lead to removal from office.[134] It seems that the purpose of the office bearers in general, and of the king in particular, was to act as exemplar for the people—to be a model Israelite and example to follow.[135] This exemplary function is accentuated even further in the period when there was no king: the poetic presentation of the ideal of obedience to Yahweh is set up as an example for all the readers and hearers of the Psalms.

Thanks to this exemplary aspect to the role of the king, it seems that the hermeneutical re-interpretation of the royal psalms was not a fraught task, but one which would occur quite naturally to both redactor and reader.[136] During the time of the monarchy the royal psalms were examples of prayer and piety, lament and thanksgiving associated with the king, but for the people as a whole.[137] The king's example of life *coram Deo*, expressed in the psalms, was exemplary for the people.[138] As the king expressed his absolute trust in Yahweh, so the people could echo his words in prayer.[139] As the king lamented over opposition, so the people could lament in the face of their own difficulties. The king in the psalms functions as a model for the people to follow,[140] therefore this

---

[134] 1 Kings 2:1-4; 11:11, 34 etc. The question of whether or not the Davidic covenant was conditional or unconditional is another area of DtrH studies which provokes a great deal of heated discussion. This is not an issue of central importance to the thesis proposed here, except to say that—based on the Kingship Law and certain texts of the DtrH—there does appear to be an expectation that the king follow the torah of Yahweh. However, this is not the only "voice" on this matter, certainly torah-obedience is of considerable importance regarding kingship, and yet words of divine grace based in the Davidic covenant are heard frequently in the OT also.

[135] Allen, "David as Exemplar."

[136] Roy F. Melugin, "Canon and Exegetical Method," in *Canon, Theology and Old Testament Interpretation: Essays in Honor of Brevard S. Childs* (ed. G. M. Tucker et al.; Philadelphia: Fortress, 1988), 55–56.

[137] Creach writes that, "late Psalms seemed to borrow from earlier writings that described... the piety of the king in order to express and encourage a personal devotion," (*Yahweh as Refuge*, 73).

[138] Soll, *Psalm 119*, 133.

[139] See Starbuck, *Court Oracles*, 103, where he writes, "the [royal] prayers that were reused were appropriated not only by monarchs but by commoners as well."

[140] Soll, *Psalm 119*, 130–31; Starbuck, *Court Oracles*, 210–11.

process of post-exilic re-interpretation of royal texts from the perspective of the people would have been quite natural.[141]

4.1.2 DEMOCRATISATION OF THE TORAH-KINGSHIP PSALM GROUPINGS

Miller develops these thoughts with regard to the reinterpretation of two of the three torah-kingship psalms groupings.[142] First, with regard to the Psalter's introduction, it is worth quoting extensively from Miller's argument:

> At this point, therefore, one recognizes a major link between Psalms 1 and 2 that is provided by Deuteronomy in its latest editorial stages. In the Deuteronomic law of the king, the ruler is given only one responsibility, one assignment. It is to have "a copy of this law" (*mišnēh hattôrâ hazzō't*, Deut 17:18) with him always, to read in it all the days of his life, and to learn to fear the Lord by keeping all its words. In the Deuteronomic ideal of human rule, the *'îš* or "one" whose delight is in the law of the Lord, and who meditates on it continually, is the king. The ideal ruler therefore is the model Israelite....
>
> There is also a reverse way of reading from these psalms into the ones that follow than the one outlined above. The dual introduction creates a certain ambiguity for the reading of the psalms. The subject introduced to us is clearly the king against his enemies. But it is also the *'îš* against the wicked, that is, *anyone* who lives by the Torah of the Lord and thus belongs to the righteous innocent who cry out in these psalms. So one may not read these psalms as exclusively concerning rulers....
>
> [T]he ruler is the *'îš* of Psalm 1, but to no greater extent than any member of the community who delights in the law of the Lord and walks in the way of the righteous. *Psalm 1 placed before Psalm 2, therefore, joins Deuteronomy in a kind of democratizing move that stands in tension with the royal one arising out of the placing of Psalm 2 as the lead into Psalms 3ff....* [T]he anointed one is simply a true Israelite even as he is a true king.... *The 'îš of Psalm 1 is as much a ruler as the ruler of Psalm 2 is an 'îš.*[143]

Miller makes the point concisely: there is a democratising principle at work in the juxtaposition of Pss 1 and 2 based around the Law of the King. The figure of the king is an example of proper piety for the people and the juxtaposition of the "person" (איש) and "king" (מלך) in Pss 1 and 2 makes this democratising principle clear. The people are expected to follow the example of piety set by the king.

---

[141] Allen, "David as Exemplar," 545.

[142] See "Beginning," 83–92, with regard to the interpretation and re-interpretation of Pss 1 and 2 and "Kingship," 127–42, concerning the re-interpretation of the royal concepts of Pss 18–21.

[143] Miller, "Beginning," 91–92 (emphasis mine).

With regard to Pss 18–21, Miller argues that a similar principle is at work (again, a more extensive citation helps to clarify the overall argument):

> [Pss 15–24] are a collection of psalms or prayers centering around loving obedience of the torah and the king as the embodiment of that way or that ideal. But it is clearly the case that this collection, introduced by Pss 1 and 2, resonates with Deuteronomy at one quite critical point: the equality of the king with other Israelites, the democratizing of kingship and the royalizing of the people. In Deuteronomy, this is especially seen in the law of the king....
>
> I would suggest the same is the case here. There is no explicit reference to the king in Ps 15 nor to the human king in Ps 24. It is only from the center [i.e. Pss 18–21] that we move backward and forward to see in those psalms a reflection of the one who fulfills the righteousness they [Pss 15 and 24] seek. If the king passes Israel's test according to the Deuteronomistic formulation and models Israelite obedience according to the Deuteronomistic law, it is also the case that any member of the community may fulfill the torah-piety that is exemplified in the king and reflected in the answers to the liturgical questions of Pss 15 and 24. Whoever lives this way may enter into the presence of the Lord in the sanctuary. Whoever meets the requirements is the 'iš of Ps 1, the torah lover and keeper.... As I have suggested, "the king, indeed David, is a representative figure, and never more so than as the one who lives by the Lord's torah."[144]

Once more, the centrality of the king in the collection of Psalms 15–24 is most significant because of the example that he sets for all of God's people. There is a democratising principle at work in this torah-kingship psalm grouping (Pss 18–21) which echoes the agenda of the Dtr Kingship Law: the king shall live as an example of commitment to Yahweh for all God's people to follow.

The same sort of democratising effect is at work in Pss 118–119, where the king leads the community in an entrance liturgy (Ps 118) and provides an example of prayerful devotion to Yahweh by way of commitment to his torah (Ps 119). Soll suggests that one of the reasons why the identity of the individual in Psalm 119 is not defined more clearly is precisely because of this process of democratisation—the prayer of the king has become the prayer of the people.[145] Frost makes the same sort of observation with regard to Ps 118.[146] As with the

---

[144] Miller, "Kingship," 130–31.

[145] Soll, *Psalm 119*, 138–39. He comments that Ps 119, though once associated with the king, has become "democratised and used in rituals for commoners."

[146] Frost ("Psalm 118," 161–62) suggests that, "[Ps 118] is itself the product of the inner court. It was the thanksgiving of the king for victory in battle and for his vindication in the eyes of the people. But when the kingship departed it was taken over for use with a wider reference and adapted for congregational use. The "I" of the psalm now

286   *The King as Exemplar*

previous two groupings, we see an association which reflects the theology of the Kingship Law: Ps 118 expresses the king's dependence upon Yahweh for deliverance and Ps 119 the king's delight in his torah. The psalmist-king is presented as the exemplar of these attitudes in Pss 118–119.

Not only the theological content, but also the pattern of democratisation is common to all three of these psalm groupings. In them the idealised figure of the king is held up as an example to the people. The piety of the king (probably seen by most post-exilic readers as David[147]) is held up as an example for the people to follow. Not only are these psalms meant to influence the Psalter's presentation of the eschatological king, but they also teach a worldview which, according to the editors of the Psalms, the people of God should adopt: one of complete reliance upon Yahweh and devotion to him through keeping his torah.

4.2 DEMOCRATISATION IN THE KINGSHIP LAW

There is (at least) a twofold sense in which the Kingship Law may be seen as democratised. First, intrinsic to the text of Deut 17:14–20 is the strong association of the king with his Hebrew "brothers"—he is no more and no less than that, one of the covenant community. Secondly, the Book of Deuteronomy has an inherently democratising quality about it, whereby officials and people alike are under the same covenant obligations.

4.2.1   THE KING AS ONE OF THE HEBREW BROTHERS

As we have seen in our examination of the Kingship Law, this association of king and individual member of the covenant community is important to a proper understanding of the monarchic office in Israel. Whilst the practice of kingship in Judah and Israel was often far too similar to the exploitative patterns of ANE

---

became not the king but the nation. It was used to express the perennial sense of the people of God that 'Zion with Babylon must cope,' and she survives in her warfare only by the grace of God, and that as constantly renewed." He goes on to add that, "the democratisation of religion is a steady factor in the life of the ancient east."

[147] Alistair G. Hunter, *Psalms* (OTR; London: Routledge, 1999), 10. "The fact that Psalm 2 forms part of the introduction to the whole Psalter, that it makes explicit reference to the anointed (Hebrew *mashiach*), and that it uses exalted language for the relationship between the king and Yahweh — "You are my son: today I have begotten you" (2:7) — might very possibly be taken to demonstrate that Psalm 2 is one of those post-exilic writings (parts of Chronicles belong to the same type) which idealises the long-vanished Davidic monarchy in terms of an apocalyptic hope."

monarchy, the Dtr ideal presents a very different picture; a picture of the king as one of the community and not exalted over his "subjects." Deut 17:15 states that the king must be one of the Hebrew brothers (מקרב אחיך תשים עליך מלך), and, whilst clearly designed to prohibit the kingship of a foreigner (one not under the covenant), this verse also indicates that, "the essential criteria for Israel's appointment are that the king should be the one chosen by Yahweh, and that he should be a 'brother'-Israelite."[148] This democratising criterion finds fuller expression in Deut 17:20, where the king is told not to "exalt himself over his brothers" (לבלתי רום־לבבו מאחיו).[149] This emphasis on equality as part of the whole community under covenant allegiance, makes it clear that the king is not greater than the people, but is essentially part of the body corporate.[150] The emphasis of his role is not as administrator, judge or general, but rather as torah-keeper.[151] The king is to excel in keeping covenant with Yahweh and as such acts as an example for all of the Hebrew community.[152]

4.2.2 DEMOCRATISATION IN DEUTERONOMY

The idea of the monarch as a model of piety broadly reflects Deuteronomy's teaching with regard to those in power.[153] The stipulations addressed to the king echo obligations placed on the people throughout the book. The limitations on the king's power (no excess in terms of "weapons, women or wealth"[154]) and his positive duty (to keep the torah) echo similar obligations placed upon the people throughout Deuteronomy:

> Finally, the law of the king places upon that figure the obligations incumbent upon every Israelite. In that sense, Deuteronomy's primary concern was that the king *be the model Israelite*. This is seen especially in the fact that the essential responsibility of the king is to read and study the law constantly... "that he may learn to fear the Lord his God, by keeping all the words of this law and these statutes, and doing them" (v 19). This is the word that Moses constantly

---

[148] McConville, *Deuteronomy*, 293

[149] See above chapter 5.

[150] Knoppers, "Deuteronomist and Deuteronomic Law of the King," 329–30; McConville, *Law and Theology*, 19.

[151] Howard, "The Case for Kingship in Deuteronomy," 102; Craigie, *Deuteronomy*, 256–57.

[152] Miller, *Deuteronomy*, 148–49.

[153] As Tigay puts it, "The law about the king continues Deuteronomy's policy of limiting the power and prestige of human authorities," (*Deuteronomy*, 166).

[154] Wright, *Deuteronomy*, 209.

places before Israel throughout his speeches. The warning "that his heart may not be lifted up" echoes the same warning to Israel in 8:14, even as the prohibition against multiplying silver and gold (v 17) is reminiscent of the words of 8:13–17 about Israel doing the same thing and then forgetting that it is the Lord who has given the wealth. So also the warning not to "turn aside from the commandment, either to the right and or to the left," is the same as or similar to words addressed to each Israelite (cf 5:32; 11:28; 17:17; 28:14; 31:29; Joshua 23:6) or to other leaders (e.g., Joshua 1:7). *The fundamental task of the leader of the people, therefore, is to exemplify and demonstrate true obedience to the Lord for the sake of the well-being of both the dynasty and the kingdom. King and subject share a common goal: to learn to fear the Lord (v 19)*.[155]

Yahweh calls upon the king to practice a worldview which has already been placed before the people. The community as a whole is expected (under the Dtr covenant) to live in accordance with the obligations and prescriptions of the Kingship Law, so what is the purpose of repeating these obligations again in the law governing the monarchy? Probably there is a dual reason for this repetition: first, to emphasize that the king does not stand above or beyond the covenant;[156] and, secondly, because the king must *excel* in that which all the people are called to do, in the keeping of the covenant with Yahweh.[157] Miller sums up these two factors in suggesting:

> [T]he point of the Deuteronomic law of the king is that the king's responsibilities are the same as those of the people. He is to keep the torah continually and completely. Thus he embodies faithful Israel and models Israel's way with the Lord.[158]

4.3 CONCLUSION REGARDING DEMOCRATISATION

So, finally, it appears that the torah-kingship psalms not only share the Dtr views on torah and kingship, but that their process of democratisation also reflects the theology of Deuteronomy and, in particular, of the Kingship Law. Deuteronomy's Law of the King sets the lifestyle which the king should follow as an example of proper conduct for the people. The torah-kingship psalms fulfil

---

[155] Miller, *Deuteronomy*, 148–49 (emphasis mine). Mayes adds the concept of taking too many wives as another expression of an obligation placed first upon the people (Deut 7), tying it in with the rules rejecting the apostasy of the neighbouring nations (the assumption being that these are foreign wives, see his *Deuteronomy*, 272–73).

[156] "Rather, for the Deuteronomist the king was clearly also subject to the covenant. The king, like any other Israelite, was expected to obey the law as it was found in Deuteronomy," (Gerbrandt, *Kingship*, 100).

[157] Lohfink, "Distribution," 349.

[158] Miller, "Kingship," 130.

the same function. Not only are these psalms to be read as influencing the picture of the eschatological king, but they should also be read as commending a particular lifestyle to the reader of the Psalter—a lifestyle of complete trust in Yahweh and immersion in his word.

5. Conclusion

What then can be concluded from this analysis? Could Deuteronomy's Law of the King have been the paradigm which led to the juxtaposition of kingship and torah psalms? It seems that it could. The analysed texts show a notable correspondence to the ideals of Deut 17:14-20 in their teaching and theology. Their views of torah, kingship and democratisation are similar to such an extent that it does, indeed, seem (at least) possible that the Kingship Law was the paradigm which inspired the book's editors to place kingship psalms alongside the Psalter's three torah psalms. It appears that they had a twofold reason for doing so: (1) to nuance the image of the expected, restored Davidic king (i.e. a king in line with the ideal and not the historical practice); and (2) that the reader of the Psalms should follow the world-and-life view represented in the Kingship Law and the torah-kingship psalms.

> It may be premature to generalize about these questions, but I do believe that the biblical books of Deuteronomy and Psalms are amenable to an interactive relationship, capable of creating or evoking a conversation between them that enlarges our perception of both and contributes to a sense of the whole that is scripture.[159]
>
> I conclude, then, with Mays... that the organizing principle of the Psalter ultimately has to do with the reign of God as King. This theme manifests itself in the dual expressions of YHWH's divine kingship and the Davidic kings' human kingship, both of which find their earthly expression at Zion. The Zion, royal, and Davidic traditions displayed prominently and placed strategically throughout the Psalter take their place alongside the traditions of YHWH as King to portray the fact that YHWH's rule extends everywhere: to the nations, the cosmos, nature, and even Israel. Its expression in Israel is through the Davidic kingship, which is centered at Zion, and it is focused on YHWH through worship at Zion. *The faithful reader of the Psalter will do as the king is supposed to do: study and meditate on YHWH's disclosure of himself in both the Torah and the Psalter (Deut 17:18-19, Psalm 1)*.[160]

---

[159] Miller, "Deuteronomy and Psalms," 3.
[160] Howard, *Structure*, 207 (emphasis mine).

Conclusion

Often, having read a doctoral thesis, one is left with the impression that much ground has been covered in the course of that study—a working hypothesis is proposed in the introduction, a method suggested, detailed exegesis carried out, a case argued and theological inferences are drawn. Drawing a brief conclusion from such a breadth of discussion is no easy job. The discussion has been *necessarily* broad in order to argue the case fully; therefore, it is difficult not to be overly reductive in summarising this discussion. However, such is the task at hand.

The working hypothesis suggested in the introduction was that the editors of the Psalter made use of the Kingship Law as an intellectual paradigm in their placement of kingship psalms alongside torah psalms at key junctures in the Book of Psalms. A two-fold rationale was suggested for this use of the Kingship Law: (1) in response to the climate of messianic expectation, the editors wished to make clear that the restored Davidic king should be one who follows the ideal of kingship rather than the historical examples found in Deuteronomic History; (2) the Law of the King defined the monarch as an example of devotion to Yahweh (by way of developing a torah-centered worldview) for the whole people, and the editors of the Psalter wished to pick up on this exemplary commitment to God, and set it as a model for the readers of the psalms to follow.

The method suggested was a comparative canonical-theological treatment of the texts of the Psalms and Deuteronomy.[1] This is perhaps best described as reflecting Miller's idea of "conversation" between two books of the OT.[2] The

---

[1] See chapter 1 above.
[2] Miller, "Deuteronomy and Psalms."

aim (whilst intertextual "in its most basic sense"[3]), was not to prove that the torah-kingship psalms were dependent upon the Law of the King, nor was it to show exact borrowing between one text and the other. Rather it was to depict a theology of the torah-kingship psalm groupings and to compare that with the theology of the Kingship Law. Miller describes this as interaction "on a larger plane of theology and hermeneutics,"[4] and our discussion has also been carried out on this level—a major element of discussion has been how the respective theologies of torah, kingship and democratisation in the Psalms and Deuteronomy compare. The text which was analysed was, necessarily, the final, canonical form of each book. Obviously, examination of the final text is key to the idea of the shaping of the Psalter, and is the necessary starting point for discussion of the central question of this thesis is whether the final form of the Psalms has been deliberately framed to reflect Dtr (perhaps, more specifically DtrN) concerns, and, in particular, to reflect the Law of the King.

The exegetical examination was carried out over four chapters,[5] looking in some detail at the text of the torah-kingship psalm groupings (Pss 1–2; 18–21; 118–119) and of the Kingship Law (Deut 17:14–20). At the risk of oversimplifying, strong echoes of the theology of Deuteronomy as a whole were found in the poems in question. Not just in the torah psalms (as one might expect), but also in the kingship psalms. The picture of the king presented in Pss 2, 18, 20–21 and 118, is of an individual entirely dependent upon Yahweh—reliant upon him for deliverance and refusing to trust in alternative sources of power. This is a central aspect of the theology of Deuteronomy and, more specifically, of the Kingship Law.[6] Paralleled with this image of a king trusting in God is the idea of an individual living according to the torah.[7] Once again, this is an important feature of Deuteronomy and one which is clearly encouraged in the Law of the King.[8] These are not the only associations apparent between the torah-kingship psalms and the Kingship Law, but they are dominant features of both the psalmic and Deuteronomic texts studied and shape the reader's understanding in each case. It seems clear from the exegetical examination of these texts

---

[3] Miller, "Deuteronomy and Psalms," 5.
[4] Miller, "Deuteronomy and Psalms," 5.
[5] Chapters 2–5 above.
[6] Miller, *Deuteronomy*, 148; Wright, *Deuteronomy*, 209.
[7] Miller, "Beginning"; "Kingship."
[8] Tigay, *Deuteronomy*, 168; Miller, *Deuteronomy*, 141.

that there is, indeed, a conversation going on between Deuteronomy and the Psalms; and this is a conversation surrounding the figure of the king, as presented in the Kingship Law.[9]

The case was then argued that these psalm groupings which reflect the Law of the King were positioned at key junctures in the final form of the Psalter.[10] The first torah-kingship pairing (Pss 1–2) introduces the whole Book of Psalms: all of the discussions of kingship and piety which follow are somehow coloured by this image of the Dtr king found in that introduction. The remaining torah-kingship groupings are central to Books I and V of the Psalms, acting as a type of bracket, calling the reader's attention back to the message of the introduction. The Dtr influence upon the psalmic picture of the king is not peripheral; rather, it is prominent and positioned in such a way as to nuance the idea of kingship throughout the whole book. This redaction, clearly, does not reflect the complete or only view of kingship found in the Psalms, but it does influence the picture of the king in significant ways.

Theological inferences were also drawn from the analysis of the texts in question.[11] In particular, discussion focussed on the three main themes apparent both in the torah-kingship psalm groupings and the Kingship Law: torah, kingship and democratisation. The analysis of these concepts in the Psalms and Deuteronomy showed a marked similarity in their usage in both books. Torah in the psalms seems to refer to the written revelation of Yahweh. Initially, this may even be a reference to the Book of Deuteronomy itself, but with the passage of time this reference expanded into the Pentateuch and beyond. Torah-piety was to be based in the study of Yahweh's revelation in written form. Similarly, the Kingship Law contains Deuteronomy's first self-reference to the speeches of Moses ultimately becoming a book to be studied by king and people alike. Analysis of the concept of kingship in these psalms and in Deut 17 also reveals notable similarities: both books indicate that he is to be one dependent on God before any alternative source of power and one who is not elevated over his brothers. This leads us to the idea of democratisation. In both the Kingship Law and the torah-kingship psalms, there seems to be an inherently democratising ideal. The king is not greater than the people; rather, he is one of them. He is

---

[9] Miller, "Deuteronomy and Psalms," 16.
[10] Chapter 6 above.
[11] Chapter 7 above.

subject to the same torah and his lifestyle is meant to be one of example for the rest of the covenant people, example of keeping that torah: the king as exemplar.

Final Words

How do the ideas of this thesis speak to the contemporary Christian community? One clear message concerns the importance of divine revelation for proper relationship with the Creator. The Law of the King and the Dtr redaction of the Psalms suggests to the reader that proper piety can only be attained through the diligent study and application of the Word. The theology of the two ways further emphasises this point in that, if one is to walk in "the fear of the Lord," one must immerse oneself in his revealed torah. This speaks to the church, particularly in the West, where sometimes it appears that we are more concerned with the application of secular marketing principles and management techniques, than we are about giving primacy to the shaping of our worldview in accordance with God's teaching. If the church is to grow in depth *and numbers*, then we must follow the example of the king and devote time and energy to the application of divine instruction to our *Sitz im Leben*. Just as the Dtr king was not furnished with a lengthy list of regal "dos and don'ts" but was expected to apply the principles of Yahweh's torah to every aspect of his life and service, so we today should engage wholeheartedly in this important hermeneutical task. We too should seek to apply the whole of God's revealed "law" in our own particular life and circumstances. As with the king and the reader of the Psalms, the inculcation of a worldview is encouraged. It is about more than just following the particulars of the "law," it is a holistic way of thinking and acting shaped by God's revelation—we too must strive to develop a biblical worldview.

A second area of application, which the Christian community should be aware of, is in terms of broader biblical interpretation. Have we, perhaps, been missing out on a messianic theme which is of broader significance than we first realised?

> Much has been written about the way the messianic passages of the royal psalms and Isaiah point us to and find their actuality in Jesus of Nazareth. It is possible we have overlooked the text that may resonate most with the kingship he manifested; he was one who sought and received none of the perquisites of kingship, who gave his full and undivided allegiance to God, and who lived his whole life by the instruction, the torah, of the Lord.[12]

---

[12] Miller, *Deuteronomy*, 149.

Conclusion

McConville points out that, "The ideal of human kingship, introduced by the story of human failure and the gracious accommodation of God to it (in 1 Sam 8-12; 2 Sam 7), remains, however, for messianic appropriation."[13] And, in another article, he adds that, "the concept of a king under Torah is not lost even in the entrance of Davidic dynastic concepts into the story. And it is instructive to observe connections with the teaching Messiah in Matthew's gospel."[14]

Here it is that we return, at last, to the "greatest mystery of religion... the representative figure that carries all the world's agony and hope."[15] In Christ we see the fulfilment of the exemplary piety endorsed both by the Kingship Law and the Dtr redaction of the Psalter. He lived the life of the king who was also the torah-keeper. Where even the best of the Davidic kings failed, he did not. He lived the life of absolute devotion to Yahweh, as an example for all the people to follow. He was the king who would not exalt himself over his brothers. He is the ultimate king and ultimate exemplar. We find the teaching in the Old Testament and the reality in the New—Ιησοῦς ὁ βασιλεύς, Jesus the King.

---

[13] McConville, *Deuteronomy*, 366.
[14] McConville, "King and Messiah," 293.
[15] Eaton, *Kingship*, preface, cited above, p xiv.

BIBLIOGRAPHY

Alexander, Desmond T. "Messianic Ideology in the Book of Genesis." Pp. 19–39 in *The Lord's Anointed: Interpretation of Old Testament Messianic Texts*. Edited by Philip E. Satterthwaite, Richard S. Hess, and Gordon J. Wenham. Carlisle/GrandRapids: Paternoster Press/Baker Book House, 1995.

Allen, Leslie C. *Psalms 101–150*. WBC. Waco: Word Books, 1983.

———. "David as Exemplar of Spirituality: The Redaction Function of Psalm 19." *Bib* 67, no. 4 (1986): 544–46.

Alter, Robert. *The Art of Biblical Poetry*. New York: Basic Books, 1985.

Anderson, A. A. *The Book of Psalms, Volume I, Psalms 1–72*. NCB. London: Marshall, Morgan and Scott, 1972.

———. *The Book of Psalms, Volume II, Psalms 73–150*. NCB. London: Marshall, Morgan and Scott, 1972.

André, Gunnel. "'Walk,' 'Stand,' and 'Sit' in Psalm I 1-2." *VT* XXXII, no. 3 (1982): 327.

Ashburn, Daniel G. "Creation and Torah in Psalm 19." *JBQ* 22 (1994): 241–48.

Auffret, Pierre. *The Literary Structure of Psalm 2*. Translated by D. J. A. Clines. JSOTSup 3. Sheffield: JSOT Press, 1977.

———. *La Sagesse a Bâti Sa Maison: Études de Structures Littéraires dans l'Ancien Testament et Spécialement dans les Psaumes*. OBO 49. Fribourg: Editions Universitaires, 1982.

Baker, Kenneth L. "Praise." Pp. 233–54 in *Cracking Old Testament Codes: A Guide to the Literary Genres of the Old Testament*. Edited by D. B. Sandy and R. L. Giese, Jr. Nashville: Broadman and Holman, 1995.

Barré, Michael L. "'Fear of God' and the World View of Wisdom." *BTB* 11 (1981): 41–43.

Barr, James. "The Theological Case against Biblical Theology." Pp. 3–19 in *Canon, Theology and Old Testament Interpretation: Essays in Honor of Brevard S. Childs*. Edited by G. M. Tucker, D. L. Petersen, and R. R. Wilson. Philadelphia: Fortress, 1988.

Barth, Christoph F. *Introduction to the Psalms*. Translated by R. A. Wilson. New York: Charles Scribner's Sons, 1966.

Bartholomew, Craig G. "A Table in the Wilderness: Towards a Post-Liberal Agenda for Old Testament Study." Pp. 19–47 in *Make the Old Testament Live: From Curriculum to Classroom*. Edited by R. S. Hess and G. J. Wenham. Grand Rapids: Eerdmans, 1998.

Barton, John. "The Messiah in Old Testament Theology." Pp. 365–79 in *King and Messiah in Israel and the Ancient Near East: Proceedings of the Oxford Old Testa-*

ment Seminar. Edited by J. Day. JSOTSup 270. Sheffield: Sheffield Academic Press, 1998.

Beckwith, R. T. "The Canon of Scripture." Pp. 27–34 in *New Dictionary of Biblical Theology*. Edited by T. D. Alexander and B. S. Rosner. Leicester: IVP, 2000.

Bellinger, William H. "Let the Words of My Mouth: Proclaiming the Psalms." *SwJT* 27, no. 1 (Fall 1984): 17–24.

———. "Portraits of Faith: The Scope of Theology in the Psalms." Pp. 111–28 in *An Introduction to Wisdom Literature and the Psalms: Festschrift Marvin E. Tate*. Edited by H. W. Ballard and W. D. Tucker. Macon, GA: Mercer University Press, 2000.

Berry, Donald K. *The Psalms and Their Readers: Interpretive Strategies for Psalm 18*. JSOTSup 153. Sheffield: Sheffield Academic Press, 1993.

Blenkinsopp, Joseph. *Prophecy and Canon*. Notre Dame: Notre Dame Press, 1977.

Blomberg, Craig L. "The Unity and Diversity of Scripture." Pp. 64–72 in *New Dictionary of Biblical Theology*. Edited by T. D. Alexander and B. S. Rosner. Leicester: IVP, 2000.

Braulik, Georg. "The Sequence of the Laws in Deuteronomy 12–26 and in the Decalogue." Pp. 313–35 in *The Song of Power and the Power of Song: Essays on the Book of Deuteronomy*. Edited by D. L. Christensen. SBTS Vol 3. Winona Lake, IN: Eisenbrauns, 1993.

Briggs, Charles Augustus, and E. G. Briggs. *The Book of Psalms*. ICC. Edinburgh: T&T Clark, 1906.

Brown, F., S. A. Driver, and C. A. Briggs. *A Hebrew and English Lexicon of the Old Testament*. Peabody, MA: Hendrickson, 1997.

Brownlee, William H. "Psalms 1–2 as a Coronation Liturgy." *Bib* 52, no. 3 (1971): 321–36.

Broyles, Craig C. *The Conflict of Faith and Experience in the Psalms: A Form-Critical and Theological Study*. JSOTSup 52. Sheffield: JSOT Press, 1989.

Brueggemann, Walter. *The Creative Word*. Philadelphia: Fortress, 1982.

———. "Futures in Old Testament Theology." *HBT* 6, no. 1 (1984): 1–11.

———. *The Message of the Psalms: A Theological Commentary*. ACOT. Minneapolis: Augsburg, 1984.

———. "Imagination as a Mode of Fidelity." Pp. 13–36 in *Understanding the Word: Essays in Honour of Bernard W. Anderson*, JSOTSup 37. Edited by J. T. Butler, E. W. Conrad, and B. C. Ollenburger. Sheffield: JSOT Press, 1985.

———. "The Costly Loss of Lament." *JSOT* 36 (1986): 57–71.

———. "Bounded by Obedience and Praise." *JSOT* 50 (1991): 63–92.

———. "Response to Mays, 'The Question of Context.'" In *The Shape and Shaping of the Psalter*. Edited by J. Clinton McCann. JSOTSup 159. Sheffield: JSOT Press, 1993.

———. *The Psalms and the Life of Faith*. Edited by P. D. Miller. Minneapolis: Fortress, 1995.

———. "A First Retrospect on the Consultation." Pp. 342–47 in *Renewing Biblical Interpretation*. Edited by C. G. Bartholomew, C. J. D. Greene, and K. Möller. SHS, Vol. 1. Carlisle/Grand Rapids: Paternoster Press/Zondervan, 2000.

Brueggemann, Walter, and Patrick D. Miller. "Psalm 73 as a Canonical Marker." *JSOT* 72 (1996): 45–56.

Bullough, Sebastian. "The Question of Metre in Psalm I." *VT* XVII, no. 1 (January 1967): 42–49.
Ceresko, Anthony R. "The Sage in the Psalms." Pp. 217–30 in *The Sage in Israel and the Ancient Near East*. Edited by J. G. Gammie and L. G. Perdue. Winona Lake, IN: Eisenbrauns, 1990.
Childs, Brevard S. "Psalm Titles and Midrashic Exegesis." *JSS* 16, no. 2 (Autumn 1971): 137–49.
———. "Reflections on the Modern Study of the Psalms." Pp. 377–88 in *Magnalia Dei: The Mighty Acts of God: Essays on the Bible and Archeology in Memory of G. Ernest Wright*. Edited by F. M. Cross, W. E. Lemke, and P. D. Miller. Garden City, N.Y.: Doubleday, 1976.
———. *Introduction to the Old Testament as Scripture*. London: SCM Press, 1979.
———. "Old Testament Theology." Pp. 293–300 in *Old Testament Interpretation: Past, Present and Future, Essays in Honour of Gene M. Tucker*. Edinburgh: T&T Clark, 1995.
Clements, Ronald E. *Deuteronomy*. Edited by R. Whybray. OTG. Sheffield: JSOT Press, 1989.
———. "Wisdom and Old Testament Theology." Pp. 269–86 in *Wisdom in Ancient Israel*. Edited by J. Day, R. P. Gordon, and H. G. M. Williamson. Cambridge: CUP, 1995.
Clines, David J. A. "The Tree of Knowledge and the Law of Yahweh." *VT* 24 (1974): 8–14.
———. "Psalm 2 and the MLF (Moabite Liberation Front)." Pp. 158–85 in *The Bible in Human Society: Essays in Honour of John Rogerson*. JSOTSup 200. Sheffield: Sheffield Academic Press, 1995.
———. "Universal Dominion in Psalm 2?" Pp. 701–07 in *On the Way to the Postmodern: Old Testament Essays 1967–1998*, Vol. 2. JSOTSup 292. Sheffield: Sheffield Academic Press, 1998.
Collins, John J. "Before the Canon: Scriptures in Second Temple Judaism." Pp. 225–41 in *Old Testament Interpretation: Past, Present and Future, Essays in Honour of Gene M. Tucker*. Edinburgh: T&T Clark, 1995.
Collins, Terence. "Decoding the Psalms: A Structural Approach to the Psalter." *JSOT*, no. 37 (February 1987): 41–60.
Cooper, Alan. "Creation, Philosophy and Spirituality: Aspects of Jewish Interpretation of Psalm 19." Pp. 15–33 in *Pursuing the Text: Studies in Honor of Ben Zion Wacholder on the Occasion of His Seventieth Birthday*. Edited by John C. Reeves and John Kampen. JSOTSup 184. Sheffield: Sheffield Academic Press, 1994.
Craigie, Peter C. *The Book of Deuteronomy*. NICOT. Grand Rapids: Eerdmans, 1976.
———. "The Role and Relevance of Biblical Research." *JSOT* 18 (1980): 19–31.
———. *Psalms 1–50*. WBC. Waco: Word Books, 1983.
Creach, Jerome F. D. *Yahweh as Refuge and the Editing of the Hebrew Psalter*. JSOTSup 217. Sheffield: Sheffield Academic Press, 1996.
———. "Like a Tree Planted by the Temple Stream: The Portrait of the Righteous in Psalm 1:3." *CBQ* 61 (1999): 34–46.
Crenshaw, James L. *Old Testament Wisdom: An Introduction*. Louisville: WJKP, 1998.
———. "The Deuteronomist and the Writings." Pp. 145–58 in *Those Elusive Deutero-*

nomists: The Phenomenon of Pan-Deuteronomism. Edited by L. S. Schering and S. L. McKenzie. JSOTSup 268. Sheffield: Sheffield Academic Press, 1999.

———. *The Psalms: An Introduction.* Grand Rapids: Eerdmans, 2001.

Crim, Keith R. *The Royal Psalms.* Richmond: John Knox Press, 1962.

Croft, Steven J. L. *The Identity of the Individual in the Psalms.* JSOTSup 44. Sheffield: JSOT Press, 1987.

Crüsemann, Franz. *The Torah: Theology and Social History of Old Testament Law.* Translated by A. W. Mahnke. Edinburgh: T&T Clark, 1992.

Dahood, Mitchell. *Psalms vol. I, 1–50: A New Translation with Introduction and Commentary.* AB. Garden City, New York: Doubleday, 1965.

———. *Psalms vol. III, 101–150: A New Translation with Introduction and Commentary.* AB. Garden City, New York: Doubleday and Co., 1970.

Dalglish, Edward R. "The Use of the Book of Psalms in the New Testament." *SwJT* 27, no. 1 (Fall 1984): 25–39.

Daude, David. "One from Among Your Brothers Shall You Set Over You." *JBL* 90 (1971): 480–81.

Davidson, Robert. *The Vitality of Worship: A Commentary on the Book of Psalms.* Grand Rapids: Eerdmans, 1998.

Day, John. *Psalms.* OTG. Sheffield: JSOT Press, 1990.

deClaissé-Walford, Nancy L. *Reading from the Beginning: The Shaping of the Hebrew Psalter.* Macon, GA: Mercer University Press, 1997.

———. "The Canonical Shape of the Psalms." Pp. 93–110 in *An Introduction to Wisdom Literature and the Psalms: Festschrift Marvin E. Tate.* Edited by H. W. Ballard and W. D. Tucker. Macon, GA: Mercer University Press, 2000.

de Pinto, Basil. "The Torah and the Psalms." *JBL* 86 (1967): 154–74.

Diamond, A. R. Pete. "שׂיח." Pp. 1234–35 in *New International Dictionary of Old Testament Theology and Exegesis, Volume 3.* W. A. VanGemeren, gen. ed. Carlisle: Paternoster Press, 1997.

Drinkard, Joel F., Jr. "The Ancient Near Eastern Context of the Book of Psalms." Pp. 67–92 in *An Introduction to Wisdom Literature and the Psalms: Festschrift for Marvin E. Tate.* Edited by H. W. Ballard and W. D. Tucker. Macon, GA: Mercer University Press, 2000.

Driver, S. R. *Deuteronomy.* ICC. Edinburgh: T&T Clark, 1978.

Durham, John I. "The King as 'Messiah' in the Psalms." *RevExp* 81 (Summer 1984): 425–35.

Eaton, John H. *Psalms.* TBC. London: SPCK, 1967.

———. "Some Misunderstood Hebrew Words for God's Self-Revelation." *BT* 25, no. 3 (1974): 331–38.

———. *Kingship and the Psalms.* SBT, Vol. 32. London: SCM Press, 1976.

———. *Psalms of the Way and the Kingdom: A Conference with the Commentators.* JSOTSup 199. Sheffield: Sheffield Academic Press, 1995.

Enns, Peter. "Law of God." Pp. 893–900 in *New International Dictionary of Old Testament Theology and Exegesis, Volume 4.* W. A. VanGemeren, gen. ed. Carlisle: Paternoster Press, 1997.

Eskenazi, Tamara Cohn. "Torah as Narrative and Narrative as Torah." Pp. 13–30 in *Old Testament Interpretation: Past, Present and Future, Essays in Honour of Gene M. Tucker.* Edinburgh: T&T Clark, 1995.

Filipiak, Marian. "Mesjanizm Królewski w Psalmie 2." *ColT* 43 (1973): 49–65.
Freedman, David Noel. *Psalm 119: The Exaltation of Torah.* BJS/UCSD. Winona Lake, IN: Eisenbrauns, 1999.
Frost, S. B. "Psalm 118: An Exposition." *CJT* VII, no. 3 (1961): 155–66.
Fulton, Robert C. "Victory from Death: What Makes the Reject Sing?" *CurTM* 14 (1987): 278–82.
Futato, Mark D. "Suffering as the Path to Glory: The Book of Psalms Speaks Today." *MR* 8 (March/April 1999): 24–27.
Gerbrandt, Gerald E. *Kingship According to the Deuteronomistic History.* SBLDS 87. Atlanta: Scholars Press, 1986.
Gerstenberger, Erhard S. "Canon Criticism and the Meaning of 'Sitz Im Leben.'" Pp. 20–31 in *Canon, Theology and Old Testament Interpretation: Essays in Honor of Brevard S. Childs.* Edited by G. M. Tucker, D. L. Petersen, and R. R. Wilson. Philadelphia: Fortress, 1988.
———. *Psalms Part I: With an Introduction to Cultic Poetry.* FOTL, Vol. XV. Grand Rapids: Eerdmans, 1988.
———. *Psalms Part II, and Lamentations.* FOTL, Vol. XIV. Grand Rapids: Eerdmans, 2001.
Gesenius, H. W. F. *Hebrew-Chaldee Lexicon to the Old Testament.* Grand Rapids: Baker Book House, 1979.
Gillingham, Susan E. "The Messiah in the Psalms: A Question of Reception History and Psalter." Pp. 209–37 in *King and Messiah in Israel and the Ancient Near East: Proceedings of the Oxford Old Testament Seminar.* Edited by J. Day. JSOTSup 270. Sheffield: Sheffield Academic Press, 1998.
———. "The Exodus Tradition and Israelite Psalmody." *SJT* 52, no. 1 (1999): 19–46.
Gitay, Yehoshua. "Psalm 1 and the Rhetoric of Religious Argumentation." Pp. 232–40 in *Literary Structure and Rhetorical Strategies in the Hebrew Bible.* Ed. L. J. de Regt, J. de Waard, and J. P. Fokkelman. Assen/Winona Lake, IN: Van Gorcum/Eisenbrauns, 1996.
Glass, Jonathan T. "Some Observations on Psalm 19." Pp. 147–59 in *The Listening Heart: Essays in Wisdom and the Psalms in Honor of Roland E. Murphy, O. Carm.* Edited by K. G. Hogland, E. F. Huwiler, J. T. Glass, and R. W. Lee. JSOTSup 58. Sheffield: JSOT Press, 1987.
Goulder, Michael. "The Shape and Shaping of the Psalter." Review. *Int* 48 (1994): 426.
Goulder, Michael D. *The Psalms of the Sons of Korah.* JSOTSup 20. Sheffield: JSOT Press, 1982.
Grant, Jamie A. "Psalms 73 and 89: The Crisis of Faith." Pp. 61–86 in *Praying by the Book: Reading the Psalms.* Edited by C. G. Bartholomew and A. West. Carlisle: Paternoster Publishing, 2001.
Gunkel, Hermann. *Introduction to Psalms: The Genres of the Religious Lyric of Israel.* Translated by James D. Nogalski. Macon: Mercer University Press, 1998.
Halpern, Baruch. *The Constitution of the Monarchy in Israel.* HSM 25. Chico, CA: Scholars Press, 1981.

Hamidovich, David. "'Les Portes de Justice' et 'la Porte de YHWH' dans le Psaume 118:19-20." *Bib* 81 (2000): 542-50.
Harding, Thomas. "Psalm 118: How Can We Sing the Lord's Song Sitting Down?" *Touchstone* 4, no. 2 (May 1986): 38-46.
Harman, Allan M. *Psalms*. Mentor Commentary Series. Fearn, Ross-shire: Christian Focus Publishers, 1998.
Harrelson, Walter. "Psalm 19: A Meditation on God's Glory in the Heavens and in God's Law." Pp. 142-47 in *Worship and the Hebrew Bible*. Edited by M. P. Graham, R. R. Marrs, and S. L. McKenzie. JSOTSup 248. Sheffield: Sheffield Academic Press, 1999.
Harrisville, Roy A. "Paul and the Psalms: A Formal Study." *WW* V, no. 2 (Spring 1985): 168-79.
Hasel, Gerhard. *Old Testament Theology: Basic Issues in the Current Debate*. Fourth ed. Grand Rapids: Eerdmans, 1996.
Healey, John F. "The Immortality of the King: Ugarit and the Psalms." *Or* 53, no. 2 (1984): 245-54.
Heim, Knut M. "The Perfect King of Psalm 72: An 'Intertextual' Inquiry." Pp. 223-48 in *The Lord's Anointed: Interpretation of Old Testament Messianic Texts*. Edited by Philip E. Satterthwaite, Richard S. Hess, and Gordon J. Wenham. Carlisle / GrandRapids: Paternoster Press / Baker Book House, 1995.
———. "The (God-)Forsaken King of Psalm 89: A Historical and Intertextual Enquiry." Pp. 296-322 in *King and Messiah in Israel and the Ancient Near East: Proceedings of the Oxford Old Testament Seminar*. Edited by J. Day. JSOTSup 270. Sheffield: Sheffield Academic Press, 1998.
Holm-Nielsen, Svend. "The Importance of Late Jewish Psalmody for the Understanding of Old Testament Psalmodic Tradition." *ST* XIV, no. 1 (1960): 1-53.
Hossfeld, Frank-Lothar, and Erich Zenger. *Die Psalmen I*. NEchtB. Würzburg: Echter Verlag, 1993.
Howard, David M. "The Case for Kingship in the Old Testament Narrative Books and the Psalms." *TJ* 9 (1988): 19-35.
———. "The Case for Kingship in Deuteronomy and the Former Prophets." *WTJ* 52 (1990): 101-15.
———. "A Contextual Reading of Psalms 90-94." In *The Shape and Shaping of the Psalter*. Edited by J. Clinton McCann. JSOTSup 159. Sheffield: JSOT Press, 1993.
———. "Editorial Activity in the Psalter: A State-of-the-Field Survey." In *The Shape and Shaping of the Psalter*. Edited by J. Clinton McCann. JSOTSup 159. Sheffield: JSOT Press, 1993.
———. *The Structure of Psalms 93-100*. BJS/UCSD 5. Winona Lake, IN: Eisenbrauns, 1997.
———. "Recent Trends in Psalm Study." Pp. 329-68 in *The Face of Old Testament Study: A Survey of Contemporary Approaches*. Edited by D. W. Baker and B. T. Arnold. Leicester: Apollos, 1999.
Hubbard, David A. "The Wisdom Movement and Israel's Covenant Faith." *TynBul* 17 (1966): 3-33.
Huie-Jolly, Mary R. "Threats Answered by Enthronement: Death/Resurrection and the Divine Warrior Myth in John 5:17-29, Psalm 2 and Daniel 7." Pp. 191-217 in

Early Christian Interpretation of the Scriptures of Israel: Investigations and Proposals. Edited by Craig A. Evans and James A. Sanders. JSNTSup 148 and SSEJC 5. Sheffield: Sheffield Academic Press, 1997.
Hunter, Alistair G. *Psalms*. OTR. London: Routledge, 1999.
Jacobson, Delmar L. "The Royal Psalms and Jesus Messiah: Preparing to Preach on a Royal Psalm." *WW* 5, no. 2 (Spring 1985): 192–98.
Jasper, F.N. "Early Israelite Traditions and the Psalter." *VT* XVII, no. 1 (January 1967): 50–59.
Jenks, Alan J. "Theological Presuppositions of Israel's Wisdom Literature." *HBT* 7, no. 1 (1985): 43–75.
Jenson, Philip P. "Models of Prophetic Prediction and Matthew's Quotation of Micah 5:2." Pp. 189–211 in *The Lord's Anointed: Interpretation of Old Testament Messianic Texts*. Edited by Philip E. Satterthwaite, Richard S. Hess, and Gordon J. Wenham. Carlisle / GrandRapids: Paternoster Press / Baker Book House, 1995.
Johnson, Aubrey R. *Sacral Kingship in Ancient Israel*. Cardiff: University of Wales Press, 1967.
Johnston, Philip S. "'Left in Hell?' Psalm 16, Sheol and the Holy One." Pp. 213–22 in *The Lord's Anointed: Interpretation of Old Testament Messianic Texts*. Edited by Philip E. Satterthwaite, Richard S. Hess, and Gordon J. Wenham. Carlisle/GrandRapids: Paternoster Press/Baker Book House, 1995.
Joyce, Paul M. "King and Messiah in Ezekiel." Pp. 323–37 in *King and Messiah in Israel and the Ancient Near East: Proceedings of the Oxford Old Testament Seminar*. Edited by J. Day. JSOTSup 270. Sheffield: Sheffield Academic Press, 1998.
Kaufman, Stephen A. "The Structure of the Deuteronomic Law." *Maarav* 1, no. 2 (1978–79): 105–58.
Kidner, Derek. *Psalms 1–72*. TOTC. Leicester: IVP, 1973.
———. *Psalms 73–150*. TOTC. Leicester: IVP, 1973.
Kirkpatrick, A. F. *The Book of Psalms*. Cambridge: CUP, 1910.
Knight, Douglas A. "Deuteronomy and the Deuteronomists." Pp. 61–79 in *Old Testament Interpretation: Past, Present and Future, Essays in Honour of Gene M. Tucker*. Edinburgh: T&T Clark, 1995.
Knoppers, Gary N. "The Deuteronomist and the Deuteronomic Law of the King: A Reexamination of a Relationship." *ZAW* 108, no. 3 (1996): 329–46.
———. "Introduction." Pp. 1–18 in *Reconsidering Israel and Judah: Recent Studies on the Deuteronomistic History*. Edited by G. N. Knoppers and J. G. McConville. SBTS, Vol. 8. Winona Lake, IN: Eisenbrauns, 2000.
———. "Prayer and Propaganda: Solomon's Dedication of the Temple and the Deuteronomist's Program." Pp. 370–96 in *Reconsidering Israel and Judah: Recent Studies on the Deuteronomistic History*. Edited by G. N. Knoppers and J. G. McConville. SBTS, Vol. 8. Winone Lake, IN: Eisenbrauns, 2000.
Knoppers, Gary N., and J. Gordon McConville, eds. *Reconsidering Israel and Judah: Recent Studies on the Deuteronomistic History*. SBTS, Vol. 8. Winona Lake, IN: Eisenbrauns, 2000.
Krause, Deborah. "The One Who Comes Unbinding the Blessing of Judah: Mark 11:1–10 as a Midrash on Genesis 49:11, Zechariah 9:9, and Psalm 118:25–26."

Pp. 141-53 in *Early Christian Interpretation of the Scriptures of Israel: Investigations and Proposals*. Edited by Craig A. Evans and James A. Sanders. JSNTSup 148 and SSEJC 5. Sheffield: Sheffield Academic Press, 1997.

Kraus, Hans-Joachim. *Theology of the Psalms*. Translated by K. Crim. Minneapolis: Augsburg, 1986.

———. *Psalms 1-59: A Commentary*. Translated by Hilton C. Oswald. Minneapolis: Augsburg, 1988.

———. *Psalms 60-150: A Commentary*. Translated by Hilton C. Oswald. Minneapolis: Augsburg, 1989.

Kuntz, J. Kenneth. "Psalm 18: A Rhetorical-Critical Analysis." Pp. 70-97 in *Beyond Form Criticism: Essays in Old Testament Literary Criticism*. Edited by P. R. House. SBTS, Vol. 2. Winona Lake, IN: Eisenbrauns, 1992.

———. "Review of 'The Psalms and Their Readers: Interpretive Strategies for Psalm 18.'" *Int* 48 (1994): 426-27.

Lacy, Graham Gordon. "'A Living Stone': An Easter Sermon." *Int* 6 (1952): 39-46.

Landon, Michael. "God and the Sciences: A Sermon on Psalm 19." *RestQ* 38, no. 4 (1996): 238-41.

Lehrman, S. M. "Psalm 119." *JBQ* 23, no. 1 (1995): 55-56.

Levenson, Jon D. "The Sources of Torah: Psalm 119 and the Modes of Revelation in Second Temple Judaism.". In *Ancient Israelite Religion: Essays in Honor of Frank Moore Cross*. Edited by P. D. Miller, P. D. Hanson, and S. D. McBride. Philadelphia: Fortress, 1987.

Levinson, Bernard M. "The Reconceptualization of Kingship in Deuteronomy and the Deuteronomistic History's Transformation of Torah." *VT* LI, no. 4 (2001): 511-34.

Lewis, Clive Staples. *Reflections on the Psalms*. London: G. Bles, 1958.

Lindars, B. "Is Psalm II an Acrostic Poem?" *VT* XVII, no. 1 (January 1967): 60-67.

———. "Torah in Deuteronomy." Pp. 117-36 in *Words and Meanings: Essays Presented to David W. Thomas*. P. R. Ackroyd and B. Lindars. Cambridge: CUP, 1968.

Lohfink, Norbert F. "Distribution of the Functions of Powers." Pp. 336-52 in *The Song of Power and the Power of Song: Essays on the Book of Deuteronomy*. Edited by D. L. Christensen. SBTS, Vol. 3. Winona Lake, IN: Eisenbrauns, 1993.

———. "Recent Discussion on 2 Kings 22-23: The State of the Question." Pp. 36-61 in *The Song of Power and the Power of Song: Essays on the Book of Deuteronomy*. Edited by D. L. Christensen. SBTS, Vol. 3. Winona Lake, IN: Eisenbrauns, 1993.

———. "Was There a Deuteronomistic Movement?" Pp. 36-66 in *Those Elusive Deuteronomists: The Phenomenon of Pan-Deuteronomism*. Edited by L. S. Schering and S. L. McKenzie. JSOTSup 268. Sheffield: Sheffield Academic Press, 1999.

———. "Which Oracle Granted Perdurability to the Davidides?: A Textual Problem in 2 Kings 8:19 and the Function of the Dynastic Oracles in the Deuteronomistic Historical Work." Pp. 421-43 in *Reconsidering Israel and Judah: Recent Studies on the Deuteronomistic History*. Edited by G. N. Knoppers and J. G. McConville. SBTS, Vol. 8. Grand Rapids: Eisenbrauns, 2000.

Longman III, Tremper. *How to Read the Psalms*. Downers Grove: IVP, 1988.

———. "Lament." Pp. 197–215 in *Cracking Old Testament Codes: A Guide to the Literary Genres of the Old Testament*. Edited by D. B. Sandy and Jr. R. L. Giese. Nashville: Broadman and Holman, 1995.

López, Félix García. "Le Roi d'Israel: Dt 17,14–20." Pp. 277–97 in *Das Deuteronomium: Entstehung, Gestalt und Botschaft*. Edited by N. Lohfink. Leuven: Leuven University Press, 1985.

Macintosh, A. A. "A Consideration of the Problems Presented by Psalm II.11 and 12." *JTS* XXVII, no. 1 (1976): 1–14.

Mason, Rex. "The Messiah in Postexilic Old Testament Literature." Pp. 338–64 in *King and Messiah in Israel and the Ancient Near East: Proceedings of the Oxford Old Testament Seminar*. Edited by J. Day. JSOTSup 270. Sheffield: Sheffield Academic Press, 1998.

Mauchline, J. "Implicit Signs of a Persistent Belief in the Davidic Empire." *VT* 20 (1970): 287–303.

Mayes, A. D. H. *Deuteronomy*. NCB. London: Marshall, Morgan and Scott, 1979.

———. "Deuteronomy 14 and the Deuteronomic Worldview." In *Studies in Deuteronomy in Honour of C J Labuschagne on the Occasion of His 65th Birthday*. Edited by F. Garcia Martinez. VTSup 53. Leiden: E. J. Brill, 1994.

———. "Deuteronomistic Ideology and the Theology of the Old Testament." *JSOT* 82 (1999): 57–82.

May, Harry S. "Psalm 118: The Song of the Citadel." Pp. 97–106 in *Religions in Antiquity: Essays in Memory of Erwin Ramsdell Goodenough*. Edited by Jacob Neuser. Leiden: E. J. Brill, 1968.

Mays, James L. "The Place of the Torah-Psalms in the Psalter." *JBL* 106, no. 1 (1987): 3–12.

———. "Psalm 118 in the Light of Canonical Analysis." Pp. 299–311 in *Canon, Theology and Old Testament Interpretation: Essays in Honor of Brevard S. Childs*. Edited by G. M. Tucker, D. L. Petersen, and R. R. Wilson. Philadelphia: Fortress, 1988.

———. "The Question of Context in Psalm Interpretation." Pp. 21–28 in *The Shape and Shaping of the Psalter*. Edited by J. Clinton McCann. JSOTSup 159. Sheffield: JSOT Press, 1993.

———. *The Lord Reigns*. Louisville: Westminster John Knox Press, 1994.

———. "Past, Present and Prospect in Psalm Study." Pp. 147–56 in *Old Testament Interpretation: Past, Present and Future, Essays in Honour of Gene M. Tucker*. Edinburgh: T&T Clark, 1994.

———. *Psalms*. IBC. Louisville: John Knox Press, 1994.

McBride, S. Dean. "Polity of the Covenant People: The Book of Deuteronomy." Pp. 62–77 in *The Song of Power and the Power of Song: Essays on the Book of Deuteronomy*. Edited by D.L. Christensen. SBTS, Vol. 3. Winona Lake, IN: Eisenbrauns, 1993.

———. "Perspective and Context in the Study of Pentateuchal Legislation." Pp. 47–59 in *Old Testament Interpretation: Past, Present and Future, Essays in Honor of Gene M. Tucker*. Edinburgh: T&T Clark, 1995.

McCann, J. Clinton, ed. *The Shape and Shaping of the Psalter*. JSOTSup 159. Sheffield: JSOT Press, 1993.

———. "Psalm 73: A Microcosm of Old Testament Theology." In *The Listening Heart: Essays in Wisdom and the Psalms in Honor of Roland E. Murphy, O.Carm.* Edited by K. G. Hoglun, E. F. Huwiler, J. T. Glass, and R. W. Lee. JSOTSup 58. Sheffield: JSOT Press, 1987.

———. "The Psalms as Instruction." *Int* 46, no. 2 (April 1992): 117–28.

———. "Books I–III and the Editorial Purpose of the Psalter." In *The Shape and Shaping of the Psalter*. Edited by J. Clinton McCann. JSOTSup 159. Sheffield: JSOT Press, 1993.

———. *A Theological Introduction to the Books of Psalms: The Psalms as Torah*. Nashville: Abingdon, 1993.

———. *The Book of Psalms*. NIB. Nashville: Abingdon, 1996.

———. "Wisdom's Dilemma: The Book of Job, the Final Form of the Book of Psalms, and the Entire Bible." Pp. 18–30 in *Wisdom, You Are My Sister: Studies in Honor of Roland E. Murphy, O. Carm., on the Occasion of His Eightieth Birthday*, CBQMS 29. Edited by Michael. L Barre. Washington D.C.: Catholic Biblical Association of America, 1997.

McCarthy, D. J. "The Inauguration of the Monarchy in Israel: A Form-Critical Study of 1 Samuel 8–12." *Int* 27 (1973): 401–12.

McConville, J. Gordon. *Law and Theology in Deuteronomy*. JSOTSup 33. Sheffield: JSOT Press, 1984.

———. *Grace in the End: A Study in Deuteronomic Theology*. Carlisle: Paternoster Press, 1993.

———. *Judgment and Promise*. Leicester: Apollos, 1993.

———. "Messianic Interpretation of the Old Testament in Modern Context." Pp. 1–17 in *The Lord's Anointed: Interpretation of Old Testament Messianic Texts*. Edited by Philip E. Satterthwaite, Richard S. Hess, and Gordon J. Wenham. Carlisle/GrandRapids: Paternoster Press/Baker Book House, 1995.

———. "Deuteronomic/istic Theology." Pp. 528–37 in *New International Dictionary of Old Testament Theology and Exegesis, Volume 4*. W. A. Van Gemeren, gen. ed. Carlisle: Paternoster Press, 1997.

———. "King and Messiah in Deuteronomy and the Deuteronomistic History." Pp. 271–95 in *King and Messiah in Israel and the Ancient Near East: Proceedings of the Oxford Old Testament Seminar*. Edited by J. Day. JSOTSup 270. Sheffield: Sheffield Academic Press, 1998.

———. "1 Kings 8:46–53 and the Deuteronomic Hope." Pp. 358–69 in *Reconsidering Israel and Judah: Recent Studies on the Deuteronomistic History*. Edited by G. N. Knoppers and J. G. McConville. SBTS, Vol. 8. Winona Lake, IN: Eisenbrauns, 2000.

———. "Deuteronomy: Torah for the Church of Christ." *EuroJTh* 9, no. 1 (2000): 33–47.

———. "'Who May Ascend the Hill of the LORD?' The Picture of the Faithful in Psalms 15–24." Pp. 35–58 in *Praying by the Book: Reading the Psalms*. Edited by C. G. Bartholomew and A. West. Carlisle: Paternoster Press, 2001.

———. "Biblical Theology: Canon and Plain Sense." *SBET* 19, no. 2 (Autumn 2001): 134–57.

———. *Deuteronomy*. Leicester: Apollos, 2002.

———. "Law and Monarchy in the Old Testament." In *A Royal Priesthood: The Use of the Bible Ethically and Politically*. Edited by C. Bartholomew, J. Chaplin, R. Song, and A. Wolters. Carlisle/Grand Rapids: Paternoster/Zondervan, 2002.
McConville, J. Gordon, and J. Gary Millar. *Time and Place in Deuteronomy*. JSOTSup 179. Sheffield: Sheffield Academic Press, 1994.
Melugin, Roy F. "Canon and Exegetical Method." Pp. 48–61 in *Canon, Theology and Old Testament Interpretation: Essays in Honor of Brevard S. Childs*. Edited by G. M. Tucker, D. L. Petersen, and R. R. Wilson. Philadelphia: Fortress, 1988.
Mettinger, T. N. D. *King and Messiah: The Civil and Sacral Legitimation of the Israelite Kings*. ConBOT, Vol. 8. Lund: CWK Gleerup, 1976.
Millard, M. *Die Komposition Des Psalters: Ein Formgeschichtlicher Ansatz*. FAT 9. Tübingen: Mohr, Siebeck, 1994.
Millar, J. Gary. *Now Choose Life: Theology and Ethics in Deuteronomy*. Leicester: Apollos, 1998.
Miller, Patrick D. "Trouble and Woe: Interpreting the Biblical Laments." *Int* 37 (1983): 32–45.
———. "Current Issues in Psalms Studies." *WW* V, no. 2 (Spring 1985): 132–43.
———. *Interpreting the Psalms*. Philadelphia: Fortress, 1986.
———. *Deuteronomy*. IBC. Louisville: John Knox Press, 1990.
———. "The Beginning of the Psalter." Pp. 83–92 in *The Shape and Shaping of the Psalter*. Edited by J. Clinton McCann. JSOTSup 159. Sheffield: JSOT Press, 1993.
———. "'Moses My Servant': The Deuteronomic Portrait of Moses." Pp. 301–12 in *The Song of Power and the Power of Song: Essays on the Book of Deuteronomy*. Edited by D. L. Christensen. Winona Lake, IN: Eisenbrauns, 1993.
———. "Kingship, Torah Obedience and Prayer." Pp. 127–42 in *Neue Wege der Psalmenforschung*. Edited by K. Seybold and E. Zenger. Freiburg: Herder, 1995.
———. "The End of the Psalter: A Response to Erich Zenger." *JSOT* 80 (1998): 103–10.
———. "Deuteronomy and Psalms: Evoking a Biblical Conversation." *JBL* 118, no. 1 (1999): 3–18.
Mitchell, David C. *The Message of the Psalter: An Eschatological Programme in the Book of Psalms*. JSOTSup 252. Sheffield: Sheffield Academic Press, 1997.
Montgomery, Robert M. "Freedom Within Obedience to the Torah." Pp. 425–37 in *Religions in Antiquity: Essays in Memory of Erwin Ramsdell Goodenough*. Edited by Jacob Neuser. Leiden: E. J. Brill, 1968.
Mowinckel, Sigmund. *The Psalms in Israel's Worship*. Vol. I. Translated by D. R. Ap-Thomas. Oxford: Basil Blackwell, 1962.
———. *The Psalms in Israel's Worship*. Vol. II. Translated by D. R. Ap-Thomas. Oxford: Basil Blackwell, 1962.
Murphy, Roland E. "Reflections on Contextual Interpretations of the Psalms." In *The Shape and Shaping of the Psalter*. Edited by J. Clinton McCann. JSOTSup 159. Sheffield: JSOT Press, 1993.
———. *The Gift of the Psalms*. Peabody, MA: Hendrickson, 2000.
Nelson, R. D. "Josiah in the Book of Joshua." *JBL* 100, no. 4 (1981): 531–40.
Nicholson, E. W. *Deuteronomy and Tradition*. Oxford: Basil Blackwell, 1967.
Niehaus, J. J. "The Theology of Deuteronomy." Pp. 537–44 in *New International Dic-*

tionary of Old Testament Theology and Exegesis, Volume 4. W. A. Van Gemeren, gen. ed. Carlisle: Paternoster Press, 1997.

Nogalski, James D. "From Psalm to Psalms to Psalter." Pp. 37–54 in *An Introduction to Wisdom Literature and the Psalms: Festschrift Marvin E. Tate*. Edited by H. W. Ballard and W. D. Tucker. Macon, GA: Mercer University Press, 2000.

Noth, Martin. *The Deuteronomistic History*. Translated by H. G. M. Williamson. JSOTSup 15. Sheffield: JSOT Press, 1981.

———. "The Central Theological Ideas." Pp. 20–30 in *Reconsidering Israel and Judah: Recent Studies on the Deuteronomistic History*. Edited by G. N. Knoppers and J. G. McConville. SBTS, Vol. 8. Winona Lake, IN: Eisenbrauns, 2000.

Oesterley, W. O. E. *The Psalms: Translated with Text-Critical and Exegetical Notes*. London: SPCK, 1959.

Olson, Dennis T. *Deuteronomy and the Death of Moses*. Minneapolis: Fortress, 1994.

Ormseth, Dennis H. "The Psalms and the Rule of God." *WW* V, no. 2 (Spring 1985): 119–21.

Östborn, Gunnar. *Tōrā in the Old Testament: A Semantic Study*. Lund: Håkan Ohlssons Boktryckeri, 1945.

Parkander, Dorothy J. "'Exalted Manna:' The Psalms as Literature." *WW* V, no. 2 (Spring 1985): 122–31.

Plantinga, Alvin. "Two (or More) Types of Scripture Scholarship." *Modern Theology* 14, no. 2 (April 1998): 243–77.

Porter, J. Roy. *Moses and Monarchy: A Study in the Biblical Tradition of Moses*. Oxford: Basil Blackwell, 1963.

———. "The Succession of Joshua." Pp. 139–62 in *Reconsidering Israel and Judah: Recent Studies on the Deuteronomistic History*. Edited by G. N. Knoppers and J. G. McConville. SBTS 8. Winona Lake, IN: Eisenbrauns, 2000.

Provan, Iain W. "The Messiah in the Book of Kings." Pp. 67–85 in *The Lord's Anointed: Interpretation of Old Testament Messianic Texts*. Edited by Philip E. Satterthwaite, Richard S. Hess, and Gordon J. Wenham. Carlisle / Grand Rapids: Paternoster Press / Baker Book House, 1995.

———. "In the Stable with the Dwarves: Testimony, Interpretation, Faith and the History of Israel." Pp. 281–319 in *Vetus Testamentum Congress Volume, Oslo 1998*. Edited by A. Lemaire and M. Sæbø. Leiden: Brill, 2000.

Reif, Stefan C. "Ibn Ezra on Psalm I 1–2." *VT* XXXIV, no. 2 (1984): 232–36.

Reimer, D. J. "Concerning Return to Egypt: Deuteronomy XVII 16 and XXVIII 68 Reconsidered." In *Studies in the Pentateuch*. Edited by J. Emerton. VTSup 41. Leiden: Brill, 1990.

Ridderbos, J. *Deuteronomy*. Translated by E. M. van der Maas. BSC. Grand Rapids: Zondervan, 1984.

Ross, J. P. "Jahweh $S^e\underline{b}\bar{a}'\hat{o}\underline{t}$ in Samuel and Psalms." *VT* XVII, no. 1 (January 1967): 76–92.

Sanders, James A. "A New Testament Hermeneutic Fabric: Psalm 118 in the Entrance Narrative." Pp. 177–90 in *Early Jewish and Christian Exegesis: Studies in Memory of William Hugh Brownlee*. Edited by C. A. Evans and W. F. Stinespring. Atlanta: Scholars Press, 1987.

Sarna, Nahum M. *On the Book of Psalms: Exploring the Prayer of Ancient Israel*. New York: Schocken Books, 1993.
Sasson, Victor. "The Language of Rebellion in Psalm 2 and in the Plaster Texts of Deir 'Alla." *AUSS* 24, no. 2 (Summer 1986): 147–54.
Schaefer, Konrad. *Psalms*. Edited by David W. Cotter. Berit Olam. Collegeville, MN: Liturgical Press, 2001.
Schafer, B. E. "The Root *Bḥr* and Pre-Exilic Concepts of Chosenness in the Hebrew Bible." *ZAW* 89, no. 1 (1977): 20–42.
Seitz, Christopher R. *Word without End: The Old Testament as Abiding Theological Witness*. Grand Rapids: Eerdmans, 1998.
———. "Christological Interpretation of Texts and Trinitarian Claims to Truth: An Engagement with Francis Watson's *Text and Truth*." *SJT* 52, no. 2 (1999): 209–26.
Selman, Martin J. "Messianic Mysteries." Pp. 281–302 in *The Lord's Anointed: Interpretation of Old Testament Messianic Texts*. Edited by Philip E. Satterthwaite, Richard S. Hess, and Gordon J. Wenham. Carlisle/GrandRapids: Paternoster Press/Baker Book House, 1995.
Seybold, Klaus. *Introducing the Psalms*. Translated by R. G. Dumphy. Edinburgh: T&T Clark, 1990.
Shepherd, Jerry Eugene. "The Book of Psalms as the Book of Christ: A Christo-Canonical Approach to the Book of Psalms." Ph.D. Dissertation. Philadelphia: Westminster Theological Seminary, 1995.
Sheppard, Gerald T. *Wisdom as a Hermeneutical Construct: A Study in Sapientializing of the Old Testament*. BZAW 151. Berlin: Walter de Gruyter, 1980.
———. *The Future of the Bible: Beyond Liberalism and Literalism*. Toronto: United Church Publishing House, 1990.
———. "Theology and the Book of Psalms." *Int* 46, no. 2 (April 1992): 143–55.
———. "The Book of Isaiah as a Human Witness to Revelation within the Religions of Judaism and Christianity." Pp. 274–80 in *SBLSP*. Atlanta: Scholars Press, 1993.
Singer, Michael A. "King/Messiah: Rashi's Exegesis of Psalm 2." *Proof* 3 (1983): 273–78.
Smelik, K. A. D. "The Origin of Psalm 20." *JSOT* 31 (1985): 75–81.
Smend, Rudolf. "The Law and the Nations: A Contribution to Deuteronomistic Tradition History." In *Reconsidering Israel and Judah: Recent Studies on the Deuteronomistic History*. Edited by G. N. Knoppers and J. G. McConville. SBTS 8. Winona Lake, IN: Eisenbrauns, 2000.
Smith, Ralph L. "The Use and Influence of the Psalms." *SwJT* 27, no. 1 (Fall 1984): 5–16.
Soll, Will. *Psalm 119: Matrix, Form and Setting*. CBQMS 23. Washington D.C.: The Catholic Biblical Association of America, 1991.
Sonnet, Jean-Pierre. *The Book within the Book: Writing in Deuteronomy*. BIS, Vol. 14. Leiden: Brill, 1997.
Starbuck, S. R. A. *Court Oracles in the Psalms: The So-Called Royal Psalms in Their Ancient Near Eastern Context*. SBLDS 172. Atlanta: Scholars Press, 1999.
Still, Judith, and Michael Worton. "Introduction." Pp. 1–44 in *Intertextuality: Theories and Practices*. Edited by M. Worton and J. Still. Manchester: Manchester University Press, 1990.

Thompson, J. A. *Deuteronomy: An Introduction and Commentary*. TOTC. Leicester: IVP, 1974.
Tigay, Jeffrey H. *Deuteronomy* דברים. JPSTC. Philadelphia: Jewish Publication Society, 1996.
Torrance, T. F. "The Last of the Hallel Psalms." *EvQ* 28 (1956): 101–08.
Tucker, Gene M. "The Law in the Eighth-Century Prophets." Pp. 201–16 in *Canon, Theology and Old Testament Interpretation: Essays in Honor of Brevard S. Childs*. Edited by G. M. Tucker, D. L. Petersen, and R. R. Wilson. Philadelphia: Fortress, 1988.
Unknown. "Litany on Law and Liberty: A Response to Psalm 119." *ExAud* 11 (1995): 151–52.
VanGemeren, Willem A. *Psalms*. EBC. Grand Rapids: Zondervan, 1991.
van Seters, John. "'Comparing Scripture with Scripture': Some Observations on the Sinai Pericope of Exodus 19–24." Pp. 111–30 in *Canon, Theology and Old Testament Interpretation: Essays in Honor of Brevard S. Childs*. Edited by G. M. Tucker, D. L. Petersen, and R. R. Wilson. Philadelphia: Fortress, 1988.
Van Wolde, Ellen. "Trendy Intertextuality?" Pp. 43–49 in *Intertextuality in Biblical Writings: Essays in Honour of Bas Van Iersel*. Edited by Sipke Draisma. Kampden: J. H. Kok, 1989.
Vincent, M. A. "The Shape of the Psalter: An Eschatological Dimension?" Pp. 61–82 in *New Heaven and New Earth: Prophecy and the Millenium, Essays in Honour of Anthony Gelston*. P. J. Harland and C. T. R. Hayward. VTSup 77. Leiden: Brill, 1999.
von Rad, Gerhard. *Deuteronomy: A Commentary*. Translated by Dorothea Barton. OTL. London: SCM Press, 1966.
———. *Wisdom in Israel*. Translated by James D. Martin. London: SCM Press, 1972.
Waddell, Chrysogonus. "A Christological Interpretation of Psalm 1? The Psalter and Christian Prayer." *Comm* 22 (Fall 1995): 502–21.
Wagner, J. Ross. "Psalm 118 in Luke-Acts: Tracing a Narrative Thread." Pp. 154–78 in *Early Christian Interpretation of the Scriptures of Israel: Investigations and Proposals*. Edited by Craig A. Evans and James A. Sanders. JSNTSup 148 and SSEJC 5. Sheffield: Sheffield Academic Press, 1997.
———. "From the Heavens to the Heart: The Dynamics of Psalm 19 as Prayer." *CBQ* 61 (1999): 245–61.
Wallis, Gerhard. "Torah und Nomos: Zur Frage Nach Gesetz und Heil." *TLZ* 105 (Mai 1980): 321–32.
Waltke, Bruce K. "A Canonical Process Approach to the Psalms." Pp. 3–18 in *Tradition and Testament: Essays in Honor of Charles Lee Feinberg*. Chicago: Moody Press, 1981.
———. "Theology of the Psalms." Pp. 1100–15 in *New International Dictionary of Old Testament Theology and Exegesis, Volume 4*. W. A. VanGemeren, gen. ed. Carlisle: Paternoster Press, 1997.
Waltke, Bruce K., and M. O'Connor. *An Introduction to Biblical Hebrew Syntax*. Winona Lake, IN: Eisenbrauns, 1990.
Walton, John H. "Psalms: A Cantata About the Davidic Covenant." *JETS* 34, no. 1 (March 1991): 21–31.

Watson, Francis. "The Old Testament as Christian Scripture: A Response to Professor Seitz." *SJT* 52, no. 2 (1999): 227-32.
Watts, James W. "Psalm 2 in the Context of Biblical Theology." *HBT* 12 (1990): 73-91.
Weinfeld, Moshe. *Deuteronomy and the Deuteronomic School*. Oxford: Clarendon Press, 1972.
———. "The King as the Servant of the People: The Source of the Idea." *JJS* 33 (1982): 189-94.
———. "Deuteronomy: The Present State of Enquiry." Pp. 21-35 in *The Song of Power and the Power of Song: Essays on the Book of Deuteronomy*. Edited by D. L. Christensen. Winona Lake, IN: Eisenbrauns, 1993.
Weiser, Artur. *The Psalms: A Commentary*. OTL. Translated by H. Hartwell. Philadelphia: Westminster Press, 1962.
Wenham, Gordon J. "Method in Pentateuchal Source Criticism." *VT* XLI, no. 1 (1991): 84-109.
———. "The Deuteronomic Theology of the Book of Joshua." Pp. 194-203 in *Reconsidering Israel and Judah: Recent Studies in the Deuteronomistic History*. Edited by G. M. Knoppers and J. G. McConville. SBTS Vol. 8. Winona Lake, IN: Eisenbrauns, 2000.
Weren, W. J. C. "Psalm 2 in Luke-Acts: An Intertextual Study." Pp. 189-203 in *Intertextuality in Biblical Writings: Essays in Honour of Bas Van Iersel*. Edited by Sipke Draisma. Kampden: J. H. Kok, 1989.
Westermann, Claus. *Praise and Lament in the Psalms*. Translated by Keith R. Crim and Richard N. Soulen. Atlanta: John Knox Press, 1981.
Whybray, R. Norman. "The Wisdom Psalms." Pp. 152-60 in *Wisdom in Ancient Israel: Essays in Honour of J. A. Emerton*. Edited by J. Day, R. P. Gordon, and H. G. M. Williamson. Cambridge: CUP, 1995.
———. *Reading the Psalms as a Book*. JSOTSup 222. Sheffield: JSOT Press, 1996.
———. "Psalm 119 Profile of a Psalmist." Pp. 31-43 in *Wisdom, You Are My Sister: Studies in Honor of Roland E. Murphy, O. Carm., on the Occasion of His Eightieth Birthday*, CBQMS 29. Edited by Michael L. Barré. Washington D.C.: Catholic Biblical Association of America, 1997.
Widengren, G. "King and Covenant." *JSS* 2, no. I (January 1957): 1-32.
Willis, John T. "Psalm 1—An Entity." *ZAW* 91, no. 3 (1979): 381-401.
———. "A Cry of Defiance—Psalm 2." *JSOT* 47 (1990): 33-50.
Wilson, Gerald H. "Evidence of Editorial Divisions in the Hebrew Psalter." *VT* XXXIV, no. 3 (1984): 337-52.
———. *The Editing of the Hebrew Psalter*. SBLDS 76. Chico: Scholars Press, 1985.
———. "The Use of Royal Psalms at the 'Seams' of the Hebrew Psalter." *JSOT* 35 (1986): 85-94.
———. "The Shape of the Book of Psalms." *Int* 46, no. 2 (April 1992): 129-41.
———. "Shaping the Psalter: A Consideration of Editorial Linkage in the Book of Psalms." In *The Shape and Shaping of the Psalms*. Edited by J. Clinton McCann. JSOTSup 159. Sheffield: JSOT Press, 1993.
———. "Understanding the Purposeful Arrangement of the Psalms: Pitfalls and Promise." In *The Shape and Shaping of the Psalter*. Edited by J. Clinton McCann. JSOTSup 159. Sheffield: JSOT Press, 1993.
———. *Psalms, Vol. I*. NIVAC. Grand Rapids: Zondervan, 2002

Wolff, Hans Walter. "The Kerygma of the Deuteronomistic Historical Work." In *Reconsidering Israel and Judah: Recent Studies on the Deuteronomistic History*. Edited by G. N. Knoppers and J. G. McConville. SBTS, Vol. 8. Winona Lake, IN: Eisenbrauns, 2000.

Wright, Christopher J. H. *Deuteronomy*. NIBCOT. Peabody, MA/Carlisle: Hendrickson /Paternoster Press, 1996.

Wyatt, N. "The Liturgical Context of Psalm 19 and Its Mythical and Ritual Origins." *UF* 27 (1995): 559–96.

Zenger, Erich. "The Composition and Theology of the Fifth Book of the Psalter." *JSOT* 80 (1998): 77–102.

Author Index

A

Alexander, T. D., 297–98
Allen, L. C., 98, 99n60, 113, 127n11, 138n50, 143n74, 171n140, 175n155, 181n170, 187n198, 228n22, 234n38, 265n58, 271, 283n135, 284n141, 297
Anderson, A. A., 80n16, 82, 84, 127n11, 128n13, 131n24, 135n39, 136n42, 142n69, 146n86, 166, 172n143, 177n160, 178n164, 184n184, 211n87, 262n42, 297
André, G., 44n7, 45n8, 297
Ashburn, D. G., 91n41, 100n65, 297
Auffret, P., 11, 24, 53n31, 57n43, 60nn53–54, 62nn64–65, 67, 64n75, 73, 74n8, 104, 224n3, 234, 297

B

Baker, K. L., 23n72, 137n49, 297, 301–303, 308
Barr, J., 297
Barth, C. F., 12n25, 60, 281n125, 297
Bartholomew, C. G., 256n17, 297–98, 301, 306–7, xiii
Barton, J., 190n4, 297, 310
Bellinger, W. H., 237n48, 240n58, 298
Berry, D., K. 28n93, 78, 81, 85, 186n192, 298
Blenkinsopp, J., 298
Braulik, G., 298
Briggs, C. A., 79n16, 80, 84, 109n80, 127n11, 137, 146n86, 260, 262n42, 270n83, 298
Brown, F., 62n63, 137, 260, 297

Brownlee, W. H., 21n60, 63nn72–73, 64n76, 128n14, 298, 308
Broyles, C. C., 298
Brueggemann, W., 9n11, 14n33, 21n61, 166n127, 211, 239n55, 250n99, 255n6, 275n99, 298
Bullough, S., 299

C

Ceresko, A. R., 8n5, 299
Childs, B. S., 8nn5, 11, 12n23, 23, 25, 36, 41, 54n34, 66n84, 97n57, 122n2, 128n15, 225n8, 227nn15, 18, 232n32, 246n88, 247nn89–90, 256n11, 262n44, 265n58, 282n129, 283n136, 297, 299, 301, 305, 306, 310
Clements, R. E., 299
Clines, D. J. A., 53n31, 57n43, 92n43, 297, 299
Collins, J. J., 299
Collins, T., 256n11, 299
Cooper, A., 299
Craigie, P. C., 57n43, 80, 109n80, 111nn86, 89, 136n43, 183n178, 195, 199, 201n40, 202n47, 203n50, 204n52, 207n64, 209n77, 210n80, 212n93, 214n98, 215n103, 256nn16, 18, 257, 271n87, 278n117, 287n151, 299
Creach, J. F. D., 23, 49, 59, 87n35, 107, 117n102, 136n41, 137n45, 145, 163–64n121, 186n191, 240nn58, 63, 245n86, 255n6, 275nn101–2, 277n109, 280n122, 283n137, 299

Crenshaw, J. L., 29n97, 172n147, 270n81, 299–300
Croft, S. J. L., 25n79, 127n11, 128n12, 172n143, 300
Cross, F. M., 27n90, 30n99, 247n89, 299, 304
Crüsemann, F., 31n102, 266n64, 300

D

Dahood, M., 127n11, 133n32, 174n151, 257n23, 277n110, 300
Daude, D., 200n39, 300
Davidson, R., 300
Day, J., 32n104, 33n106, 90, 140, 297–302, 304–5, 310
deClaissé-Walford, N. L., 16n39, 17n43, 35n112, 58n46, 63n74, 228n22, 232, 233n34, 237n48, 242, 255n8, 272n88, 300
Diamond, A. R. P., 261n37, 300
Drinkard, J. F., 246n89, 300
Driver, S. R., 137, 205n56, 207n67, 209n77, 211, 256n15, 260, 266n66, 298, 300
Durham, J. I., 8n10, 59, 300

E

Eaton, J. H., 21n60, 25n79, 26n87, 38n124, 57n43, 59, 77n9, 94n50, 127n11, 128n11, 133n32, 138n50, 145, 171n142, 174n151, 229n25, 257, 270, 271n84, 274n97, 277n110, 295n15, 300
Enns, P., 257n19, 265n60, 300
Eskenazi, T. C., 300

F

Filipiak, M., 301
Freedman, D. N., 9n14, 123n6, 124, 160n107, 186, 224n4, 228n20, 257, 260n32, 264n52, 265n58, 270n82, 301
Frost, S. B., 130n22, 177n160, 285, 301
Fulton, R. C., 301
Futato, M. D., 301

G

Gerbrandt, G. E., 31–32, 59n51, 63n74, 197nn25, 27, 199n31, 201n40, 206, 208n71, 210nn78, 81, 220nn126–27, 234n38, 278, 279nn119, 121, 288n156, 301
Gerstenberger, E. S., 256n11, 274n97, 301
Gesenius, H. W. F., 137, 182n176, 260, 261n36, 301
Gillingham, S. E., 8n7, 33n106, 38, 301
Gitay, Y., 99n61, 181n173, 301
Glass, J. T., 301, 306
Goulder, M. D., 301
Grant, J. A., 301
Gunkel, H., 12n26, 15n38, 20, 21n62, 25n79, 41, 274n97, 301

H

Halpern, B., 12n26, 15n38, 20, 21n62, 25n79, 41, 274n97, 301
Hamidovich, D., 302
Harding, T., 302
Harman, A. M., 255n8, 277n109, 302
Harrelson, W., 302
Harrisville, R. A., 302
Healey, J. F., 302
Heim, K. M., 302
Holm-Nielsen, S., 51n28, 302
Hossfeld, F.-L.,16n40, 112n90, 223–24n3, 225n9, 229n26, 234, 235nn42–43, 236–37n52, 239, 244–45, 264n57, 265n58, 302
Howard, D. M., 8n9, 9n11, 15, 18n49, 22n63, 23, 26n86, 31–32n103, 37, 47n15, 60n53, 62n64, 66n84, 68, 97, 199n31, 225nn6, 8–10, 227nn15, 18, 228, 249n97, 251n100, 273n93, 287n151, 289n160, 302
Hunter, A. G., 286n147, 303

J

Jacobson, D. L., 22n64, 33n105, 303
Jasper, F. N., 303
Jenson, P. P., 303

Johnson, A. R., 127n11, 303
Johnston, P. S., 303
Joyce, P. M., 303

K

Kaufman, S. A., 303
Kidner, D., 303
Kirkpatrick, A. F., 62n66, 73n6, 80n16, 96n54, 104n72, 111, 127n11, 130n22, 142n69, 146n86, 158n99, 161n108, 162nn111, 113, 168n132, 184n185, 242, 257n23, 264n55, 271n85, 303
Knoppers, G. N., 30n99, 32n104, 47n15, 58n44, 190n5, 192, 278, 287n150, 303–4, 306, 308–9, 311–12
Kraus, H.-J., 21n61, 44, 46, 48, 51–52n29, 73n6, 80, 83, 88n36, 93n48, 104n72, 106, 107n75, 108n79, 113n91, 114n95, 128n13, 130n22, 135n39, 136n42, 138n50, 139, 159–60n105, 161n108, 162n111, 167, 168n130, 169n133, 177n160, 178nn163, 165, 181n170, 184n183, 186n194, 215n103, 234n37, 240n56, 257n23, 260n32, 262n43, 264, 303
Krause, D., 303
Kuntz, J. K., 77, 81n20, 172n147, 304

L

Lacy, G. G., 304
Landon, M., 91n41, 304
Lehrman, S. M., 304
Levenson, J. D., 27n90, 158, 159n102, 258, 304
Levinson, B. M., 58n45, 266n66, 278, 304
Lewis, C. S., 90, 91n39, 304
Lindars, B., 266n62, 272n88, 304
Lohfink, N. F., 29n97, 47n15, 53n30, 189n2, 193n13, 208n70, 279n120, 288n157, 304–5
Longman III, T., 305
López, F. G., 305

M

Macintosh, A. A., 57n43, 144n76, 305
Mason, R., 305
Mauchline, J., 304
Mayes, A. D. H., 47n16, 55n37, 59n51, 190n6, 200n36, 202–4n54, 206, 209n77, 212, 267n67, 288n155, 305
Mays, J. L., 4n4, 8, 12n24, 14n33, 18n52, 20n59, 23, 24n78, 33n105, 44, 50n22, 51, 54n32, 60n53, 62n65, 65n80, 66n84, 67n86, 68, 72n3, 73n6, 78n12, 79, 81, 82n22, 84n29, 86, 91, 96, 100n64, 104n72, 106n74, 109nn80, 82, 112n90, 114n94, 115n97, 117n101, 122n3, 123n4, 127n11, 128n15, 129n16, 132n29, 133n32, 135n40, 137, 138n50, 139n58, 140n61, 141n63, 142, 143n73, 144nn75, 78, 146n87, 158n98, 159n103, 161n108, 177nn160, 162, 178nn163, 165, 182, 183n180, 185n189, 186nn193, 195, 187n199, 214nn97–98, 225nn6, 8–9, 227n15, 228n22, 231nn30–31, 232n32, 237n48, 242nn68–69, 244n83, 245nn85–86, 247n89, 255nn6, 10, 260n32, 263n49, 264, 265n58, 272n88, 274n96, 275nn99, 102, 277n109, 280, 289, 297, 305
McBride, S. D., 198n30, 202n44, 207n63, 209n75, 265n61, 266n63, 272–73n89, 279n118, 304–5
McCann, J. C., 8, 14nn32–33, 16n39, 17n44, 22n63, 23, 24n74, 33n107, 34n111, 37, 54nn33–34, 58n46, 60n53, 62n64, 65n80, 73n6, 80n16, 81–82n23, 89, 93, 94n49, 96n54, 104n72, 110n85, 112n90, 117, 127n11, 133n32, 136n42, 137n47, 141n65, 147n90, 166n123, 170, 177n160, 178n164, 182, 183nn177–78, 184n183, 185n188, 186n194, 187nn197–98, 214nn97–98, 215n103, 225nn8–9, 227n15, 231n31, 237nn48, 51, 239n54,

240n58, 244nn81, 83, 247n89, 248n94, 249nn96–97, 255nn6, 8–9, 258, 281n126, 298, 302, 306–7, 311
McCarthy, D. J., 306
McConville, J. G., xiii, 30n99, 32n104, 47n15, 50n23, 58n45, 95, 106n75, 107n76, 110n83, 130n21, 134n38, 138n57, 169n134, 192, 193n12, 194n15, 195, 197, 200n38, 201, 202n45, 211nn83, 88, 254n4, 256n17, 273, 277n112, 279n118, 287nn148, 150, 295, 303–4, 306–9, 311–12
Melugin, R. F., 283n136, 307
Mettinger, T. N. D., 25n79, 256n12, 307
Millar, J. G., 107n75, 141n64, 163n114, 212, 307
Millard, M., 23, 307
Miller, P. D., 5, 8, 9n11, 11, 22n65, 23–24n78, 25n79, 27n90, 28–29n98, 45, 46n15, 47nn15, 17, 53n31, 56n42, 60n53, 61nn59–60, 65n80, 66n83, 68, 70, 73, 74n8, 82n23, 94, 95n52, 99n59, 104–5, 106n73, 108–9, 110n83, 113, 114n95, 115n96, 116n99, 124, 129nn17, 19, 130n20, 131, 132n27, 133nn31, 33, 141n68, 145n79, 147nn88–89, 93, 148n95, 163n114, 166n127, 171n139, 175n154, 183n179, 185n189, 186n193, 187n201, 193n13, 200n37, 203n50, 204nn52, 55, 206, 208n72, 209n76, 211, 214nn97–98, 224nn2–3, 227n15, 229nn23, 26, 230n29, 232, 233n33, 234, 237nn48–49, 239n55, 240n58, 246n88, 249n97, 250n99, 254n5, 256n15, 262n43, 265n59, 266n66, 271n87, 275nn100, 102, 276, 277n108, 281nn124, 128, 282n129, 284–85n144, 287n152, 288, 289n159, 291–92n8, 293n9, 294n12, 298–99, 304, 307
Mitchell, D. C., 1n1, 8n11, 13, 27n91, 31n102, 33n105, 36, 37n118, 53n31, 60n56, 61nn57–58, 62nn64–65, 64n78, 66n84, 69, 104n70,

124n9, 127n11, 129n18, 224n4, 225n9, 230, 231n31, 299, 307
Montgomery, R. M., 307
Mowinckel, S., 22n66, 25n79, 41, 172, 180n167, 246n89, 247n89, 308
Murphy, R. E., 9n11, 14n33, 19n56, 55, 158n100, 172n147, 225nn8–9, 226n12, 237n48, 302, 308, 311

N

Nelson, R. D., 47n15, 308
Nicholson, E. W., 190n4, 195, 196n23, 198n28, 199n32, 308
Niehaus, J. J., 308
Nogalski, J. D., 12n25, 20n58, 64n78, 227n18, 243n77, 246n88, 248n92, 262nn41, 45, 301, 308
Noth, M., 30n99, 190n4, 308

O

Oesterley, W. E., 92n43, 127n11, 275n98, 308
Olson, D. T., 266n62, 267n67, 272n88, 279n117, 308
Ormseth, D. H., 33n105, 308

Ö

Östborn, G., 308

P

Parkander, D. J., 308
Pinto, B. de, 272n88, 300
Plantinga, A., 308
Porter, J. R., 47n15, 308
Provan, I. W., 308

R

Rad, G., von, 30n99, 82, 114, 190n4, 195, 198n28, 199n32, 202n47, 209n77, 310
Reif, S. C., 45, 309
Reimer, D. J., 203n50, 309
Ridderbos, J., 203n50, 207n64, 256n15, 266n66, 309

Ross, J. P., 91n40, 123n5, 255n8, 302, 308, 310

S

Sanders, J. A., 123n5, 128n14, 130n23, 133n32, 140n62, 142, 147n91, 177n160, 249n97, 303–4, 308, 310
Sarna, N. M., 47n17, 62n62, 91nn41–42, 92, 93nn46–47, 207n65, 208n69, 255nn8, 10, 257n23, 258n28, 259–60n33, 261n38, 262nn41, 46, 263n50, 264n56, 269, 309
Sasson, V., 144n76, 309
Schaefer, K., 264, 271n85, 274n96, 277n110, 309
Schafer, B. E., 197n24, 201n40, 309
Seitz, C. R., xiii, 35n114, 111n88, 309, 311
Selman, M. J., 309
Seybold, K., 5n5, 53, 54n33, 178n163, 240n63, 243n77, 244nn79, 82, 84, 245n84, 247n91, 248nn92, 94, 249n98, 250nn98–99, 307, 309
Shepherd, J. E., 15, 22n64, 246, 247n90, 309
Sheppard, G. T., 8n5, 23, 65n81, 99n60, 101, 224n2, 227n15, 228n22, 229n26, 231nn29–31, 233nn35–36, 237n49, 256n12, 263n51, 265n58, 282n130, 309
Singer, M. A., 25n79, 310
Smelik, K. A. D., 310
Smend, R., 30n99, 31n102, 310
Smith, R. L., 19n54, 181n168, 249n97, 310
Soll, W., 21n60, 158nn98, 101, 160, 164, 165n122, 167n129, 171n141, 172, 173n150, 174, 181nn169, 172, 185, 209n74, 277n110, 283nn138, 140, 285, 310
Sonnet, J.-P., 46n12, 63n71, 256n13, 266nn64–65, 267–69n80, 271, 279n121, 281n123, 308
Starbuck, S. R. A., 25n79, 231n29, 248n93, 281n127, 282–83 n140, 310
Still, J., 310

T

Thompson, J. A., 256n14, 267n67, 279n117, 310
Tigay, J. H., 136n43, 193n12, 195, 198n29, 200n35, 201nn39–40, 202n47, 203n51, 204n52, 205, 207n66, 208n69, 209n77, 211–12n92, 256n15, 279n118, 287n153, 292n8, 310
Torrance, T. F., 123n5, 310
Tucker, G. M., 12n25, 128n15, 237n48, 246n89, 256n11, 265n61, 283n136, 297–301, 303, 305, 307–8, 310

V

VanGemeren, W. A., 54n34, 127 n11, 173n148, 225n9, 257n19, 261n37, 299, 310
Vincent, M. A., 9n11, 26n85, 35n113, 37, 38n120, 237n51, 265n58, 282nn130–31, 310

W

Waddell, C., 310
Wagner, J. R., 91, 93n48, 101, 123n5, 183n179, 234n39, 240nn57–58, 310
Wallis, G., 310
Waltke, B. K., 33n105, 45n11, 51 n27, 173n148, 274n97, 281n129, 310
Walton, J. H., 310
Watts, J. W., 61nn57–58, 311
Weinfeld, M., 85n31, 131n25, 134, 172n145, 174n152, 189n3, 311
Wenham, G. J., xiii, 297, 302–3, 306, 308–9, 311
Westermann, C., 12n26, 21–22n65, 72n2, 73n4, 181n168, 237n49, 243nn76–77, 244n84, 245n84, 248nn94–95, 249n98, 311
Whybray, R. N., 9n12, 18, 65, 158n100, 161, 162n109, 170, 181n171, 184, 187n200, 227n16, 255n10, 256n12,

261n37, 263, 264nn52, 56, 299, 311
Widengren, G., 47n15, 311
Willis, J. T., 64n77, 311
Wilson, G. H., 7, 8n3, 12nn24–25, 13–18n51, 19n55, 24n77, 25–26n84, 33n107, 34, 35n112, 37, 53n31, 54, 59n47, 60n55, 67n85, 97, 113, 122n2, 124, 127n11, 176, 190n8, 225, 226n13, 227n18, 228, 230, 240–43, 246nn88–89, 247n91, 249, 250n98, 255n6, 262n44, 296, 300, 304, 306, 311
Wolff, H. W., 30n99, 312
Wright, C. J. H., 79n14, 129n19, 130n21, 131n26, 132n28, 133n33, 146n84, 163n115, 169n135, 193nn12–13, 194–95n19, 198n30, 201, 202n47, 203nn50–51, 204n53, 206, 207n67, 209n73, 210, 211nn89–90, 212, 247n89, 278n117, 287n154, 292n6, 298, 312
Wyatt, N., 92n43, 312

Z

Zenger, E., 5n5, 8nn6–7, 16n40, 17, 24n77, 112n90, 124n7, 176n158, 223–24n3, 225n9, 229, 234, 235nn42–43, 236–37n52, 239, 240nn59, 61–62, 241–43, 245, 264n57, 265n58, 302, 307, 312

SCRIPTURE INDEX

Genesis

Genesis, 92n43, 264, 297, 303

Exodus

Exodus, 8, 121, 124, 139, 142, 198n30, 203n50, 209n77, 241, 256, 262, 264, 301, 310
15, 142
18:18, 198n30
20:6, 129

Deuteronomy

Deuteronomy, 2, 5, 8n6, 10–11, 24n78, 28–32n104, 43, 45–47n17, 50, 52, 55–56n42, 58, 59n51, 63, 65–66n83, 68, 70, 71n1, 74, 78–80, 82nn23, 25, 84–85n31, 87, 92, 94–97, 100, 105–10n83, 116, 118, 123, 128–41n68, 142n70, 145, 146n84, 148, 157–61, 163, 165–66, 167n128, 168–71n139, 172n145, 173, 184, 187–97, 198nn29–30, 199–200n36, 201nn39–40, 43, 202–12n96, 222, 253–56n18, 258–59, 262–74, 276, 277n112, 278, 279nn117–18, 281, 284–89n159, 291–93n9, 294n12, 295n13, 298–300, 302–12
1:5, 46n12, 264
1:16, 200
3:12–20, 200
3:18–20, 200, 204
4, 96
4:1–6, 159
4:1–8, 96, 264, 271
4:5–8, 94, 168
4:5–14, 207
4:6, 172n145
4:9, 170
4:10, 132
4:10–14, 131
4:11, 80
4:18, 266n66
4:26, 171
4:29, 165
4:39, 159
4:44, 268
4:44–5:1, 267
4:45, 165
5:1–26:19, 268
5:1–28:58, 268
5:10, 130
5:11, 105
5:15, 211
5:22, 80
5:32, 170, 288
6, 44–45, 202
6:1–9, 207
6:2, 44, 131–132
6:4–5, 45,
6:4–9, 167n128
6:4–13, 44–45
6:6, 159
6:6–9, 45
6:7, 44, 208
6:7f, 159
6:13, 45
6:14, 196
6:10–12, 202, 204
6:17, 165
6:20, 165
6:24–25, 83n28, 131–132

Deuteronomy, cont'd.
6–8, 163
7, 139
7:3, 204
7:3–4, 206
7:3–6, 203n51
7:9–12, 130
8, 203
8:6, 85n31, 131, 166
8:13, 204, 206
8:13–17, 288
8:14, 288
8:19, 171
9:4, 196
10:9, 200
10:12, 85n31, 131, 166
10:16, 95, 169
10:19, 208
11:16, 170
11:22, 85n31, 166
12, 138, 138nn52–53
12:5, 106n73
12:10, 195
12:11, 106n73
12:21, 106n73
12:29–31, 138, 138n55
12–26, 209n77, 256, 266, 269
13:1, 138n54
13:7, 195
14, 55n37
14:23–24, 106n73, 132
15:3, 200
15:7, 200
15:9, 200
16:18, 194
16:18–18:22, 4, 82, 92n45, 193, 196, 208n70
17, 42, 58, 67, 108, 148, 163, 190, 206, 221, 275, 293
17:1, 194n15
17:14, 193–97, 199, 210
17:14–20, 2, 4–5, 9, 66, 68–69, 71–72, 108, 118, 148, 162, 173–74, 188, 189, 189n2, 191–93, 197–201, 203, 207, 211–12, 220–21, 229, 253–54, 266, 277, 286, 289, 292
17:15, 193, 196–98, 200–2, 204, 211, 287
17:16, 218
17:16–17, 134n35, 193, 201, 203n50
17:17, 137, 162, 170, 204, 210, 287–88
17:18, 63, 100n62, 148, 266–69, 276, 280, 284
17:18–19, 193, 207, 212, 251, 256
17:18–20, 200–1, 209
17:19, 46, 46n19, 63n68, 82, 100n62, 131–132, 208–9, 216, 269, 272, 279, 288
17:20, 48, 82, 170, 193, 207, 210, 220, 280, 287
18:9–13, 92, 138n55
18:13, 82
19:1, 138n51
19:9, 85n31, 166
20, 163
20:14, 106n73
25:19, 195
26:7, 85n31
26:16, 140
26:17, 166
27:1–8, 129
27:9–10, 140
27:15, 129
28, 141, 169
28:9, 166
28:29, 141
28:58, 131
28:58–68, 272
28:68, 203n50
29:16–18, 138n55
29:19, 196
30, 52
30:1–10, 139, 169
30:10, 46n12, 100n62
30:11–20, 52
30:14, 159
30:15–16, 140, 166
30:16, 85n31, 95, 166
30:18, 171
30:19, 166
31, 268
31:9, 268
31:12-13, 132, 272
31:24–29, 169
31:29, 288

32, 78, 135, 138n55, 169
32:4–5, 79, 84, 85
32:12, 131
32:15, 139
32:18, 79
32:30–31, 79
32:36–43, 169
32:37, 79, 135, 164
32:38, 139
33, 134–35
33:5, 198
33:7, 126, 139
33:10, 100n62
33:26, 134, 139, 169
33:29, 134, 139, 169

Joshua

Joshua, 1, 47, 209n77
1:6–9, 134–135, 212
1:7, 82, 288
1:8, 46, 48, 167, 258, 260
3:7, 140
23:6, 82
24:15, 140

Judges

8:23, 198n23
8:29–9:57, 201n39

1 Samuel

8:5, 199n32
8:5–9, 195
8:19–20, 195
8–12, 206, 295
12:14, 206

2 Samuel

7, 38, 110, 295
7:15, 129
22, 77

1 Kings

2:1–4, 283
2:3, 166

3:5ff., 114
11:1–8, 204
11:1–13, 137n44
11:11, 283n134
11:34, 283n134
16:29–33, 204

2 Chronicles

6:31, 166

Nehemiah

18:13ff, 264

Job

Job, 179n166

Psalms

1, 2–3, 13, 20–24, 41, 43, 45, 49–50,
    52–55, 58, 60, 63, 83, 85–88, 123,
    159, 176, 181, 214, 219, 251,
    254–55, 257–63, 275–76, 280, 284,
    289
1:1, 44, 61–62, 183–84, 219
1:1–2, 82, 182, 219
1:1–3, 50
1:2, 45–46, 61–62, 99, 169, 181–82, 184,
    208n69, 258–60
1:3, 48–49, 51, 64, 87, 141, 167, 183, 258
1:4–5, 50, 64
1:5, 51–52
1:6, 52, 170, 184
1–2, 5, 10, 13n30, 16n40–18, 27, 42, 55,
    60–65, 67–72, 74, 81, 84, 96–101,
    104, 111, 113–17, 121, 133, 140,
    143–45, 148, 186–88, 190–91, 213,
    217, 219, 221, 224, 227–34,
    244–45, 248–50, 253, 292–293
1–14, 239
1–41, 239
2, 2n2, 3, 8, 25, 34n112, 37, 56–71, 87,
    89, 105–6, 143–45, 176, 214, 217,
    274–76, 284, 292
2:1, 61–65, 91
2:1–3, 64, 217

Psalms cont'd.
2:1–5, 38
2:2, 59, 114, 215–16
2:4, 62
2:4–5, 59
2:4–9, 217
2:6, 59, 64, 114, 215
2:7, 60, 62, 144, 185, 215, 286n147
2:7–9, 59–60, 64, 115
2:8–9, 38, 114
2:12, 49, 59, 61–62, 64, 86–87, 145, 186, 215
3–14, 235–36, 245
3–41, 229, 232, 237–38, 248
3–72, 228
7, 63
8, 235
9–10, 228
10, 228
15, 11, 68, 122, 128, 131, 235–36
15:1, 129
15–24, 5, 15, 17, 24, 71, 73, 99, 102, 104, 113, 129, 147, 234–36, 238–39, 245, 247, 250, 276, 285
16, 235
17, 235, 239
18, 2, 4, 11, 71–92, 103, 105, 141, 143–48, 214, 216–17, 235, 275, 292
18:1, 98, 216
18:3, 79, 86, 215
18:4–5, 89, 185
18:4–7, 217
18:6, 115
18:8–16, 81
18:8–25, 217
18:9–16, 81
18:10, 80–92
18:17–25, 81
18:19
18:20–22, 68
18:21–25, 81, 187, 219
18:22, 88
18:23–25, 99, 187
18:26–30, 83, 187
18:27, 84, 98
18:29, 98
18:31, 98, 187
18:31–37, 84
18:33, 186
18:38–46, 88
18:47, 86, 215
18:50, 186
18:51, 85, 101, 215
18–19, 33n105, 90, 97, 103–5, 111, 181
18–21, 5, 27, 42, 70–74, 89–101, 112–14, 121–22, 129, 133, 143–45, 148, 186–88, 190–91, 213, 215, 221, 224, 234, 239, 245, 247, 250, 253, 285, 292
19, 4, 20–22, 24, 68, 72–74, 83, 91–92, 101, 103, 123, 159, 214, 235, 237, 255, 262–64, 266, 290
19B, 159
19:1–7, 91–92
19:7, 165
19:7–12, 181
19:7–14, 99
19:8–9, 98, 187
19:8–12, 91
19:8–15, 91
19:11, 100, 218–19
19:11–12, 183
19:12, 98, 100, 216, 219
19:13, 99
19:13–15, 91, 185–87, 240, 261n39
19:14, 216, 219
19:15, 100
19:14, 98
19:15, 98
20, 2, 71–74, 141, 143–44, 185, 217
20:1, 106
20:2, 105, 114, 186
20:4–5, 115
20:5, 106
20:6, 109, 186
20:7, 106, 109, 114, 216
20:7–8, 110
20:8, 106, 108, 186
20:10, 110
20–21, 11, 71–74, 99, 101–2, 104–19, 214, 216, 235, 275, 277, 280, 292
21, 2, 71–74, 103, 143–44, 217–18
21:2, 107, 109–10, 186
21:3–5, 114, 185

21:6, 109, 186
21:7, 111, 216
21:8, 110
21:9–13, 110, 115
21:14, 107, 218
22, 103, 235, 239
22:1, 15
22:8, 81
23, 103, 235
23:1, 15
24, 11, 122, 128, 131, 235–36
24:3, 129
25, 164, 236
25–41, 239
25–177, 245
33, 228
34, 164, 236
34:12, 132
35–41, 235–36
37, 164
40:68, 174n152
41, 25, 230–32
41:8, 230
42:8, 169
42–43, 228
43, 228
45:7, 68
47:11–12, 81
56, 142
63:6, 169
71, 228
71:1–7, 82
72, 8, 25, 119n103, 277
73, 66
78:1, 264
78:5, 167
78:10, 167
89, 26, 35n114, 144, 228
89:3, 215
89:30–33, 68, 111
93–99, 8, 15, 225n10
96, 35n 113
98, 35n113
101, 35, 35n114
103, 35
105:45, 167
105–106, 241–43

106:1, 241
107, 176, 241–43
107–112, 241
107–145, 241
108–110, 242–43
110, 8, 26, 35, 119n103, 277
111–117, 124, 175, 224, 243
113–117, 123
113–118, 124, 241
114, 123
115, 131
115:9–13, 130
117, 17
118, 2, 4, 121–48, 172, 175–76, 214, 275, 277, 280, 286, 292
118:1, 180
118:1–4, 147, 177
118:4, 177
118:5, 185, 218
118:5–7, 133–135
118:5–14, 277
118:5–21, 146
118:8–9, 136, 145, 180
118:10–12, 137–38, 186, 218
118:13–14, 139, 180
118:14–15, 177–78
118:17, 179
118:19, 180, 218
118:20, 143, 146, 218
118:21, 177, 180
118:22–23, 140, 277
118:24–26, 140
118:25, 145
118:25–27, 141
118:26, 142, 144, 216
118:28, 147, 180
118:29, 177, 180
118–119, 5, 9n4, 11, 27, 33n105, 118–19, 121–24, 133, 143, 146, 179, 188, 190–91, 213, 216, 218–19, 221, 224, 240, 243–45, 251, 253, 285, 292
119, 2, 4, 20–22, 24, 46, 54, 100, 130, 132, 146, 148, 157–88, 214, 220, 240–41, 255, 257–64, 266, 271, 277, 280, 286

Psalms cont'd.
119:1-2, 178, 184, 187
119:2, 160
119:3, 166
119:4, 160
119:7, 180
119:10, 160, 165
119:12, 170, 179, 184
119:15, 167, 182
119:17, 173, 178, 216
119:17-24, 170
119:21-23, 164, 184, 186
119:23, 161, 167, 173, 182, 216
119:26, 179
119:27, 167, 169, 182
119:29-30, 165, 168, 170
119:31, 170
119:34, 160, 168
119:35, 170, 181
119:40, 178
119:41, 177
119:44, 168
119:46, 173
119:48, 167, 182
119:50, 178
119:55, 162, 168, 182-83, 186
119:59, 169
119:61, 164, 168-69
119:62, 180, 182-83
119:64, 177
119:65, 180
119:66, 180
119:68, 180
119:69, 160
119:69-70, 164, 168
118:71, 180
119:72, 161, 166, 173, 180, 182, 186
119:73, 167
119:76, 177
119:77, 168, 178
119:78, 167, 182
119:80, 187
119:81, 170, 183
119:88, 177-78, 183
119:92, 181
119:97, 169, 182-83
119:98, 173
119:103, 167
119:107, 178
119:109, 168
119:113, 168
119:114, 161, 186
119:116, 173, 178
119:117, 170
119:120, 177
119:122, 180
119:123, 177
119:124, 177
119:127, 167, 173, 182
119:132, 162, 186
119:144, 178
119:148, 182-83
119:149, 177, 178
119:157, 168
119:159, 177, 178
119:160, 168
119:165, 168
119:166, 177-78
119:167, 173
119:173, 180
119:174, 168, 177-78
119:175, 180
119:176, 170
120-134, 36, 124, 175, 224-25n10, 242-44
120-137, 241
120-150, 245
134, 243
134:1-2, 242
135, 243
135:2, 242
135-37, 241-44
136, 176
137, 176, 240
138-145, 243-44
146-150, 17-18, 27

Proverbs

8, 270
8-9, 52
24:13-14

Song of Songs

2:3, 183
2:7–9, 204
4:11, 183
5:1, 183
5:16, 183
7:9, 183

Isaiah

12, 142
48:17, 166

Jeremiah

17, 50
17:7–8, 49
29:19–23, 50
30:21, 114
31:33, 50
32:23, 50

Ezekiel

47:12

Daniel

7:12, 51

Micah

5:10, 204

Malachi

4:4, 264

Matthew

Matthew, 295

Mark

11:23–24, 115

Luke

11:5–13, 115

Acts

13:33

Romans

8:31, 133, 137

GENERAL INDEX

A

acrostic psalms, 157n97, 158, 160n107, 228, 236, 240–41
aggrandisement, of king, 200, 205
anointed, king as, 10–11, 34, 55, 57, 59, 61–64, 67–68, 73, 77, 85–86, 88, 97, 101, 103, 109, 111, 114–15, 117–18, 129, 143–44, 185–86, 215, 217–18, 230, 232n32, 274–75, 284, 286n147
appellatives, 78–80, 85–87, 91, 97, 144, 186, 215, 217
Autumn Festival, 138n50, 227n18, 246n89, 299, 306

B

beatitudes, 43–44
blamelessness, 77, 81–84, 92, 99, 114, 128, 157, 165, 178, 184, 187
brothers, king as one of Israelite, 46, 192–93, 196, 199–200, 205–06, 210–11, 213, 215, 220, 276n105, 286–87, 293, 295

C

canon, 53–54, 116, 128n15, 247n90, 256n11, 267, 269, 283n136, 297–99, 301, 305–7, 310
canonical method, 5, 7, 8n7, 9n12, 11–20, 21n60, 22–25, 27–28,
canonical shaping of Psalter, 31, 33n105, 34, 36, 38, 41, 51n27, 58n46, 60n53, 63, 65, 72, 78n12, 88, 97–98, 103, 111, 119n103, 122–24, 128n15, 166n127, 167, 172n147, 175–76, 180, 190–91, 213, 221, 223–26n13, 227n16, 230, 233, 237, 239n54, 242, 243n77, 245, 247–48n92, 249n97, 253, 255, 258, 262, 274–75n99, 277, 291–92
chariots, 103, 108–9, 201, 203n50, 205, 218
chiastic structures, 11, 22n64, 24, 73, 81–82, 98, 104–5, 219, 224, 234–36, 238, 243
chosenness, of king, 196, 197n24, 199–200, 201n40, 213–16n106, 232n32, 261n37, 275, 287
collections of psalms, 1, 8, 10–12n26, 17–19, 21n62, 22, 24, 30n99, 31n100, 38, 41, 54–55, 69, 71, 73–74, 94–95, 99–100, 104, 111, 113, 115, 123–24, 129, 147–48, 164, 175–76, 224, 231n29, 232n32, 233, 235–37, 239–42, 243nn76–77, 244, 247–48n92, 249nn97–98, 250, 257, 262–63, 274, 276, 285
commandments, 90, 105, 108, 130, 141n68, 158, 160, 166, 192, 204, 211–12, 271n86
concatenation, 4, 15–16n40, 72, 73n7, 97, 104–5, 114, 176, 225–26, 236, 238
constitution, torah as, 82n25, 134n36, 189n1, 194, 202n44, 209, 266, 273n92, 301
court settings, 85n31, 173n149, 189, 231n29, 248n93, 281n127, 282n133, 283nn139–40, 285n146, 309
covenant, 37, 64, 66, 82–83, 85, 96, 110–11, 113–14, 129–30, 132, 141, 147, 173, 177, 198–99, 201–2, 204, 206,

208–13, 215, 220, 232n32, 264, 269, 272, 275, 276n105, 279, 283n134, 286–88n156, 294
cult settings, 12n24, 20, 22, 25n79, 41, 44n6, 51, 54, 66, 128, 182, 247n89, 249n98, 275n97, 282

D

David, 1, 3, 8nn9, 11, 9n14, 15, 22n63, 23, 25n79, 26, 27n87, 32n103, 34n112, 35n114, 36–37, 42, 57n43, 67–68, 77, 86, 88, 90, 98, 99n60, 101, 103, 110, 113n92, 117, 138n56, 142–43n74, 175n155, 187n198, 200n39, 215, 222, 225n8, 227n18, 228–30, 231n30, 232–34n38, 240, 246n88, 248n92, 250–51, 254n4, 262n41, 264n57, 266n62, 273, 274n97, 277, 283n135, 284n141, 285–86, v, xiv

Davidic Covenant, 110n84, 111, 283n134
  framework 17n44, 27n88, 240–44
  kingship, 3, 11, 16n41, 21n60, 26, 27n87, 33–39, 42, 59, 63n74, 66, 68–69, 104n70, 111, 121, 127n11, 129, 142–45, 162n110, 174–75, 188, 190, 219, 221, 246n88, 249–51, 282, 286n147, 289, 291, 295
  psalters, 11, 18, 21, 148, 228n22, 231–33, 239–40, 247–48
  superscriptions, 35, 60, 97, 127n11, 173, 227n18, 228–33, 237, 243–44
  Torah, 263

death, 52–53, 77, 114n95, 126, 133n32, 141n64, 166, 178, 254n5, 260, 268n73

democratisation, 5, 46n13, 68, 89, 117–18, 147n88, 148, 164, 193, 199, 200–202, 205–6, 208n69, 211, 213, 222, 253–54, 280–81, 285–86n146, 276n105, 281, 284–89, 292–93

dependence, attitude of, 2, 29, 49, 55n36, 58–59, 79, 85, 89, 95, 104–5, 107–10, 112, 139–40, 144–45, 147, 161–64, 170, 177–78, 180, 186, 193, 202–3, 205, 217–18, 220, 235, 245, 277, 279–80, 286

Deuteronomic, themes and theology, 2, 4, 8–9, 24, 27, 30, 32n104, 39, 42–50, 52–53, 55–58n44, 60, 65–66n82, 68–69, 71, 78–85n31, 87, 89, 91–96, 104–7, 109–10, 116, 118–19, 121–22, 125, 127–31n25, 134, 139n59, 157–61, 166–67, 172n145, 174, 180, 185–86, 190, 192, 198nn28, 30, 202, 204, 209, 239, 244, 258, 265n58, 267, 270n83, 272, 276, 278n113, 284, 287n150, 288, 291–92, 303, 305–7, 311

Deuteronomist(s), the, 29n97, 32, 53, 58n44, 96, 116, 159, 174, 190n5, 192n11, 208n71, 210, 257, 270n81, 278, 279n121, 280, 287n150, 288n156, 299, 303

Deuteronomistic, themes and theology, 5, 29n97, 30–32n104, 46–47n15, 49–50, 53n30, 58n45, 59n51, 92, 94, 106, 110, 134, 158, 160, 173–74, 190n4, 191, 197, 200, 204, 206, 258, 276, 285, 301, 303–6, 308–9, 311–12
  DtrH, 3, 30n99, 31–32n104, 47, 107, 110, 118, 133–34, 138, 140–41, 145, 148, 166, 168, 190–91, 193, 199n32, 208n71, 209n77, 211, 221, 232n32, 258, 278, 283n134
  DtrN, 30n99, 31n102, 32, 42, 58, 65, 96, 123, 172, 258, 292

Deuteronomistic worldview, 4, 10, 45, 50, 52–53, 55, 59, 61, 64, 65, 68, 78, 80, 89, 93, 96, 105, 116–17, 129, 134, 147, 160, 165, 171, 173, 198n28, 221, 265n58, 270, 286, 288, 291, 294

devotion, to Yahweh, 9, 11, 42–43, 46, 47n15, 65, 67, 95, 116, 137–38, 159–61, 164, 202, 205, 209–10, 213, 265n58, 270–71, 277, 280, 283n137, 285–86, 291, 29

E

editing, of Psalter, 7, 8n3, 12, 13nn28–29, 17n49, 15n38, 16nn 41–42, 18n51, 23n73, 25n81, 26nn82–84, 28n96, 29n96, 33n107, 35n112, 37–38, 53n31, 59n47, 60n55, 67n85, 97n57, 122n2, 190n8, 225n6, 226n13, 227n18, 228n19, 230n28, 246n89, 247n91, 249nn97–98, 262n44
editor(s), 2–4, 11, 13–14, 26, 19n56, 31–32, 34, 36, 42, 78, 87, 91, 101, 104–5, 112–13, 116, 124, 127, 132, 188, 190, 213–14, 221, 231, 250n98, 253–54, 263, 280, 282n131, 286, 289, 291
editorial activity in Psalter, 2, 7, 10, 13–18n51, 24n78, 26, 28n96, 29n96, 33–34, 36–37, 41–42, 46, 59, 67–68, 71–72, 74, 87n35, 88, 97–98, 101, 104n70, 105, 124, 127n11, 143, 163, 172, 176n158, 187–88, 215n101, 225–28, 234, 238, 239n54, 249, 253, 262n44, 263, 274, 276, 284, xiii
indicators, of editing, 13, 15, 18, 25n79, 39, 41, 80, 122, 133, 140, 146, 173, 190, 216, 219, 226–27, 262n44, 263–64
keywords, 15, 97, 225–26
eschatological, readings of the psalms, 3, 8–10, 26–27, 33, 35n113, 36–39, 42, 51–52, 66–67, 69, 89, 104n70, 111–12, 118, 119n103, 122, 188, 190, 221, 232n32, 241, 253, 274n97, 280, 282, 286, 289
exemplar, king as, 2, 10, 67–68, 95, 98n58, 99nn59–60, 101, 112, 113n92, 122, 132, 134, 143, 175n155, 187n198, 190, 203, 208–9, 213, 218, 228n22, 234, 250, 254, 283, 286, 294–95

F

fear, of Yahweh, 45, 46n15, 57, 66, 90, 99, 126, 131–32, 134, 143, 146, 157, 172, 176–77, 192, 207–8, 216, 269, 276, 279n120, 280, 284, 287–88, 294
fearer(s) of Yahweh, 130–31, 143, 145, 177
festal frameworks, 241, 243–44
festival settings, 124, 126, 128, 130, 132, 138n50, 141, 176, 246n89, 247n89
foreigner(s), 192, 196, 200, 201n39, 206, 215, 287
frameworks, within Psalter, 16, 17n44, 21, 169, 193, 241, 249n98, 266

G

genre, 12–13, 15, 20–21n62, 41, 64, 73n4, 78, 105, 112–13, 164, 165n122, 172, 226n13, 249n97, 262, 274n97
Gattungen, 23, 73n4, 78
Gattungsforschung, 12
grace, 162, 169–71, 177n160, 197, 205, 283n134, 286n146
guidance, 101, 233, 236n47, 261n37, 276

H

Hallel, Great or Egyptian, 121, 123–24, 130, 139, 176, 310
Closing, 17
happiness, 43–46, 48n17, 52, 61, 115, 182–84
hermeneutical paradigms, 10, 21–22, 42, 51, 56, 65, 68, 83n26, 113, 115, 123, 180, 224, 231, 233, 244–45, 248, 283, 292, 294
hope, 9, 27, 33–34, 36–37, 39, 42, 50, 66–67, 69, 104n70, 109, 111, 115, 118, 121, 132, 141, 157, 161, 163, 167–69, 202, 233n32, 280, 286n147, 295
horses, trust in, 103, 108–9, 192, 201, 203–5, 218
humility, 198n28, 220
hymnbook, Psalter as, 54

I

ideal, of kingship, 2–3, 5, 27n89, 58, 66–69, 82, 86, 101, 111–12, 115, 118–

19, 122, 133–34, 143, 147n93, 184, 188, 198, 211, 221, 234, 254, 276–78, 280, 283–85, 287, 289, 291, 293, 295
idolatry, 135, 212–13
imprecations, 274
inclusio, 22n64, 61n59, 86, 107, 218, 230, 232, 236, 244–45
instruction, Torah as, 11, 49n19, 53–56, 63, 67–68, 82, 93–94, 96, 99–100, 143, 163–64, 168, 182, 204, 207, 221, 232, 251, 255, 257, 259, 260n32, 271–73n90, 276n105, 283, 294
intercession, 104n72, 109, 122
intertextuality, 28–29, 49–50, 77, 229, 292
introduction, Psalms 1–2 as, 10, 13, 17–18n49, 21, 23–24, 30n99, 31n100, 34, 41–42, 48, 50–51, 53–57, 60, 64–71, 83, 86–89, 94–95, 99–101, 104, 113–17, 121, 123, 128, 130, 140, 180, 188, 194, 196, 199, 219, 227, 229–34, 239, 244–45, 248, 249n96, 250, 265n58, 267n72, 268, 275–76, 284, 286n147, 291, 293
Israel, 2, 4–5, 8–9, 20n58, 24n78, 25n79, 26n87, 30n99, 31nn100, 102, 32, 33n106, 34, 35n114, 36–38, 42, 47, 48n17, 54n35, 63n74, 66–67, 69, 79, 82, 92, 93n46, 94–97, 107, 109–13, 114n95, 117–19, 123n5, 126, 127n11, 129–30, 132, 134–36, 138n51, 169–70, 172n147, 189nn1–2, 192–98n30, 199n32, 200–202, 203nn49–50, 204–9, 211n89, 212–13, 234, 241, 246n88, 247n89, 254, 258, 260, 262n41, 263–64, 271, 273, 276, 278–79n121, 281–82, 285–89, 297, 299, 301–12
Israelite, 8n7, 10, 27n90, 46, 68, 108, 112, 131–34, 136n42, 137, 161–62, 164, 166, 168, 172n147, 189, 197, 200–201, 205–6, 208–10, 234, 246n89, 256n12, 272, 276, 279n120, 282–85, 287–88n156, 301, 303–4, 307

Israelites, 52, 85, 134n36, 200–202, 206–7n68, 210, 220, 268, 275, 279, 285

J

Jesus, 22n64, 294–95, 303
Josiah, 47n15, 58, 67, 85n31, 93n47, 189
Judah, 2, 9, 30n99, 31n100, 34, 47n15, 118, 278n116, 286, 303–4, 306, 308–9, 311–12
Judaism, 27n90, 121, 256n11, 257n24, 259, 299, 304, 309
judge, the office of, 21n60, 157, 193, 198n30, 281, 287
judges, 57, 138n56, 194, 198n30, 199n32, 201n39, 208, 313
juxtaposition, of psalms, 2–4, 9–11, 34, 69, 71–72, 73n4, 74, 97, 113, 119, 121, 130, 143, 148, 176–77, 214, 221–22, 228, 253, 274, 276–77, 280, 284, 289

K

keeping the torah, 9, 47, 52, 68, 83, 90, 95, 130–31, 157, 167–68, 170–71, 177–78, 192, 203n49, 208–10, 212, 261n37, 279, 287–88
torah-keeper, king as, 4, 9, 42, 49, 89, 99n59, 101, 209, 211, 285, 287, 295
king, 2–4, 8–11, 25–27n88, 33–39, 42, 47n15, 51, 57–60, 61n61, 62–63n74, 65–69, 72, 77–89, 94–95, 97–98, 99nn59–60, 100–101, 103–19, 121–22, 127–48n95, 162, 164, 170, 173–75n153, 178–80, 182–83, 185–90, 192–222, 228n22, 229–30, 232n32, 234, 246n89, 251, 254, 256, 258, 266, 268–69n78, 272, 274–89, 291–95
King, Law of, 2–5, 8n10, 9, 28–29, 39, 67, 69, 71n1, 72, 112, 121–22, 188–95, 197–203, 205–8, 210–14, 216, 218, 220–22, 253–54, 270, 274, 277–79, 284, 288–89, 291–95
Yahweh as, 26, 34, 58, 59n50, 194–96, 288–89

General Index 331

kings, 10, 56–57, 62, 88, 115, 150, 173, 198n30, 215, 217, 220, 230, 276n105
  ancient Near Eastern, 83, 201, 204
  Israelite, 36–37, 46, 47n15, 67–68, 86, 99–100, 110–12, 118, 134, 196, 204–5, 211n89, 279n120, 289, 295
Kingship Law, the, 2–5, 9–11, 27–32n104, 39, 46n15, 47n15, 58, 60, 63, 66–67n87, 69, 71–72, 74, 85n33, 86–87, 92nn43, 45, 95, 105, 109, 112, 116–17, 119, 121–23, 132, 136–37, 138n57, 162–63, 168, 186, 188–95, 197–203, 205–7, 209n77, 210–15, 218–22, 234, 250, 253–56n17, 257n19, 258, 263–64, 265n60, 266–67, 269–71, 273–81, 283n134, 284–86, 287n150, 288–89, 291–95
kingship psalms, 2, 4–5, 10–11, 16–17, 22, 25n79, 26–30, 32–33, 36, 37, 39, 42, 58–59, 67–69, 73, 117, 125, 133, 143–44, 161, 163, 166–67, 175, 184, 186–88, 190, 198, 214, 216, 224, 226, 234–35, 244, 247–48, 253–55, 267, 271, 274–75, 277, 280–81, 284, 288–89, 291–93
  in Psalter, 2–5, 8–11, 16–17, 18n49, 22–23, 25–34n112, 35nn112, 114, 36–39, 42, 52, 55, 58–60, 63, 66–74, 82, 86, 97, 99, 100n62, 101, 104–5, 108, 110–19n103, 121–23, 125, 127n11, 128n11, 132–34n36, 142–44, 146–47, 161–63, 166–67, 175, 184, 186–88, 190–99n32, 201, 203, 207–16, 217n110, 219–22, 224, 226, 229, 234–35, 243–45n84, 246n88, 247–48, 250, 253–55, 266–67, 271, 273–81, 283n134, 284–89, 291–95

L

lament, 18n49, 25, 34, 53, 55, 73, 122, 164–65n122, 168, 173, 235–37n51, 239, 250, 283
land, 3, 55n38, 79, 96, 138n51, 157, 171, 192–94n15, 196, 203, 205, 209–10, 267, 268n73, 278n117
law, 9–10, 20n58, 22–23, 27, 43, 45, 46n13, 47–48, 55n38, 63, 67–68, 82, 83n28, 90, 94, 100n62, 101, 108–9, 129–30, 132, 134n36, 141, 148n95, 157, 159–60, 162–63, 167–71, 173–74n151, 178, 180n167, 181–85, 190n6, 192–96, 198n30, 199–200, 202, 203n49, 204–10, 211n89, 212–13, 219–21, 239, 249n98, 255–58n27, 259n29, 261n37, 262n43, 263–66, 268–69, 271–73n90, 275n101, 276, 278–79n120, 284–85, 287–88n156, 294
leader, king as, 36, 46n15, 47n15, 63n74, 67, 127n11, 128n11, 134–35, 198n28, 201n39, 203, 206, 208, 279n119, 288
leadership, in Israel, 47n15, 82n23, 133, 174, 193n14, 209, 260
legalism, Torah and, 21, 66n82, 82n25, 94, 187, 219, 257–58, 271–72
linkage, between psalms, 19, 60n54, 88, 226n14, 230, 258
liturgy, 108, 111, 113, 117, 124, 216, 218, 285

M

marriage, kingship and, 137n44, 162, 201, 203, 206
meditation, on torah, 43, 47, 53–54, 61, 68–69, 90, 94, 100, 134, 141, 157, 162, 167–69, 171, 174, 182–83, 185, 208–9, 213, 219, 251, 256, 258, 260–61, 265, 268–69, 276, 280, 284, 289
memorisation, of torah, 207, 259
messiah, 9, 25n79, 27n87, 35, 38, 51, 66, 68–69, 85, 88–89, 101, 106, 110–11, 114, 144, 215n101, 216, 232n32, 291, 294–95
military, 68, 104–8, 115, 127, 133, 136, 138, 143, 162, 186, 201, 203, 205, 209, 213, 217n110, 220, 279, 282

monarchy, in Israel, 2, 16n41, 21n60, 25n79, 26, 27n87, 33, 34n112, 35–36, 38, 47n15, 58n45, 189n3, 190, 192, 195–97, 199n32, 202, 205, 209, 221, 249, 274, 275n97, 277–78n116, 283, 286n147, 287–88

Moses, 46, 47n15, 48n17, 52, 79–80, 84, 85n31, 96, 130, 132, 134n36, 135, 138–39, 141nn64, 68, 166, 169, 208, 258, 260, 262n41, 263–64, 266n62, 267–69, 271n86, 272, 279n117, 287

N

name, of Yahweh, 45, 60n53, 77, 98, 103, 105–8, 126, 128n11, 137–40, 142, 144, 146, 157, 162, 180, 186, 216, 218, 248, 254n5, 272–73

nations, 10, 37–38, 57, 59, 61–62, 77, 85–86, 88, 94, 107, 109, 126, 127n11, 136–39, 141, 144, 185, 192, 194–97, 204, 215, 217–18, 220n126, 230, 275, 279n119, 288n155, 289

nomism, 257, 272

O

obedience, to torah, 46n15, 47n15, 48, 49n19, 52, 63n74, 82, 94–95, 101, 131, 134, 138, 141–42, 148n95, 166–71, 174, 177, 180, 184, 187, 198n28, 208–9, 211, 213, 221, 234, 245n85, 263, 271n86, 275, 280, 283, 285, 288

offices, laws concerning, 4, 127n11, 191n9, 208n70

ordering, of psalms in Psalter, 1, 7, 12–13, 18, 21, 41, 61n57, 122, 134n 36, 191, 239n54, 249n97

P

paraenetic, passages in Deuteronomy, 79, 138, 158–59, 167n128, 169, 266, 270n81

Pentateuch, 53, 56, 171, 195, 203n50, 256–57, 259n29, 261–65n58, 267, 269, 293

piety, torah-based, 2–3, 9, 20n58, 39, 42, 46, 48, 53, 55, 59, 66–69, 87, 94–95, 99n59, 105, 112, 117–19, 122, 131–32, 142–43, 147–48, 159–61, 164, 166–67, 169, 171–72, 175, 178, 180–83, 185, 187–88, 190, 198n28, 208, 220–21, 245, 250–51, 253, 257–58, 261, 265, 269, 283–87, 293–95

placement, of psalms in Psalter, 2, 4–5, 8, 10, 13–18, 21n60, 22–23, 24n78, 25, 28n96, 29, 31–32, 36n116, 37, 53–54n35, 64n78, 65, 67, 73n4, 94, 99, 104–5, 112–13, 117, 122, 132, 163, 167, 175, 188, 190–91, 213, 221–22, 225, 228, 230, 238, 247–48, 253, 255, 271, 274, 291

polity, torah as, 118, 198, 202, 209, 213, 215, 221, 266, 279n120

power, and kingship, 59–60, 83, 118, 137, 139, 145n80, 180, 182, 184n182, 186, 189, 192–95, 198, 201–6, 213, 217, 245n85, 270n82, 275, 278, 280, 287, 292–93

prayer, 56, 85, 89, 91, 95–96, 99n60, 101, 112, 114–15, 118–19, 122, 141–42, 146–47, 162, 170–72, 174–75, 178–80, 183, 185–87, 216, 218–19, 228n22, 236n47, 240, 246n88, 261n39, 280, 283, 285

prosperity, 37, 43, 51–52, 64, 66, 83n28, 94, 111, 115, 126, 140–42, 147, 166, 180, 183, 258

psalmist(s), 35n114, 50, 57n43, 73, 78–80, 83–85, 87, 91, 94–95, 97–98, 100, 106–7, 116, 118, 127n11, 132–133n32, 134–39, 144, 147, 158, 161–71, 173–75n153, 177–78, 181–84n182, 185n187, 186–87, 215–20, 236, 240, 242, 257, 259, 261, 263, 264n52, 265n58, 270nn82–83, 271, 275, 286

psalm groupings, 2–5, 10n20, 13, 15n38, 16–17, 23, 28–30, 42, 67n87,

69n93, 71, 86, 89, 92, 96–97, 99, 104–5, 109n81, 110, 116, 124–25, 133, 143–47, 160n107, 163, 167, 175–76, 180, 185–88, 190–91, 193, 198, 213–15, 218–19, 220–22, 224–229, 234–39, 242–44, 246–49, 253–54, 267, 274n95, 275, 277, 280, 284–86, 292–93

Psalter, 1–5, 7–28, 31–34, 35nn112–14, 36–39, 41–43, 45–48, 49n19, 50–56, 59–61n57, 64–69, 71–73n4, 77–79, 86–91, 94, 97–101, 103–6, 111–13, 115n98, 116–19n103, 121–25, 136n42, 139n59, 140–43, 145, 147, 161, 163–64, 166, 175–78, 180–81, 183, 185, 187–88, 190–91, 194, 198, 213–14, 216, 219, 221, 223–27n18, 228n22, 229–34, 236–37n51, 239–51, 253–55, 257, 259, 260n32, 261–63n48, 265, 270, 274–77n108, 280–81, 282nn130–31, 284, 286, 289, 291–93, 295

R

Rabbinic literature, 45, 123, 261

randomness, of the Psalter, 1, 13, 18, 19, 123, 160n107, 239n54

redaction(s), of Deuteronomy, 30–32, 37
of Psalter, 5, 9, 12–13, 18, 24, 26–28, 33, 37, 39, 42, 50, 56, 71, 78, 86, 89, 94–95, 97, 104, 112, 118–19, 121–23, 125, 143, 185n186, 191, 198, 231n29, 233 244n84, 250n98, 263, 276, 283, 293–95

redactors, 2–3, 7, 9, 15, 35–36, 39, 104n70, 112–13, 116, 124, 185, 190, 280

refuge, Yahweh as, 23, 34, 49, 57, 59, 61, 64, 77–79, 86–88, 107, 115, 117, 126, 135–37, 145–46, 163–64, 180, 186, 245n85, 263, 275

representative, king as, 11, 25n79, 35n113, 84, 104n72, 114, 122, 127n11, 132, 232n32, 237, 282, 285, 295

rereadings, of psalms, 33, 38–39, 50, 52, 66

righteous, the, 9–10, 43–45, 50, 52, 61, 64, 68–69, 82, 84, 88–90, 94, 96, 101, 126, 128, 134, 142–43, 146, 148, 157, 162, 172, 175, 178, 187, 218, 229, 233, 250, 284

righteousness, 53, 68, 73, 77, 81–84, 96, 100–101, 126, 128–32, 138n54, 144, 146, 148, 157, 163, 175, 179–80, 219, 239–40, 263, 285

royal psalms and themes, 2–3, 5, 7, 10, 13n30, 16n41, 22, 24n78, 25–26n87, 33–34, 35n114, 36–39, 52, 57–59, 63, 66–67, 69, 71–73, 85n31, 88, 94n51, 97–99n60, 104–5, 111–13, 116, 119n103, 121–23, 127, 135, 148, 162, 164, 173–75n153, 187–88, 190–91, 192n10, 193, 197, 201, 204–5, 208n71, 211, 216, 220, 229, 237n51, 241, 246n89, 268n74, 274, 276–77n111, 279–84n142, 289, 294

rule, of king/messiah, 8, 10–11, 35, 65–69, 86, 88, 111, 113, 148n95, 198n28, 207, 211, 215, 217, 276
of Yahweh, 10–11, 36, 38, 55, 59, 65–69, 84, 106n75, 111, 113, 118–19, 197, 210–13, 215, 217, 275, 279–80, 284, 289

ruler, king as, 3, 35n113, 68, 108, 174n151, 229, 275–76n105, 284

rulers, 10, 34, 57, 62, 88, 100, 115, 157, 184, 192, 194, 217, 284

S

salvation, 54, 77–78, 81, 83–84, 86, 103, 105n72, 109–10, 115, 126, 128–29, 139–40, 143–46, 157, 165n122, 169, 171, 176–78, 180, 186, 203n50, 216, 220

seam, psalms, 8, 13n30, 16, 18n49, 26, 237n51

shape, of Psalter, 1–2, 4, 7, 9–10, 12–13, 21–23, 42, 56, 60n53, 96, 110–11,

113, 161, 185, 207, 232, 237n51, 249n97, 264, 292, 294
Shema, 43–45
Solomon, 35n114, 38, 109, 137n44, 183, 204, 303
son, king as, 25n79, 57, 58n43, 63, 115, 215, 217, 228n22, 274n97, 275, 286n147
statute, 157
statutes, 82, 84, 90, 94, 99, 131, 157, 158n99, 167, 185, 196–97, 208, 210, 271n86, 287
structure, of Psalter, 11–12, 14–16, 18–19, 43n4, 44, 57n43, 60n54, 77n9, 81–82, 85, 94, 98, 104, 157n97, 158, 193, 195, 219, 224, 235, 238, 240–43, 245n84, 262–63, 278n117, 279n117
superscription(s), 13, 15, 35, 42, 60, 94, 97–98, 101, 112, 121, 123–24, 127n11, 172–73, 175–76n158, 220, 227–29, 230–33, 237, 242–44, 246n88, 248n95

T

tabernacle, 269
tacit indicators of editing, 13, 18n51, 92, 142
Talmud, 61
Tanakh, 255n7, xvii
Targum, 111
teaching, 23, 46n13, 53, 96, 109n80, 132, 159, 161–62, 168, 170, 173–74, 179, 207, 221, 255–57, 259, 260n32, 261, 264–65, 271–72, 281, 287, 289, 294–95
Temple, 4, 11, 24n78, 25n79, 27n90, 49n20, 107n75, 127n11, 128, 132, 138n54, 139–40, 142–43, 146, 148, 175, 178–79, 186–87, 216, 218, 246n88, 256n11, 277, 299, 303–4
theophany, 78, 80–81, 217
torah psalms, 2–5, 8–11, 16–17, 20–24n78, 27–30, 32, 33n105, 39, 41–44, 46–54n32, 55n36, 56–58, 60–63n69, 65, 66n82, 67–74, 81–82n23, 86–87, 89, 90n38, 91–96, 98–101, 104–5, 112–19, 121–25, 130–34n36, 138, 140–43, 146–48, 157–71, 173–75, 177–78, 180–88, 190–93, 198, 201, 202n44, 203n49, 205n57, 206–14, 216, 218–22, 224, 226, 229, 234–35, 240, 243–45n85, 247–48, 250, 253–81, 283n134, 284–89, 291–95
Torah, 20, 23, 41, 54, 62–63, 68–69, 71, 81, 87, 93, 95–96, 99, 113, 116, 118, 121, 147, 157–59, 167–68, 174, 181, 188, 195, 206–7, 209, 218–19, 223, 232–34, 240–41, 244, 251, 253, 256–59, 261, 263–70, 274, 277, 279n120, 280–81, 284, 289, 293, 295
  tôrâ, 49n19, 117, 160, 163–64, 181n169, 212, 257, 260n32, 264, 270n82, 272, 280
  tôrâh, 264
treaties, 129, 136–37, 162, 195, 279
trust, in Yahweh, 34, 60, 79, 103, 106–9, 110n84, 111, 115, 117, 126, 127n11, 133–37n44, 139, 142, 145, 157, 161–63, 168, 171, 186, 202–5, 207n68, 213, 217–18, 234, 245n85, 261n37, 263, 276, 279n121, 280, 283, 289, 292

V

victory, 11, 37, 66, 77, 85, 105n72, 107, 109, 114, 117, 127, 135, 138, 285n146
vindication, 38, 51, 59, 84–86, 140, 175, 247n89, 285n146

W

war, 69, 107–10, 162–63
Ways, Two, 43, 45, 51–52, 60, 62, 64–68, 77, 83–85n31, 88, 95, 99, 105, 115–16, 118–19, 122, 131n25, 138, 141, 146, 157, 165–66, 170, 179–81, 184–85, 187, 254, 271, 282, 294

wealth, 78, 108, 118, 133, 162–63, 184n182, 201–6, 210, 213, 274, 279, 287–88
weapons, 108, 139, 162, 201–3, 205, 287
Wisdom Literature, 25n79, 43, 44n6, 52, 54, 56n40, 65n81, 85n31, 131n25, 179, 184, 233, 236, 270
wisdom themes, 8, 20, 24, 41, 53, 56n41, 66, 91, 96, 100, 121, 162, 164, 170–72n145, 173n149, 179, 182, 210, 233, 241, 259n29, 264, 270n82

Z

Zion, 11, 33, 34n108, 36–39, 42, 51, 57, 86, 103, 107n75, 124, 128, 144, 215, 217, 222, 229, 241, 254n4, 273, 274n97, 275, 277, 286n146, 289, 299

www.ingramcontent.com/pod-product-compliance
Lightning Source LLC
Chambersburg PA
CBHW021817300426
44114CB00009BA/211